D1551467

God, Passion and Power

THOMAS AQUINAS ON CHRIST CRUCIFIED
AND THE ALMIGHTINESS OF GOD

Vol. I   Henk J.M. Schoot, *Christ the 'Name' of God: Thomas Aquinas on Naming Christ*, 1993
Vol. II   Jan G.J. van den Eijnden ofm, *Poverty on the Way to God: Thomas Aquinas on Evangelical Poverty*, 1994
Vol. III   Henk J.M. Schoot (ed.), *Tibi soli peccavi: Thomas Aquinas on Guilt and Forgiveness*, 1996
Vol. IV   Harm J.M.J. Goris, *Free Creatures of an Eternal God: Thomas Aquinas on God's Infallible Foreknowledge and Irresistible Will*, 1996
Vol. V   Carlo J.W. Leget, *Living with God: Thomas Aquinas on the Relation between life on Earth and 'Life' after Death*, 1997
Vol. VI   Wilhelmus G.B.M. Valkenberg, *Words of the Living God: Place and Function of Holy Scripture in the Theology of Thomas Aquinas*, 2000
Vol. VII   Paul van Geest, Harm Goris, Carlo Leget (eds.), *Aquinas as Authority: A Collection of Studies Presented at the Second Conference of the Thomas Instituut te Utrecht, December 14 - 16, 2000*, 2002
Vol. VIII   Eric Luijten, *Sacramental Forgiveness as a gift of God: Thomas Aquinas on the Sacrament of Penance*, 2003

Vol. X   (to be published soon) Stefan Gradl, *Deus beatitudo hominis: Evangelische Annäherung an die Glückslehre des Thomas von Aquin*, 2003

Mark-Robin Hoogland cp

GOD, PASSION AND POWER

THOMAS AQUINAS ON CHRIST CRUCIFIED AND THE ALMIGHTINESS OF GOD

PEETERS
LEUVEN
2003

© Stichting Thomasfonds - Nijmegen
ISBN 90-429-1306-1
D. 2003/0602/60

One morning that autumn, Thangbrand went out early
and ordered a tent to be pitched.
Then he sang Mass with great ceremony,
for it was an important feast-day.
Hall asked him: "In whose honour are you celebrating this day?"
"The angel Michael," replied Thangbrand.
"What power has this angel?" asked Hall.
"Great power," said Thangbrand. "He weighs everything you do,
both good and evil, and he is so merciful
that the good weighs more heavily with him than the evil."
"I would like to have him as my friend," said Hall.
"You can do that easily," said Thangbrand.
"Give yourself to him in God's name this very day."
Hall said: "I want to stipulate
that you plegde your word on his behalf
that he shall become my guardian angel."
"I give you my promise," said Thangbrand.
After that, Hall and all his household were baptized.

Njal's Saga, chapter 100 (Iceland, 13th century)

TO MY BELOVED

A friend is a friend at all times (Pr 17,17)

TABLE OF CONTENTS

INTRODUCTION

How can grown-up people still believe? How are contemporary Christians living in this post-modern time, the time after Auschwitz, Hiroshima, Vietnam, Rwanda and New York September 11th, able to connect their experiences of suffering and death in this world and in their personal lives with their faith in God, whom we profess to be the Almighty? The questions concerning suffering in people's lives, and this in respect to God, especially His involvement in it, did not just rise in Western Christianity during the last century or so. The struggle with faith in God (or the gods) in view of the reality of suffering and death, especially when it strikes a just or innocent person, is found in all religions at all times. However, because of the use of methods and weapons of mass destruction, because of the economical, ecological and medical problems that still outrun ingenious technological developments and because of the increased knowledge through the modern means of communication of misery close by and far away, this question has become pressing. For a growing group of (Western) Christians it becomes more and more difficult to live in a relation of faith to God and to experience this relation as a source of living hope and life-giving love. Faith may become disconnected from every day life, and thus lose its meaning.

"Almighty" as a name of God is part of this crisis of faith, it seems. The question "If God is good and almighty, why is there so much suffering in our world", since Leibniz[1] the theodicy question, has changed from a starting point of an inquiry of one's faith into a reason to turn one's back on God and so to let go of one's faith.

At the same time "almighty" is the only property of God mentioned in the Creed. For this reason it has an extra emphasis. All the greater is the contrast with the experience of many, that God is powerless in this world full of evil. Others refrain from speaking of God's almightiness and use a term like "vulnerable power" instead.[2] Yet

---

[1] G.W.F. von Leibniz, *Essais de Théodicée sur la Bonté de Dieu, la Liberté de l'Homme et l'Origine du Mal* (1710). The word theodicy, from Greek, means "justification of God".

[2] This is the translation of the Dutch term "weerloze overmacht", in: Schillebeeckx (1987), 381. A more literal translation would be "defenceless supremacy". This - rather confusing - term was introduced by Berkhof (1973[1], 1985[5]), later on taken over by Wiersinga (1975), and Schillebeeckx (*l.c.*).

because God's almightiness is an essential part of the Christian faith, someone who calls him/herself Christian, cannot simply deny that God is almighty. Still, in the light of the experiences of suffering mentioned, one has to ask what "almighty" means as a name of God (*fides quaerens intellectum*).

Another name of God is love, as we read in Scripture (1 Jn 4,8, 16). It is a name that may be more appealing; "love" is associated with warmth and closeness, whereas "almighty" may rather be regarded as a cool and distant term. Still, ignoring the name almighty and speaking of God as love instead does not dissolve the question of the relation between God and suffering. For if He is love and loves us, why then all our suffering? This question becomes even more pressing in respect of the sufferings of Christ, who is called the beloved Son, by God Himself (Mt 3,17 par., 17,5 par.), and who was without sin (2 Co 5,21, Heb 7,26, 1 P 2,22, 1 Jn 3,5).

For me it is not far-fetched to approach this crisis of our faith from the angle of the Passion of Christ. For after living for four years in a Passionist community, I entered the Congregation of the Passion in 1991 and took vows in 1992. In the course of time I made the spirituality of this religious congregation my own and it became the centre, the point of orientation of my life. The living memory of the Passion of Christ forms the very heart of this spirituality.

The Congregation of the Passion (abbreviated as C.P.) is a religious order in the Roman Catholic Church, founded by St. Paul of the Cross (Ovada 1694 - Rome 1775) in 1721, the members of which are called Passionists. The purpose of this Congregation was and is to strive for a Christian form of living together and to proclaim the Word of the Cross in words and in deeds of charity.[3] St. Paul of the Cross was deeply moved by the sufferings of the poor living, or rather barely surviving, in

---

The term *superpotens* is used for God by Thomas, citing Pseudo-Dionysius in CDN c.8 l.3, but not as an alternative for the name *omnipotens*, but rather as a synonym of it.

[3] *Constitutions of the Congregation of the Passion of Jesus Christ*, Rome 1984, n.1, cf. *Rule of the Discalced Clerics of the Most Holy Cross and Passion of our Lord Jesus Christ*, Rome 1775, Chapter 1.

the swamps of Western Central Italy. These swamps, called the Maremmas, were in those days constantly war-stricken and famine- and malaria-infested. Civil and religious authorities had left these people to their devices. St. Paul of the Cross saw the name of Jesus written on the foreheads of these poor people (*Processi* I, 572). Inspired by the living memory of Christ's Passion he decided to answer God's call by living, in a religious community, close to them and working for and with them.

Passionists want to live in the spirit of their founder. In order to do so, Passionists take a fourth vow, in addition to poverty, chastity and obedience, called the *Memoria Passionis*. This so called "special vow" implies "recalling to mind the Passion of our Lord and to promote its memory by word and deed."[4] Characteristic for Passionist spirituality is the connection between the sufferings of people today and the sufferings of Christ and the love, wisdom and power of God, that He reveals to us in the Passion of Jesus Christ.[5] Living my life as a Passionist I grew in sensitivity of this connection.

But would it not be obvious for any Christian theologian or philosopher of religion to consider the relation between God, whom we profess as almighty, and human suffering from a christological perspective? After all, the sufferings of Christ take up a major part of the gospel narratives[6] and in Scripture they are explicitly connected with our sufferings, redemption and rising from the dead[7] as well as with God's role in it (see chapter 1 of this study). The more remarkable is it that in many Christian theodicies and considerations of the almightiness of God

---

[4] *Constitutions* (1984), n.96.

[5] *Constitutions* (1984), nn.3-6.

[6] From the very beginning of the gospels we find allusions to Christ's Passion, death and resurrection. In Ac 2,22-40, 3,11-26 we even read that it forms the centre of the proclamation of the gospel. In the letters of Paul and in the letters to all Christians it is referred to constantly.

[7] E.g. Lk 1,68, 24,19-27, Rm 3,24f, 5,6-11, Ga 3,13f, 24f, Ep 1,7, Ph 3,10f, Heb 2,10, 1 P 1,18, 1 Jn 4,10, 19, Rv 5,9.

Christ's Passion is discussed only briefly, on the side or as an appendix[8], or even not at all.[9]

    This study aims to be a contribution to an answer to the crisis in our faith as it is described above. For this some distance is taken from the present crisis as such, in order to inquire into the deeper theological roots. It is in view of this that in this study we are not merely interested in what "God is almighty" means as such, but primarily in how His almightiness shows (or does not show) in the Passion of Christ. The main question of this study, therefore, concerns a *nexus mysteriorum*: How in the Christian faith are the mystery of the Passion of Christ and the mystery of the almightiness of God interrelated?

    In order to find an answer to this question the theological writings of Thomas Aquinas (1224/5 - 1274) are studied, especially his *Summa Theologiae* (1266-1273), his latest, and although unfinished, most comprehensive and systematic work, which he wrote as *magister in Sacra Pagina*. Other works are used because they contain additional information needed for this study (for instance in chapter 2 on God's love), to show a development (for instance in chapter 1, on the place of satisfaction) or a change (for instance in chapter 3, Thomas' use of Lk 1,37) in Thomas' thoughts or an example or explanation by which the text in the *Summa Theologiae* is understood better.

    One of the inducements to the choice of this great Doctor of the Church is that this study has taken place and was written at the Catholic Theological University at Utrecht (KTU) in the context of the Thomas Instituut. After ten years this originally KTU institute was established as an inter-university institute, on the 7th March 2000. It functions as a centre for academic research into the life and the works of Thomas

---

    [8] Recent exemples: Richardson, Bowden (1991), 414 (last sentence), Van den Brink (1993) (only in the last subparagraph of the book (267-275) he recognizes that (268) "Christian theodicy cannot *in the end* do without *an appeal* to God's working in Christ to overcome evil" (italics added, MR), Schwartz (1995), 79-81 (he mentions Christ's sufferings, but they play no distinct role in his argument), Schoberth (1997), 66f.

    [9] Recent exemples: Van Driel (1988), Van der Ven (1990), chapter 5, Ammicht-Quinn (1992), Bonk (1996), Stackhouse jr. (1998), Lacroix (1998), Swinburne (1998), Kress (1999), Simonis (1999).

Aquinas. Characteristic for this research is the attention to Thomas'
profound theocentric orientation and his special attention to the language
we use when we speak of God and the things connected with Him.

Thomas' texts are approached using what Pesch calls the "method
of a double estrangement".[10] The first estrangement takes place when we
begin to read his texts with our questions in mind, which are not the same
as Thomas'. Therefore also his answers may not quite fit. The second
arises by reason of the often different context in which a subject is
considered, and Thomas' different associations and interests. We follow
this method in order to gain a better insight into what Thomas is saying
and what it may mean to us. Therefore, contemporary theologians and
philosophers of religion, reacting to Thomas, are also put upon the scene.

In earlier studies published by the Thomas Instituut it came to the
fore that Thomas was foremost a negative theologian, who also employs a
negative christology,[11] as well as a Scriptural theologian.[12] In this study
I will build on these two hypotheses. They will be tested in the inquiry
into this theme and evaluated in the general conclusion. The word theologian implies that Thomas poses a believer's questions regarding the
content of the faith of the Church. His questions concern the mysteries of
faith rather than (purely) philosophical problems. The word Scriptural
implies that Scripture functions in this proces as a guiding principle. The
word negative does not imply that we cannot say anything positive about
God. It rather refers to God's self-revelation in Scripture as a hidden God
(cf. Is 45,15), whom we can never have, possess or fathom fully and
adequately. Since God reveals Himself as a mystery, we cannot speak of
Him as if He were a problem (to be) solved. Negative theology is
employed to express this. We will see whether Thomas in discussing the
Passion of Christ follows the same line in his christology.

At the end of this study we will answer two more questions. One

---

[10] Pesch (1988), 40: Methode einer doppelten Entfremdung.

[11] Henk Schoot, *Christ the 'Name' of God, -Thomas Aquinas on Naming Christ*,
Leuven, Utrecht 1993

[12] Pim Valkenberg, *Words of the Living God, -Place and Function of Scripture in the
Theology of Thomas Aquinas*, Leuven, Utrecht 2000

is about a further characterisation of Thomas' theology. Jüngel[13] holds that Christian theology fundamentally is a theology of the Crucified One. He responds to Thomas' theology as one of the classical theologies which he does not recognize as such.[14] Can we, after examining how, in Thomas' theology, the connection is explained between the Passion of Christ and God's almightiness, characterize Thomas' theology as a *theologia crucis* in which God is thought of in the light of the Crucified, or does his theology rather emerge as a kind of speculative theology whereby a clear link to the Crucified is absent in the *theologia*?[15]

The second extra question that we want to answer at the end of this study comes from Christian art (and from the discussion on whether God suffers or is able to suffer). In depictions of the mercy seat, in which the Father upholds the cross on which the Son is crucified, we see the Father suffer; He is saddened. This image was never condemned; it is fully part of the Christian tradition. But what does this mean? How would Thomas answer our question whether we can say in faith, and if so, what it means, that God suffered, when Christ suffered?

In order to answer the main question of the book, four steps are taken in this study. First we review how Thomas speaks of the *passio* (the suffering) of Christ and whether and, if so, how he connects this with the almightiness of God. In chapter 2 the way Thomas speaks of the *passio* of God is expounded. Here we look at the use of metaphors *in divinis*. The third chapter, on the almightiness of God in Thomas' theology, contains the central part of this study. In the third paragraph lines in chapters 1

---

[13] Eberhard Jüngel, *Gott als Geheimnis der Welt, -Zur Begründung der Theologie des Gekreuzigten im Streit zwischen Theismus und Atheismus*, Tübingen 1977, 15 (English translation: 13).

[14] Jüngel, *o.c.*, 50f (40): "Der Tod Jesu hatte für den Gottesbegriff selber in der Regel überhaupt keine Bedeutung. Nicht nur in der metaphysischen, sondern auch in der christlichen Überlieferung wurde der Begriff des göttlichen Seins so sehr vom Gedanken der Absolutheit beherrscht, daß die christologische Identität Gottes mit dem gekreuzigten Jesus zu denken am besten Fall zu einem das Denken selber sprengenden Paradox führen konnte. Cf. esp. 6f, 139-141, 193f, 334, 347, 362, 378f (7, 106f, 145f, 245, 254f, 266, 277f).

[15] *Theologia* is the theology of what is in God, as distinct from the *oikonomia*, which concerns God's acting in the history of salvation.

and 2 come together with the ones of chapter 3. In the final paragraph of the third chapter the word almightiness itself is subject to examination: its place and how it functions in the Christian tradition (Scripture and negative theology; analogous language). In chapter 4 we consider the almightiness of Christ and the negative use of language in Thomas' christology.

Finally, in this study the Latin words *potentia* and *potestas* are translated as "might", whereas the word *virtus* is translated as "power". To us they may be synonyms and speaking of God Thomas sometimes uses these words as equivalents, but in paragraph 4.1 it is elucidated that there is a difference. So for the sake of clarity this translation is employed consistently. As a consequence of this choice *omnipotens* and *omnipotentia* are translated as "almighty" and the more unusual "almightiness". Translations of Thomas' texts are by the author. The English translation of the *Summa Theologiae* in the Blackfriars edition was consulted. The quotes from Scripture are taken from the New Jerusalem Bible, unless indicated otherwise.

Haastrecht, 17th December 2002

CHAPTER 1

THE *PASSIO* OF CHRIST

If God is almighty, why then the *passio* of Christ? Was God unable or unwilling to avoid it? What good did it do? If the *passio* were for any purpose, could God then not have achieved this aim in any other, better way? What kind of a God is that, that He allows or even wills the torment and the injury and the disgraceful death of not just someone, but of His only Son, Jesus Christ? The *passio* of Christ raises questions about God.

In the same way the event of Christ's *passio* and death on a cross raises questions about Christ Himself and His *passio*, as happened amongst His disillusioned first disciples, for instance the two leaving Jerusalem for Emmaus (Lk 24,14, 19-22): how and why could this have taken place? And who actually was this Jesus of Nazareth? It is the crucified and resurrected Jesus Himself, joining them in disguise, who reveals to them that He is the Christ and that His sufferings were necessary in order to enter into His glory (Lk 24,26). Unfortunately the gospel does not record Christ's own explanation, except that He used Scripture to demonstrate the reason: the fulfillment of the Scriptures (Lk 24,44 cf. 1 Co 15,3f etc.). Yet this reason alone may not provide a satisfying answer for us to the initial question.

As I said in the introduction to this study, Thomas' thoughts concerning the second part of the initial question, the *passio Christi*, will be examined first. In order to gain a clear understanding of the structure and the content of Thomas' theology concerning the *passio* of Christ, one could follow the order of Thomas' inquiry of the *quaestiones* "De passione" (46 to 49) in the *Tertia Pars* of the *Summa Theologiae*. The structure as described by Thomas in the introduction to *quaestio* 46, is indeed very clear: the first *quaestio* is about Christ's *passio* itself; the second on the efficient cause of His *passio*; the last two *quaestiones* on the fruits of His *passio* (with respect to the role of Christ in bringing them about, in *quaestio* 48, and with regard to the ones benefitting from it, namely we and Christ Himself, in *quaestio* 49).

But since in this study Thomas' texts are being read in view of the question about the relation between the *passio* of Christ and the almightiness of God, it is more obvious to begin with the discussion of the texts on how God, "the Almighty", Christ and others involved in this event, are related to Christ's *passio* and death (1.1). Therefore the first

step of this inquiry consists of the analysis of the first three *articuli* of
quaestio 47, also in order to draw up an inventory of the issues at stake.

Instead of starting off by discussing the relation between God and
Christ as efficient causes of Christ's *passio*, I will begin by discussing the
relation between Christ and His pursuers, for three reasons. Firstly, this
order of inquiry takes the historical fact that Christ was crucified seriously. Secondly, it is more logical if one takes Scripture as the basis and the
starting-point for theological reflection, for in the Passion narratives
"God" is not directly mentioned as an agent, whereas Christ and His
pursuers are. Thirdly, and I believe that this reason includes the first two,
it is Thomas' own order. This approach will take us to the very heart of
the matter and will lay open where Thomas' attention is focused as well
as what some of His presuppositions and choices are. At the same time
the outcome will raise quite a few questions, *our* questions which will be
the guideline, when the order of the *articuli* of *quaestio* 46 is pursued in
the following paragraphs.[1] Although the structure of Thomas' *quaestio*
"on the *passio* itself" may evoke in us a sense of surprise or even
estrangement, reading this *quaestio* in Thomas' order is preferable, since
by doing so Thomas' intentions, the line of his exposition and its
coherence, at times not so easily recognized or understood, may become
clearer. Hence in paragraph 1.2 the purpose and the suitability of Christ's
passio will be discussed, as Thomas considers it in *articuli* 1 to 4. Only
then - to us it may seem more logical to take this issue as a point of
departure - Thomas considers the *res* of the *passio*: what Christ
underwent and in what way, *articuli* 5 to 8, in paragraph 1.3. The next
three *articuli*, 9 to 11, are quite unexpected: on whether Christ suffered
and was crucified at the right time, in the right place and with the right
people. However, on further consideration these questions are not that
strange; after the internal aspects of Christ's *passio* Thomas reflects upon
the external aspects. Since the content of these *articuli* is either beyond
the scope of this study or closely connected with questions in 1.2, it will
only be discussed very briefly, in subparagraph 1.2.3. *Quaestio* 46
culminates in the, for this study crucial question "whether the *passio* of
Christ must be attributed to His divinity". Crucial, since the answer to

---

[1] This method is used by Corbin (1980) and Pesch (1988). Pesch (1988), 40, speaks of
the "Methode einer doppelten Entfremdung", the method of a double estrangement: We
read *Thomas'* works with *our* questions in mind *and* Thomas considers issues often in a
different way, in a different context and with different associations than ours.

this question touches upon the very foundations of our faith. In the final paragraph of this chapter this 12th *articulus* will be extensively discussed.

1.1 Who Caused Christ to Die?

In the gospels we read that after Christ had celebrated the Passover with His disciples, during which Judas, one of the Twelve, had left the group, He went with them to Gethsemane, on the Mount of Olives. According to the Synoptics He prayed that God's will would be done. While He was there with them, Judas came, accompanied by a large number of armed men, sent with Judas by the chief priests, the scribes and the elders, in order to arrest Him. After Judas had betrayed Him with a kiss, He was apprehended. The other disciples fled. Christ was led away. After a process before the Sanhedrin, that very same night, He was sentenced to death. For that they took Him to the Roman governor Pontius Pilate. After an interrogation he handed Christ over to be crucified. Christ was stricken and ridiculed by the Roman soldiers and thereupon burdened with the cross-bar. As they arrived at the mountain Golgotha, outside Jerusalem, they crucified Him and two others with Him. And after a loud cry He died.[2]

On the basis of this information it seems to be clear that Christ suffered and died by the agency of particular Jews and Romans. Apart from these two groups of people Thomas also distinguishes the roles of Christ Himself and of God in the event of the *passio* of Christ,[3] leading to His death on the cross; Thomas highlights that Christ was not only the object, but takes an active part in this event, and that similarly God was actively involved in it. Thomas takes one step at the time. First he

---

[2] Mt 26,20-27,50, Mk 14,17-15,37, Lk 22,14-23,46, Jn 13,2-19,30.

[3] In C1C c.2 1.2 (on 1 Co 2,8) Thomas mentions the role of the demons, which is persuading Judas: *Sed etiam daemones operati sunt in mortem Christi, persuadendo, secundum illud Ioan. XIII: "Cum diabolus iam misisset in cor, ut eum traderet, etc."* (Jn 13,2). They knew, Thomas continues, that He was the Christ, which is evident in Mk 1,24 and Lk 4,34 and in Mt 8,29 and Lk 4,41, although they did not fully grasp the mystery of Christ's divinity; *Augustinus dicit* [in IX *De civ. Dei*] *quod innotuit daemonibus, non per id quod est vita aeterna, sed* per quaedam temporalia sua virtute effecta.

considers the human relations: what was the role of Christ and what was
the role of His pursuers (*quaestio 47 articulus* 1)? Next Thomas reflects
upon the relation between Christ and God, with regard to respectively the
role of Christ and the role of God (*articuli* 2 and 3, in 1.1.2). Note that
Thomas speaks of the death of Christ as a part, namely the completion, of
His *passio*.

1.1.1 Christ and His Pursuers

As was said already, from Holy Scripture it seems to be clear that
Christ suffered and died by means of the hand of others than Himself.
Thomas points this out by quoting Lk 18,33 in the *sed contra* of *quaestio
47 articulus* 1: "And when they have scourged Him, they will put Him to
death," implying that this third prophecy of the Passion was fulfilled. It is
the most obvious conclusion drawn from the gospel stories. But this
seems to be contradictory, Thomas says in the *obiectiones*, to what we
read in other places in Scripture, that Christ was killed by Himself
(*occisus a seipso*). This is a theological question concerning the deep
structure of Christ's death. Thomas mentions three passages. First Jn
10,18, where Christ says that no one takes His soul (*anima*) away, but
that He will lay it down Himself. This verse refers to Jn 19,30, where it
says that Christ gave (up) (*tradidit*) His Spirit/spirit, actively that is; it
does not say that His Spirit/spirit escaped from Him, as something that
happened to Him, passively.[4] Thomas explicates in *obiectio* 1 that taking
someone's soul away is the definition of killing someone; "the soul is the
cause and the principle of a living body."[5]

The second passage brought forward by Thomas is about the way
Christ died. In Mt 27,50 we read that Christ died crying out in a loud
voice (*magna voce*). This loud voice is interpreted by contemporary
exegetes in divergent ways, varying from a cry of victory, in the light of
Mt 27,51f (the earth quaked, the rocks were split, the tombs opened and

---

[4] The same applies to Mt 27,50, where it says that Christ sent (*emisit*) the Spirit/spirit.

[5] ST Ia q.18 a.3 ag.2: [A]*nima est viventis corporis causa et principium*, cf. Aristotle
in II *De anima* c.4 n.3. And therefore in bodies death, ST IaIIae q.72 a.5co: *est per
remotionem principii vitae*. Hence, ST IIIa q.50 a.2 ag.3: [C]*orpus* [*Christi*] *mori non
poterat nisi anima separata*.

the bodies of many holy people rose from the dead), and a cry proclaiming to all the world (the veil of the Sanctuary was torn) the death of the Son of God[6], to a cry of utter despair, in the line of Ps 22,2.[7] Thomas is more interested in the christological meaning of the text and therefore he cites Augustine's interpretation in *De Trinitate* of Christ's loud voice[8]: people crucified died slowly, while their natural powers declined. The strength of Christ's voice then seems to indicate that Christ was, just before He died, not weakened like other people crucified who were eventually overcome by death, but that He laid down His life, by Himself.

The reader of Thomas' work is assumed to know that Christ died of His own free will.[9] Thomas refers to the content of these passages where he formulates the third argument, that someone who dies by being killed by someone else, dies by force (*per violentiam*) and therefore not of one's own free will. So that, since Christ died of His own free will, he cannot also have died by force; these two ways of dying seem to be incompatible. The argumentation is brought to a head by Thomas by quoting Augustine's words from the same chapter of *De Trinitate*, saying that "the spirit of Christ did not leave the flesh unwillingly, but because He willed it, when He willed it and in the way He willed it."

We might feel more comfortable with the emphasis on Christ having been killed by others than by Himself; in the Passion narratives we read that He died after His pursuers had crucified Him. Besides, would He otherwise not be a suicide? - a suspicion already found in Jn 8,22 (Jesus' audience thought Jesus alluded to killing Himself when He said "Where I am going, you cannot come."). But at the same time, although the second argument is less strong since it may admit of more interpretations, we cannot ignore Jn 10,18 - which already caused a division among Christ's audience (Jn 10,19-21) - and what Scripture and

---

[6] E.g. Senior, 141f resp. Gnilka, 476.

[7] E.g. Brown, 1078 and Nielsen, 167.

[8] IV *De Trin.* c.13, ML 42,899

[9] As it is expressed in Jn 4,34 and Mt 26,39, 42 and 44. In his commentary on Mt 26,42 in REM c.26 n.5 Thomas refers to Ps 40,9 (Vulg-Ps 39,9); not to be confused with Jonah's desire, in Jon 4,3; a different motive (see below).

an authority like Augustine say about Christ's free will.

In the *corpus* of the *articulus* Thomas argues that we are dealing with a paradox here: both views are in accordance with Scripture, both views of Christ's death are correct, provided that the one is not separated from the other; Christians must hold that Christ died both because He was killed by others *and* because He willed it. Therefore Thomas distinguishes between two ways of being effective, namely directly and indirectly. Now the first way is not difficult to grasp: to act upon something in order to bring something about. In this sense Christ's pursuers killed Him, for they afflicted Him so badly, that death followed, which was their purpose. Thomas does not pay much attention to this obvious explanation. Yet he underlines the role of Christ's free will[10], because that needs further clarification. The indirect way of causing something is by not preventing it, although one could. For instance when someone does not shut the window when it starts raining and this person is subsequently said to be the cause of the carpet being soaked. And in this way, Thomas says, Christ was the cause of His own death.

This second way needs further clarification, for it concerns a view on Christ's *passio* which is not intelligible without it: how could Christ have hindered His pursuers from crucifying Him? Thomas mentions two possibilities - fleeing is not one of them. The first is stopping His adversaries, in such a way that they would not want or be able to kill Him. Thomas does not elaborate this here, but it seems that he refers to what he recalls later on, that if His persecuters had known who He was, they would not have made Him suffer unto death (1 Co 2,8).[11] The second possibility is based on christology:

> "The spirit of Christ had the might (*potestas*) to preserve
> the nature of His flesh, so that it would not be over-
> powered by whatever inflicted injury. And the soul of

---

[10] ST IIIa q.47 a.1co: *Quia ergo anima Christi non repulit a proprio corpore nocumentum illatum, sed* voluit *quod natura corporalis illi nocumento succumberet, dicitur suam animam posuisse, vel* voluntarie *mortuus est.* Whilst in REI c.2 1.3 n.2 Thomas iuxtaposes the two aspects: *Christus enim mortuus fuit* et *ab aliis occisus; Matth. XVII,22: "Et occident eum": eo* tamen *volente: quia, ut dicitur Isa. LIII,7, "oblatus est quia ipse voluit".*

[11] ST IIIa q.47 a.5co.

Christ did have this [might] indeed, since it was connected to the Word of God in unity of person, as Augustine (l.c.) says."[12]

This raises quite a few questions. But what is important for this moment, is to see that Thomas points here to a fundamental difference between Christ as a human being and us: on account of the union in one person and *suppositum* between the incarnated Word of God and the human being Christ[13], this Christ had the might to protect His body from any harm. Therefore, unlike in us, *all* that belongs to human nature is in Christ subject to His will and might, as Thomas states in this context explicitly in the *Quaestiones quodlibetales* and in the *Compendium theologiae*.[14] The consequence of this is that, since Christ did suffer and die, it must have been because He did not thwart the plans of His pursuers; He wanted to suffer and die. And in this sense we say that Christ also died "*a seipso*", indirectly. He was the subject, laying down His life, of His own free will.

By this explanation Thomas has shown how texts like Lk 18,33 and Jn 10,18 are not conflicting, but reflect a different aspect of the same truth. And Thomas endorses Augustine's emphasis on Christ's ultimate

---

[12] ST IIIa q.47 a.1co: *Secundo, quia spiritus eius habebat* potestam conservandi *naturam carnis suae, ne a quocumque laesivo inflicto opprimeretur. Quod quidem habuit anima Christi, quia erat Verbo Dei coniuncta in unitate personae, ut Augustinus dicit, in IV De Trin.* (l.c.).

[13] ST IIIa q.2 aa.2, 3.

[14] QDL I q.2 a.2co, explaining Jn 19,30 (sc): *Sed ad videndum causam mortis eius considerandum est quod, cum Christus fuerit* verus Deus et homo, *eius potestati suberat* quidquid *pertinet ad humanam naturam in Christo; quod in aliis puris hominibus non contingit: voluntati enim eorum non subiacent quae naturalia sunt*; OTT c.230, explaining Jn 10,18: *Nos enim morimur quasi morti subiecti ex necessitate vel naturae vel alicuius violentiae nobis illatae. Christus autem mortuus est non ex necessitate, sed potestate et propria voluntate. Unde ipse dicebat Ioan. X (v.18): "Potestatem habeo ponendi animam meam, et iterum sumendi eam." Huius autem differentiae ratio est, quia naturalia voluntati nostrae non subiacent; coniunctio autem animae ad corpus est naturalis, unde voluntati nostrae non subiacet, quod anima corpori unita remaneat, vel quod a corpore separatur, sed oportet hoc ex virtute alicuius agentis provenire. Quidquid autem in Christo secundum humanam naturam erat naturale,* totum *eius voluntati subiacebat propter divinitatis virtutem, cui subiaceret* tota *natura.*

freedom, most explicitly where he concludes that "no one takes away My soul from Me" (Jn 10,18) must be understood with the addition "against My will (*invito*)", i.e. under duress.

But a question already posed remains: is Christ in this way not a 'spitting image' of a suicide? Thomas refutes this thought in his *Quaestiones quodlibetales*. First he states the general truth that our earthly body exists for the sake of the soul and not the other way round. This is not an expression of contempt for the body[15], but because the soul is the life giving principle of the body, without which the body is dead and not the other way round.[16] Therefore, Thomas calls it injustice to the soul that it is forced to leave the body, when the body is inflicted with injury unbearable for that body. Here he presupposes that the desire to live is natural to a human being, a desire absent in someone with a distorted will, who therefore becomes self-destructive. If Christ's will was well-ordered and if His soul had the might to withdraw from- *and* to return to the body (cf. Jn 10,18), then definitely leaving His body would be an act of self-destruction, comparable to a man destroying his own house.[17] This holds also for Christ, unless dying, or letting the soul leave the body, would be in accordance with His, not distorted, will.

This explanation by Thomas maybe leaves the reader with more questions than answers. Quite a few issues need to be clarified in the

---

[15] Thomas stresses the importance of taking good care of the body in e.g. ST Ia q.85 a.7co: *Manifestum est enim quod quanto corpus est melius dispositum, tanto meliorem sortitur animam*; cp. IaIIae q.63 a.1co, IIaIIae q.81 a.7co, qq.146 - 156. N.B. that Thomas in IIaIIae q.55 aa.1, 2 only speaks of *prudentia carnis* as a sin resp. a mortal sin in as far as it causes a human being to turn away from God (as in Ph 3,19).

[16] ST Ia q.75 a.1co: [*A*]*nima dicitur esse* primum principium vitae *in his quae apud nos vivunt: "animata" enim viventia dicimus, res vero "inanimatas" vita carentes*; IIaIIae q.100 a.1 ad 6: [*S*]*icut anima vivit* secundum seipsam, *corpus vero vivit ex unione animae.*

[17] QDL I q.2 a.2co: *Nec tamen culpandus est quasi sui homicida. Est enim corpus propter animam, et non e converso. Unde iniuria fit animae, cum propter nocumentum corpori illatum de corpore expellitur contra* naturalem appetitum animae, *sed forte non propter depravatam voluntatem se interficientis. Sed si anima in sui potestate haberet recedere a corpore quando vellet, et iterum advenire, non maioris esset culpae si corpus desereret, quam quod habitator deseruit domum; culpae tamen est quod inde expellatur invitus.*

course of this study: that Christ had a well-ordered will and what this means, and why His will to die was in accordance with it. In other words: why did He not avert His violent death, which, Thomas says, He could have done? Moreover, the way in which Thomas speaks of Christ undergoing violence unto death does not so much highlight Christ's weakness, but rather His strength and that He even had everything under control. This evokes the question of the extent of His might: was Christ almighty?

These questions are closely connected with those concerning Christ's *passio*. In his explanation of Christ's loud cry in Mt 27,50 (and Mk 15,37) Thomas underlines how remarkable His death was. Citing Jn 19,32f, he even contends that it must be reckoned amongst His miracles that Christ saved His strength until the very end, so that He could cry out in a *loud* voice and die so soon;[18] and that this is the reason that the centurion recognized Him as the Son of God (Mk 15,39); and that Pilate was astonished (Mk 15,44). But, one may ask, did Christ then really suffer? Does Thomas do justice to the faith of the Church that Christ truly suffered (*vere passus*)?[19]

Moreover, if Christ did not *die* like any other human being, one may ask whether He actually *lived* as a human being: was Christ a true human being (*verus homo*)? In the *Questiones quodlibetales* (note 14) Thomas speaks of Christ as truly God and man (*verus Deus et homo*), which seems to imply that the man Christ was human as we are. But in the same text he speaks of us, other human beings, as pure human beings (*pures homines*), as distinct from Christ. Apparently Thomas makes this distinction because of the hypostatic union of the Word of God with the man Christ in one person and *suppositum*. In this study we will inquire what it means for a correct interpretation of Christ's *passio* that He was not a "pure" human being. A question that comes up in this context is that in this *articulus* Thomas considers the *passio* of Christ's body (note 12: *carnis*); what does Thomas say about the *passio* of Christ's soul?

---

[18] ST IIIa q.47 a.1 ad 2: *Sicut enim eius voluntate natura corporalis conservata est in suo vigore ad extremum, sic etiam quando voluit,* subito *cessit nocumento illato.*

[19] A question also in the light of what we read (note 14) in QDL, that everything concerning His human nature is subject to His might and will, and in OTT - more precisely, as will be shown in chapter 4 - that everything concerning His human nature is subject to His will by reason of divine power.

Furthermore, since the soul of Christ is united with the Word of God as was said above (ibidem), how does the *passio* affect His divine nature?

1.1.2 Christ and God

The relation between Christ and God with regard to the *passio* of Christ is designated in Scripture by two actions: the one being Christ's obedience (Ph 2,8), to God that is, and the other God's handing Christ over (Rm 8,32) to the *passio* that ended with His death. In particular this second Scriptural text may evoke the image of Christ being the victim of the abuse of power and authority by a peremptory, cruel and angry god, and not only nowadays, but in the 13th century as well. However, this misunderstanding is short-circuited by Thomas in two ways, namely by discussing Rm 8,32 distinct but not separated from Ph 2,8; both pauline texts approach the same event from a different point of view. Further Thomas, following on Christ's own addressing of God as Father, emphatically speaks of God *the Father* in *articuli* 2[20] en 3 - a word implying "Son" as well as (source of) life and concern.

In Respect of Christ, the Son

Thomas presents the question how to understand Christ's obedience as an inner Scriptural issue. The problems rise from the word obedience itself and the understanding of it.[21] For obedience presupposes a precept or an order. But where in Scripture do we read that God commands Christ to suffer? Connected with this is the apparent contra-distinction between the necessity to obey, which goes with a precept, and

---

[20] The word *Pater* is as remarkably absent in the *obiectiones* as it is present in the Thomas' answers; he even adds, citing Ph 2,8, *Patri* to *obediens* (a.2sc).

[21] Eder (1993), 17, in discussing ST IIIa q.47 aa.2, 3, fails to see that Thomas examines the meaning of biblical texts; according to him "*Thomas* hat auch kein Bedenken zu erklären: 'Christus empfing vom Vater den Auftrag zu leiden,' und *er* beruft sich dafür auf Jo 10,18." (italics added, MR) Since Eder similarly fails to explore both the deep structure of Christ's obedience and the context in which Thomas poses these questions, Thomas' theology remains totally incomprehensible to him.

Christ's voluntariness regarding the *passio*, which came forward in the former subparagraph. And thirdly, since we read in Ep 5,2 that Christ handed Himself over out of love for us, is it not better to speak of His love than of His obedience as the motive for His *passio*?

In the *corpus* of the *articulus* Thomas mentions three reasons why Christ's obedience in respect of His *passio* was "most becoming" or "most becoming (*convenientissimum*)". This is a way of argumentation not by solid evidence, but by showing the multi-layeredness and the harmony of God's abundant goodness in events or in the state of things. In this case Thomas on the basis of Scripture tries to convince his readers of this, that Christ's obedience is good and just in view of God's plan with us. First He shows that it was becoming in view of our justification, citing Rm 5,19 while the verses 12 to 21 resound, where a parallel is drawn between Adam's disobedience, through which many became sinners, and Christ's obedience, through which many are justified (cf. 1 Co 15,21f). It recalls the image of a pair of scales put into balance again. After this most obvious reason Thomas moves to a deeper, somewhat less obvious level, citing the text just preceding Rm 5,12-21: "We are reconciled with God through the death of His Son" (Rm 5,10, cf. Col 1,22). This text refers to the Old Testament sacrifices, that were made for the peoples' reconciliation with God. St. Paul interprets Christ's voluntary death as a sacrifice pleasing to God (Ep 5,2 again). Thomas underlines that this sacrifice was so pleasing to God especially because of Christ's obedience, citing 1 S 15,22: "Obedience is better than sacrifices." The third reason is on an even deeper level:

> "This [i.e. that He died out of obedience] was in keeping with His victory, whereby He triumphed over death and the author of death. For a soldier cannot conquer, unless he obeys the commander-in-chief. And so the man Christ obtained the victory through this, that He was obedient to God: in accordance with Pr 21,28: 'An obedient man speaks of victories.'"[22]

---

[22] ST IIIa q.47 a.2co: *Tertio, hoc conveniens fuit eius victoriae, qua de morte et auctore mortis triumphavit. Non enim miles vincere potest nisi duci obediat. Et ita homo Christus victoriam obtinuit per hoc quod Deo fuit obediens: secundum illud Prov. 21,28: "Vir obediens loquitur victorias."*

Yes, Thomas is still discussing Christ's death on the cross. Yet the terms he is using here may be somewhat strange to us. Although, on second thoughts this idea and the terminology is perfectly in keeping with 1 Co 15,54f ("Death is swallowed up in victory. Death where is your victory", a reference by St. Paul to Is 25,8), which Thomas does not cite here, but which clearly resounds; he takes 1 Co 15 here to be common knowledge.[23]

So Thomas began with the conclusion: that Christ's obedience was "most becoming", for he sees three reasons why it was "becoming". Now these three reasons and the order in which they are presented designate a purposiveness in Christ's *passio*. Thomas draws our attention to deeper levels, where we may descry God's underlying plan, being our salvation (*salus*), and the order in which it is brought about: our justification, *leading to* our reconciliation with God, *the consequence of which is* the defeat of death and its author. The superlative Thomas uses at the beginning of his exposition makes the reader aware that he considers something of utmost importance. The importance here is not that Christ's *passio* was to our salvation - he has already discussed this in *quaestio* 46 - but that Christ's obedience was "most becoming" in this respect.

After the conclusion that there is no tension between "Christ" and "obedient", on the contrary rather, Thomas continues to expound how to understand the Scriptural texts in the light of one another. First he must establish that there was indeed an order: that "the Father" ordered Christ to undergo the crucifixion is said by Christ Himself, in Jn 10,18b.[24]

---

[23] The insight that Thomas presupposes a basic knowledge of Scripture in his readers, contains a warning to us: We cannot determine how Scriptural Thomas' theology is just by counting how often he explicitly cites texts from the First or Second Testament. The importance of this awareness for a good understanding of Thomas' theology will also be shown in 3.2 and 3.3.

[24] Until here Thomas only cited the first part of the verse. Thomas elaborately shows how Christ fulfilled all the precepts of the Old Law, cf. Jn 19,30, *Consummatum est*: the moral (stressing Christ's love for the Father and for His neighbour, resp. Jn 14,31 and Ga 2,20), the ceremonial (the sacrifices of the Old Law prefigured Christ's, citing Col 2,16f; cf. Ex 29,18 and Ep 5,2) and the judicial (satisfaction, cit. Ps 69,5; see 1.2) precepts. By the way, Thomas says that Jn 19,30 can (*potest*) be understood in this way, which means that this is not the only possible interpretation, as Thomas shows in REI c.19 l.5 n.2: apart from the *consummatio Scripturarum* (Lk 18,31) he first mentions the *consummatio mortis* (Heb 2,10) and *sanctificationis* (Heb 10,14).

This verse already implies voluntariness. The word obedience does imply necessity, but only with regard to the thing prescribed; an order demands obedience. But obeying an order is a matter of the will; and Christ wanted to obey His Father, as was shown above.

And Christ obeyed the Father out of love (Ep 5,2). In the *Secunda Secundae* Thomas enunciates how intertwined the virtues of love and obedience are, as in 1 Jn 2,4f: "Whoever says 'I know God' without keeping His commandments, is a liar and truth has no place in him. But anyone who keeps His word, in such a one God's love truly reaches its perfection."[25] And hence Thomas can conclude that we must say that for the same reason (*eadem ratione*) Christ suffered out of love and out of obedience.

In his commentary on Ph 2,8 Thomas stresses how great this obedience actually was. It was much more than 'simply' doing the good the Father willed Him to do, since accepting death on a cross goes against any person's natural inclinations, which are directed towards the good of life and honor.[26]

It is important to see that Thomas brings into the limelight that Christ's obedience was a free and conscious act, as an answer to what His Father willed Him to do. At the same time it shows that the Father's will was not arbitrary. For in the *corpus* of the *articulus* Thomas speaks of God's plan and purposes, namely our justification, our reconciliation with God and the defeat of death and its author. And in his commentary on Ph 2,8 he quotes 1 P 3,18 concerning Christ's death for our sins (*pro peccatis nostris*). Further on in this chapter this purposiveness will be analysed in greater detail.

No matter how Scriptural it is, the image of the conquering hero

---

[25] Cited in ST IaIIae q.104 a.3co, cf. CRO c.5 1.5 (on Rm 5,19, citing Ph 2,8 and Ep 5,2). And the same connection is found where Christ urges His disciples to remain united in Him and with one another by means of obedience and love, Jn 15,1-17. Since love is the first and most excellent virtue (1 Co 13,13, cited in q.23 a.6sc), without which no other virtue can be (1 Co 13,3, W 8,7, cited in q.23 a.7sc), q.104 a.3sc: [O]*bedientia habet laudem ex eo quod ex caritate procedit* (quotation from Gregory, ult. *Moral.* L.35 c.14, ML 76,765).

[26] RPL c.2 1.2 v.8, citing 1 P 3,18 and W 2,20; also Dt 21,23 and Ga 3,13 come to mind. For the desire for life and honor see resp. ST IaIIae q.35 a.6 ad 1 and q.31 a.5co. Cf. Vosman (1996) 63-85.

used by Thomas may sound an alarm: is Thomas' theology on the *passio* of Christ a *theologia gloriae*? Does he take the cross seriously? Is Christ in the *Summa Theologiae* an unaffected hero, a victorious saviour, a kind of superman? And if not, what then is Thomas saying in his discussion of His *passio*? But before going any deeper into this, the role of "God the Father" will be considered first: *articulus* 3.

In Respect of God, the Father

In Rm 8,32[27] we read that God did not spare His own Son, but handed Him over. It does not say: it was a mistake or a blunder; it did not slip through God's fingers. Neither do we read anywhere in Scripture that God was powerless to do anything to hinder Christ's infliction and crucifixion[28] nor that He tried or willed to. Handing over (*tradere*) is an act, of God in this case. But how then could this have come to pass?

> "For it is wicked and we consider it cruel that an innocent person be handed over to *passio* and death. But, as it is said in Dt 32,4: 'God is faithful and without any iniquity.' Hence He did not hand the innocent Christ over to *passio* and death."[29]

This argument's power of expressiveness has not diminished over the

---

[27] And also in Rm 4,25 and Is 53,6, read as referring to Christ (as in CIS c.53).

[28] Still Hedinger (1983), 57-61, holds that God was powerless with regard to this; that He did not, for He could not, preclude Pilate from crucifying Christ. It is not quite clear what he means when he thereupon says, that God does protest against the crucifixion. Hedinger contrasts God's powerlessness with regard to the crucifixion with God's power in the event of Easter and Pentecost (pp 61-63). Hedinger leaves his readers with at least two questions, one concerning the scriptural basis of this view of God and the crucifixion, and the other concerning God at one time being powerless and at another powerful.

[29] ST IIIa q.47 a.3 ag.1: *Videtur quod Deus Pater non tradiderit Christum passioni. Iniquum enim est crudele esse videtur quod innocens passioni et morti tradatur. Sed sicut dicitur Deut.* [32,4], *"Deus fidelis et absque nulla iniquitate." Ergo Christum innocentem non tradidit passioni et morti.*

centuries; it is still a question very much alive.[30] It touches upon the very heart of our faith in God: is He really good, if He allows evil to happen or even acts wickedly Himself?

In the *Summa Contra Gentiles* this objection is sustained, where the argumentation is that

> "it was not befitting to God that He made a human being undergo death, since death seems to be contrary to divinity, which is life."[31]

How can God, the giver of life,[32] essentially being life itself, *make* someone endure death? Next Thomas even makes the argumentation heavier, saying that Scripture itself, namely Ezk 18,23 and 32, testifies that God does not will the death of *any* person; He wills even a sinner to repent and *live*.[33] So God as the one handing Christ over to His *passio* seems to act contrary to who and what He is.

Further it is problematic to say that *God* handed Christ over, for two reasons. First since, as was just shown above, Christ handed Himself over (Ep 5,2). And also Is 53,12, read by Thomas as referring to Christ, speaks of the initiative (*tradidit*, hif'il of ה ר ע) of the servant of YHWH. Secondly, since we read in Scripture that Judas, being a devil - Thomas cites Jn 6,70f here - is held responsible for handing Christ over. In the same gospel we read that Pilate says to Christ: "It is your own people and the chief priests who have handed you over to me" (Jn 18,35). And further on (Jn 19,16) it is Pilate himself who hands Him over to be crucified. The acts of these people are reckoned amongst the iniquities. And therefore, says Thomas, showing the complexity of the matter, handing over Christ cannot be an act of the Just one, it seems (2 Co 6,14). As in the third *obiectio* of *articulus* 2 Thomas presents the problem

---

[30] E.g. Wiersinga (1974), 218-221 (221: "God is geen vampier"); Wissink (1993), 151-154.

[31] SCG IV c.53 n.14: [*N*]*on fuit conveniens Deum hominem* factum *mortem pati, quia mors contraria esse videtur divinitati, quae est vita*. Again, *facere* denotes an act, by God.

[32] Cf. Gn 2,7, Jn 5,26.

[33] SCG IV c.53 n.15.

here of how to interpret paradoxical texts from Scripture in the light of one another. The problem is similar to the one in the former *articulus*, only now the focus is on the role of God the Father instead of on Christ.

Thomas begins his answer by repeating the conclusion of the former *articulus*, that Christ suffered voluntarily out of obedience. Thomas then explains that this conclusion has three consequences (*Unde...*) for how we are to conceive the Father's role in the event of Christ's *passio*. In order to unearth these consequences Thomas analyses the elements of the conclusion.

"Obedience" presupposes a precept or an order (cf. Jn 10,18), as was said. And precepts and orders presuppose the will of the one who prescribes and orders, i.c. God the Father. So it (somehow) was the Father's will that Christ suffered. Thomas cites Is 53,6 and 10 as referring to Christ to confirm this. Yet two elements mentioned by Thomas in his explanation do not emerge from these verses from Isaiah, namely that this will is eternal and that He ordered, from eternity, Christ's *passio* to the liberation of the human race.[34] The reason why the will that Christ suffers is eternal, is because it is the will *of God*. God Himself is eternal, which means that there is no earlier and later in God. For the correct understanding of this it is crucial to see that this is beyond our imagination, for everything we observe and experience is subject to time; being subject to time is proper to all creation. Since God is the Creator and not a creature, He is not subject to time and to the change that is inherent in it. And this is what we call eternal.[35] This means that it is incompatible with God's eternity that He begins to will something

---

[34] ST IIIa q.47 a.3co: *Uno quidem modo, secundum quod sua* aeterna *voluntate* prae*ordinavit passionem Christi* ad humani generis liberationem. Thomas subsequently cites Is 53,6, 10.

[35] ST Ia q.10 a.1co: *[S]icut in cognitionem simplicium oportet nos venire per composita, ita* in conitionem aeternitatis oportet nos venire per tempus. [....] *Sicut igitur ratio temporis consistit in numeratione prioris et posterioris in motu, ita in apprehensione uniformitatis eius quod est* omnino extra *motum, consistit ratio aeternitatis*. This means that according to Thomas eternity is a negative term, i.e. a word that designates something of which we do not exactly know what it is, but only what it is not. In q.10 a.3 Thomas argues that *aeternitas vere et proprie in solo Deo est*; everything else called eternal participates in God's eternity, or is called eternal because it is undetermined (like the eternal fire in Mt 25,41).

that He earlier did not will or that He stopped willing what He does will.[36] The consequence of this is that, if it was God's will that Christ underwent *passio* unto death, He must have willed it from eternity - although we do not quite know what this means, since we do not know what eternity is, but only what it is not.[37]

The other element that does not stem from Is 53, the liberation of the human race, is another instance of Thomas speaking of the purpose of Christ's *passio*: "for us (*pro nobis*)". A closer look at this will be taken in the next subparagraph.

The second consequence relates to the word "voluntarily". This implies that handing Christ over as in Rm 8,32, cannot be understood as that God the Father forced Christ in any way. Therefore Thomas says:

> "He [i.e. God the Father] has inspired His will to suffer
> for us, by infusing love into Him. Therefore we read in
> the following verse: 'He has become obedient, because He
> willed it.' (Is 53,7)"[38]

And in his commentary on Rm 8,32 Thomas stresses even more how spontaneous Christ's response was.[39] And again the close interrelatedness of love and obedience is shown here. But what's more, it catches the eye that Thomas speaks here in terms of inspiration, love and will, words that allude to the Holy Spirit (see also paragraph 2.1). In this formulation Thomas brings to our attention that the handing over and the obedience are not an entre-nous so to say between the Father and the Son; the bond

---

[36] Cf. Ps 33,11, 119,89-91.

[37] As in ST Ia q.19 a.7 on the changeability of God's will, where he explaines Nb 23,19. In the *corpus* Thomas makes a clear distinction between changing one's will and wanting that first something happens and that next the opposite comes about. See also q.9 a.1 on God's immutability in general (where he cites W 7,24, Jm 4,8, which seem to imply change, and Ml 3,6) and q.14 a.15 regarding God's knowledge (sc cit. Jm 1,17). For a detailed study on this matter: Goris (1996), 34-52.

[38] ST IIIa q.47 a.3co: *Secundo, inquantum inspiravit ei voluntatem patiendi pro nobis, infundendo ei caritatem. Unde ibidem* (Is 53,7) *sequitur: "Oblatus est quia voluit."*

[39] CRO c.8 l.6: *Tradidit eum Deus Pater in mortem, eum incarnari et pati statuendo et humanus eius voluntati inspirando caritatis affectum, qua passionem* spontaneus *subiret.*

between Father and Son is described as through the Holy Spirit.[40] The handing over is an act of the Triune God, as Thomas says in his commentary of the *Sententiae Magistri Petri Lombardi*: "God the Father, yes even the whole Trinity has handed Him over."[41]

But, the third consequence, not only did the Father hand Christ over *to* the *passio*, He also handed Him over *in* the *passio*, namely by exposing Him to the might (*potestas*) of His pursuers. In his commentary on the *Sententiae* this is Thomas' explanation of Jn 19,11a: "You would have no power over Me at all, if it had not been given you from above" (note 41). However, in the *Summa Theologiae* Thomas, following Augustine, says that this is how the loud cry of the Crucified, "My God, My God, why have You abandoned Me?!" (Mt 27,46), must be understood. This exegesis by Thomas of Christ uttering these first words of Psalm 22 is a rather unusual one nowadays. Is he not too formal here? Does Thomas take this cry seriously as a cry from the depth of Christ's heart? Does he do justice to the true abandonment? For the sake of the clarity of the discussion of this third *articulus*, I will first consider Thomas' answers to the *obiectiones*, before going deeper into these questions concerning this abandonment.

It cannot come as a surprise that Thomas denies that God is bloodthirsty.[42] But the ground for this denial is not that handing over Christ to and in the *passio* was for a good purpose: "The end justifies the means" is not the device of our God. No, Thomas underlines, the reason why God cannot be called wicked and cruel, is that this handing over is not against Christ's will. Christ's will was inspired, Thomas says in the

---

[40] And if this is the case, we have found here the seed for what Schoonenberg centuries later (1991) calls Spirit-christology (Geest-christologie), i.e. a reflection on Christ's life and death in which the bond between Christ and God is seen as through the Spirit. See also Rikhof (2000), esp. 95-100.

[41] SN III d.20 a.5a co: *Deus Pater, immo tota Trinitas, eum tradidit. Uno modo, praeordinando passionem eius a salutem humani generis. Secundo Christo homini voluntatem dando, et caritatem ex qua pati voluit. Tertio dando potestatem et non cohibendo voluntatem occidentium, sicut dicitur Joan. XIX,11: "Non haberes in me potestatem, nisi fuisset tibi data desuper."*

[42] Besides the texts from Ezk 18 also Ps 78,38, 86,15, 111,4, 112,4, Ezk 33,11, 1 Tm 2,4 and 2 P 3,9 as well as Ps 5,7 and Pr 6,16-19 may come to mind.

corpus, not forced. In other words, whoever only looks in a superficial way and does not see on a deeper level, does not notice the involvement of the Holy Spirit here and may therefore deem God cruel indeed. Hence this deeper level is vital for a correct understanding of God the Father handing over Christ.[43]

In order to grasp how Christ can be handed over by Himself and by God, Thomas distinguishes two wills in Christ, a human, inspired will, and a divine will, which is the same as the Father's will. With His human will He complied with the will of God the Father. Now on a deeper level we see that Christ is not only human, but also the divine Son. And since there are not three wills, but only one will in God, Christ handed Himself over with the same will and with the same action as the Father did it; the human being Christ complied with the one will of the Father, the Son and the Holy Spirit.[44] And in this way Thomas has shown how Rm 8,32 and Ep 5,2 are not in any way conflicting texts.

That Christ allowed His pursuers to crucify Him was already set out by Thomas in *articulus* 1 (1.1.1). Here he elucidates why, although they wanted the same as God and the man Christ, namely Christ's death by crucifixion, *their* act was impious, whereas God's and Christ's were not. Again a level under the surface of the event is uncovered by Thomas:

---

[43] Note that Thomas explicitly states that, ST IIIa q.47 a.3 ad 1: *innocentem hominem passioni et morti tradere contra eius voluntatem, est impium et crudele.* Also, Thomas states in CDN c.10 l.1: *Contingit autem aliquem aliquibus principari dupliciter. Uno modo per modum timoris, et iste modus principandi non est efficax ad subditos tenendum. Qui enim contra propriam voluntatem subduntur, qui timore serviunt, data opportunate, servitutis iugum excutiunt. Alio modo* per modum amoris *et hic modus principandi est* efficax *ad tenendum subiectos qui* voluntarie *subduntur, et* hunc modum principandi Deo attribuit.

[44] ST IIIa q.18 a.1: Since Christ was truly human, He must have had a human will. In sc Thomas cites Lk 22,42, where Christ speaks of the will of the Father and His own. Since He was the Son of God, He must have had 'a' divine will. And since God is *maxime indivisum* (Ia q.11 a.4co), this must have been the one divine will, the same as the Father's. Thomas speaks of the man Christ's obedience to God *the Father* following on Christ's own addressing God as Father.
This explanation resounds Jn 5,19 and 30, two texts that will be discussed in greater detail in chapter 4, considering the almightiness of Christ.

the origin of their action was sinful[45]; greed was Judas', envy was the Jews' and fear of the emperor was Pilate's according to respectively Mt 26,14-16, Mt 27,18 and Jn 19,12.[46] In the *Sententiae* Thomas mentions God's and Christ's motives: the salvation (*salus*) of the human race respectively love (*caritas*).[47] Both will be discussed in the next sub-paragraphs.

My God, My God, Why Have You Abandoned Me?!

Thomas is very compact in his exegesis of this text in the *Summa Theologiae*. Reading his exposition on Mt 27,46 in his commentary on the gospel according to St. Matthew gives some insight into his method of reading a text from Scripture. Since some key elements are important for understanding what Thomas is doing when he considers Christ's *passio*, a major part of the text is quoted here. With regard to the cry itself, as distinct from its effect, he says:

"According to Origen that Christ cries out in a loud

---

[45] They wanted the same, but in a different way, in SN III d.20 a.5a ad 3: [C]onformitas voluntatis humanae ad divinam, non est simpliciter in volendo quod Deus vult, sed in volendo eodem mod, id est ex caritate, sicut Deus vult, vel ad eumdem finem, vel in volendo id quod Deus vult nos velle.

[46] It must be noted that Thomas is in the ST much more balanced than in the SN. In the latter (III d.20 a.5a ad 3) he only speaks of "the Jews" and without referring to texts from Scripture he mentions the origin and the purpose of theirs, being wickedness (*nequitia*) and obstructing the salvation of humankind, despite the fact that they saw it following from Christ's preaching (*impedientiam salutem quam ex eius praedicatione sequi videbant*). Judas and Pilate are not mentioned here. In the ST IIIa he distinguishes not only between Judas, the other Jews and Pilate, but also between the ordinary Jews and their leaders (q.47 a.5) and he broadens "Pilate" to "Pilate" and "(the) gentiles" (q.47 a.4). Yet since he still speaks in ST about "Jews" or "the Jews" being guilty of killing Christ, which is, as Thomas nota bene says, "so to say murdering God Himself" (q.46 a.12), and being much more guilty than "(the) gentiles" (q.47 a.6), it is a small step from his exposition to a persecution of Jews, ST IIIa q.46 a.12 ag.3: *Iudaei puniti sunt pro peccato occisionis Christi tanquam homicidae ipsius Dei*. See also the article of Valkenberg (2002), 43, 47-50, on Thomas' interpretation of Jn 8,12-59.

[47] SN III d.20 a.5a co, ad 3.

voice, also designates a multitude of mysteries. Is 6,3:
'Seraphim cried out to one another: Holy, holy holy, the
Lord, God of the hosts.' Therefore, who wants to understand this as that He has cried out of sadness about His
death, has not understood it as a mystery. Hence it must
not be understood in that way; but since He wanted to
give to us the understanding that He is equal to the
Father, He has said in Hebrew: 'Eli, Eli, lama sa-
bacthani?' Further, since He wanted to indicate that the
passio was announced in advance by the prophets,
therfore He has used the words of Psalm 22,2: 'My God,
look at me; why have You abandoned me?' Therefore
Hieronymus says that those who want to explain this
Psalm in a different way than in respect of the *passio* of
Christ, are impious.

Note that some have misunderstood it. Therefore you
must know that there have been two heresies: one, Arius',
that holds that the Word was not united in Christ, but that
the Word had taken the place of the soul. It belongs to the
other one, Nestorius', that the Word was not naturally
united but by grace, as in a righteous person, like the
prophets."[48]

Then Thomas explains why these are heresies: according to Arius the
words are of the Word of God, which he perceives as a creature; hence
the Word cries out saying "God" instead of "Father". The Nestorian
interpretation rightly understands these words as coming from the man

---

[48] REM c.27 n.2: *Secundum Originem Christus voce magna clamat, et signat*
multitudinem mysteriorum. *Isa. cap. VI v.3: "Seraphim clamabant alter ad alterum:*
'Sanctus, sanctus, sanctus Dominus Deus exercituum." Unde qui vult hoc intelligere, quod
taedio mortis clamavit, non intellexit mysterium; *ideo non sic intelligendum est, sed quia*
voluit dare intelligere se aequalem Patri, *lingua hebraea dixit: "Eli, Eli lamasabacthani?"*
Item voluit signare quod praenuntiata *est* a prophetis, *ideo dixit illud Psal. XXI,2: "Deus*
meus, respice in me, quare me dereliquisti?" Unde dicit Hieronymus quod impii sunt qui
aliter Psalmum illum exponere volunt quam de passione Christi.
Notate, quod quidam male intellexerunt. Unde debitis scire quod fuerunt duae haereses.
Una quae in Christo non posuit Verbum unitum, sed quod Verbum fuit loco animae, et hoc
posuit Arius. Alii vero, quod Verbum non fuit unitum naturaliter, sed per gratiam, sicut in
aliquo justo, ut in prophetis, et sic Nestorius.

Christ. But since according to Nestorius the union of the divine Word and the man Christ was only by grace, Nestorians erroneously interpret the cry as out of sadness, since the divine Word would be leaving the human body and the soul of Christ, which cannot be, even not in His death.[49] Hence, Thomas concludes that the words must be understood as referring to Christ's exposure to the *passio* (as in the *Summa Theologiae*), for a short time, as in Is 54,7. Thomas ends this exposition by giving two possible answers to the question why God had abandoned Him in this sense: referring to the former verse, Mt 27,45, the compassion (*compassio*) with His people, as if Christ is saying: "Why have You willed to hand Me over to the *passio* and (*et*, in one and the same breath) why did You blot out the sun for them?" Further it also shows God's love for us, while we were still sinners, as in Rm 5,8.

A contemporary theologian, exegete or any person interested in this subject may at least be tempted to leave Thomas' exegesis for what it is and concentrate on a more "serious' explanation of this text. No doubt, considering Mt 27,46 nowadays one cannot simply repeat Thomas' words as a by itself convincing or sufficient exegesis.[50] But from the viewpoint of the interest in the contribution of Thomas' theology to ours, a first question could be why his exegesis is so very different. One reason is that he was of course not acquainted with modern methods like the historical critical method, which had and has a tremendous impact on current

---

[49] Thomas cites Jn 7,29, where he reads: *Qui me misit, mecum est.* Although at first sight the Greek text says something quite different, "I know (οιδα, not γιγνωσκω) Him who sent Me", according to Kittel, 1954, Band 5, 121f, the word "to know" here refers to the connectedness of Christ with God.
If Christ in His death had been separated from God, Christ's death would have undone the incarnation and we would not be able to say that the Son of God died and was buried, which we do in the Creed, according to the rule of the *communicatio idiomatum*: see paragraph 2.3.3. Therefore Christ's death is to be understood as a human death, i.e. the separation of His soul from His body (cf. ST IIIa q.50 aa.1, 2). Since even in His death Christ was not separated from God, we say, REI c.3 1.3 n.1: *Christus mortuus est. Sed nota, quod dicit, non pereat. Perire namque dicitur aliquid quod impeditur ne perveniat ad finem ad quem ordinatur. Homo autem ordinatur ad finem, qui est vita aeterna; et quamdiu peccat, avertit se ab ipso fine. [....] [V]ita aeterna nihil aliud est quam frui Deo.* However, this distinction between *morire* and *perire* becomes problematic in Is 57,1, where it reads: *Iustus autem perit* (cited in ST IIIa q.46 a.6 ad 5).

[50] Cf. Hoogland (2000), 158; Leget (2002), 21-26; Menken (2002), 29-36.

theologies. Another reason, on our side, is that, since the historical critical method and even methods approaching the Bible as a literary document are so dominant in present-day exegesis, that many have grown away from a (more) theological reading of the Bible. A theologian reads the Bible as Holy Scripture, that is as containing the word of God in the community of faith (its theology and liturgy[51], contemporary and in the tradition), (re)kindling faith. This means that the faith of the Church, coming forth from how the Bible functions in this community, namely as Holy Scripture, is implied in this method. In the earthly reality of the biblical stories the theologian seeks traces of- and references to the mystery of God. This is not so strange as it may sound, for Christians speaking or hearing of Jesus imply that He is the Christ and likewise "YHWH" and "God" are understood as the triune God.

What foremost estranges Thomas' exegesis from us, is that he employs a christological way of reading Mt 27,46. In his commentary on Psalm 22 Thomas sets out what this means for the approach of a text:

"As in other prophets, here the text is on some things that were present then as a prefiguration of Christ and that are connected with this very prophesy. And therefore particular things that are connected with Christ, were once written down, which as it were exceed the historical content. And in particular this Psalm treats the Passion of Christ. And therefore this is its litteral meaning. [....] So, although David figures as the subject of this Psalm, especially in the litteral sense this Psalm refers to Christ.[52]

---

[51] Ps 22 is prayed during Midday Prayer in the Liturgy of Hours on Good Friday; Is 52,13-53,12 is read that evening in the liturgy; Is 54,5-14 is read in the Easter Vigil. This influences how we understand these scriptural texts just as these texts influence our view of Christ's *passio*.

[52] RPS ps.21 n.1: [S]*icut in aliis prophetis, ita hic agitur de aliquibus tunc praesentibus inquantum erant figura Christi et quae ad ipsam prophetiam pertinebant. Et ideo quandoque ponuntur aliqua quae ad Christum pertinent,* quae excedunt quasi virtutem historiarum. *Et inter alia specialiter iste psalmus agit de passione Christi. Et ideo hic est eius sensus litteralis.* [....] *Et ideo licet* figuraliter *hic psalmus dicatur* de David, *tamen* specialiter ad litteram *refertur* ad Christum.

Hence characteristic of this method is that the Old Testament, and especially the Psalms and Isaiah, are read as announcing Christ[53] and that the text contains an abundance of - theological, hidden - meaning, not instead of, but beyond the historical purport. Hence Thomas is not so much interested in the literary or in the psychological aspects of Mt 27,46. This feature makes Thomas' approach insufficient for us today. Yet at the same time, its weakness is also its strength. For reading his exegesis, we see deeper layers of this Scripture text. It makes us realize that according to our faith this man dying on a cross, exclaiming why God has abandoned him, is also the Son of God, which has far- reaching consequences for how we interpret this text.[54] In the next paragraph, discussing Thomas' view of "the *passio* itself" (*quaestio* 46) this will be

---

[53] E.g. RPS ps.21 n.1: *Sciendum est autem quod quinque psalmi agunt de passione Christi prolixe: Quorum iste psalmus* [Vulg-Ps 21 = Ps 22] *primus est. Alii enim brevius tangunt passionem Christi,* namely Psalms 35, 55, 69 and 109. E.g. CIS c.52: *"Consurge, consurge."* [....] *Primo enim praedicit liberationem Iudaeorum a Babyloniis; secundo liberationem gentium a peccatis.* We already find this method with regard to Christ's *passio* in the Passion stories in the gospels (e.g. many references, the use of the word fulfill(ment)) and in Lk 24,25-27, 44-46, Ac 3,17f, 8,32-35, 17,2f, 26,22f, 1 P 1,10-12.

[54] And it is in this sense that Vercruysse, in Gregorianum 55 (1974), 376f, criticizes the overaccentuation of Moltmann (in: Der Gekreuzigte Gott (1972), 140) of the historical aspect of Christ's cry in Mk 15,34 (citing Ps 22,2) and Heb 5,7. He argues that Moltmann's view is too narrow-based, namely on the abandonment and the cry of Jesus, and therefore fails to see Christ's motives for undergoing the *passio* unto death. Hence Moltmann cannot perceive the crucifixion also as the revelation of God's love and as a consequence of Christ's faithful life.

But for catholic Christians the fundamental problem of Moltmann's view of Christ in respect of His crucifixion is his denial of what the oecumenical Council of Constantinople, specifying Nicaea, says about the hypostatic union. For he sees this as incompatible with the historical Jesus: "Das Schema von Inkarnation und Auferstehung, von Erniedrigung und Erhöhung bringt das Geheimnis Jesu zwar mit dem Geheimnis Gottes selbst zusammen. Es macht aber die Besonderheiten des wirklichen, geschichtlichen Menschen Jesus von Nazareth und die Zufälligkeiten seiner Geschichte unwesentlich. [....] [Gottes] Menschwerdung in Jesus von Nazareth und sein Tod in dessen Sterben auf Golgotha lassen sich schwerlich deduzieren und auch mühsam rekonstruieren" (o.c., 89). Although Chalcedon's christological dogma results from a centuries long reflection on the *meaning* of Scripture, the life and the death, the humanity and the divinity of Christ, Moltmann speaks of it as "Aufhebung", yes even "Vernichtung der geschehenen Geschichte" (o.c., 89f). Moltmann apparently does not conceive Chalcedon as providing a grammar rule for how to read Scripture.

elaborated in more detail.

A second striking element in the text quoted above is how
Thomas emphasizes that considering the meaning of Christ crying out the
words of Ps 22,2, we are dealing with a mystery. In fact, *all* that Christ
was and did and underwent is treated by Thomas as a mystery. "Mystery"
is a word many feel uncomfortable with in our scientific world. For
Western culture is aimed at solving problems. The Scriptural term
"mystery" signifies, according to Thomas, something beyond our
intellectual understanding, something veiled.[55] Mysteries are not problems. They cannot be "solved"; they are to be believed (in); as a
Christian one has to learn to live with them, relate to them, growing in
understanding them *as* mysteries. Characteristic of a mystery is that the
more you know about it, the greater it becomes.[56]
The greatest of mysteries is God Himself:

"Since we cannot know about God what He is, but we can
what He is not, we cannot consider with regard to God
how He is, but rather how He is not."[57]

This has a great impact on how we talk about mysteries, including God,
for

"Something can be named by us, in as far as it can be

---

[55] ST IaIIae q.101 a.2 ad 1: [D]*ivina non sunt revelanda hominibus nisi secundum
eorum capacitatem: Alioquin daretur eis praecipitii materia, dum contemnerent quae
capere non possent. Et ideo utilis fuit ut* sub quodam figurarum velamine *divina mysteria
rudi populo tradentur*.

[56] As in Weinandy (2000), 33: "Christians believe that Jesus revealed God to be a
trinity of persons - the Father, the Son and the Holy Spirit. Christians now know more
about God than did Moses, but *in coming to a greater knowledge of God, God has become
even more mysterious* than he was for Moses." (italics added, MR). More on the
distinction between problems and mysteries o.c., 27-39 (based on Maritain and Marcel).

[57] ST Ia q.3 intr.: *Sed quia de Deo scire non possumus quid sit, sed quid non sit, non
possumus considerare de Deo quomodo sit, sed potius quomodo non sit.*

known by our intellect."[58]

And the same applies to knowing and speaking of Christ:

> "We must say that the mystery of Christ cannot be
> believed explicitly without belief in the Trinity: for in the
> mystery of Christ it is implied that the Son of God
> assumed flesh [i.e. the Incarnation], that the Holy Spirit
> will have renewed the world by grace, and further that He
> [i.e. Christ] was conceived by the Holy Spirit."[59]

And it will be expounded in what way Thomas speaks of Christ's *passio*
as a mystery. Hence, in order to talk about the mysteries of God *and*
Christ Thomas uses what is called negative theology (cf. also note 35).
The implications of this conclusion for our understanding of Thomas and
what this means for our own way of reading Scripture will be shown in
the continuation of this study.

Surveying what has been said until now, it seems that Thomas
reads the Bible as a theologian and apparently as a negative theologian. If
this is the case, the discussion of *quaestio* 46 must elucidate that he
indeed speaks of the *passio* of Christ as a mystery. It already caught the
eye how Thomas, beginning with what we see on the surface when
reading about Christ's *passio*, then lays open the deep structure of it. By
doing so he makes the reader sensitive to the mysteries in the life and
death of Christ. This will be explored further in the continuation of this
study.

It is clear that Scripture is the basis of Thomas' considerations
regarding the *passio* of Christ: how to understand what we read in
Scripture? It is conspicuous how Thomas not only explains the texts (and

---

[58] ST Ia q.13 a.1co: *Secundum igitur quod aliquid a nobis intellectu cognosci potest,
sic a nobis potest nominari.*

[59] ST IIaIIae q.2 a.8co: *[D]icendum quod mysterium Christi explicite credi non potest
sine fide Trinitatis: quia in mysterio Christi hoc continetur quod Filius Dei carnem
assumpserit, quod per gratiam Spiritus Sancti mundum renovaverit, et iterum quod de
Spiritu Sancto conceptus fuerit.* Schoot (1993), 11-40, demonstrates that Thomas foremost
speaks of "mystery" regarding Christ.

their implicit contexts) as such, but also how he explains them in the light of one another: apart from texts from the Passion stories Jn 10,18, Ep 5,2, Ph 2,8 are present in the whole of Thomas' exposition. What hampers the (post-)modern reader in understanding Thomas, is that he seems to presuppose a certain familiarity with Scriptural texts and their meaning, for instance 1 Co 15,54, when quoting Pr 21,28. Whether or not this assumed familiarity is characteristic in Thomas' theology may become clear in the course of this study.

Reading these first three *articuli* of *quaestio* 47 many things regarding the relation between God and Christ concerning the *passio* are elucidated, but at the same time quite a few questions remain. What really stands out is how Thomas speaks of the *passio* not only having a cause, but also having a purpose, namely our salvation, described as our justification, our reconciliation (with God) and the conquest of death. But what does this mean; how is our salvation brought about by Christ's *passio*?

In respect of this purposiveness it is salient how the situation of Christ's *passio* and death seems to be never out of control - on a deeper level at least, for Christ's disciples did truly experience fear (Mk 14,50-52), distress (Jn 20,11, 13-15) and despair (Lk 24,21) and Christ Himself was sorrowful to the point of death (Mk 14,34) and prayed in anguish (Lk 22,44). It raises the question about the nature of God's *and* Christ's might. For God had everything under control, it seems, but at the same time evil happened, as was said above. Does this not contradict almightiness and His goodness? Moreover, if God is almighty indeed, was there then not another, a better, way for Him to achieve the aim? Moreover, as Christ is said to be suffering with (*compassio*) His people (- an act of solidarity? -), did God suffer with Christ, when He underwent *passio* unto death? Did it affect God? After all, "God is love" (1 Jn 4,8) and Christ was His beloved Son (Mk 1,11, 9,7 par.). How then is His love - with or without *com-passio* - related to His almightiness?

And similarly with regard to Christ, which are the deeper reasons and further consequences of how Thomas speaks of Christ as having been able to prevent His *passio* and preserving the body? Does Thomas do justice to Christ's human weakness when he explains Christ's loud voice from the cross? Was He not "crucified in weakness" (2 Co 13,4)? Did Christ according to Thomas' exposition truly suffer; does he take Christ's *passio* seriously? (Or) was Christ almighty too? How then is His (al)might(iness) related to His *passio*? Can or must we eventually call

Thomas' theology a *theologia gloriae*? Moreover, concerning Christ's human will, of what did Christ's ultimate freedom consist; did He really have a choice? What is the consequence of the union by nature with the divine Word for His human will?

1.2 Liberating Passion

If people of the 21st century start reading the first *articulus* of *quaestio* 46, expecting to find an exposition on the *passio* itself (*de ipsa passione*), as Thomas announces in the introduction to *quaestio* 46, they may be baffled by the first question formulated by Thomas: "Whether it was necessary that Christ suffered for the liberation of humankind." This question as the *opening* question of the section of the *Summa Theologiae* on the *passio Christi*, may not sound too inviting to continue reading. For a word like "necessary" and the phrase "the liberation of humankind" are not the terms which come to mind directly when contemporary believers, theologians and others interested, consider the *passio* of Christ. The strangeness of this question may well prevent us from going more deeply into this subject.

That the phrase "for the liberation of humankind" returns in the questions of the two following *articuli*, may well open our eyes to Thomas' approach of the matter. Apparently his first interest is not a kind of philosophical knowing of what the *passio* of Christ *is*, but what it *means for us*. In other words, his concern here is the history of salvation, the *oikonomia* (as in Ep 3,9: "I have been entrusted with this speacial grace [....] of throwing light on the inner workings of the mystery kept hidden through all the ages in God, the Creator of everything"). For this study the questions of the first four *articuli* are of importance, since the form and the content of the answers also reveal how in Thomas' theology almightiness and *passio* are interconnected. Although God's almightiness is only mentioned once, that God is the Almighty is clearly assumed in Thomas' approach.

In order to clarify the meaning of Christ's *passio* for us, Thomas, in line with Scripture and the tradition as will be shown, first considers the *passio* of Christ in terms of necessity. Eventually he opts for another terminology in his questioning: *conveniens*, becoming (1.2.1). By doing so Thomas is able to lay open in a better way the richness of the mystery of the *passio* of Christ and the revelation of God's abundant goodness for us in it. And elaborates this in the three subsequent *articuli*: was another way of salvation possible (q.46 a.2: 1.2.2) and why is the way chosen by God the best way (q.46 aa.3, 4: 1.2.3)?

1.2.1 Necessity

"Whether it was necessary that Christ suffered for the liberation of humankind." Judging from the blunt way he opens *quaestio* 46 and the fact that he does not explain this question at all, this must have been an obvious opening question for Thomas *and* for the freshmen in theology he is writing for.[60] And maybe it is, if one hears the Scriptural background resounding in this question. For "for us" is an interpretative frequently used in Scripture to expound the meaning of Christ's *passio*. In the former paragraph one came already accross it in Ep 5,2 and Rm 5,8.[61] This "for us" is specified as being liberating us from our sins[62] and having eternal life in Christ (Jn 3,15). Going deeper into this here is beyond the scope of this study. The attention of this subparagraph must be directed towards the necessity already mentioned. For necessity seems to contradict the almightiness of God and the free will of both Christ[63] and God.

But first, what kind of a question is this actually; what is the ground for asking about necessity in this context? If we are not used to think and speak in terms of necessity with regard to the *passio* of Christ, it may surprise us that Scripture does. In the synoptic gospels we hear Christ announcing His crucifixion thrice and once in Jn 3,14; not only in Lk 24,26, as was said above, but also elsewhere it is referred to the Scriptures or "Moses and the prophets" foretelling His *passio* and that

---

[60] ST Ia intr.: (citing 1 Co 3,1f); *propositum nostrae intentionis in hoc opere est, ea quae ad Christianam religionem pertinent, eo modo tradere, secundum quod congruit* ad eruditionem incipientium.

[61] It is also found in Is 53,5; Mt 20,28, Jn 10,11, 15, 11,50-52, 15,13, Rm 8,32, 2 Co 5,14f, 1 Tm 2,6, Tt 2,14, Heb 9,26-28, 1 P 2,21, 3,18, 4,1, 1 Jn 3,16; in the context of the Eucharist in Mt 26,28, Mk 14,24, Lk 22,19f and 1 Co 11,24.

[62] Is 53,6, 11; Jn 1,29, 1 Co 15,3, Ga 1,4, 1 P 2,24, 1 Jn 3,5, 4,10.

[63] ST IIIa q.46 a.1 ob.1, 2.

they are fulfilled by it[64], in accordance with God's previously determined plan.[65]

Besides, Thomas' question is certainly not unique in his time; posing this question he joins a tradition, common since Anselm of Canterbury's *Cur Deus homo* (1098). Anselm develops in this work the so called satisfaction theory[66]: a human being who does not do God's will, i.e. does not give God the honour due to Him, robs (*rapuit*) God of His honour. This is called sin. This disturbed relationship between the human being and God cannot be restored by giving back what was robbed, "but for the inflicted indignity he is indebted to give back more than he has taken." And until then the person remains indebted.[67] Anselm stresses the gravity of the sin and the impossibility for a human being to give God back more than he robbed, since *all* honour is due to God anyway (I cc.20-24). This dark situation is hopeless: no human being - for *all* are sinners[68] - *can* in fact meet the requirements and yet a human being - for one of the human race sinned - *must* (II c.6). Anselm contrasts this with God's goodness: in no way being obliged, He gave us Jesus Christ, truly human and truly divine, to satisfy for our sins. Satisfaction includes obedience to God's will, giving back to Him what was robbed and restoring the goods lost by reason of sin. The remarkable term "to rob" in this context originates from Ps 69,5, understood as said by Christ:

---

[64] Mt 26,24, Mk 9,11f, Ac 3,18, 17,3, 26,22f, 1 P 1,10 resp. Mt 5,17f, 26,31 par, 27,9f, Mk 15,28, Jn 19,24, 28, 36f, Ac 13,29, 33.

[65] Lk 22,22, Ac 2,23, 4,28.

[66] Before Anselm another theory was common (Origen, Augustine, Gregory the Great), known as the *casus diaboli*: Due to the sin of the first human beings the devil was entitled to keep the human race ensnared. Deliverance could only come to pass, if the devil would *unjustly* entrap someone, namely a person without sin. By laying violent hands on Christ - the devil was deceived, since Christ looked like any other, sinful, human being, but was not - the devil lost his previous right.

[67] *Cur Deus homo* I c.11: *Quamdiu autem non solvit quod rapuit, manet in culpa. Nec sufficit solummodo reddere quod ablatum est, sed pro contumelia illata plus debet reddere quam abstulit.*

[68] Cf. Rm 3,23; 3,9.

"Must I give back what I have never stolen (robbed)?"[69]

Over the years there has been much critique on Anselm's satisfaction theory (or on the commentators' understanding of it), for instance that God looks here more like an 11th century prince concerned about his honour than like the God of Israel.[70] The reason why I briefly outline Anselm's *Cur Deus homo* in this paragraph, is twofold: first of all it helps us to understand Thomas better. Without citing or even mentioning him even once, Thomas is in fact involved in a discussion with Anselm. Thomas accepts the ground-structure of Anselm's satisfaction theory, but, unlike Anselm, satisfaction is not *the* key term in his exposition on the *passio* of Christ. Note that, although both Anselm and Thomas may seem to be from 'the dark Middle Ages', Thomas is writing the *Tertia Pars* of his *Summa Theologiae* 174 years after *Cur Deus homo*, in circumstances quite different (Naples, the university, the movement of the mendicant friars) from Anselm's (feudal, totally agrarian society, abbeys).[71]

Secondly, although Anselm's exposition evokes many questions, it contains an underlying thought which most people would agree with, namely that some kind of punishment is required for trespasses. Otherwise our world would become chaotic (*inordinatum*), there would not be a difference between a sinner and a just person before God (moral consequence), and injustice would be made alike to God, i.e. good (theological consequence) (I c.12). And what's more this thought is in

---

[69] Vulg-Ps 68,5: *Quae non rapui, tunc exsolvebam.*

[70] However, Southern (1990), 226f, points out that in *Cur Deus homo* "God's honour is simply another word for the ordering of the universe in its due relationship to God [....] Anselm used the language of feudal relationships, not because he approved every aspect of them, but because they provided an exemple of hierarchy, which both philosophically and morally he found most satisfying." It is just as when we use examples from our society to explain something about the relation between us and God. Cf. Evans (1989), 17, 23, 76. Cf. also Kasper (1974), 261f: "Es geht bei der Verletzung der Ehre Gottes also gar nicht um Gott, sondern um den Menschen, um die Ordnung und Schönheit der Welt [....] um Freiheit, Friede, Ordnung und Sinnerfüllung der Welt."

[71] Southern (1990), esp. 221-227, 232-234, 270-274, 289-351.

accordance with Scripture.[72]

Hence Scripture itself evokes the question of how to understand
the necessity of Christ's *passio* and by posing it Thomas stands in the
tradition of the Church.

The catholic understanding of Jn 3,14f (cited in sc and co) is at
stake in this *articulus*: "As Moses lifted up the snake in the desert (Nb
21,8), so must (*oportet*, δεῖ) the Son of man be lifted up, so that (*ut*, ἵνα)
everyone who believes may have eternal life in Him." How to understand
this "must": is it a rigid necessity, like the divine δεῖ in ancient Greek
tragedies? Is it a fatalistic "there was no other way"? If Jn 3,14f is
understood in this way, Thomas distinguishes three[73] problems: we
cannot be saved but by God alone, according to Is 45,21 ("There is no
other god exept Me, no saving God, no Saviour except Me!"). So, if
necessity is conceived in this sense, God Himself would be subject to this
necessity. However Thomas emphatically states:

> "Yet in God cannot be any necessity, since this is in-
> compatible with His almightiness. Hence it has not been
> necessary that Christ suffered."[74]

From this reasoning it seems that Thomas speaks of almightiness as
opposed to being forced or compelled; almightiness seems to cohere with
God's (absolute) freedom.

A second problem rising from the Scriptural δεῖ with regard to
Christ's *passio* is Christ's voluntariness (Thomas cites Is 53,7); what is
necessary cannot be voluntary at the same time.[75] And a third problem is
how to understand God's mercy (*misericordia*) and justice in the light of

---

[72] Lv 26,18, Ezr 9,13, Pr 22,3, Is 13,11, Jr 13,22, Lm 4,22, Mt 25,41-46, 2 Co 2,5-8, 1 Th 1,5-9, 2 P 2,9f; Ps 135,14, Pr 17,26a.

[73] The fourth, that Christ did not suffer for us, since He did not suffer for the angels either, is not relevant for this study.

[74] ST IIIa q.46 a.1 ag.1: *Humanum enim genus liberari* non poterat nisi a Deo, *secundum illud Is 45,21* [....] In Deum autem non cadit aliqua necessitas: *quia repugnaret omnipotentiam ipsius. Ergo non fuit necessarium Christum pati.*

[75] Cf. CMP V l.6 nn.829f: *Tertium modum ....*

the necessity in Jn 3,14f: there was no necessity because of God's mercy, for just like God distributes His gifts for nothing (*gratis*), He could have liberated the human race simply because He willed it, so without Christ's satisfaction. And since the human race by sinning *deserved* to be eternally damned, there was no necessity in respect of God's justice either to liberate the human race. So, because all God's ways are mercy and justice (Thomas cites Ps 25,10[76]), in what way could Christ's *passio* have been necessary?

These three *obiectiones* are ordered after the structure of Thomas' answer. Following Aristotle, Thomas distinguishes between two types of necessity, the first being a necessity inherent in the nature of something: implicitly referring to the first two *obiectiones*, Thomas says that it is beyond any doubt (*manifestum*) that necessity is not to be understood in this way, regarding neither God nor Christ. The second type is a necessity on the basis of something extrinsic. He makes a subdivision between something being necessary because it is forced or hindered, which for the same reasons befit neither God nor Christ, and because of an aim:

> "Namely, when an aim either cannot be achieved any other way or cannot be achieved in a becoming way unless such an aim is presupposed."[77]

In fact this is not too surprising an answer, for Jn 3,14 itself already contains purposiveness: "must ...., so that (*oportet, ut*)". In the elaboration of this answer Thomas shows the richness of the mystery of Christ's *passio* by mentioning three aims being achieved by the *passio*. His interest in our salvation shows again, when he first mentions our

---

[76] Thomas reads: *Universae viae Domini misericordia et veritas.* God's justice, understood as the order of things established by Him in conformity with His wisdom, is truth. For truth can be conceived as the equality of the image of a thing in our intellect with the thing itself; in this sense *res sunt regula et mensura intellectus.* But truth can also be conceived as the equality of a thing with the image in someone's intellect, for instance when an artist makes a true work (*vere opus*). And in this sense all God's works are rightly called truth (ST Ia q.21 a.2co).

[77] ST IIIa q.46 a.1co: [N]*ecessarium ex suppositione finis: quando scilicet finis aliquis aut nullo modo potest esse, aut non potest esse* convenienter, *nisi tali fine praesupposito.*

liberation to eternal life (Jn 3,14). Next he mentions, citing Lk 24,26, the exaltation of the man Christ in glory. And finally, citing Lk 22,22, 24,44, 46, the fulfillment of the Scriptures. And in the answer to the third *obiectio* he demonstrates the suitability of the *Passio* in respect of God's justice and His mercy;

> "It was becoming in respect of His justice, because by means of His *passio* Christ satisfied for the sin of the human race. And so the human being is liberated by means of the justice of Christ."[78]

More words are dedicated to explaining that Christ's *passio* was not only in accordance with God's mercy (Rm 3,24f), but that through it God showed Himself to be abundantly merciful (*abundantioris misericordiae*: Ep 2,4f).

This answer of Thomas may at first not seem to be too shocking, but his approach is a true upheaval in comparison to Anselm's. Reading Anselm's *Cur Deus homo* one stumbles over words like *oportet*, *debet*, *indigeo* and especially *necessitas/necessarium*. And this makes his reasoning quite solid and coercive. It even creates the impression that God Himself is subject to necessity. In comparison to Anselm, Thomas makes two sweeping changes in this *articulus*. He distinguishes between different types of necessity. This way a misinterpretation of necessity in respect of God and Christ is avoided; an aim-necessity (*necessitas finis*) so to say is only a relative necessity, namely for as far as the aim has been determined. And this is done in freedom, by God and by Christ. This means that aim-necessity is not a necessity in the common sense of the word. But no matter how one interprets the word necessity, it is associated with some kind of compulsion or constraint. And this can in no way be in God (*obiectio* 1, note 74). And this is why Thomas changes the atmosphere: in his answers he does not speak in terms of necessity anymore, but in terms of being becoming (*conveniens*, notes 77 and 78). Reading Thomas' earlier works one can follow the development: in his

---

[78] ST IIIa q.46 a.1 ad 3: [C]onveniens *fuit et misericordiae et iustitiae eius. Iustitiae quidem, quia per passionem suam Christus satisfecit pro peccato humani generis: et ita homo* per iustitiam Christi *liberatus est.*

Sententiae the question whether there was a necessity for Christ to die, is answered in terms of necessity.[79] But in *De rationibus fidei* he already makes a stand against "those who say that everything comes out of necessity from God," in favour of the use of "becoming" in this context.[80] In the *Compendium* he even designates an absolute irreconcilability of necessity with the *passio* of Christ.[81] Yet in the *Summa Theologiae* this contradistinction is not found anymore.

The second change is the place of satisfaction in the *Summa Theologiae*. Here satisfaction is not a category of its own anymore. It is classified under justice, a property of God, which in the *Summa Theologiae* is always bracketed together with God's mercy.[82] This prevents God being regarded as a bloodthirsty and rigid god. In comparison, in the *Sententiae* satisfaction is a separate category and even the main focus of the inquiry.[83] In the *Compendium* Thomas, on the basis of Scripture, already broadened satisfaction as the motive for Christ's *passio*

---

[79] SN III d.16 q.1 aa.1, 2.

[80] OCG c.7: *Ad eos autem qui omnia ex necessitate provenire dicunt a Deo operiosus a nobis alibi* [e.g. CMP V 1.6 nn.827-841, VI 1.3 nn.1192-1222] *disputatum est.* Here Thomas speaks of aim-necessity only once; he uses the word *conveniens* 10 times.

[81] OTT c.227: *Manifestum igitur est secundum praedicta, quod Christus aliquos defectos nostros suscepit* non ex necessitate, sed propter aliquem finem, *scilicet propter salutem nostram.* Ibidem c.230: *Christus autem mortuus est* non ex necessitate, sed potestate et propria voluntate. *Unde ipse dicebat Io 10,18* [....].

[82] E.g. In one *quaestio* (ST Ia q.21) Thomas considers the *iustitia Dei* (aa.1, 2) and subsequently in coherence with it the *misericordia Dei*.

O'Leary (1952), interested in the question whether Thomas' teaching on Christ's Passion is "consistent" throughout his theological works, overlooks the first development and wipes away the second, 110f: "In the *C.S.* [SN] and in the *D.V.* [QDV], St. Thomas insists on the penal and on the moral side of satisfaction (poenalitas-charitas). The *C.G.* [SCG] points out the efficacy of charity in satisfaction. In the *S.T.*, we have the fully developed *synthesis* of the two aspects of the two aspects of satisfaction. [....] No other element occurs more *constantly* in St. Thomas' teaching than that of satisfaction." (italics added, MR)

[83] SN III d.20 (5 *articuli*), where Thomas does cite Anselm. Also in his questioning Thomas is closer to *Cur Deus homo* (e.g. I cc.11, 19f, 22, 24). The *misericordia Dei* only occurs in a.1b ag/ad 2 (but not in connection with the *iustitia Dei*) and in a.1c ag.3 (but is remarkably absent in the ad 3)

to many motives.[84]

Because of these changes, the total orientation of the inquiry shifts from the means (*satisfactio* in SN) to the aim (*liberatio humanae generis* in ST).[85] For this reason it is not enough to establish that in the *Summa Theologiae* Anselm's term necessity has been replaced by Thomas' term becoming. Even adding that Aquinas "*refined* Anselm's satisfaction model"[86] does not do justice to Thomas' fundamental change in the approach of the matter.

Because of this shift the questions in the subsequent *articuli* of *quaestio* 46 are about the *passio* as the way to attain the aim: was there no other way to attain the aim (1.2.2)? And if so, why was the *passio*, and in particular the *passio* on a cross most becoming in respect of the aim (1.2.3)?

1.2.2 Was no Other Way Possible?

If there were no other way for God to achieve the liberation, He would not be free, but coerced to do it that way. Then there would be necessity in God. And this would raise the question what "al-mighty (*omni-potens*)" means, if something were beyond God's might (*potentia*). But since "no word is impossible (*impossibile*) for God", according to Lk

---

[84] OTT c.227: *Mori etiam voluit, non solum mors eius esset nobis satisfactionis remedium, sed etiam salutis Sacramentum* [....] (1 P 3,18). *Mori etiam voluit, ut nobis mors eius esset perfectae virtutis exemplum*: love (*caritas*) cf. Jn 15,13; firmness that despite adversity does not recede from justice (*fortitudo*) cf. Heb 2,14; patience (*patientia* i.e. not being absorbed by sadness or being confused) cf. *de Christo Propheta praedixit*, Is 53,7; obedience cf. Ph 2,8 ("*obediens Patri*").

[85] SN III d.20 a.4a, 4b: *Videtur quod alius modus non fuerit possibilis*; *Videtur quod alius modus fuisset convenientior*; ST IIIa q.46 aa.2, 3: *Utrum fuerit possibilis alius modus* liberationis humanae naturae *quam per passionem Christi*; *Utrum alius modus convenientior fuisset* liberationis humanae *quam per passionem Christi*.

[86] Mertens 1992, 76f, italics added MR

1,37, we must hold that the crucifixion was not the only way for God.[87]

This answer of Thomas evokes some questions. A first question could be concerning the use of Lk 1,37 here. It seems like this verse is coming out of the blue; is it not treated completely outside the original context, the Anunciation? Or is there something else going on here? Since Thomas cites this verse also in the discussion on the almightiness of God in the *Prima Pars*, this question will be dealt with in paragraph 3.2.

Thomas' own questions are about how to understand texts from Scripture, which seem to say that there was no other way possible. First he mentions Jn 12,24f, where Christ, referring to Himself as the grain, says that the grain *only* yields a rich harvest if it dies. Following on the first *articulus* the focus of this first *obiectio* is the aim. The other three questions concern respectively God, Christ and faith. That there was no other way in respect of God is suggested by Christ's prayer in Gethsemane: "My Father, if this cup *cannot* pass by, but I *must* drink it, Your will be done" (Mt 26,43).[88] And even more with Church Father Hilary's comment on this text, that we could not be restored but by means of Christ's *passio*. And in respect of Christ it seems that there was no other way, for He does not act contrary to the Father's will. Ps 25,10, that all God's ways are justice, cited in the former *articulus*, is obviously presupposed here. And Scripture testifies that even if we act unjustly (by not believing and thus not obeying), Christ will not disown His own self (by not obeying): 2 Tm 2,13. The last reason Thomas formulates, a stranger one to us, is referring to what has been said about the fulfilment of the Scriptures: the ancestors in the faith (*antiqui Patres*, i.e. Abraham and his descendants (Lk 1,55)), believed that Christ would suffer. Now, what belongs to the faith cannot be false. Their faith would have been false, if Christ had not suffered. And therefore it seems there was no other way possible in respect of the faith either. The formulation of this problem shows how much these four elements are intertwined.

That our liberation took place as it did, through Christ's *passio*,

---

[87] ST IIIa q.46 a.2co: *Simpliciter igitur et absolute loquendo, possibile fuit Deo alio modo hominem liberare quam per passionem Christi: Quia non est impossibile apud Deum omne verbum, ut dicitur Lc. 1,37.*

[88] Thomas could have increased the tension by citing Mk 14,36, for in Mt it does not say "Father, for You everything is possible." Mt is cited because of Hilary's exegesis (*In Mt.* c.31, ML 9,1069), quoted in the *obiectio*.

and that we recognize this as "good and in accordance with God's dignity", does not mean that another way was not possible for Him, because "everything is in the same way subject to His might"[89] - a strong formulation of Augustine, endorsed by Thomas. Yet that the *passio* of Christ as it came to pass, was good and in harmony with who and what God is, leads to the conclusion that it was what God willed. And what God wills, as was said above, He wills from eternity.

> "Under the supposition of God's foreknowledge and preordination regarding Christ's *passio* it was not at the same time possible that Christ had not suffered and that humankind had been liberated in another way, for it is impossible that God's foreknowledge is deceived and that His will or regulation is caused to totter."[90]

Thomas' point of departure for his inquiry clearly is not an abstract idea of what God wills or what is good or becoming; it is what we read in Scripture, that Christ *did* suffer. And that same Scripture tells us that this *passio* was for an aim and that all this was known and preordained, i.e. "from eternity", by God. And so Thomas brings to our attention that the texts from Scripture mentioned in the *obiectiones* are to be read in this light.

In the discussion of *quaestio* 47 it was said already that there is no change in the will of God. But here a further step is set: God's foreknowledge and will are *unfailing*; God willed the *passio* of Christ and

---

[89] ST IIIa q.46 a.2sc citing Augustine's XIII *De Trin.* c.10, ML 42,1024: bonum *et* divinae dignitati congruum [....] cuius potestati cuncta aequaliter subiacent.

[90] ST IIIa q.46 a.2co: *Sed ex aliqua suppositione facta, fuit impossibile. Quia, enim impossibile est Dei praescientia falli et eius voluntatem sive dispositionem cassari,* supposita praescientia et praeordinatione Dei de passione Christi, non erat simul possibile Christum non pati, *et homo alio modo quam per eius passionem liberari.* Since *necessarium* is a central term in questions *and* answers in SN, Thomas is even firmer there, SN III d.20 a.1c ad 2: [N]*ecessitas quae est ex suppositione voluntatis immutabiliter aliquid volentis, non minuit rationem voluntarii,* sed auget *tanto magis quanto ponitur firmius inhaerens volito ut moveri non possit.*

so it came to pass.[91] The consequence of this is that the interpretation of God being forced to bring about the liberation of humankind and to bring it about in this way is precluded: it is the foreknowledge and the will *of God* that excluded other possibilities.

> "Even this justice [according to which Christ acts because He wants to] depends on the divine will that demands from the human race satisfaction for sin. Although, if He had willed to liberate humankind from sin without any satisfaction, He would not have acted contrary to justice."[92]

And this distinguishes God from a judge or a prince, who is bound to the rules of justice or a higher prince.[93]

> "But God does not have anyone higher than Himself, for He is the supreme and common good of the whole universe."[94]

Hence God is not accountable to anyone or anything, *because* He Himself is *the* criterion of what is good and just, any time, any place. Scripture is

---

[91] Note that according to Thomas (ST Ia q.14 aa.8, 9, 12, 13) this does not exclude, but rather *in*cludes creaturely contingency and therefore human, c.q. Christ's, freedom. God's foreknowledge is eternal; He knows the - temporal - future from eternity. Since we do not know what eternity is, but only what it is not, as was said above, we only understand what God's eternal foreknowledge concerning the future is *not*, namely that He would know the future in a temporal way. Hence God's eternal foreknowledge does in no way presuppose a static, in time determined future. See also Goris (1996), 125-254.

[92] ST IIIa q.46 a.2 ad 3: *[H]aec etiam iustitia dependet ex voluntate divina ab humano genere satisfactionem pro peccato exigente. Alioquin, si voluisset* absque omni *satisfactione hominem a peccato liberare, contra iustitiam non fecisset.*

[93] Also king Darius in Dn 6 may come to mind, who, clearly lacking any foreknowledge, was fatally tied hand and foot to his own promulgation.

[94] ST IIIa q.46 a.2 ad 3: *Sed Deus* non *habet* aliquem *superiorem,* sed ipse est supremum et commune *bonum* totius *universi.* Hence the addition, in SN III d.20 a.1c ad 3: *Sed ex parte illius qui peccavit, secundum ordinem quem nunc Deus rebus imposuit, non potest peccatum congrue sine poena dimitti.*

permeated with this testimony.[95] Therefore arbitrariness cannot be implied when we say that God is the Most High. The issue of being the Highest and His will being unfailing seems to be closely connected with almightiness. And also Thomas' frequent use of words derived from *posse* and the quotation of Lk 1,37 seem to indicate that an aspect of God's almightiness is being discussed here.

Thomas then shows a consequence for the *theologia* and one for the *oikonomia*: when God forgives without satisfaction, He is not like a judge acting unjustly, but more like anyone (*quicumque*) who forgives someone who perpetrated an offence against him/her. And that is not injustice, but what we call merciful. The connection between Christ's *passio* and God's mercy and almightiness will be considered in the course of this study (paragraph 3.2).

A further consequence regards prayer. That God's will cannot be changed, may convey the idea that God is static. And why would we pray, if God is static? Yet the use of the unusual word "to make someone or something totter (*cassari*)", indicates something quite different. It is a rare word, also in Scripture. Therefore this word may remind someone who daily prays the Psalms and is *Magister in Sacra Pagina* on the Psalms[96], of Psalm 46,3: even when the mountains - pre-eminently symbols of being steady[97] - are made to totter (*concussi*) and even tumble into the sea, YHWH Sabaoth is our citadel. Therefore "not being made to totter" rather signifies God's constancy - not an obstacle for prayer, but indeed the very basis of it. Accordingly, Thomas concludes, David's Psalm 51 must be interpreted as a petition for God's mercy (and

---

[95] E.g. Ex 34,6f, Ps 34,8, Mt 19,17, Rm 2,4.

[96] Thomas was very familiar with the Psalms: As a Dominican Friar he prayed the Psalms daily in the liturgy of the hours. He taught as *Magister in Sacra Pagina* the Psalms in Naples througout the academic year 1272-3 and the first two months of the academic year, i.e until the 6th December 1273: the very same time he worked on the Tertia Pars of ST. Both works were terminated abruptly on the 5th December 1273; during morning Mass on the morning of the 6th he was "struck (*commotus*) by something"; he never wrote or dictated again until his peaceful death, the 7th March 1273 (Weisheipl (1983), 110f, 321, 327, 361, 368f).

[97] In the context of prayer cf. Ps 121,1f, Mt 17,20, 21,21f.

not, for instance, as an attempt to make God change His mind[98]).

Hence the impossibility to liberate the human race in another way is *only* an impossibility under a supposition, namely the supposition that God willed it this way. But if God was absolutely free to choose and and did so with eternal foreknowledge, and if He is not an arbitrary god, why then did He choose the *passio* of Christ?

1.2.3 "Most Becoming"

Thomas poses the question somewhat differently, or actually he poses a 'slightly' different question. For, instead of trying to read God's mind, again his point of departure is what we read in Scripture about the crucifixion. On the basis of these data he inquires how "becoming" the *passio* of Christ was.

> "Augustine says in XIII *De Trinitate*: 'There has not been another way more becoming to cure our misery' than by means of the *passio* of Christ. I answer that we must say that some way is more becoming to attain an aim, as through it many things come along that serve the purpose."[99]

Alongside (*praeter*) our liberation from sin Thomas mentions five interconnected benefits: that through Christ's *passio* we know how much God loves humankind (Rm 5,8f); He gave us an example of virtuosity

---

[98] Cf. ST IIaIIae q.83 a.2 ad 2: *[O]ratio nostra non ordinatur ad immutationem divinae dispositionis: sed ut obtineatur nostris precibus quod Deus disposuit.*

[99] ST IIIa q.46 a.3sc, co: *Augustinus dicit, XIII De Trin.* [c.10 n.5, ML 42,1024] *"Sanandae nostrae miseriae convenientior modus alius non fuit" quam per Christi passionem. Respondeo dicendum quod tanto aliquis modus convenientior est ad assequendum finem,* quanto per ipsum plura concurrunt quae sunt expedientia fini.

("obedience, humility[100], constancy, justice and others," 1 P 2,21[101]); Christ gained for us also justifying grace and the glory of beatidude;[102] we realize how necessary it is to refrain from sinning (1 Co 6,20); a human being, once deceived and enslaved by the devil, now defeats him (1 Co 15,57, see note 66).[103]

Apart from the aim, in respect of Christ Himself, who He was, a natural death would have been even less becoming, says Thomas citing Chrysostom: since He was life itself (Jn 14,6), He did not come to undergo His own death, but ours. Moreover, it was unbecoming that He who cured many from the weariness of life (*languor*) would Himself be

---

[100] Humility is a new element in Thomas' exposition. Humility does not imply that we should not stand up against evil. It refers to the pride of the devil, called (ST IIIa q.46 a.3 ad 3:) "the desertor of justice the lover of might", since his ultimate goal was not God; he sought after his own honour and wielding power over others (cf. IaIIae q.2 aa.2, 4). Thomas indicates pride as the first sin of humankind (IIaIIae q.162f). Hence, IIIa q.1 a.2co: [S]*uperbia quae maximum impedimentum est ne inhaereatur Deo.*

[101] In R2C c.5 l.3, on 2 Co 5,14, Thomas elaborates on the love of Christ: *Caritas Christi quasi stimulus stimulat nos ad faciendum ea quae caritas imperat,* ut scilicet procuremus salutem proximorum. *Hic est effectum caritatis,* citing Rm 8,14 and Sg 8,6. Later on in l.3 Thomas cites 1 P 4,21 and Lk 9,23 as references that exhort us to follow the suffering Christ (cf. note 103, on CIS c.57).

[102] Thomas refers here to q.48 a.1 and q.49 aa.1, 5, where he discusses many texts from Scripture.

[103] Remarkably enough Thomas does not explicitly mention here Augustine's own clarification that all these are closely connected with the incitement of our hope (*tam necessarium fuit ad erigendam spem nostram*). Also not at the end of his commentary on Is 57, where he mentions four aspects of the Passion to be considered. He connects them explicitly with consequences for the Christian life (*ad ...*), whilst he refers to Scripture, CIS c.57: [*I*]*n passione Christi homo debet cogitare primo dilectionem* ad reamandum, citing Sg 8,6; cf. the first and the fourth (but now formulated positively) benefit mentioned in ST IIIa q.46 a.3co. *Secundo, amaritudinem,* ad compatiendum, citing Lm 3,19; when we suffer, we suffer with Christ (*compassio*). *Tertio, fortitudinem,* ad fortiter patiendum, citing Heb 12,3; cf. the second benefit mentioned in *l.c.. Quatro, utilitatem,* ad gratias agendum, citing Sg 7,9a; cf. the third benefit mentioned *l.c.* and q.49.

affected by it.[104] Furthermore, since so many saw that He truly died,
His resurrection became more credible - although Mt 28,11-15 ("His
disciples stole the body") shows that also another interpretation is
possible.

According to this line of reasoning, realizing how abundant God's
goodness is for us through the *passio* of Christ, may strengthen a human
being in a virtuous life.[105] These extra benefits would not have been
bestowed on us, if we were liberated through God's will c.q.[106] His
might alone or by means of an infinitesimal *passio* of Christ, which
would have been sufficient in the light of the satisfaction, since the human
being Christ Himself was without sin.[107] Hence our liberation through
Christ's *passio* was *more* becoming (*conventient*ior) *than* by God's will or
power alone.

After this exposition on the relative suitability of Christ's *passio*
unto death on a cross Thomas inquires how becoming it was as such. His,
remarkably extensive, answer is that it was *most* becoming (*con-
venient*issimum). The cross is mentioned explicitly, as in Ph 2,8. This,
exactly because the cross raises some questions in respect of Christ's
dignity - was the cross not a most disgraceful (*turpissima*) execution
(citing W 2,20, cf. Dt 21,23)? - and the prefiguration of this sacrifice of
His in the First Testament.[108]

---

[104] in: ST IIIa q.46 a.3 ad 2. This argument seems to refer to Mt 27,39-43 par.. Also
the interpretation of the old and weak (and disobedient) Christ in the film The Last
Temptation of Christ comes to mind.

[105] Thomas speaks of it in terms of *promotio hominis in bono*, ST IIIa q.1 a.2co: *ad
fidem, spem, caritatem, rectam operationem, plenam participationem divinitatis*, and *ad
remotionem mali, ne sibi diabolum praeferat et eum veneratur.*

[106] One's will is being executed by one's action, the principle of which is one's might
(ST Ia q.14 intr.), see chapter 3.

[107] SN III d.20 a.3 ag.4: *Bernardus dicit quod "una gulla sanguinis Christi fuit
sufficiens pretium nostrae redemptionis."*

[108] ST IIIa q.46 a.4 ag.1: As in the First Testament the sacrifices were for
reconciliation with God, so did Christ's *passio* unto death reconcile us with God, but in a
unique way (Rm 6,10, Heb 9,28, 10,10, 1P 3,18, 4,1, see also q.49) But the sacrificial

Thomas walks in two ways: in the *corpus*, drawing on works of the Church Fathers Augustine, Chrysostom and Gregory of Nyssa, he confirms the abundance of the fruits that the *Passio* yields and the harmony of it.[109] And in the answers to the *obiectiones* he refutes the argumentations. He counters the opinion that prefiguration means that *everything* must be similar[110]: a caution for us seeking prefigurations in the First Testament.

About the disgrace of the Crucified:

"Christ has refused to assume the *passiones* that could distract Him, those which are allied with a defect of knowledge or grace, or even of virtue. However He did not refuse those allied with injustice which were inflicted

---

animals were killed by the sword and subsequently burned. Therefore, is this not incongruent with the crucifixion?

[109] He names seven reasons why it was most fitting, fruits (2) and signs (5): First the example of a virtuous life, without fear of any form of death, ST IIIa q.46 a.4co: *nihil enim erat, inter omnia genera mortis, illo genere* [*scilicet in cruce*] *execrabilius et formidabilius* (Augustine). Only secondly - in earlier works this is, also in this context, the first fruit (SN III d.20 a.4b ad 1, OTT c.228) - he mentions the satisfaction (Augustine). Further: As Christ purified and sanctified the earth by walking on it, He did likewise with the air by being exalted on the cross (Chrysostom). The next is that in this way [He revealed to us that] He prepared our exaltation, i.e. our ascension into heaven (Chrysostom). A fifth is that the form of the cross corresponds with the four quarters of the world to which Christ's power and providence extends (Gregory of Nyssa) and Christ's outstretched arms refer to Him gathering the people of the Old Covenant with His one hand and the gentiles with the other. This interpretation of Chrysostom does not exclude Augustine's interpretation of the outstretched arms on the breadth, the length, the height and the depth (Ep 3,18) of the cross, referring to resp. Christ reaching out to good works, the constancy (the cross stands firmly on the ground), heaven, in which we place our hope, and the depth of gratuitous grace.

[110] ST IIIa q.46 a.4 ad 1: "*Non autem oportet quod quantum ad* omnia: *quia iam non esset similitudo, sed veritas,*" *ut Damascenus dicit* [*De fide orth.* III c.26, MG 94,1096]. But one has to look carefully, Thomas says: according to Ex 27,1 sacrifices' altars were made of wood, as the cross was. And in Christ's case the fire was the fire of His love (cf. Lk 24,32, MR). Thomas also cites Chrysostom, saying that Christ was not beheaded like St. John the Baptist or sawn into two like Isaiah (according to the tradition), so that the integrity and unity of His body may symbolize the unity of the Church intended by God.

on Him from without, as Heb 12,2 says."[111]

Hence the disgrace of the crucified, of which Dt 21,23 speaks (male*dictus a Deo est qui pendet in ligno*) cannot be with regard to who Christ is, according to Mt 21,9 (bene*dictus qui venit in nomine Domini*). His disgrace must therefore be understood in the sense of 2 Co 5,21 ("For our sake He made the sinless One a victim for sin") and Ga 3,13 ("Christ redeemed us from the curse of the Law by being cursed for our sake"), as Augustine also says.

Quite elaborately the suitability of the external circumstances of Christ's *passio* are discussed by Thomas: three *articuli* (9 - 11) at great length. We may shrug our shoulders reading his questions: whether Christ suffered at the right time, in the right place and whether it was becoming that He was crucified with bandits. The *obiectiones* as well as the *sed contra*s in these *articuli* are texts from Scripture, texts which seem to conflict with one another. For instance, if Christ's death was prefigured by the sacrifices of the Torah, would the temple not have been the proper place for Christ's sacrifice, instead of outside the gate of the city? Thomas' answer is threefold: in Lv 16,27 it says that on the great Day of Atonement the sacrifice must be taken outside the camp to be burnt, cf. Heb 13,11f; He gave us an example of turning away from worldly things, cf. Heb 13,13; now everyone can know that the sacrifice is for the whole world (Chrysostom).[112]

Thomas does two things here: first he shows his readers how to read these texts from Scripture. And through his explanation, referring to W 8,1 ("Strongly (*Fortiter*) She [i.e. God's Wisdom] reaches from one end of the world to the other and She governs the whole world for its good"), he shows how in Christ's *passio* everything reveals God's

---

[111] ST IIIa q.46 a.4 ad 2: *Christus detractibiles passionis assumere* renuit *quae pertinebant ad defectum scientiae vel gratia, aut etiam virtutis. Non autem illas quae pertinent ad iniuriam ab exteriori illatam: quinimmo, ut dicitur Heb.12,2.*

[112] ST IIIa q.46 a.10 ad 2.

wisdom, will, justice and goodness.[113]

Reading the *articuli* 3 and 4, I find it intriguing how Thomas lets the tension mount in and between these *articuli*.[114] Another thing that catches the eye is, not only how elaborate, but also how figurative Thomas' exposition is, in particular in *articulus* 4: no air-tight arguments here, but rather seeking God's hand in the harmony of the events. Taking his readers by the hand, he approaches the mystery of the *passio* from different angles. Explaining Scripture and using all kinds of images, he is building up his argumentation: it was most becoming. The reader is led into the multi-layeredness of the awe-ful mystery of Christ's *passio* as well as the superabundance of God's and Christ's loving goodness. This is why we speak of *Good* Friday and why in the Roman Catholic Church we *celebrate* the Exaltation of the Cross (14th September).[115]

But in the context of this study the answer in this last *articulus* raises questions that have come up before: does Thomas, speaking of Christ's *passio* in this way, take it seriously? Here he says that Christ

---

[113] ST IIIa q.46 a.9co: [S]*icut supra* [a.1] *dictum est, passio Christi* subiecta *erat* eius voluntati. *Voluntas autem eius regabatur divina* sapientia, *quae* omnia *convenienter et suaviter disponit, ut dicitur* Sap.8,1, cf. a.10co; ad 1: *Christus* convenientissime *in Ierusalem passus est*; a.11co: *Christus inter latrones crucifixus est, alia quidem ratione quantum ad intentionem Iudaeorum, alia vero quantum* ad Dei ordinationem.

[114] In a.3 ag.1 - 3: *conveniens - convenientius - convenientissimum*; in sc: *convenientior modus alius non fuit*. And aa.1 and 2 are in terms of the positive degree (a.1 ad 3: [*Q*]*uod hominem liberari per passionem Christi conveniens fuit*); a.3 of the comparative degree (intr.: *Utrum alius modus convenientior fuisset*); in a.4 of the superlative degree (co: *Respondeo dicendum quod convenientissimum fuit*).

[115] Already by the end of the 4th century a cultus is found in Jerusalem (Veneration of the Cross and the feast of the Exaltation of the Cross on the date of the consecration of the church on the holy grave, the consecration date of the church on Golgotha and the feast of finding the holy Cross), which attracted many pilgrims, by whom it was spread to Constantinople (6th century) and Rome (7th century; Pope Sergius I instituted these feasts by the end of that century); Sepiere (1994), 20-22.

The Passionist Congregation also celebrates, on the Friday before Ash Wednesday, its titular feast: the "Solemn Commemoration of the Passion of Our Lord Jesus Christ". The readings for the Eucharist are (morning) Gn 3,9-15, Ps 130, Rm 5,12, 15-21 and Mt 16,21-27 or Mk 10,32-34 and (day time) Is 53,1-12, Ps 22, 1 Co 1,18-25 or Ph 2,(5)6-11 and Jn 19,17-30 or Lk 23,33-46.

"refused" and allowed; what does this mean? Does this not imply that Christ did not truly suffer and that He was not truly human? And why does Thomas mention Christ's knowledge, grace and virtue here? Why were these not affected, whereas His body was? And with regard to almightiness one may ask what kind of might Christ's is, that He could refuse and allow?

Another pressing question is what Thomas means when he, with Augustine, says that our misery has been cured by means of the *passio* of Christ (note 99). For although Christ suffered and died "for us", is not our world still full of misery? Thomas' answer to this question will be considered in paragraph 3.3.

1.3 *Vere passus*

In the preceding paragraphs is shown that in Thomas' theology the relation between the Father and Christ in the *passio* of Christ is described in terms of handing over and obedience, that God's and Christ's absolutely free will is emphasized and that the *passio* as it came to pass was salutary for us. And the crowning touch (for us) may be that Christ even allowed to be affected by certain *passiones* and refused to be affected by other *passiones*. On account of the texts read until now, one cannot but come to the tentative conclusion that in Thomas' theology Christ is a great hero. He is more like Michelangelo's "Cristo ligneo" (Casa Buonarroti, Florence) than the crucified Christ on Grünewald's "Isenheimer Altar" (Musée d'Unterlinden, Colmar). This is the more remarkable, because since the ecumenical Council of Chalcedon (451), and especially since the Council or Synod in Trullo (Constantinople, 692) there had been a growing attention for the sufferings of the man Christ. And in Thomas' days a popular devotion around it was widespread.[116]

---

[116] The ecumenical councils of the 4th century (Nicaea I, Constantinople I) formulated the *homoousion*, which resulted in images of Christ sitting on a throne. But even after Chalcedon (451) only the divinity of Christ was stressed in art (probably under the influence of the Monophysitism against Nestorianism, that underlined Christ's human and divine nature, but denied the unity of Christ's person). During a Council in Constantinople called Quinnisext or Trullanum (Council or Synod in Trullo) in 692 it was determined that Christ was to be depicted as a human being, not as a lamb, on the cross (canon XI). The crucifix became the pre-eminent sign of the incarnation, i.e. Christ's true humanity. But,

In the terminology of Luther (Heidelberger Disputation, 1518) Thomas' theology on the *passio* of Christ has been and still is regarded by some as "theology of the glory (*theologia gloriae*)", as distinct from "theology of the cross (*theologia crucis*)".[117] A theology of the cross is a theology which starts with Christ's *passio* as the primary or even the

---

in line with Chalcedon, Christ on the cross had to remain recognizable as divine as well, for instance head up and with open eyes, in accordance with Ps 121,3f. Yet hardly any representation of a cruelly suffering Christ is known until the Carolingian era. By order of Charlemagne a David-cycle was painted in Müstair as a paralell to a Christ-cycle: David as the *alter-Christus* ("Son of David", Mt 21,9) and Charlemagne saw himself as a kind of David: king under God. Inspired by these paintings Christ was often depicted in the 9th century as a king on the cross in Western Europe, from Italy to Sweden. In Rome, 8th century, the Pope carried a wooden cross from the church of San Giovanni in Laterano to the church of Santa Croce in Gerusalémme; on the way a deacon took over (cf. Lk 23,26 par.). In the 9th century the tradition of the Stations of the Cross started: In Jerusalem's Santo Sepulcro the Patriarch carried round a relic of the holy Cross, stopping each time to commemorate an aspect of Christ's crucifixion - a tradition soon taken over in the West. It made people more sensitive to the mystery of Christ's human suffering. Especially through the Franciscans, devotions concerning the *passio Christi* expanded enormously in the 13th century: When we suffer, we suffer with the suffering Christ, as formulated in the *Stabat mater* (±1300): *Sancta mater, istud agas, Crucifixi fige plagas cordi meo valide.* Under the influence of the interpretation in the theology of the sacraments of Christ's death on the cross as a sacrifice (Ps 116, Is 53, Jn 19,33f) (mid 800's), Christ was also depicted as being worn out, marked by the heavy burden (our sins) he bore or had born, with a crown of thorns (instead of a golden crown), almost naked (instead of the regalia; two cases of a completely naked Christ are known of) and dead; in particular in the liturgical books, on the page of the Consecration. In some of these pictures one or more angels are holding a Eucharistic chalice at Christ's wounds, in order to collect His Blood. Carter (1936), 34, Constantini (1911), 28f, 102f, Dirks (1963²), 94f, Henderson (1972), 236-8, Hinz (1973), 84-172, 253-352, Louis (1957), 98-110, Sepiere (1994), 1-26, 127, De Solms (1995²), Väterlein (1977).

[117] Lippi (1982), 86: "Secondo san Tomasso, dalla Sacra Scrittura risulterebbe *solo* una finalita soteriologica" (italics added, MR). And although Lippi says that "San Tomasso non sviluppa una vera e propria teologia della gloria" (20), he discusses Thomas' theology as a theology of the glory (paragraphs 1.4 and 4.4). His conclusion, however, is merely based on his interpretation of ST IIIa q.1 a.3. Not even once in the book does he refer to ST IIIa q.46.

only source of theology.[118] Theology of glory is a theology that does not take suffering seriously; Easter is already present on Good Friday, so to say.[119] In this paragraph an answer will be sought to the question whether Thomas' theology should be seen as "glorious" theology or not. Does he take the suffering of Christ seriously? And if so, how then are the *articuli* that were considered hitherto and the four to be read in this paragraph interrelated?

In the *Summa Theologiae* Thomas first surveys which were the *passiones* of Christ. Then he distinguishes between Christ's bodily *passiones* and the *passiones* of His soul. For we profess in the Creed that Christ suffered. Now if Christ was truly human, He must have had a human, possible body[120] and a human, possible soul. But what does it mean for His *passio* of body and soul that Christ was conceived by the Holy Spirit and existed in union with the divine Word - two aspects of Christ's humanity that distinguish Christ from other human beings? Hence, in *articulus* 5 Thomas sums up the *passiones* (1.3.1). Then, in the next *articulus*, he considers in depth the nature of His bodily *passiones*, by comparing them to the sufferings of other human beings; Lm 1,12 ("Look and see: is any sorrow like the sorrow inflicted on me?") read as an expression of Christ in His Passion, induces Thomas to do so (1.3.2). Finally Thomas considers in two *articuli* the *passiones* of Christ's soul

---

[118] Salvati (1992), 143: "La croce è per i credenti *soglia* cioè luogo di ingresso e di contatto con il Dio cristiano, anzitutto dal punto di vista della participazione alla vita di Dio: 'sine cruce, nulla grazia'. Questo principio non vale solamente per il momento iniziale della vita della Chiesa, ma sempre. [....] [I]l vero teologo è solo colui che parla di Dio a partire dal Crocifisso (Lutero)." Cf. Moltmann (1972), 77.

[119] Hedinger's reproach to staurology, (1993), 59-61. Cf. Metz (1995), 84: "Wer z.B. die theologische Rede von der Auferweckung so hört, daß in ihr die Schrei des Gekreuzigten unhörbar geworden ist, der hört nicht Theologie, sondern Mythologie, nicht Evangelium, sondern eine Siegermythos." Cf. Janßen (1996), 81f. A clear example of *theologia gloriae* is Dillistone's Jesus Christ and His Cross, - Studies on the Saving Work of Christ (1953). The titles of its chapters speak for themselves: The Mystery of the Cross, The Saviour-Hero, The Great Shepherd of the Sheep, The Son Who Was Not Spared, The Sin Bearer, The Great High Priest, The Servant of the Lord, The Glory of the Cross.

[120] A heavenly body is impassible and incorruptible. Hence, ST IIIa q.5 a.2co: *Si Filius Dei corpus caeleste assumpsisset, non vere esuriisset nec sitiisset, nec etiam passionem et mortem sustinuisset.*

(1.3.3).

1.3.1 All *passiones*?

In comparison with the *Summa Theologiae* Thomas does not devote a separate *articulus* to an inventory of Christ's *passiones* in the *Sententiae*. Besides, in the latter he discusses the *passiones* of His soul *before* the *passiones* of the body.[121] The structure and the content of the *Summa Theologiae* has at least two advantages: the starting point is what we read in the gospel, namely the story of the Passion. In the *Summa Theologiae* it is clearer that Scripture is the starting point of, and the criterion for, further evaluation on the deep structure of the *passio* of Christ. And secondly there is more attention for Christ's bodily sufferings in the *Summa Theologiae* than in the *Sententiae*.

Which were the *passiones* that He did and did not experience? Since Hilary, a Doctor of the Church, interprets Christ's words "It is fulfilled" (Jn 19,30) as that He was tested by every kind (*genus*) of human *passio* and had completed it by His death, and since the text of Is 52,13f says that He even bore the *passiones* that took all His glory from Him, it seems that He underwent all *passiones*. But on the other hand, Scripture itself testifies that Christ did not bear all *passiones*: Thomas cites Jn 19,32f, where it says that the soldiers did not break His legs.[122] Moreover, no one can undergo all *passiones*, for some exclude one another, like death by being burnt and death by drowning.

The clue for finding a refined answer to the question which *passiones* Christ underwent, is the distinction between sort or type (*species*) and kind or category (*genus*). Thomas introduces the term "kind" in the third *obiectio*:

> "The *passio* of Christ is ordered to the liberation of humankind from sin, as was said above. But Christ has

---

[121] SN III d.15 q.2 a.3c resp. a.1c/a.3b.

[122] ST IIIa q.46 a.5sc. In fact a remarkable argument, since Christ had already died and thence would not have undergone this *passio* as a human being anyway.

come and liberated human beings from every *kind* of sin. Hence He had to undergo every *kind* of *passio* [....] and not every single *passio*."[123]

It is quite surprising that Thomas just after making the distinction, excludes a whole group of the bodily *passiones*, namely the ones that are caused from inside a person. Another surprise: Thomas designates the bodily illnesses as such. We commonly consider illnesses as coming from outside. If Thomas had known of bacteria and viruses, he might have agreed. But on the other hand, we all know that when there is an epidemic in a certain place and time, some people do not fall ill: either because they live in such a way that they cannot contract it or because they are not sensitive to it. And this is why Thomas speaks of bodily illnesses as coming from within a person (*ab intrinsico causatas*). Now with regard to Christ, although we do not find in Scripture that He was ever ill, the reason is much deeper: illnesses do not *befit* Christ. For they are caused, Thomas says in an earlier *quaestio*,[124] either by unordered conduct (*ex inordinatione victus*, as in Ps 38,6) or by what we call sensitivity to an illness, or in other words, a weakness caused whilst a person was formed in his/her mother's womb (*ex defectu virtutis formativae*) (as in Ps 139,13). Yet since Christ's body was conceived by the Holy Spirit, "which is of infinite wisdom and power," His human body was without any ailment, and since His life was irreproachable, illnesses do not befit Christ.

However, the consequence of this is not that there was a kind of suffering which Christ did not bear. For illnesses are not a category (*genus*) of their own, but a sort (*species*), a subdivision, of a category[125]; illnesses belong to the category of the *passiones* in the body (*in corpore*). The sort of the *passiones* in the body that Christ *did* bear, were the ones inflicted upon Him from outside: the bruises, the wounds from

---

[123] ST IIIa q.46 a.5 ag.3, co: *Praeterea, passio Christi ordinata est ad liberationem hominis a peccato, ut supra dictum est* [aa.1-3, q.14 a.1]. *Sed Christus venit liberare homines ab* omni *peccatorum* genere. *Ergo debuit pati* omne genus *passionum*. [....] [*Q*]*antum ad* speciem. *Et sic non oportuit Christum omnem humanam passionem pati*.

[124] ST IIIa q.14 a.4co.

[125] ST Ia q.30 a.4co; q.7 a.3 ad 2, q.15 a.3 ad 4.

the nails etc.

Next Thomas sets out how extensive Christ's *passio* was; He underwent every category of human *passio*. He distinguishes between three kinds: *passio* in respect of the people inflicting it upon Him; *passio* in respect of the aspects of being human; *passio* of the limbs. This arrangement is a rather odd one - it is not found in earlier theological or philosophical works; there is not even one reference to any Doctor of the Church in the *corpus* - *until* one begins to read his enumeration. For Thomas basically follows the order of Scripture and lets Scripture even determine the categories. This elucidates why there is so much attention to Christ's bodily *passiones* in the *Summa Theologiae*.

Thomas reckons among the first kind what Christ suffered because of gentiles and Jews, men and women[126], and, in conformity with Ps 2,1b - 2, leading figures as well as their servants and ordinary people, and even confidants, like Judas who handed Him over and Peter who disowned Him. Of the aspects of being human that can cause someone to suffer Thomas mentions Christ's friends (deserting Him), the public opinion (the blasphemies uttered against Him), honour and glory (the mockery and the grievous bodily harm), objects[127] (He was even stripped of His clothes), the soul (sadness, aversion and fear) and the body (wounds and bruises). These bodily aspects Thomas classifies under a separate category (for the reason mentioned above): His head was crowned with a crown of thorns, His hands and feet were attached to a wooden pole by nails, His face was hit and spit upon, He had bruises all over His body; "He even suffered in respect of all His senses": the touch (the bruises and the nails), taste (sour wine and vinegar He drank), smell (the place stank after dead bodies), hearing (He was taunted by

---

[126] ST IIIa q.46 a.5co: ... *ut patet de ancillis accusantibus Petrum*. But to us this is not clear at all. Peter was driven into a corner by their questions and Christ suffered because of his denial. So it seems that these women only caused *passio* indirectly. However, in Thomas commentary on Mt 26,69-72 the questions of these women are heavily reckoned against them, REM c.26 l.7: *Et convenit casus Petri casui primi hominis; Eccli. 25,33* [= Si 25,24]: *A muliere initium peccati*. More convincing that Christ also suffered through women may be e.g. to assume that there were not only men in the crowd shouting for His crucifixion (Mt 27,22f).

[127] It seems that Thomas, being a Dominican, i.e. a member of a mendicant order, is keen on avoiding the word "possessions" (cf. Mt 8,20) here.

blasphemers and mockers) and sight ("While He saw His mother and the disciple whom He loved crying"[128]).

And it seems that Thomas by this exposition has formulated a positive answer to the third *obiectio* quoted above. But he has not. He rather refutes the argumentation as regards two points:

> "As to what would have been enough: one, minimal *passio* would have been enough to redeem the human race from all sins."

This was discussed in the former paragraph: justice through satisfaction is not a matter of how much Christ underwent, but *that* He, the just One, underwent it, of His own free will. Similarly Thomas says with regard to Is 52,13f that Christ was not exalted because of the amount (*numerus*) of *passiones* he bore, but because of their quality (*magnitudo*), i.e. their ignobility.

The second point, also discussed in paragraph 1.2, concerns the way of thinking, namely in terms of "had to" instead of what is becoming:

> "But as to the suitability, it was sufficient that He underwent all kinds of *passiones*, as was said already in the *corpus*."[129]

So the suitability is here not with regard to the aim, but with regard to who Christ is. And in this way Thomas says that *passiones* caused from within, from how a person is, do not befit Him; He is as a human being a perfect human being (cf. Ep 4,13).

---

[128] In Jn 19,26, where Thomas is referring to, it does not say that they are crying. Thomas is in all probability referring to the tradition that at least Mary cried at the foot of the Cross, as it is also written in the first stanza of the *Stabat mater*: *Stabat mater dolorosa iuxta crucem* lacrimosa, *dum pendebat Filius*; cf. the fifth stanza: Quis est homo qui non fleret, *Christi Matrem si videret in tanto supplicio?*

[129] ST IIIa q.46 a.5 ad 3: *Secundum sufficientiam,* una minima *passio Christi suffecit ad redimendum genus humanum ab* omnibus *peccatis. Sed* secundum convenientiam *sufficiens fuit quod pateretur omnia genera passionum, sicut iam dictum est* [in co.].

From this it is clear that Thomas did not need the enumeration of the *passiones* to find an answer to the *obiectiones*. But by drawing up this inventory he has prepared the next step: for if one wants to inquire about the quality of Christ's *passio*, one needs to know what His actual *passiones* were. Yet it cannot escape one's attention that Thomas, by doing so, is highlighting the largeness of the *passio* of Christ.

1.3.2 No Greater Pain Can Someone Have...

In the 13th century there was a growing attention to the mystery of the humanity of Christ and in particular to His *passiones*, as a reaction to a primary interest in His divinity (note 116). In our days it may seem the other way round: to many not the humanity but rather the divinity of Christ is a stumbling block for believing. At the same time the humanity of Christ and therefore His *passio* is so obvious, that it may not be a point of discussion; if Christ was truly human, then He truly suffered.[130] But in order to see how *passio* and almightiness are interrelated, the nature of Christ's pain caused by His *passio* must be examined first.

Of old Christians have heard Lm 1,12, "Look and see: is any sorrow like the sorrow inflicted on me", as being also an exclamation of Christ.[131] This could relate to Christ's bodily pain as well as to the pain in His soul. Thomas first focuses our attention on Christ's bodily pain, its quality that is, as was said above. He does so by comparing these sufferings of Christ with those of other human beings. Thomas lists as many as six points of comparison. The first three are the body, the soul and the body in relation to the soul. The second series of three are about the relation between pain and loss, respectively pain and innocence and pain and the aim of the salvation of humankind. Here the concentration will be on the first two, because the first reveals Thomas' serious attention for Christ's humanity and the second concerns the power of

---

[130] And, as Weinandy points out, in this way the soteriological import of Christ's suffering is overlooked. Weinandy (2000), 214-242.

[131] That is why we find it e.g. in the liturgical Lamentationes Prophetae Hieremiae (lectio III), in the Matins Responsories for Good Friday (n.6) and thence in e.g. Händel's Messiah (part II, n.30).

Christ's soul.

With regard to the body one could say that some people suffer more gravely and for a longer time. Thomas mentions the - in his days popular - martyrs Laurence, who was roasted alive, and Vincent, whose flesh was torn up by iron torture hooks. And the second argument too has not been robbed of its strength over the years:

> "The power of the mind mitigates pain. Even so much
> that the Stoics asserted that 'sadness does not occur in the
> soul of a wise person.' And Aristotle asserted that moral
> power keeps the state of mind balanced. But in Christ was
> a most perfect power of the mind. Hence it seems that in
> Christ was minimal pain."[132]

Christ had a great inner strength, so to say. But what was the nature of it? And how far did it reach? And how is it related to His *passio*? Another question is why Thomas introduces the Stoics in this *obiectio*. It strengthens the suspicion that some of the readers might already have, that Christ in Thomas' view was stoic.

The fourth argumentation, or rather Thomas' answer to it, is also of importance for this study: assuming that the greater the good lost, the greater the pain, Christ seems to have had not as much pain as sinners do, since the latter not only lose the natural life, but, contrary to Christ, the life of grace as well.[133]

---

[132] ST IIIa q.46 a.6 ag.2: [V]irtus mentis est mitigativa doloris: in tantum quod Stoici posuerunt "tristitiam in animo sapientis non cadere" [in Augustine's De civ. Dei L.4 c.8, ML 41,411]. Et Aristoteles posuit quod virtus moralis medium tenet in passionibus [Ethic. II c.6 n.9, Bk 1106b14]. Sed in Christo fuit perfectissima virtus mentis. Ergo videtur quod in Christo fuerit minimus dolor.

[133] The other three relative *obiectiones* (ag.3, 5, 6) are not as important for this study. They are listed here, so that Thomas' approach to Christ's *passio* may be evaluated better: The third *obiectio* reads that someone who is more sensitive feels more pain. Since sensitivity is based in the soul (*corpus sentiat ex anima*), it seems that Adam before the Fall (Thomas refers to the state of innocence, ST Ia q.91 a.3co: *Deus instituit corpus humanum in optima dispositione secundum convenientiam ad talem formam* [= *animam eius*] *et ad tales operationes*) and the souls suffering in purgatory or hell suffer more (nl. directly and not through the body) than Christ. The basic assumption of *obiectio* 5 is strange; it says that innocence diminishes the pain of a *passio*. And since Christ was

Answering these argumentations Thomas takes two steps. First, he refers to earlier *quaestiones*, where he clearly establishes that the body of Christ was such that He underwent true pain (*verus dolor*) in body and soul: in the Passion narratives we read that Christ's body was injured and that He died eventually. That His wounds were real is emphatically confirmed by the story of Christ's appearances to His disciples (Jn 20,19-29).[134] And since this injury and death signify that Christ's body was passible and mortal, Thomas firmly concludes that it is beyond a shadow of doubt (*nulli dubium debet esse*) that there was true, human pain in Christ, as also Is 53,4[135] says. In brief: *Christus verus homo*.

His second step is the explanation why we must hold that and in what way Christ's pain was the greatest of the pains of today's life (*praesentis vitae*). Four reasons are put forward. The first is the most obvious to us: the causes of the pain. He distinguishes between the pain Christ felt through the bruises inflicted upon Him and the pain He felt from within. Thomas is remarkably detailed on how painful crucifixion was, much more painful than being killed by the sword.[136] From within He felt the pain of all the sins of the people for whom He suffered, as if He felt their pain (*quasi sibi adscribit*); he took their situation to heart, as we say, or in other words, it hurt to see them in their miserable situation.[137] And this is what Thomas calls *com-passio*[138], as will be

---

innocent (Thomas cites Jr 11,19: *"mansuetus"*, cf. Js 53,7, applied to Christ in Ac 8,32-35, cf. Mt 26,63, 2 P 2,23), His pain was not the greatest. The last *obiectio* has in fact been met with already in the first *articulus* of *quaestio* 46, that the greatest pain was not needed (and therefore would have been cruel) for the liberation of humankind; Christ could as well have brought it about by divine might.

[134] Cited in ST IIIa q.14 a.1co.

[135] ST IIIa q.15 a.5co; cited in sc: *Vere languores nostros ipse tulit, et* dolores nostros *ipse portavit.* (also cited in q.14 a.1co).

[136] ST IIIa q.46 a.6co: [M]ors confixorum in cruce est* acerbissima*: [1] *quia configuntur in locis nervosis et* maxime *sensibilibus, scilicet in manibus et pedibus;* [2] *et ipsum pondus corporis pendentis continue* auget *dolorem;* [3] *et* cum hoc *etiam est doloris* diuturnitas, *quia non statim moritur, sicut hi qui sunt gladio interfecti.*

[137] As in Mt 9,36, 14,14 15,32.

further explained in the next chapter. Two other pains from inside are mentioned by Thomas: the absence of His people, in particular His disciples[139], and the prospect of losing his life, "which is naturally horrific for a human being".[140]

The second reason refers to what was said in the former sub-paragraph, that Christ's body was very susceptible; it

> "was composed very well, because His body was formed by the miraculous operation of the Holy Spirit, just as those things that are done or made by miracles are better than other things. Chrysostom says so concerning the wine into which Christ changed the water at the wedding in Cana. And therefore in Him the tactile sense, from which the perception of pain follows, was developed to the highest extent."[141]

---

[138] Cf. REM c.15 1.3, on the text *misereor turbae*: *Misericordia est* passio, *quia misericors est miserum cor habens, qui repugnat alienam miseriam suam* (citing Ps 103,8); c.14 1.1, citing Ps 86,15 with regard to Christ: *Miserator et misericors Dominus*, patiens, *et multae misericordiae et verax*. ST Ia q.95 a.3co: [*M*]*isericordia, quae est* dolor *de miseria aliena* (cf. ST IaIIae q.102 a.6 ad 8). IIaIIae q.30 a.1co: (cit. Augustine's IX *De civ. Dei* c.5, ML 41,261) *Misericordia est alienae miseriae in nostro corde* compassio, *qua utique, si possumus, subvenire compellimur.*

[139] Christ called them "friends" (Lk 12,4, Jn 15,15). Thomas' answer to the question [*u*]*trum dolor et tristitia mitigentur per compassionem amicorum* (ST IaIIae q.38 a.3) is affirmative. Thomas adds, in IIIa q.46 a.6co, that Christ was ashamed about the absence of them (*scandalum passi fuerant*), which at the same time sounds like an appeal to his readers not to desert friends in their misery.

[140] For every human being's natural inclination is towards life, ST Ia q.18 a.2 ad 2, cf. q.IaIIae q.35 a.6 ad 1 (cf. Ps 34,13). And, IaIIae q.31 a.6co: [*I*]*d quod est naturale in unoquoque, est potentissimum.*

[141] ST IIIa q.46 a.6co: *Secundo potest magnitudo considerari ex perceptibilitate patientis. Nam et secundum corpus erat* optime *complexionatus, cum corpus eius fuerit formatum miraculose operatione Spiritus Sancti: sicut et alia quae per miracula facta sunt, sunt aliis potiora, ut Chrysostomus dicit de vino in quod Christus aquam convertit in nuptiis* [*In Io. homil.* 22, MG 59,136]. *Et ideo in eo* maxime *viguit sensus tactus, ex cuius perceptione sequitur dolor.*

And the same applies to Christ's soul - with the same consequences for
the causes of sadness (*dolor interior*). It is noticeable that Thomas speaks
in superlatives here.[142]

In comparison to the *Sententiae* (and his other earlier works) it is
clear that in the *Summa Theologiae* Thomas stresses Christ's pain much
more: these two reasons in the *Summa Theologiae* are one reason in
Sententiae; and in the *Summa Theologiae* he elaborates the bodily pain in
more detail.[143]

The purity of the pain is the third respect in which Christ's pain,
of body and soul, was greater. For when we suffer, we look for

> "a certain diversion or for an overflow from higher
> powers to the lower. But this was not so in Christ when
> He suffered, for each and every power He 'allowed to act
> according to its nature', as John of Damascus says."[144]

The first part is recognizable right away; Thomas appeals to what is
usual: when we feel pain, we try to suppress it or look for distraction.
Further, it is not that strange that Christ did not act like this, if one takes
into account that His sufferings had a purpose, as was said above. That
Christ "allowed" the powers to torture Him, as was said before, remains,
also in this context, unclear. Even more so because of a new element
introduced here, that there was no "overflow from the higher to the lower
powers". What Thomas means by this and whether this also was because
Christ Himself did not allow it to happen, will be looked at in the next
subparagraph, about the *passio* of Christ's soul. Since Thomas repeats
this point in his reply to the second *obiectio* it appears to be an important
element. Thomas presents Christ in His *passio* not as a languid and

---

[142] It may remind us of Scriptural texts like Mt 26,38 (cited in ST IIIa q.15 a.6sc), Jn
12,27 and Heb 5,7 (cited in ST IIIa q.7 a.6co).

[143] SN III d.15 q.2 a.3c co. Since in SN the pain of the soul is discussed before the
pain of the body (aa.3a, b), the *dolor interior* is absent in a.3c.

[144] ST IIIa q.46 a.6co: *quandam derivationem seu redundantionem a superioribus
viribus ad inferiores. Quod in Christo patiente non fuit: unicuique enim virium* "permisit
agere quod est sibi proprium," *sicut Damascenus* [De fide orth. 1.3 c.19, MG 94,1080, cf.
cc.14, 15, MG 94,1037, 1045] *dicit.*

powerless victim, and yet at the same time he underlines that His pain was not diminished. For, that there was in Christ no overflow from the higher to the lower powers is the basis of His pain being beyond all other human pains.[145]

Having gained a comprehensive view of Christ's pain in His *passio*, Thomas comes to the conclusion that when all respects are considered together, Christ's pain was the greatest. But then the pains of others can be greater in a certain respect. With this comment Thomas refers to Laurence' and Vincent's pains in respect of the causes of the pain.

Regarding the second *obiectio*: in the *corpus* it became clear that we say that Christ's power of mind was so perfect because His humanity, body and soul, was composed by the Holy Spirit and that this does not mean that therefore His pain was less. In his reply to the second *obiectio* Thomas denies the Stoic presupposition that *passiones* are morally wrong, for totally distracting from reason (*ratio*); *passiones* can even be praise-worthy (*laudabilis*),

> "as Augustine demonstrates in XIV *De civitate Dei*, namely when it comes forth from holy love, like, for instance, when someone is sad because of his own or someone else's sins."[146]

Thomas then quotes 2 Co 7,10 ("For to be distressed in a way that God approves leads to repentence and then to salvation with no regrets; [it is the world's kind of distress that ends in death]"). And so *passio* can even incite someone to do good. The best example of this is of course Christ Himself, who, being deeply touched by our misery, suffered "for us".

---

[145] The fourth reason is a revision of reason 3 in SN III d.15 q.2 a.3c co. It has the character of a *conveniens* agrument: The quantity of the pains parallels the greatness of the fruits (in SN it parallels the sins of all humankind). However, it is not clear why Thomas stresses Christ's voluntariness so much here. Further, it is remarkable that Thomas does not come back to this parallel in ST IIIa q.49, on the effects/fruits of Christ's *passio*.

[146] ST IIIa q.46 a.6 ad 2: *ut Augustinus probat, in XIV De civ. Dei* [cc.8, 9, ML 41,411, 413]: *quando scilicet procedit ex sancto amore, ut puta cum aliquis tristatur de peccatis propriis vel alienis.*

And this was neither irrational nor unreasonable, as became clear in this study already.[147] But apparently whether a *passio* is morally good depends on whence it originates. This will be considered in the next chapter, where the *passio* of God will be discussed: does the same apply to Him?

This same question comes up due to Thomas' reply to the fourth *obiectio*: Christ's pain was greater than that of others in respect of the loss, because He lost something greater, namely a body that through the union with the divine Word had a greater dignity. And therefore He loved (*diligit*) His body accordingly. Hence handing it over caused great pain.[148] As in his response to the second *obiectio* Thomas points here to the relation between love and pain: the greater the love, the greater the pain. Two interconnected questions come forth from this with regard to God: does God's love for Christ (Mt 3,17, 17,5, Joh.15,9 etc.), imply that when Christ undergoes pain, God experiences pain too; does *compassio* befit God? And if not, what then does it mean that "God is love" (1 Jn 4,8, 16)?

What is clear from Thomas' exposition in the *Summa Theologiae* is that he discusses Christ's bodily *passio* at great length; it is important in his theology. Further, it is clear that he discusses the pain of Christ's *passio* as truly *human* pain, even as pain in all parts of His body. The differences between His pain and that of others is conveyed in terms of gradual difference - "more than" - instead of categorical difference.[149]

---

[147] And so Thomas confirms what Aristotle says (ag.2), cf. ST IaIIae q.64 a.2 and IIaIIae q.58 a.10.

A fine example of a balanced moral consideration on our *passiones* is found in ST IaIIae q.44: *De effectibus timoris* (4 *articuli*).

[148] Cf. Jr 12,7. And Christ's pain is even aggravated, because, ST IIIa q.46 a.6 ad 5: An innocent person has less pain in respect of the quantity (only *poena*, no *culpa*), but an innocent's pain is more intense (quality), when he/she realizes how undeserved (*indebitum*) the pain is. Implied is in this answer is that humankind owes the loss of the life of grace through sin to itself; God cannot be held responsible for our faults (ST Ia q.49 a.2, q.114 a.3).

[149] Christ's pain is comparable to the pain of other human beings who have a body and a soul; not to the pain of the (body-less) souls in purgatory and hell. The case of Adam feeling pain before the Fall is hypothetical; but because of the reasons mentioned in the

At the same time he takes our pains seriously; in certain respects the pains of other people can even be worse than Christ's.

Further, a relation between love and *passio*, is indicated briefly here. In chapter 2 this relation will be explored in more detail.

1.3.3 With Heart and Soul

Christ's inner pain during His physical pain was already mentioned by Thomas in the *articuli* 5 and 6: sadness, aversion and fear. And in this, that He experienced these inner pains, Christ did not differ from any other human being. But in some respects His *passiones* and pains of His soul were different. Question is whether they are such that we can still say that He truly suffered as a human being.

In order to understand what Thomas is saying about the *passio* of Christ's soul, one needs to know that Thomas has an Aristotelian understanding of what the soul is: the soul is the life giving principle (*forma*) of the human body.[150] It is not a body, but is the first principle of the life of a body. Without it the body is dead.[151] Thomas distinguishes two ways of looking at the soul. The one is the soul in its essence:

> "In every body the soul is fully in the whole of the body
> as well as fully in whatever part of the body."[152]

So the soul is one and as such present in the whole of the body. And the

---

corpus Christ's pain would have been more anyway (ad 3).

[150] ST Ia q.70 a.3 ag.2: *Nobilissima autem forma est anima, quae est principium vitae* (cf. IaIIae q.51 a.1co, q.56 a.1 ad 1), cf. Aristotle's II *De anima* c.1 n.5 (Bk 412a27), cited in ST Ia q.76 a.4 ad 1; c.4 n.3 (Bk 415b8), cit. ST Ia q.18 a.3 ag.2.

[151] ST Ia q.75 a.1co: *[A]nima, quae est primum principium vitae, non est corpus, sed corporis actus.* IIIa q.50 a.4co: *Mors enim hominis vel animalis provenit ex separatione animae [a corpore], quae complet rationem animalis vel hominis.*

[152] ST Ia q.76 a.8sc: *Augustinus dicit in VI De Trin.* [c.6, ML 42,929] *quod "anima in quocumque corpore et in toto est tota, et in qualibet eius parte tota est".*

soul directs the body.[153] The other way of looking at the soul is with regard to its parts:

> "It suffices to say that the whole soul is present in the whole of the body in the sense of the totality of its perfection and essence; not however in the sense of the totality of its power, since the soul is not in whatever part of the body by way of any of its mights, but by way of sight in the eye and by way of hearing in the ear etc."[154]

In other words, the soul makes that the parts of the body function (or not, in case of a defect). The parts of the soul are called mights (*potentiae*) or powers (*virtutes*)[155], since they can make the body do or undergo something. Thomas underlines in addition that this distinction in the soul must be seen in the light of the essence of the soul (*per posterius, secundum quod habent ordinem ad totum*); they are all rooted in it, founded upon it. The mights of the soul are distinguished after their acts or what they undergo on the one hand and after their objects on the other.[156] The (parts of the) mights that are naturally directed towards God are called higher (*superior*) and the ones naturally directed towards what is not God (creation) are called lower (*inferior*). Since our intellect and our will are directed towards the truth and the good and these are found in God as well as in creation (coming forth from Him, ST Ia q.44 aa.1-3) they are directed towards both. Therefore we speak of the higher

---

[153] QDA a.10 sc.3: [*A*]*nima non operatur nisi ubi est.* ST IaIIae q.17 a.8 ad 2: [*S*]*icut Deus movet mundum, ita* anima movet corpus. *Non quantum ad omnia: non enim anima creavit corpus ex nihilo, sicut Deus mundum; propter quod totaliter subditur eius imperio*; a.9sc: *Augustinus dicit, VIII Confess.* [c.16, ML 41,425]*: "Imperat animus ut moveatur manus, et tanta est facilitas, ut vix a servitio discernatur imperium.*

[154] ST Ia 76 a.8co: *Sufficit dicere quod anima tota est in qualibet parte corporis secundum totalitatem perfectionis et essentiae; non autem secundum totalitatem virtutis. Quia non secundum quamlibet suam potentiam est in qualibet parte corporis; sed secundum visum in oculo, secundum auditum in aure, et sic de aliis.*

[155] Thomas uses these words as synonyms at times, e.g. in ST Ia q.77 a.2 ag.2. However, Thomas does distinguish them, as will be discussed in chapter 4.

[156] ST Ia q.77 a.3.

and of the lower part of the intellect and the will - not of two intellects and wills.[157]

A human being has a human body and a human soul. Since the soul is the *forma* of the body, they are one being (*esse*) in such a way, that when the body is shaken up (*perturbato*), the soul also is shaken up, accidentally or indirectly (*per accidens perturbetur*).[158] This applies to Christ too, since He was truly human. Since Christ suffered in His whole body, as was said in 1.3.2, and since the soul is fully in the whole of the body (note 152), the logical conclusion is that the whole of Christ's soul suffered when His body suffered. This is true regarding the essence of the soul.[159]

Thomas expounds in the *corpus* of *articulus* 7 that when the whole of Christ's soul is understood as the footing of all its mights or its proper operations, this is equally true in sofar as the so called lower parts are concerned, as was shown in 1.3.1 already; they suffer directly, through their temporal objects. But it seems that this cannot be said of the higher parts of the soul of Christ, the object of which is God. The higher part of the reason for instance, that turns to the eternal thoughts in order to contemplate and consult them[160], did not undergo anything harmful (*nocumentum*) from them, because, as was shown before, Christ's thoughts and will were in conformity with them: He neither was forced nor felt forced by God in any way to undergo the crucifixion. Hence in respect of its proper object we cannot say that this might or any higher part of the soul suffered directly, by reason of its object.

In the light of the introductory words of this subparagraph one would expect that Thomas holds that the higher parts of Christ's soul did suffer indirectly:

---

[157] ST Ia q.79 a.9.

[158] ST IIIa q.15 a.4co. Very recognizable to me, having been a hospital chaplain ("geestelijk verzorger") at a Utrecht hospital for more than three years.

[159] ST IIIa q.46 a.7sc (Ps.88,4, *ex persona Christi: "Replata est malis anima mea."* *Glossa: Non vitiis, sed doloribus*), co (*Sic igitur dicendum .... tota anima patiebatur*).

[160] ST IIIa q.46 a.7 ag.2, as Augustine says in XII *De Trinitate* c.7, ML 42,1005.

"For the soul is, in its essence, the life giving principle of the body. Now all mights of the soul are rooted in its essence. Therefore it remains that when the body of Christ suffered, somehow one or another might of the soul suffered."[161]

The word "somehow" in the *Compendium* should warn the reader. And in the *Summa Theologiae* Thomas cites the commentary on Mt 26,37 of Hieronymus, who uses the word "*propassio*" to signify the *passio* of Christ's soul. Hieronymus, Doctor of the Church, denies that in Christ the sensory *passiones* affected reason; he says that there was no *completa passio* or *passio perfecta* in Christ. Thomas does not take over the term *propassio*. It seems that he does not, because the term may suggest that the *passio* in Christ was not real or not human. Thomas maintains that it was. But he agrees with Hieronymus and with Dionysius that Christ only underwent these *passiones* insofar as He allowed them.[162] In other words, Christ does not lose control over His *pas-siones*, as we do when we undergo something terrible,

"when a *passio* of the sensory part causes the reason to turn away from the rectitude of its act justly, so that it follows the *passio* and cannot make a free decision on it."[163]

Which means that Thomas holds that the higher part of Christ's soul suffered with regard to its subject (the soul, in the essential sense of the word, in which it is rooted), but not with regard to its object (God) - for

---

[161] OTT c.232: *Est enim anima forma corporis secundum suam essentiam: in essentia vero animae omnes potentiae radicantur, unde relinquitur quod [Christi] corpore patiente quaelibet potentia animae* quodammodo *pateretur.*

[162] ST IIIa q.46 a.7 ag.3, In the words of Pseudo-Dionysius, *Epistolae* 10, MG 3,1117: *passiones sibi illatas patiebatur* secundum iudicare solum. For Hieronymus: In Mt. 26,37 l.4, ML 26,205.

[163] ST IIIa q.46 a.7 ad 3: *quando passio sensitivae partis pertingit usque ad* immutationem rationem a rectitudine sui actus, *ut scilicet sequatur passionem, et non habeat liberum arbitrium super eam.*

the reason mentioned - nor with regard to its effect - since Christ did not allow that.[164] This applies to all higher mights of Christ's soul.

But not only is *passio* absent in them with regard to their object, they are in this respect even full of joy, for instance the speculative intellect,

> "for 'no sadness is opposite to the pleasure that stems from consideration,' as Aristotle says."[165]

The might that is called the speculative intellect considers the truth as such (*verum absolute*). Now for Thomas, or rather for all Christians, the purest, first and highest truth is God.[166] And to Christ's soul God does not cause any sadness, but rather joy,[167] since His will is congruent with God's as was said.

But nevertheless the formulation of Aristotle remains enigmatic; how does Thomas understand this sentence? In the argument it is implicit

---

[164] cf. ST IIIa q.15 a.4co, where Thomas quotes Hieronymus explaining "*propassio*", saying that it therefore says in Scripture that [*Christus*] coepit *contristari* (as opposed to completa *passio*).
In IIIa q.46 a.7co Thomas gives a general example of how a *potentia animae* suffers by reason of its object: One's sight suffers from a superabundance of light. And by reason of its subject: One's sight suffers when the eye (*super quem fundatur visus*) is stung by something sharp.

[165] ST IIIa q.46 a.7 ag.4: *Sed in intellectu speculativo non est dolor: quia* "delectationi *quae est ab eo quod est considerare*, nulla tristitia opponitur," *ut Philosophus dicit* [I *Topic*. c.18 n.5, Bk 106a38].

[166] SCG I cc.60-62, where Thomas cites Jn 14,6 and Rm 3,4, Nb 23,19 (also 2 Tm 2,13 comes to mind), 1 Jn 1,5, cf ST IaIIae q.4 a.2 ad 3: [*V*]*eritas prima, quae est fidei obiectum, est finis omnium desideriorum et actionum nostrarum*, as Augustine says in *De Trin*. cc.8, 10 (ML 42,831, 834); q.9 a.3co: [*P*]*rima veritas est etiam ultimus finis, propter quem operamur*. IaIIae q.3 a.5 ad 3:[*U*]*ltimus hominis finis est aliquod bonum extrinsicum, scilicet Deus, ad quem per operationem intellectus speculativi attingimus*, cf the fifth *via* in Ia q.2 a.3co.

[167] ST IIIa q.46 a.7co: *Sed secundum hoc superior ratio non patiebatur in Christo ex parte sui obiecti, scilicet Dei, qui non erat animae Christi causa doloris, sed delectationis et gaudii*. But to us it can cause pain, e.g. Mt 19,21f par..

that in our created world we find opposites, but not *in divinis*; in God
there is no good *and* bad, light *and* darkness etc., but only goodness and
light, as in Ex 34,6 and 1 Jn 1,5.[168] Hence the person whose soul
considers God - with the speculative intellect that is - will be filled with
joy, and more as he/she 'enjoys *(frui)*' Him to a higher extent.

However, this explanation raises the question how the whole soul
of Christ could have rejoiced and at the same time have been sad[169],
since these are opposites. In 1.3.2 it became clear that His pain was even
the greatest or maximal *(maximus)*. Thence it seems that we cannot say
that Christ's soul enjoyed God when He suffered, for the joy of enjoying
God is also the greatest *(maxima)*; greatest joy and greatest pain seem to
exclude one another.[170] Moreover, what is the Scriptural basis for
maintaining that Christ enjoyed God when He suffered?

Thomas finds a solution to this problem by embroidering what
John of Damascus says and what has been cited before. But here it is
formulated with an addition:

> "The divinity of Christ 'allowed the flesh to do and to
> undergo the things that are proper to flesh.' Hence, in like
> fashion, the *passio* of His soul did not hinder the
> enjoyment of the soul, because the enjoyment was proper

---

[168] We see this throughout the ST, e.g. in q.5 a.3sc, ad 2 and a.6, and in q.48 a.1.

[169] As in OTT c.232. Here Thomas discusses the objection that Christ did suffer also
in the higher part of the reason, because He loved His neighbours who suffer with the
higher part of the reason, since He loved them because of *(propter)* God: *[S]uperior tamen
ratio in Christo de proximorum defectibus tristitiam habere non potuit, sicut in nos habere
potest. Quia enim ratio superior Christi plena Dei visione fruebatur, hoc modo
apprehendebat quidquid ad aliorum defectus pertinet, secundum quod* in divina Sapientia
continetur*, secundum quam decenter ordinatum existit et quod aliquis peccare permittatur,
et quod pro peccato punietur. Et ideo nec anima Christi, nec aliquis beatus Deum videns,
ex defectibus proximorum tristitiam pati potest.* However the reasoning in the objection *is*
true for *viatores*, those who are deprived of the view of God as He is and therefore of His
wisdom, ibidem: *Secus autem est in viatoribus, qui ad rationem sapientiae videndam non
attingunt.*

[170] ST IaIIae q.34 a.3. Also Aristotle says that profound sadness does not only
preclude profound joy, but even any joy, *et e converso* (VII *Ethic.* c.14 n.6, Bk 1154b13,
cited in ST IIIa q.46 a.8 ag.2).

to the soul for as far as it was beatic."[171]

As such this is not shocking, since the line of reasoning is the same as with regard to the flesh. Yet what *is* new here, is that Thomas speaks in this context of the divinity of Christ. He does not work it out here, but he does in *De veritate*: the power of the divine Word keeps the *passio* of His soul and the fruition of His soul separated.[172]

The other new element in this context is beatitude:

"For perfect beatitude is required that the intellect reaches to the very essence of the first cause. And so it will have its perfection through the union with God as with an object."
"We must say that enjoyment of God consists in an act by which God is being seen and loved."[173]

Thomas' answer to the question posed, whether the whole of Christ's soul enjoyed this beatic joy, is basically an application of the answers he found before: just like the whole soul, in the essential sense of the word, being the subject of the lower mights of the soul, suffered fully, so the whole soul, in the essential sense of the word, being the subject of the higher mights of the soul, fully enjoyed the beatic joy. This

---

[171] ST IIIa q.46 a.8sc: *Damascenus dicit, in III libro [De fide orth. c.19, MG 94,1080; also cited in a.6co] quod divinitas Christi "permisit carni agere et pati quae propria." Ergo pari ratione, cum proprium esset animae Christi, inquantum erat beata, quod frueretur, passio eius fruitionem non impediebat.*

[172] QDV q.26 a.10co: *In Christo autem secus est. Nam* propter divinam virtutem Verbi, *eius voluntati subiectus erat ordo naturae; unde poterat hoc contingere ut non fieret praedicta redundantia sive ex anima in corpus vel e converso, sive ex superioribus viribus in inferiores vel e converso,* virtute Verbi id faciente, *ut comprobaretur veritas humanae naturae quantum ad singulas partes eius, ut decenter impleretur quantum ad omnia nostrae reparationis mysterium.*

[173] ST IaIIae q.3 a.8co: *Ad perfectam igitur beatitudinem requiritur quod intellectus pertingat ad ipsam essentiam primae causae. Et sic perfectionem suam habebit per* unionem *ad Deum sicut ad obiectum.* QDL VII q.2 a.1co: *Dicendum quod fruitio in actu quodam consistit, quo Deus videtur et amatur,* cf ST IaIIae q.34 a.3co: *[U]ltimus finis hominis dici potest vel ipse Deus, qui est summum bonum simpliciter, vel fruitio ipsius, quae importat* delectationem *quandam in ultimo fine.*

is not a contradiction, because the pain and the joy are not about the same thing (*non sunt de eodem*). But just as the whole soul of Christ, in the sense of all its mights together, did not fully suffer - for the higher parts did not - so it did not fully enjoy either; the lower parts did not. And to this applies to what John of Damascus says in the *sed contra*. In Thomas' own words, there was no

> "overflow, because, whilst Christ was a *viator*, neither an overflow of glory occured from the higher into the lower part, nor from the soul into the body. But since it neither was the other way round - the higher part of the soul was not hindered in what is proper to it by the lower part - the consequence is that the higher part of His soul perfectly enjoyed, while Christ suffered."[174]

At first this may sound strange. Yet by this explanation Thomas points to the central aspects of our faith concerning the *passio* of Christ. First of all that He *truly* suffered as a human being.[175] But if that is the case, He must have truly suffered concerning His body and truly suffered concerning His soul. And this means that what naturally happens in us[176], that the higher parts of the soul mitigate the pains of the lower parts, did not occur in Christ; otherwise Christ's body would have been glorified as soon as or even before it had begun to suffer. By using the word *viator*, person on the way, a word used for people living on earth, Thomas emphasizes Christ's true humanity.

At the same time we profess that Christ *freely* underwent this *passio* unto death; His will did not suffer from pressure from outside,

---

[174] ST IIIa q.46 a.8co: [*N*]*ec per redundantiam, quia, dum Christus erat* viator, *non fiebat redundantia gloriae a superiori parte in inferiorem, nec ab anima in corpus. Sed quia nec e converso* superior pars animae non impediebatur circa id quod est sibi proprium, per inferiorem, *consequens est quod superior pars animae* perfecte *fruebatur, Christo patiente.*

[175] If Christ had not truly suffered, He would not have freed us, cf. ST IIIa q.46 aa.1-4; paragraph 1.1, see also note 172: ut *comprobaretur...*

[176] E.g. SN III d.15 q.2 a.3c ag.2: *In aliis sanctis dolor passionis mitigabatur ex divina contemplatione et amore, sicut de Stephano cantatur: "Lapides torrentis illi dulces fuerunt"* [in eius officio, II antiphona Laudum].

neither from God (who did not force Him, but inspired Him, as was said in paragraph 1.1.2, nor from His pursuers. But this can only be, if His will, one of the higher mights of the soul, is protected from influences from the lower, mights of the soul. And this is done by the power of the divine Word, to which He is united through the Incarnation. For in other people the will is influenced by what we see with our eyes, feel with our hands etc. (*appetitus sensitivus*). But in Scripture we read about Christ that He came to do the will of the Father and that that is what He has done. The temptations by the devil in Mt 4,1-11 and Lk 4,1-13 may come to mind and also Mt 26,39.[177] Hence Christ must have had a clear view of the good, the enjoyment of God. And on the basis of this we must conclude that the *passiones* which He truly experienced did not affect the higher mights of the soul, amongst which the will, as well as His knowledge, grace and power (mentioned in subparagraph 1.2.3). And this is why Christ is not only called *viator*, but also *comprehensor*.[178]

Thomas leaves his readers somewhat puzzled. For on the one hand it is clear that he holds that Christ truly suffered, that is as a human being, body and soul[179], even to the highest extent. The true humanity of Christ, the vulnerability of His body and soul is emphasized by Thomas: *vere homo; vere passus*; Christ was crucified in human weakness (2 Co 13,4). Yet at the same time he underlines that the so called higher parts of the soul were not affected by what He underwent. By saying this Thomas brings to our attention that no matter how grave the pains inflicted upon Him were, He constantly was fully in contact with the Father (*fruitio beata*). But if Christ suffered in human weakness whereas

---

[177] See for a further discussion on this text and Lk 22,41-44 paragraph 4.2.2.

[178] QDV q.10 a.11 ad 3: simul *viator et comprehensor. Quod ei competebat ex hoc quod erat Deus et homo: unde in eius potestate erant* omnia *quae ad humana naturam spectabant, ut unaquaeque vis animae et corporis afficeretur secundum quod ipse disponebat.* Unde *nec dolor corporis contemplationis mentis impediebat, nec fruitiomentis dolorem corporis minuebat: et sic intellectus eius, luce gloriae illustratus, Deum per essentiam vidbat, ut inde ad inferiores partes gloria non derivaretur,* cf. q.26 a.10 ad 14. Being *viator* and *comprehensor* is a *proprium* of Christ, ST Ia q.62 a.9 ad 3: *Christus, qui* solus *fuit viator et comprehensor* (as distinct from the angels, cf. q.113 a.4 ad 1, IIaIIae q.175 a.4 ad 2).

[179] Which is also brought to our attention by Gondreau (2002), esp. 141-259, 375-455.

at the same time no one and nothing could have counteracted the contact between Christ and the Father, it seems that it was the power of the divine Word with whom the humanity of Christ was united, that prevented the higher parts of His soul from turning away from the Father (Heb 4,15) by reason of being affected by them, as it could occur in us. Hence Ph 2,7, that Christ emptied Himself, is neither interpreted by Thomas as that He let go of His divinity[180], nor that He let people interfere in the purpose of His earthly life, i.e. in what He wants, namely fulfilling the will of the Father, for these would be equal to disowning Himself, which He cannot do (2 Tm 2,13). And the consequence of this is that the situation was never out of control.

However, this is beyond our imagination. And therefore Thomas' approach of the matter may not be very appealing and satisfying to us; what Thomas says is not really biographically imaginable. And it is even indigestible, if one does not realize that Thomas speaks of a mystery *of faith*: the mysteries of God, of the Incarnation and of the Passion, beyond our understanding, beyond our imagination, yet revealed to us in Jesus Christ through Scripture. In this chapter it becomes clear how Thomas struggles to find the words to indicate what is beyond our intellect, more distinguishing and comparing one (divine) thing to another (created) thing, by saying what it is not or what it is like, than describing how it is. By doing so he shows the richness or multilayeredness of the mystery as well as the strangeness of it. What would be paradoxes or incompatibilities within our created world, remain. For instance that Christ suffered and died by reason of Himself as well as of God and of others; that He died out of obedience and freedom; the cruelty of His *passio* and death as well as its goodness and suitability; His *passio* and pain to the full and full enjoyment and thus the unaffected higher powers of the soul at the same time; that He truly suffered, but unlike other human beings, since He kept control over His *passiones*; and the weakness and the strength of Christ during His *passio*. These formulations cannot be solved as problems, without denying what Scripture says. Even more, the more is said about it, the more questions arise: *vere homo*, *vere Deus*.

---

[180] According to Thomas it rather refers to the incarnation and His *passio*, RPL c.2 1.2: *Sicut enim descendit de caelo, non quod desineret esse in caelo; sed quia incepit esse novo modo in terris, sic etiam se exinanivit,* non deponendo divinam naturam, *sed assumendo naturam humanam.* [....] And in His *passio* it shows in His obedience (cf. Ph 2,7f).

1.4 Christ: The Suffering God?

During the last decades much has been written, by theologians and philosophers of religion, about whether God can suffer and suffers. The underlying issue is most of the time whether God is concerned with us, expressed in questions like: does God suffer when His beloved people suffer or sin? To me it seems rather obvious that when a Christian considers the suffering of God, he/she begins with Christ, the beloved Son of God (Mt 3,17 (Baptism), 17,5 (Transfiguration)), when He suffered: the *passio* of Christ as an avenue to the consideration of the *passio* of the Father and the triune God. Although, this approach is not as obvious as it may seem, neither for contemporary authors[181] nor for the Doctors of the Church, Thomas included.

In the previous paragraphs it became clear that Thomas emphasizes that Christ truly suffered and died, whereas we believe that this Christ was not only truly a human being (*vere homo*)[182] but also truly God (*vere Deus*).[183] But not only "Christ" is said to have suffered on the cross; in Scripture we even read that when Christ was crucified, "the Lord of glory" was (1 Co 2,8).[184] Since "Lord of glory" seems to

---

[181] Surprisingly I found that in some studies on the suffering of God (the suffering of) Christ is a marginal or just one of the subjects (e.g. Sarot (1992), 91-96) or even not at all a subject (e.g. Johnson (1993), 246-272, i.e. the 12th and last chapter on the suffering of God), whilst in other studies it is (in) the *last* chapter(s) of the book (e.g. Weinandy (2000), 172ff).

[182] In ST IIIa q.2 a.5co Thomas cites Ph 2,7 (*Pertinet autem ad rationem speciei humanae quod anima corpori uniatur*) and in ad 2 Lk 24,39 - affirmed by the Church in the first antiphon of the Laudes for the feast of Christ's cicumcision, cited in sc: "*Animatum corpus assumens, de Virgine nasci dignatus est.*"

[183] from the very beginning of His human life, cf. Lk 1,35; therefore it is said in Jn 1,16f that Christ is the source of our grace (cf. ST IIIa q.2 a.11co, ad 2).

[184] Cited in ST IIIa q.46 a.12 ag.1. Strangely enough not knowing that Christ was the Lord of glory is in ST applied to "the Jews" (ag/ad 3), whereas in C1C c.2 1.2 first and extensively the gentiles (citing Ps 2,2) are discussed and subsequently the ignorance of prominent (*principes*) and ordinary (*populus*) Jews and (referring to Mk 1,24 and Lk 4,34) of demons is called into question.

refer to God rather than to a human being, one may ask whether we therefore can or should say that when Christ suffered and died, God suffered and died? It is the question of the *communicatio idiomatum*, the interchange of words that signify what is proper to the specific natures. The answer to this question depends on what is understood by the union in the Incarnation. The Catholic understanding of the union is that in Christ

> "the true divine nature is united with the true human nature, not only in person, but also in the supposit or hypostasis."[185]

"Nature" denotes the essence (*essentia*) of a thing, what it is, to which category and type the thing belongs (*quidditas*). The nature of something is put into words in the definition of the thing.[186] So two people have the same nature, namely the human nature. "Supposit" or "hypostasis" denotes the being (*esse*) of an individual thing, something that exists by itself. "Person" denotes a rational supposit.[187] Hence two people are not and cannot be the same person, supposit or hypostasis.

The union in Christ is a hypostatic union and a union in person, yet cannot be a union of natures. For a union of natures would result in a new kind of being, with a new kind of nature, a *tertium quid*, neither divine nor human. Thus, if the union were a union of natures, incarnation would imply a change not only in the human, but even in the divine nature, which cannot be, as will also be shown in chapters 2 and 3. Besides, since the divine nature excedes the human nature immeasurably,

---

[185] ST IIIa q.16 a.1co: [S]ecundum veritatem Catholicae fidei, quod vea natura divina unita est cum vera natura humana, non solum in persona, sed etiam in supposito vel hypostasi.

[186] ST IIIa q.2 a.2co: Natura enim singnificat essentiam speciei, quam significat definitio.

[187] ST IIIa q.2 a.2co: [I]n supposito [vel hypostasi] includitur ipsa natura speciei, et superadduntur quaedam alia quae sunt praeter rationem speciei. Unde suppositum significatur ut totum, habens naturam sicut partem formalem et perfectivam sui. [....] Et quod est dictum de supposito, intelligendum est de persona in creatura rationali vel intellectuali: quia nihil aliud est persona quam rationalis naturae individua substantia, secundum Boetium [De duabus naturis c.3, ML 64,1343].

the human nature would be swallowed up in the divine as a drop of water in an amphora of wine.[188] But if the union had not been in person and in supposit or hypostasis, we would not be speaking of God becoming a man, of Incarnation, but of an accidental union, as Nestorius and Theodore of Mopsuesta held.[189]

No positive words can be found to circumscribe this union, since it is unique; no union in the created world resembles this union. It is significant that the terms used in the formulation of Chalcedon to clarify this hypostatic union, are all negative: unmixed and unchangeable (are the divine and the human nature), undivided and inseparable (are the divine Word and this human being in one hypostasis and person), never is the distinction between the natures removed *because of* the union.[190] And hence one can only compare the hypostatic union of Christ to what is similar *in a sense*.[191] Yet the consequence of this is that, when we faithfully profess that Christ is "one being", we know what we deny, but we do not exactly know what we say; we formulate a mystery, the mystery of the incarnation, that is at the very heart of our faith:

> "Hence, if the human nature is not united in person with the Word of God, it would not be united with it in any way. And so the belief in the Incarnation would be totally abolished; and this is tantamount to undoing the whole of

---

[188] ST IIIa q.2 a.1co. This image is used in the Eucharist with regard to the hypostatic union and our eschatological union with Christ's divinity. A drop of water is added to the wine in the chalice. This is interpreted as the humanity (water) and the divinity (wine) become one - the Word of God made a man; we come to share in the divinity of Christ - in such a way, that although we know that they are two, we do not know how to separate them.

[189] For a more detailed history of this issue: Weinandy (2000), 172-213.

[190] ST IIIa q.2 a.1sc: *"Confitemur in novissimis diebus Filium Dei unigenitum inconfusse, immutabiliter, indivise, inseparabiliter agnoscendum, nusquam sublata differentia naturarum propter unionem."* [Determinatio Concilii Chalcedonensis p.2 act.5]

[191] *comparatio non aequalitatis, sed similitudinis*, as in ST IIaIIae q.105 a.2 ad 1, cf. Ia q.6 a.2 ad 3: *[E]a quae non sunt in eodem genere [....] nullo modo comparabilia sunt.* For a more detailed exposition of Thomas' doctrine of the hypostatic union: Schoot (1993), 110-133.

the Christian faith. Consequently, since the divine Word
has united the human nature to itself, yet not in such a
way that it extends to the divine nature, the union is made
in the person of the Word, but not in the nature of the
Word."[192]

And this is why Thomas most emphatically says that the opinion that

"there is one hypostasis of God and man, must not be
called 'an opinion', but "an article of Catholic faith". And
likewise, the opinion that there are two hypostases and the
opinion that the union is accidental, must not be called
'opinions', but 'heresies, condemned in the (ecumenical)
Councils by the Church'."[193]

This understanding of the oneness of Christ forms the basis for
the hermeneutical rule of the *communicatio idiomatum*. It is a
hermeneutical rule for reading Scriptural texts. The rule of the
communicatio idiomatum says that because of Christ's unity in supposit,
hypostasis and person, everything that belongs to or befits human nature
can be said of the second Person of the Trinity and therefore of God, and
everything that belongs to or befits the second Person of the Trinity can
be said of the man Christ.[194] According to this rule we say *Deus est*

---

[192] ST IIIa q.2 a 2co: *Si ergo humana natura Verbo Dei non unitur in persona,* nullo
modo *ei unitur. Et sic* totaliter *tollitur incarnationis fides: quod est subruere* totam *fidem
Christianam. Quia* igitur *Verbum habet naturam humanam sibi unitam,* non autem *ad
suam naturam divinam pertinentem, consequens est quod unio sit facta in persona Verbi,*
non autem *in natura [Verbi].*

[193] ST IIIa q.2 a.6co: *Sic igitur patet quod secuna trium opinionum duas Magister
ponit, quae asserit unam hypostasim Dei et hominis, non est dicenda opinio, sed* sententia
Catholicae fidei. *Similiter etiam prima opinio, quae ponit duas hypostases, et tertia, quae
ponit unionem accidentalem, non sunt dicendae opiniones, sed* haereses in Conciliis ab
Ecclesia damnatae.

[194] ST IIIa q.16 a.4co: [C]um sit eadem hypostasis utriusque naturae,* eadem
hypostasis supponitur nomine utriusque naturae. *Sive ergo dicatur homo, sive Deus,
supponitur hypostasis divinae et humanae naturae.* Et ideo de homine dici potest ea quae
sunt divinae naturae: et de Deo possunt dici ea quae sunt humanae naturae.

homo, as in Ph 2,6f.[195] And in this sense we say that God was crucified, as in 1 Co 2,8, and that the virgin Mary is called the mother of
God. In these proposotions "God" supposits for "the Son of God" (see
paragraph 2.3.4). And in the same way we say *homo est Deus*, as in Rm
9,5.[196] And in this sense we call this human being Saviour, as in Heb
2,10.[197] And for instance in Col 1,16 and 1,18 Christ is spoken of in
one breath as respectively divine and human.

> "Thus the Word of God and the man Christ are one
> supposit and consequently one person and therefore it
> must be that whatever is said of this human being, is said
> of the Word of God and vice versa."[198]

And by these examples Thomas makes clear that Scripture itself calls for
this rule; otherwise contradictions and incredible things follow.

Hence, according to the rule of the *communicatio idiomatum* we
say that, when Christ suffered and died, (the Son or the Word of) God
suffered and died. In the *Summa contra Gentiles* Thomas comes to this

---

[195] ST IIIa q.16 a.1sc: [D]*icitur Phil.:* "*Qui* cum in forma Dei esset *exinanivit
semetipsum, formam servi accipiens,* in similitudinem hominum factus et habitu inventus
ut homo." *Et sic ille qui est in forma Dei est homo. Sed ille qui est in forma Dei, est
Deus. Ergo Deus est homo.*

[196] ST IIIa q.16 a.2sc: [D]*icitur Rom.:* "*Ex quibus est* Christus *secundum carnem,* qui
est *desuper omnia* Deus *benedictus in saecula.*" *Sed Christus secundum carnem est homo.
Ergo haec est vera. Homo est Deus.*

[197] Whilst there is but one Saviour, namely God, cf. Ps 37,39, Is 43,11 etc..

[198] SCG IV c.34 n.29: *Sic igitur Dei Verbum et homo Christus sunt unum suppositum,
et per consequens una persona; et oportet quod* quicquid *dicitur de homine illo, dicatur de
Verbo Dei, et e converso.* In the same chapter Thomas mentions many (pairs of) texts like
Jn 8,29 and 1 Co 6,17, Jn 1,14, Jn 8,59 and 10,30, Jn 6,51, Ac 1,9 and Ep 4,10, Jn
16,28 and 1,10f, Heb 10,5, Ps 24,8.10 and 1 Co 2,8, Rm 8,32 and Jn 3,14.16, Rm 5,8f,
Ga 4,4f, Ps 31,6, Rm 9,5, Ph 2,6f, Lk 4,1 and Ph 2,5f (ibidem n.25: *Verum est igitur
dicere quod homo ille est in forma, idest in natura Dei, et aequalis Deo. Licet autem
homines dicantur dii, vel filii Dei,* [implicit reference to Ps 58,2, 82,6 and Jn 10,34]
*propter inhabitantem Deum, numquam tamen quod sint aequales Deo. Patet igitur quod
homo Christus non per solam inhabitationem dicitur Deus*), Heb 3,1-4, Ac 2,33 and Ph
2,7, 1 Co 8,6.

conclusion also by another way. Here Thomas asks whose body Christ's suffering and dying body was:

"Every change or *passio* that meets someone's body, can be attributed to the one whose body it is. For, if Peter's body is injured, flogged or dies, one can say that Peter is injured, flogged or dies. Now the body of that man was the body of the Word of God, as is said in Heb 10,5. Hence every *passio* that occured in the body of that man, can be attributed to the Word of God. And thus one can rightly say that the Word of God, and God, suffered, was crucified, died and was buried."[199]

But before jumping to further conclusions, one must notice that Thomas cautions (*tamen*) a correct interpretation of propositions that are made according to what is called the *communicatio idiomatum*. For although we use words that signify the human and the divine (*quid*) indiscriminately for the one suppositum, Christ, we are to make a distinction according to what (*secundum quid*) they are used for in Him. Thus the words used for Christ because He is God signify His divine nature, whereas words used for Christ because He is a human being signify His human nature.[200] Thomas' addition, a quote from August-

---

[199] SCG IV c.34 n.11: *Omnis mutatio vel passio conveniens corpori alicuius, potest attribui ei cuius est corpus: Si enim corpus Petri vulneretur, flagelletur aut moriatur, potest dici quod Petrus vulneratur, flagellatur aut moritur.* Sed corpus illius hominis fuit corpus Verbi Dei, *ut ostensum est. Ergo omnis passio quae in corpore illius hominis facta fuit, potest Verbo Dei attribui. Recte igitur dici potest quod* Verbum Dei, et Deus, est passus, crucifixus, mortuus et sepultus.
Ibidem n.10: *Apostolus dicit* [Heb 10,5]*: "Ingrediens mundum dicit: Hostiam et oblationem noluisti, corpus autem aptasti mihi." Ingrediens autem mundum Verbum Dei est, ut ostensum est* [Jn 1,14, 16,28]. *Ipsi igitur Dei Verbo corpus aptatur, ut scilicet sit* proprium *corpus eius. Quod dici non posset nisi esset eadem hypostasis Dei Dei Verbi et illius hominis* [cf. n.9, citing Ep 4,10]. *oportet igitur esse eandem hypostasim Dei Verbi et illius hominis.*

[200] ST IIIa q.16 a.4co: *Sciendum tamen quod in propositione in qua aliquid de aliquo praedicatur, non solum attenditur* quid *sit illud de quo predicatur predicatum, sed etiam* secundum quid *de illo praedicetur. Quamvis igitur non distinguantur ea quae praedicantur de Christo, distinguuntur tamen quantum ad id secundum quod utrumque praedicantur. Nam ea quae sunt divinae naturae, praedicantur de Christo secundum divinam naturam; ea*

ine's *De Trinitate*, that the "the proficient, precise and devout reader" understands what is being said in what way, may easily be ignored by the reader. But in fact it is an important instruction for how to approach this issue: with knowledge of the data, meticulously and in faith.[201]

As was said above, according to the rule of the *communicatio idiomatum* human and divine attributes can be used for Christ, since He is the one and the same hypostasis of both natures. For

"the things that are proper of one thing cannot truly be predicated of another, unless that other is the same."[202]

Now in the mystery of the incarnation the hypostasis of the divine and the human nature is the same, but not the divine and the human nature; they remain two. This distinctness is expressed in our religious language:

"Some things are said of the Son of God which are not said of the divine nature. We say for instance that the Son of God was begotten, and nevertheless not that the divine nature was. And similarly we say in the context of the incarnation that the Son of God suffered, yet not that the divine nature did."[203]

Hence, applied to 1 Co 2,8:

---

autem quae sunt humanae naturae, *praedicantur de eo* secundum humanam naturam.

[201] ST IIIa q.16 a.4co: *Unde Augustinus dicit in I De Trin.* [....] [c.13, ML 42,840]*: Quid propter quid, et quid secundum quid dicatur, prudens et diligens et pius lector intelligit.* Thomas explains in the *corpus* why Nestorius does not match this description; he does not adhere to the Catholic understanding of the incarnation.

[202] ST IIIa q.16 a.5co: *[E]a quae sunt proprie unius, non possunt vere de aliquo praedicari, nisi de eo quod est idem illi.*

[203] ST IIIa q.16 a.5 ad 1: *[Q]uaedam dicuntur de Filio Dei quae non dicuntur de divina natura: sicut dicimus quod* Filius Dei *est genitus,* non tamen *dicimus quod* divina natura *sit genita, ut in Prima Parte* [q.39 a.5] *habitum est. Et similiter in mysterio incarnationis dicimus quod* Filius Dei *est passus,* non autem *dicimus quod* natura divina *sit passa.*

"We must hold that what is said, that the Lord of glory
was crucified (1 Co 2,8), cannot be understood in respect
of Him being the Lord of glory, but in respect of this that
He was a human being who could suffer."[204]

Or, in the words of Doctor of the Church Cyril, *the* opponent of Nestorius: God, the Son of God, suffered *as man*.[205]

Thomas' formulation of this mystery catches the eye: as he
stresses and carefully tries to find the right words to express the one-ness
in Christ, he does so in respect of the two-ness in Christ. Scripture itself
is starting point and criterion for it and for further reflection. Because of
the incomprehensibility[206] and uniqueness of the hypostatic union,
Thomas, in the footsteps of Chalcedon and Doctors of the Church, sees

---

[204] ST IIIa q.46 a.12 ad 1: [*E*]*rgo dicendum quod Dominus gloriae dicitur crucifixus,*
non secundum *quod Dominus est gloriae,* sed secundum *quod erat homo passibilis.*

[205] Weinandy (2000), 191 (italics added, MR). ST IIIa q.46 a.12co: *Unde in Epistola
Synodali Cyrilli dicitur: "Si quis non confitetur Dei Verbum passum carne et crucifixum
carne, anathema sit"* [*Ep. ad Nestorium* anath.12, MG 77,121].

[206] C1C c.1 l.3 (on 1 Co 1,18): [*S*]*tultum aliquid videtur "pereuntibus quidem", id est
infidelibus qui se secundum mundum existimant sapientes, eo quod praedicatio crucis
Christi aliquid continet, quod* secundum humanam sapientiam impossibile *videtur,* puta
quod Deus moriatur, *quod* Omnipotens violentorum manibus subiiacitur. Cf. OCG c.6:
*Quia ergo secundum quantitatem virtutis, quam Deus exercet in creaturam magis et minus
dicitur creaturae uniri, patet quod,* cum efficacia divinae virtutis humano intellectu
comprehendi non possit, sublimiori modo *Deus potest creaturae uniri* quam intellectus
humanus capere possit. *Quodam ergo* incomprehensibili et ineffabili modo dicimus *Deum
unitum esse humanae naturae in Christo,* non *per inhabitationem,* sicut *in aliis sanctis,* sed
quodam modo *singulari,* ita quod *humana natura esset* quaedam *Filii Dei natura, ut Filius
Dei qui ab aeterno habet naturam divinam a Patre, ex tempore per assumptionem*
mirabilem *habeat humanam naturam ex genere nostro, et sic quaelibet partes humanae
naturae ipsius Filii Dei* dici possunt *Deus, et quidquid agit, vel patitur quaelibet parte
naturae humanae in Filio Dei,* potest attribui *unigenito Dei Verbo.* This is a fine example
of how Thomas does not try to solve the mystery of the Incarnation as if it were a
problem, but how he thinks through the consequences (*ita quod*) of this mystery of faith
for our speech (*dicimus, dici possunt, potest attribui*).

no other way than to use negative formulations to signify it.[207] In Thomas' discussion of 1 Co 2,8 it shows how a dogma functions as a grammar rule for reading Scripture as a book of faith. Again, this is beyond our imagination: though Christ, truly God and truly a human being, suffered, truly and to the full, as was shown in the former paragraphs, the divine nature did not suffer at all; Christ did not undergo any *passio* as God. Yet we cannot but make this distinction in Christ, in order to adhere to His full humanity and His full divinity.

At the end of this chapter, the question as to whether Thomas' theology on Christ's *passio* should be called *theologia gloriae* can be answered. I can imagine that, when someone examines the first *quaestio* of the *Tertia Pars* of the *Summa Theologiae* only, with this question in mind, he/she arrives at a positive answer. For in that first *quaestio* he enunciates the framework in which he considers the *passio* of Christ: our salvation; in accordance with Scripture. Yet at the same time, the purposiveness of Christ's *passio* and death does not result in trivializing the pain and the evil. On the contrary. Nor does Thomas obscure that the suffering and dying Christ was indeed the Son of God (Mt 27,54), and this while repudiating every fatalism and masochism of God and Christ[208] and underlining their love and freedom. The purposiveness of Christ's *passio*, His true humanity, and therefore His true suffering *secundum quod hominem*, and the true divinity of Christ, and therefore His impassibility *secundum quod Deum*, are three elements of the one mystery of Christ's *passio*. Thomas does not play down to his readers in the sense that he wants to make us understand what is not understandable. Instead he makes us understand the *passio* of Christ as a mystery of faith.

---

[207] In ST IIIa q.46 a.12 ad 3 Thomas cites a homily of Theodotus of Ancyra, held during the Council of Nicaea (where the dogma of the ὁμοούσιον was formulated). It is a fine example of negative theology (N.B. the Latin words quoted). The preacher draws a comparison between killing Christ and tearing up the document on which a king's decree is written: Not just a piece of paper is torn up, but in a sense (*tanquam*) the royal word itself; the word is concealed (*celabatur*) in the paper. Similarly, in Christ not a pure human being (*non purus homo*) was crucified. The association with Christ as the divine Word made a man (Jn 1,14), goes without saying here. A contemporary example would be ostentatiously burning the flag of a country, which is much more than just burning a piece of fabric.

[208] As in Huberfeld (1976), 476-484.

    In view of this study this not-suffering of Christ's divine nature during the Passion raises the question as to God's *passio* when Christ underwent His *passio* unto death. For was God not lovingly related to Christ? And if God did not suffer when Christ suffered, did or does or can He then suffer at all? And if the answer to this question is negative, would this then not be inconsistent with, for contrary to, what we read in Scripture? Therefore the *passio* of God is to be considered in the next chapter.

    In the third and fourth chapter a closer look at almightiness will be required in this respect: in this first chapter it became clear that according to Thomas neither God nor Christ were powerless or deprived of their might when Christ suffered unto death; for God and for Christ things were not pretty much, but completely, under control during the Passion. In *articulus* 9co of *quaestio* 46 Thomas even cites W 8,1 ("She" - God's wisdom that is - "governs the whole world for its good"). Still Thomas does not deny that evil happened to Christ. This raises the question of how Thomas understands almightiness, in respect of the *passio* of Christ and the *passio* of God.

CHAPTER 2

THE *PASSIO* OF GOD

In chapter 1, in the context of Christ's crucifixion, the word *passio* is translated as "suffering". Yet in the context of love *passio* may denote suffering as well as an emotion and an ardent desire, just like our word "passion"[1]. It seems that we cannot separate passion from love, since we cannot imagine love without some kind of suffering, emotion and desire. Still Thomas does speak of love with and without *passio*.

Passion is generally regarded as inherent to love. This view of love underlies the tendency found in our days to attribute suffering to God: "A God who cannot suffer, cannot love either. In virtue of the Biblical testimony we must hold that God is love. Hence God must (be able to) suffer, desire etc., especially when His Beloved/beloved suffer(s)." It is a consistent and to many persuasive argumentation, found in the works of quite a few contemporary theologians and philosophers of religion.[2] And in the line of this argumentation it logically follows that if God does not or cannot suffer, He does not or cannot love either. To many this argumentation may be even more compelling because of their own experiences of pain coming forth from love.

One of these contemporary theologians is Eberhard Jüngel. For this study of Thomas' thoughts about the *passio* of Christ and of God he is a suitable discussion partner. He characterizes his most comprehensive book, "Gott als Geheimnis der Welt", as an attempt to exposit "God is love" (1 Jn 4,8 = 4,16).[3] Jüngel speaks of the love of the triune God - and His almightiness - in the context of Christ crucified. He does not

---

[1] Webster's vol. II, 1651, col. 2: resp. nn.1-3, nn.4-5 and n.6.

[2] E.g. Albrecht (1976), 20; Boff (1987), 114f; Brantschen (1986), 46; Fiddes (1988), 16-25; Galot (1976), 50, 172f; Hartshorne (1967), 75; Johnson (1993), 265f; Kamp (1971), 83; Kitamori (1965), 178-181, 254-261; Macquarrie (1984), 180, McWilliams (1985); Moltmann (1972), 217; (1980), 39, 75; Peacocke (1984), 77f; Redmond (1964), 156, Robinson (1940), 176f; Sarot (1992), 80-91; Sobrino (1978), 197 (citing Bonhoeffer and Moltmann), 198, 224-226; Sontag (1986), 13-17; Surin (1982), 98-102; Thaler (1994), 16ff; Vann (1947), 60; Varillon (1974), 65-71; Zahrnt (1996), 79.

[3] Gott als Geheimnis der Welt, -Zur Begründung der Theologie des Gekreuzigten im Streit zwischen Theismus und Atheismus, Tübingen 1977[2] (1977[1]), XIII, translated: God as the Mystery of Our World (1983), X. The references to this work are to the original German version, followed by the reference to the English version between brackets.

shun a serious discussion with the tradition. Moreover, in his book he demonstrates the strangeness of Thomas for us. In respect of the negativity of Thomas' theology Jüngel is of the opinion that Thomas goes too far; what Thomas says would not be Christian, not Scriptural anymore. Specifically as regards God's love: what is Thomas talking about, when he speaks of God's love as being without *passio*? For, Jüngel holds, "love includes the desire or lust of love."[4] With this in mind Thomas' thoughts will be reviewed in the subsequent subparagraphs, followed by an examination of Jüngel's critique of them.

2.1 The Love of God

This is why the point of departure for the analysis of Thomas' thoughts on the *passio* of God is the Scriptural testimony that God is love. But in order to understand what Thomas says, one should first see that Thomas is a negative theologian and what this means (2.1.1). With this in mind the *articulus* from the *Summa Theologiae* is read, in which Thomas explains 1 Jn 4,16 (2.1.2). Since we understand by "God" the triune God and since in our tradition the Holy Spirit is associated or even identified with God's love, a closer look is taken at how we are to understand that God and the Holy Spirit are said to be love (2.1.3).

The results of this first inquiry prompt us to examine in further detail what Thomas understands by *passio* and why he thinks it incompatible with God's divinity (2.2). But why then do we, and even Scripture indeed, ascribe *passio* to God? (2.3)

2.1.1 God Is ....

Contemplating God in the *Summa Theologiae*, Thomas does not start with the Crucified one, as was said above. Still one does not do justice to his theology by calling it "theology from above". For, as a careful reader notices, where Thomas considers what is proper to God and what is not, he begins with how it is in human beings and other creatures. Two principles underlie this approach. The first is that we

---

[4] Jüngel, *o.c.*, 435 (318): "Zur Liebe gehört das Liebesbegehren."

know what God is only indirectly, and therefore imperfectly, through what He brings about in creation, and so we read in Rm 1,19f ("What can be known about God is perfectly plain to them, since God has made it plain to them: ever since the creation of the world the invisible existence of God and His everlasting power have been clearly seen by the mind's understanding of created things") and, with regard to human beings, in Gn 1,26 ("Let us make the human being in Our own image, in the likeness of Ourselves"). The second principle, in line with the first, is that we cannot know what God's essence is, but that we can know what He is not. At the root of this principle lie texts like Ex 33,20, Jn 1,18 and 1 Tm 1,17: no one has ever seen God.[5] On the basis of these principles Thomas employs his method of thinking and speaking of God:

> "For as far as something can be known by us through the intellect, it can be named by us. Now it was shown above that in this life God cannot be seen by us regarding His essence. But we get to know Him from creatures, of which He is the principle, by way of excellence as well as by way of removal."[6]

That an effect is similar to its cause, may sound like a purely philosophical argument, but it has a Scriptural basis, for instance in Si 27,6, Mt 7,16, 20 and Jm 3,12: by its fruits we know about the tree. This approach determines the content and the structure of Thomas' discussion of God's being and actions. "By way of removal" means that things that are proper to creatures must be denied of God, since God is not a creature, but the Creator. This means that Thomas comes to conclusions

---

[5] ST Ia q.2 a.2co: *Cum enim effectus aliquis nobis est manifestior quam sua causa, per effectum procedimus ad cognitionem causae.* Rm 1,20 cited in ST Ia q.2 a.2sc, q.13 a.5co; Gn 1,26 cited in q.3 a.1 ag/ad 2, q.4 a.3sc, q.13 a.5 ag.2.
ST Ia q.3 intr.: *[Q]uia de Deo scire non possumus quid sit, sed quid non sit, non possumus considerare de Deo quomodo sit, sed potius quomodo non sit.* Ex 33,20 cited in ST Ia q.12 a.11sc, IIIa q.45 a.4 ad 4; Jn 1,18 cited in ST Ia q.12 a.1 ag.1, q.88 a.3sc; 1 Tm 1,17 cited in ST Ia q.31 a.3sc, q.39 a.4co.

[6] ST Ia q.13 a.1co: *Secundum igitur quod aliquid a nobis intellectu cognosci potest, sic a nobis potest nominari. Ostensum est supra [q.12 aa.1, 12] quod Deus in hac vita non potest a nobis videri per suam essentiam; sed cognoscitur a nobis ex creaturis, secundum habitudinem principii, et per modum excellentiae et remotionis.*

by means of negations. "By way of excellence" means that perfections that befit human beings and God, are said of God, in superlatives, yet, for the same reason, in an analogous way. Our categories, our terminology, do not befit God properly. Therefore we find in Thomas' texts, where he draws comparisons between human beings or other creatures and God, phrases like "in us", "like ... but without", "as if", "for instance", "according to/for as far as", "in the proper sense", "such as", "but not".[7] And this applies not only to the content, but to the structure as well: when he speaks of God's actions, he distinguishes between actions that remain within a person and actions that result in an effect outside a person. And this is the reason (*Et quia*) why Thomas in the *Summa Theologiae* first considers God's knowledge and will and thereafter God's might[8] and why he considers God's love in the context of His will.[9]

These ways of removal and of excellence are two ways to express the greatness, the transcendence, the otherness, the incomprehensibility and the ineffability of God's being.

Thomas emphasizes that Christ is the ultimate revelation of God,[10] but, as is obvious from what has been said above, not the only revelation. Thomas recognizes the revelation of the name of God at the burning bush, in Ex 3,14, as a very important one: YHWH. In this name a promise is expressed that God is there, meaning that He is actively

---

[7] *in nobis, sic(ut) .... sed absque, quasi, puta, secundum quod (est), proprie, tanquam, sed non.*

[8] ST Ia q.14 intr.

[9] ST Ia q.20 a.1 intr.: *In parte autem appetitiva [voluntatis] inveniuntur* in nobis *et passiones animae, ut gaudium, amor et huiusmodi; et habitus moralium virtutum, ut iustitia, fortitudo et huiusmodi.* Unde *primo considerabimus de amore* Dei; *secundo de iustitia* Dei *et misericordia* eius.

[10] Jn 1,18 cited in ST Ia q.88 a.3sc, ad 3 (cf. SCG IV c.54 n.3, where Jn 1,18 and 18,37 are seen as fulfilling Is 11,9); Jn 14,9 cited in ST IaIIae q.1 a.8 ag/ad 3 (also: q.2 aa.7, 8); Col 1,15 cited in ST Ia q.33 a.3 ag.3/ad 2, q.35 a.2co, q.93 a.1 ag.2 (ad 2: *imago Dei perfecta*); Heb. 1,3 cited in ST Ia q.35 a.2co, IIIa q.63 a.2 ad 2.

present in favour of His people. Kasper[11] points out that Thomas equates the Name of God with the philosophical term of being, but that he interprets it in a theological way: God is not the highest of all beings (as in Neo-Platonism), but *ipsum esse subsistens*, subsisting being itself, in which all beings participate as their source and aim.[12] Thomas underlines that YHWH signifies universal and active presence of the eternal God[13], while at the same time he interprets the Name as an expression of God's trancendence, otherness, incomprehensibility and ineffability:

> "It is the most proper name of God, first because of its meaning. For the Name does not signify a form of being, but being itself. Therefore, since God's being is the same as His essence, and this does not befit anyone else, as was said above, it is clear that amongst other names this one names God in the most proper way; for everything is being named by its form."[14]

By saying that God's being is the same as His essence, Thomas refers to the mystery of God's simplicity, i.e. His non-composedness. With this term Thomas makes a metaphysical distinction, based upon Dt 6,4:

---

[11] Kasper (1982), 187-193, criticizing Brunner's interpretation of Thomas and all theo-ontology.

[12] Texts like Rm 11,36 and Heb 2,10 may come to mind as well as 1 Co 8,6. In SN I d.2 divisio textus Thomas cites Rv 22,13, in SN III intr. Thomas cites Qo 1,7 and Jos 4,18.

[13] ST Ia q.13 a.11co: [*H*]*oc nomen "Qui est" triplici ratione est maxime proprium nomen Dei.* [....] *Secundo propter eius* universalitatem [....] *"Qui est" nullum modum essendi determinat, sed se habet indeterminate ad omnes; et ideo nominat* [John of Damascus, in *De fide orth.* L.1 c.9, MG 94,836] *ipsum "pelagus substantiae infinitum". Tertio: [Hoc nomen] [s]ignificat enim esse* in praesenti; *et hoc maxime proprie de Deo dicitur, cuius esse non novit praeteritum vel futurum, ut dicit Augustinus in V De Trin.* [c.2, ML 42,912], cf. q.9 a.1 ad 2.

[14] ST Ia q.13 a.11co: *Primo quidem propter significationem. Non enim significat formam aliquam, sed ipsum esse. Unde, cum esse Dei sit ipsa eius essentia, et hoc nulli alii convenit, ut supra* [q.3 a.4] *ostensum est, manifestum est quod inter alia nomina hoc maxime proprie nominat Deum: unumquodque enim denominatur a sua forma.*

YHWH is one.[15] From this point of view being composed is a fundamental characteristic of creation: everything in our created world is
composed. By saying this Thomas does not refer to the composition of
different parts, but to compositions on a deeper level: of form and matter
(*forma*, *materia*), essence and existence (*essentia*, *esse*), substance and
accidents (*substantia*, *accidens*), on the basis of which all things can be
classified. So in this sense the word composedness neither refers to
quantitative characteristics like "having arms and legs" nor to qualitive
characteristics like "good" and "beautiful", but to the characteristics of
the ground structure of what is created. What Thomas does at the
beginning of his *Summa Theologiae* (*quaestio* 3) is clarify that this
composedness does not befit God, since it implies being one of the
beings. Moreover, it implies being caused, that is being created, and a
process of becoming, i.e. change (growth or decline, increase or
decrease, e.g. in goodness, love or power).[16] It is on the basis of this
that Thomas emphatically *and* stammering (*balbutiendo*) formulates the
simplicity of God[17] and His perfection. And by doing so he expresses
that God is not a creature, but the Creator.

     This is typical for Thomas' negative theology. His theology is not
called negative, because he would not know anything about God, but
because he is aware that our knowledge falls short - we only know insofar
and in the way that God has revealed Himself *in* creation and in the

---

[15] *Audi Israhel Dominus Deus noster Dominus* unus *est*, cited in ST Ia q.11 a.3sc.

[16] In ST Ia q.3 a.4 Thomas explains why we must hold that in God *essentia* and *esse*
are identical: Every property in an individuated being which is not identical with its
nature, is caused, either as a consequence of belonging to a type or category (like having
(not: being) a certain degree of intelligence follows from being human) or from outside.
So if the existence itself of something (*ipsum esse rei*) is not identical with its nature, its
existence must be caused from outside, since there is no nature from which existence
follows. But of God we believe that He is not caused; God is the first and uncaused cause
of all, the Creator. *Impossibile est ergo quod in Deo sit aliud esse, et aliud eius essentia*,
cf. ibidem a.3sc: *Deus est ipsa deitas.*

[17] ST Ia q.3 a.7sc, co: *Augustinus dicit, VI De Trin.* [c.6, ML 42,928], *quod Deus*
vere et summe *simplex est. Respondeo dicendum quod Deum* omnino *esse simplicem.*

manner we understand it[18] - and thus our words, our categories do not fit *in divinis*. "Simplicity" and "perfection" used for God are non-descriptive terms; Thomas does not, for he cannot, explain what the simplicity and perfection of God are. However, he does not surrender easily. We can know what it is not, by way of removal: a composed unity and an advancing perfection as in created things cannot be in God, for these are proper to creatures. The Eternal One cannot become a better (or worse) God, so to say,[19] as we can become better (*perfectio*) or worse (*corruptio*) human beings. That we do not have words to say what God's simplicity is, is because there is nothing in our created world which is totally singular (*omnino simplex*) in this sense. "Simple" and "perfect", therefore, are used in an analogous way.

In order to speak about the simplicity of God, we cannot but make distinctions in our mind and in our speech between God's essence and His existence, while we are to realize that this distinction is not a distinction in God (*distinctio realis*), but a distinction only in our thinking (*distinctio rationis tantum*). The same applies for God's perfection: everything in our world that is perfect to a certain extent, has *become* or has been *made* perfect. And although God is not, we are to hold that God is singular and perfect, in order to express that God and God alone is the Creator, not part of all, but the source of all that is, and not a creature.[20]

---

[18] ST Ia q.13 a.2co: *Significant enim sic nomina Deum*, secundum quod intellectus noster cognoscit eum. *Intellectus autem noster, cum cognoscat Deum* ex creaturis, *sic cognoscit ipsum, secundum quod creaturae ipsum repraesentant.*

[19] QDV q.2 a.3 ad 13: *[D]icendum quod perfectionis nomen, si stricte accipiatur, in Deus non potest poni; quia nihil est perfectum nisi quod est factum. Sed in Deo nomen perfectionis accipitur* magis negative *quam positive; ut diciatur perfectus, quia* nihil deest *ei ex omnibus;* non *quod sit in eo aliquid quod sit in potentia ad perfectionem, quod aliquo perficiatur quod sit actus eius; et* ideo non *sit in eo potentia passiva.*

[20] It is not a matter of *whether* or not God is perfect, cf. Mt 5,48, but rather what it *means* that we call God perfect, for, ST Ia q.4 a.1 ag.1: *Videtur quod esse perfectum non conveniat Deum. Perfectum enim dicitur quasi totaliter factum [perfectum* is the perfect of *perficere*; as in Webster's II, 1677B, [1]perfect: nn.1, 4 and 8a]. *Sed in Deo non convenit esse factum.* Ibidem ad 1: *[S]icut dicit Gregorius [Moral.* 5,36 + 29,1, ML 75,715 + 76,477] "*balbutiendo ut possumus, excelsa Dei resonamus: Quod enim factum non est, perfectum proprie dici non potest." Sed quia in his quae fiunt, tunc dicitur esse aliquid perfectum, cum de potentia educitur in actum,* transumitur hoc nomen "perfectum" ad significandum omne illud cui non deest esse in actu, *sive hoc habeat per modum factionis,*

This fundamental distinction for Christian theology is what Sokolowski calls "the Christian distinction".[21]

This infers that, in order to understand Thomas correctly, one must see that "God is totally simple" and "God is perfect", as well as for instance "God is infinite" and "God is totally immutable"[22] are elocutions of a different kind, of a different order, than "God is love": the former are deep structure formulations, concerning God; the latter is a first order formulation signifying the nature (*essence*) of God. That this "totally singular, perfect, infinite, eternal and unchangeable" God is "love" then does not mean that He *has* a totally singular, perfect, infinite, eternal and unchangeable love, distinct from His divinity[23], but that God

---

sive non. Note therefore that perfection in this sense is not a moral description, but a *negative* ("*non deest*"), second order or deep structure word.

And God's perfection and being the Creator are inextricably bound up with one another, cf. ibidem co: *Deus autem ponitur* primum principium, *non materiale, sed in genere causae efficientis: et hoc* oportet esse perfectissimum. *Sicut enim materia, inquantum huiusmodi, est in potentia, ita agens, in quantum huiusmodi, est in actu. Unde* primum principium activum, *oportet maxime esse in actu; et per consequens maxime esse perfectum. Secundum hoc enim dicitur aliquid esse perfectum, secundum quod est in actu.* Cf. Thomas' exegesis of Dt 6,4 in ST Ia q.11 a.3co: *Impossibile est igitur esse plures Deos.*

[21] Sokolowski (1982), 32f: "In the Christian distinction God is understood as 'being' God entirely apart from any relation of otherness to the world or to the whole. God even could and would be God even if there were no world." Therefore God, though present and active in our world, is not part of this world. That also Heraclitus and Xenophanes make a similar distinction, is reason for Jüngel, to call this distinction neoplatonic, by which he means to say that it should not be part of Christian theology, *o.c.* 316ff. Thomas rather sees a similarity of an aspect of pagan philosophy or theology with Christian doctrine as a sign that God leads also people who are not Christian (a fine example of which is found in ST Ia q.20 a.1 ad 1: *Unde dicit Philosophus in VII Ethic.* [c.14 n.8, Bk 1154b26] *quod "Deus una et simplici operatione gaudet"*). And this same thought we see reflected in *Lumen Gentium* n.16 (citing Ac 17,25-28).

[22] Resp. ST Ia q.3 a.7, q.4 a.1, q.7 a.1 and q.9 a.1.

[23] SCG IV c.19 nn.5, 6: [*U*]*t in Primo* [c.44] *ostensum est: oportet quod in ipso* [= *Deo*] *sit voluntas:* non *quidem quod voluntas Dei sit* aliquid eius essentiae superveniens, *sicut nec intellectus, ut supra* [I cc.45, 73] *ostensum est, sed voluntas Dei* est ipsa eius substantia. *Et cum intellectus etiam Dei sit ipsa eius substantia, sequitur quod una res sint in Deo* intellectus et voluntas. *Qualiter autem quae in aliis rebus plures res sunt, in Deo*

is totally singular, perfect, infinite, eternal and unchangeable love. Therefore God is not called (the most) perfect etc. in the sense of "more perfect than the most perfect thing we know" (as in perfect being philosophy, see below: Sarot). For there is no gradual difference between created perfection and divine perfection, but a categorical difference. And this, again, is beyond our comprehension,[24] but as such crucial for a correct understanding of what Thomas says about the mystery of God and about God and *passio*.[25]

Jüngel's critique is leveled against what he sees as pushing the negativity to extremes. In Thomas' theology God becomes uncannily alien ("unheimlich fremd"), inaccessible and distant; how can such a God be love?[26] Jüngel formulates a second argument, more against negative theology in general, where he says:

> "Of course, the thesis of the ineffability and incomprehensibility of the divine is given its biblical grounds - for example, in John of Damascus with reference to John 1,18 and Matthew 11,27. But this reasoning came after the fact. It is in the spirit of Plato which is expressed in this fundamental statement, 'The Deity, therefore, is ineffable and incomprehensible.' Mediated by Neo-Platonism, the basic Platonic decision about the

---

sunt una res. [....] [*S*]*equitur quod in Deo non sit voluntas secundum potentiam vel habitum, sed secundum actum. Ostensum est autem quod omnis actus voluntatis in amore radicatur. Unde oportet quod in Deo sit amor.*

[24] In OTT c.13 l.1 Thomas expounds in what way *perfectio* in God is different from what we call *perfectio* in a creature: Perfection in a human being for instance is according to his/her humanity and thus this perfection is inextricably bound up with being limited; God is called perfect according to His divinity and therefore it is an infinite perfection. Hence, this perfection cannot be fathomed by a human, and ipso facto limited, mind. Hence: *Deus autem sic dicitur perfectus,* quod tamen a nullo capitur aut comprehenditur. In Scripture we find this expressed in e.g. Jb 36,26ff and Ps 139,6.

[25] For a typical caricature of Thomas' view of God's immutability: Sia (from the school of Hartshorne) (1994), 92-94.

[26] Jüngel, *o.c.*, 314-317, 378f (231-233, 277f).

speakability of God made its way into Christian
theology."[27]

In other words, that negativity was already employed in theology by
Platonists, is for Jüngel as such a point of critique directed against.

It is true, Jüngel continues, negative theology safeguards the
mystery of God, but he conjectures that at the same time the mystery of
God is being constructed by the boundaries of human knowledge and
language.[28] In the course of this chapter Jüngel's arguments will be
inspected.

2.1.2 God Is Love (1 Jn 4,16)

"Whether there is love in God," is the title question of the first
articulus of *quaestio* 20. Since Holy Scripture itself says that God is love
and loves, the answer is obviously "yes". But then the question is: what
does this mean?

Prior to reading this text Thomas' terminology must be clarified,
for he uses four words to refer to God's love: *caritas* and *dilectio*, two
words used in Scripture; Thomas seems to equate these terms with
amor.[29] And a fourth term he uses to signify God's love is *amicitia*.
Amor is the common or the generic word for love. In the context of
God's love Thomas defines love as

---

[27] Jüngel, *o.c.*, 318 (233): Zwar wird diese These von der Unsagbarkeit und
Unbegreiflichkeit des Göttlichen ihrerseits biblisch begründet, bei Johannes Damascenus
etwa mit Johannes 1,18 und Matthäus 11,27. Doch diese Begründung ist nachträglich. Es
ist Geist von Platons Geist, der sich in dem fundamentalen Satz ausspricht: "Unsagbar ist
das Göttliche und unbegreiflich." Durch neuplatonische Vermittlung gelangte die
platonische Grundentscheidung hinsichtlich der Sagbarkeit Gottes in die christliche
Theologie.

[28] Jüngel, *o.c.*, 334 (245).

[29] ST Ia q.20 a.1sc, co: *[D]icitur I Io. 4,16: "Deus* caritas *est." Respondeo dicendum
quod necesse est ponere* amorem *in Deo*; q.38 a.2 ad 1: *Hoc enim ipsum quod Filius
datur, est ex Patris* amore, *secundum illud Io. 3,16: Sic Deus* dilexit *mundum, ut Filium
suum unigenitum daret*; in REI c.3 1.3 n.1 Thomas uses all three interchangeably.

"the first movement of the will and of whatever appetitive power."[30]

This definition makes clear why love is discussed in connection with the will: God has a will[31] and according to this definition of love, the inference of having a will is having love; for without a first movement there is no movement at all. Love directs the will and all appetitive powers which naturally tend to what is good.[32] Hence Thomas also calls joy and delight kinds of love, namely love for a good owned, as well as desire and hope, in respect of a good not (yet) owned. This additional explanation may take away some of the peculiarity of Thomas' definition of love. For in our ordinary speech we may not consciously associate "love" with the will, but more with "warm attachment, enthusiasm, devotion" or "the attraction based on sexual desire".[33] Still Thomas' definition is not that different from ours; our contemporary associations seem to be rather a narrowing of the wide range of meanings of Thomas' use of the word "love"; what or whom you want is what or whom you love.

Thomas indicates *caritas*, *dilectio* and *amicitia* as three kinds of *amor*. This is why he can interchange the three words with *amor*, but not *amor* indiscriminately with one of these three words. He describes *dilectio* as love at the root of which lies a choice; the choice precedes the first

---

[30] ST Ia q.20 a.1co: *Primus enim motus voluntatis, et cuiuslibet appetitivae virtutis, est amor.*

[31] ST Ia q.19 (*De voluntate Dei*), where Thomas cites, amongst others, W 11,25f, Mt 6,10, Rm 12,2, Ep 1,11 and 1 Th 4,3.

[32] Therefore the good (*bonum*) is the prime, *per se* object of love. Of course a human being - not God, cf. Mt 19,17, as in ST Ia q.6 - can love what is not good (*malum*) or hate (*odium*) what is good. Thomas designates these kinds of loves as acts *per aliud*, that is secondary or re-actions to a primal, natural movement, without which they could not even exist, cf. q.20 a.1co: [A]*ctus voluntatis* [....] *tendat in bonum et malum, sicut in propria obiecta; bonum autem principalius et per se est obiectum voluntatis et appetitus, malum autem secundario et per aliud, inquantum scilicet opponitur bono*; IaIIae q.29 a.2co: [O]*mne odium ex amore causatur*; cf. q.77 a.4co: [I]*nordinatus amor sui est causa omnis peccati.*

[33] Webster's, vol.II, 1340, col. 1.

movement of the will. Thomas connects *dilectio* etymologically with
legere, eligere. That he designates this choice as being rational, means
that it is not influenced by desire, but that it is a choice made by the will
alone. Therefore he speaks in *De divinis nominibus* of the *free* choice
(*libera electione*), that distinguishes this kind of love.[34] The consequence
of this is that by definition *passio* is not included in *dilectio*. And
therefore, Thomas argues, this word is very suitable to signify God's
love. But since all our love is influenced or even directed by our senses
(*appetitus sensibilis*) and our natural desire (*naturalis appetitus*), which is
without consideration anyway, *dilectio* in its pure form seems not to befit
the love a human being has. However, it must be clear that Thomas does
not attach a value judgement to this; being without *passio*[35] does not
make *dilectio* a better kind of love, contrary to what Stoics say.[36]

Also in the case of *caritas* the etymology is used to describe its
meaning: it is the love for someone or something of great value (*carus*,
cf. the Italian and Spanish "caro", the French "cher"). That Thomas calls
caritas the perfection of this love is an implicit, but clear reference to 1
Co 12,31ff, the so called "Hymn to love".[37] Thomas' use of *caritas*

---

[34] CDN c.4 l.9, cf. ST IaIIae q.26 a.3co: [A]*mor communius est inter ea: Omnis enim
dilectio vel caritas est amor, sed non e converso. Addit enim dilectio supra amorem
electionem praecedentem, ut ipsum nomen sonat. Unde dilectio* non est in concupiscibili,
sed in voluntate tantum, et est sola in rationali natura.

[35] In his commentary on Pseudo-Dionysius' *De divinis nominibus* Thomas refutes the
opinion of those who find that *amor* is an unsuitable word for God for the reason that it
seems to implicate *passio*, and therefore prefer *dilectio*. Thomas answers by distinguishing
between the use of the words and what they signify, c.4 l.9: *conditores sacrae Scripturae*
communiter et indifferenter *utuntur nomine dilectionis et amoris* - and this is enough
reason for us to use the words likewise.

[36] ST IaIIae q.24 a.3: Stoics hold that every *passio* is bad (*malum*), yet Thomas holds
that from a moral point of view *passio* can be for the better as well as for the worse of an
act.

[37] Aγαπη, an obsolete word in pre-Christian times used by Christians to signify a
perfect Christian love, is translated in the Vulgate with *caritas*. But in the Latin translation
of Pseudo-Dionysius' *De divinis nominibus* the words *amor* and *dilectio* are used for εϱος
and αγαπη, for unclear reasons (Aertsen, 2000, 382f). One of the consequences is, that
the neoplatonic connotations of εϱος in Pseudo-Dionysius' exposition, esp. the union with
God through ecstasy, have disappeared in Thomas' commentary. There is, however, one

does not only signify the love of a human being for God, as Aertsen says, but also the love for one's neighbour[38] and the love of God Himself of course (1 Jn 4,16).

Amicitia is the name of the *habitus* of mutual love, in which the one *wants* the good for the beloved other.[39] By saying this Thomas cuts across Aristotle preconception that love between a human being and God is absurd.[40] In his commentary on Jn 15,10 ("If you keep My commandments, you will remain in My love"), 14 ("You are My friends, if you do what I command you") Thomas underlines, citing Pr 8,17 ("I love those who love Me"), the mutuality of this love and that our love for Him is expressed in willing the good, as it is set down in God's, wise, precepts. He subsequently cites W 6,19 and 1 Jn 2,4, which form the foundation of this thought.[41] Thomas holds that *amicitia* is personal (*aliquem*) love. From the Scriptural texts it is clear that God's love has

---

exception, namely where in Pseudo-Dionysius' Latin text the word *extasis* occurs (c.4 1.9, cited in ST IaIIae q.28 a.3sc). And since *dilectio* signifies a love without *passio* and Thomas uses the word *amor* in the Aristotelian sense, almost half the text (c.4 1.9) is devoted to the question whether *amor* always means a *materialis passio* (the answer to which is negative, as will be shown in the course of this chapter).

[38] Aertsen (2000), 390, referring to ST IaIIae q.23 a.1co: [C]*aritas amicitia quaedam est hominis ad Deum*. Yet, a bit further Thomas adds, q.25 a.1co: [H]*abitus caritatis* non solum *se extendit* ad dilectionem Dei, *sed etiam ad dilectionem proximi*, on the basis of 1 Jn 4,21 (cited in sc).

[39] ST IaIIae q.23 a.1co: *Non quaelibet amor habet rationem amicitiae, sed amor qui est cum benevolentia; quando scilicet sic amamus aliquem, ut ei velimus;* [....] [*et*] *requiritur* quaedam mutua amatio. ST Ia q.18 a.2 ad 2: [*S*]*unt* habitus *inclinantes ad quaedam operationum genera quasi per modum naturae, et facientes illas operationes esse delectabiles. Caritas* and *dilectio* can exist as a *habitus* as well as in acts. The relation of *amicitia* presupposes an attitude.

[40] *Magna moralia*: Ἄτοπον γὰρ ἂν εἴη εἰ τις φαίη φιλεῖν τον Δία; cited in Moffatt (1929), 9. Aristotle's argument is that friendship can only be between two equals. See also Wadell (1989), 125f.

[41] REI c.15 1.2 n.3 (Vulg-W 6,20: *Incorruptio autem facit esse proximum Deo*), 1.3 n.1 (1 Jn 2,4: *Qui dicit se nosse Eum et mandata Eius non custodit mendax est in hoc veritas non est*). This friendship is also mentioned with regard to Abraham, in 2 Ch 20,7, Is 41,8 or Jm 2,23, texts not explicitly referred to by Thomas here (nor in for instance ST IaIIae q.23 a.1co).

everything to do with, or even that it is highlighted in the Incarnation and Passion of Christ: for "God is love (*caritas*)" is written in the context of 1 Jn 4,14-16; "God loved (*dilexit*) the world" is said in the context of Jn 3,11-21; and Rm 5,8 "It is proof of God's own love for us, that Christ died for us while we were still sinners" (instead of lovers or friends), is written in the context of Rm 5,1-11. Not in the *Summa Theologiae*, but in the *Summa contra Gentiles* Thomas connects *amicitia* explicitly with the Incarnation: since friendship cannot exist between two persons who are too different - as also Aristotle says (note 40) - and is more intimate the more equal the two are, the friendship between humankind and God has become more intimate ever since God became like us, through the Incarnation[42] and will be made perfect when He unites us to Him in the hereafter.[43]

On the basis of this one can say that the breadth of the meaning of the word love of God and of human beings in Thomas' works is similar to that of the word love in Scripture.[44]

Yet looking at the deep structure of "God is love", questions arise. Thomas formulates three arguments according to which "God" and "love (*amor*)" appear to be incompatible:

> "It seems that there is no love in God. For there is no *passio* in God. Love is a *passio*. Hence there is no love in

---

[42] SCG IV c.54 n.6: *Cum amicitia in quadam aequalitate consistat ea quae multum inaequalia sunt, in amicitia copulari non posse videtur. Ad hoc igitur quod* familiarior *amicitia esset inter hominem et Deum, expediens fuit homini quod* Deus fieret homo, *quia* etiam naturaliter *homo homini amicus est* [ibidem c.1 n.3]: *ut sic "dum visibiliter Deum cognoscimus, in invisibilium amorem rapiamur"* [Praefatio Missae, In nativitate Domini].

[43] ST IaIIae q.65 a.5co: [D]*icitur I Io. 4,16: "Qui manet in caritate, in Deo manet, et Deus in eo." Et I ad Cor. 1,9 dicitur: "Fidelis Deus, per quem vocati estis in societatem Filii eius." Haec autem societas hominis ad Deum , quae est quaedam familiaris conversatio cum ipso, inchoatur quidem hic in praesenti per gratiam, perficietur autem in futuro per gloriam.* Cf. 1 Co 13,12.

[44] The word אֲהַב is used to signify the love of God for human beings, of human beings for God, neighbourly love, love of people who are in love and love in other personal relationships (parent - child, master - servant, friends, political allies) as well as for love in respect of animals, things, situations and actions (Jenni/Westermann (1978), I, 60-73).

God."[45]

In this first argument we find the same line of reasoning as with the contemporary theologians and philosophers mentioned above, only with another point of departure - "There is no *passio* in God", instead of "Love presupposes suffering" - and therefore with the opposite conclusion. To us Thomas' argument quoted here is strange and not at all convincing, for why would we assume that there is no *passio* in God? For in paragraph 1.1.2 it became clear that *compassio* is a kind of *passio*. And in Scripture we read that YHWH is a compassionate God.[46] We see this expressed in art as well, for instance in representations of the mercy-seat, in which the Father is depicted as suffering with the Son; the Father's face expresses sadness.[47]

Also the second argument could make us frown. This argumentation is based on our way of signification. "Love" in "God is love" would only be a metaphor, just like when we say that God is angry or sad.[48] But to us it is not self-evident that a sentence like "God is angry" would be merely metaphorical.

The third and final argument is in respect of the deep structure of "God" and of "love" in view of simplicity:

> "Pseudo-Dyonisius says in chapter 4 of his *De divinis nominibus*: love is a unifying and welding force. Yet, since God is non-composed, this does not befit God.

---

[45] ST Ia q.20 a.1 ag.1: *Videtur quod amor non sit in Deo. Nulla enim passio est in Deo. Amor est passio* [cf. VIII *Ethic.* c.5. n.5, Bk 1157b28, cit. ST IaIIae q.26 a.2sc]. *Ergo amor non est in Deo.*

[46] E.g. Ex 34,6, Ne 9,17, 31 ("great compassion"), Si 2,11, Jl 2,13, Jon 4,2, Jm 5,11.

[47] Boespflug (1990), 124-159.

[48] As in Ps 30,6, 106,40 (*locus classicus*), Is 1,24, 57,17 resp. Gn 6,6, Ps 78,40, Ep 4,30.

Hence, there is no love in God."[49]

For according to this definition love brings about a union between the loving God and the beloved creature, which seems to imply composition. And this cannot be in God, as was explained above.

In his reply to these arguments Thomas formulates in which way we are to understand that God is love and in which way not. The distinction he makes between love as a *passio* and love without *passio* is crucial for this. In his method of explanation Thomas proves himself again a negative theologian: first he discribes how in human beings love is intrinsically connected with *passio*. On the basis of this, he concludes that God's love cannot be like that; God cannot but be love without *passio*.

Our will, or intellectual appetite, is moved through the appetite of the senses; through (*mediante*) our senses we perceive something, by which love, the first movement of the will, is kindled. This kindling or excitement is always (*semper*) accompanied by a physical change, in particular one's heartbeat. Not only do we know this from experience, we also find this in the prophet Isaiah, who speaks of the throbbing and delating of the heart for joy (Is 60,5). Until here it is all very recognizable. Now this physical change is why Thomas speaks of *passio*. Yet a physical change, Thomas argues, is not constitutive of love. For, if love is the first movement of the will, it is as such not necessarily mediated through the senses, as in *dilectio*. So, although in us love is always a re-action to our senses, it does not belong to the deep structure of love as such that it is a re-action to the senses.

Because of God's simplicity and because of His perfection His love cannot be a reaction. We are to deny that God's love is caused by anything outside God; it is a *simplex operatio*. This does not mean that God would be unconcerned. It rather says that God's love is as such a first and autonomous movement of God, absolutely free and not to be forced, manipulated or stopped. *God* takes the initiative. This free love of God is expressed in for instance Ex 3,10, Ezk 16,6, Jn 15,16, Rm 5,5-11, Tt 3,3-5 and 1 Jn 4,7-11. It is *in this sense* that God is called the

---

[49] ST Ia q.20 a.1 ag.3: *Dionysius dicit, 4 cap. De div. nom* [par. 15, MG 3,709]: *"Amor est vis unitiva et concretiva."* Hoc autem in Deo locum habere non potest, cum sit simplex. Ergo in Deo non est amor.

unmoved Mover.[50] And it is therefore that Thomas denies that God's love is with *passio*, with a (physical) change in God[51]. At the same time we cannot imagine this love without *passio*, since in creatures we do not find love without *passio*.[52] In his commentary on Rm 5,5, Thomas emphasizes the freedom of God's love in this way, referring to Jr 31,3 ("I have loved you with an *everlasting* love") and 1 Jn 4,10 ("Love consists in this: it is not we who loved God, but God loved us and sent His Son"): that God is the first in loving us is revealed in the gift of "the Holy Spirit, who is love," by whom we participate in God's love.[53]

But the two texts from the First Testament seem to contradict what Thomas says. For in Ex 3,7, 9 God hears (the cry of His people) and sees (their oppression) and in Ezk 16,5, 7 God is moved with pity, while He sees. This seems to indicate a love as mediated through the senses. The same problem arises with regard to *passiones* like anger and sadness. These also cause a physical change in a human being: the boiling of one's blood (*ascensio sanguinis*) and feeling down. Yet in Scripture

---

[50] ST Ia q.9 a.1 (in sc is cited Ml 3,6, "I, YHWH, do not change", cf. Ps 102,27f, Jm 1,17 (cited in Ia q.14 a.15sc, IIIa q.61 a.4 ag.3); contrary to human beings, cf. Nb 23,19 (cited in Ia q.19 a.7sc), 1 S 15,29 (cited in Ia q.23 a.8co, IaIIae q.83 a.2 ag.2), Rm 1,23). If one does not understand *Deum esse omnino immutabilem* as concerning the deep structure of "God", "God" would indeed be perceived as unconcerned and inert as a rock. However, it is obvious that no Christian conceives for instance Ps 18,3, 31,3 and 71,3 in this way.

[51] ST Ia q.20 a.1 ad 1: *Et eadem ratione* sine passione *amat*, cf. q.82 a.5 ad 1: *Alio modo* [*amor, concupiscentia et huiusmodi*] *significant simplicem affectum* absque passione vel animi concitatione. *Et sic sunt actus voluntatis. Et hoc etiam modo attribuuntur angelis et Deo.* In SCG I c.91 n.10 Thomas cites Ps 16,11, Pr 8,30 and Lk 15,10 to confirm this. Yet, from these texts it is not obvious that God's love is without *passio*.

[52] ST IaIIae q.26 a.2.

[53] CRO c.5 l.1: *Charitas Dei autem dupliciter accipi potest. Uno modo pro charitate qua diligit nos Deus; "Charitate* perpetua *dilexi te"* [Jr 31,3]; *alio modo potest dici charitas Dei, qua nos Deum diligimus. "Certus sum quod neque mors neque vita separabit nos a chartate Dei"* [Rm 8,38]. Utraque autem caritas Dei in cordibus nostris diffunditur per Spiritum Sanctum qui datus est nobis. *Spiritum enim Sanctum, qui est amor Patri et Filii, dari nobis, est nos adduci ad participationem* amoris, qui est Spiritus Sanctus. *A qua quidem participatione efficimur Dei amatores. Et hoc, quod ipsum amamus, signum est, quod ipse nos amet. "Ego diligentes Me diligo"* [Pr 8,17]. *"Non quasi nos primo dilexerimus Deum, sed quoniam* ipse prior dilexit nos," *ut dicitur I Io 4,10.*

also anger (Ps 106,40) and sadness (Gn 6,6) are ascribed to God.

Besides the, so to say, corporeal (*quasi materiale*) aspect, a *passio* can be considered in respect of how it is related to the beloved (*quasi formale*). And in this way a *passio* may imply an imperfection: for instance not having what is good, as in desire for something good one does not have, or having what is evil, as in sadness and anger. God's perfection implies that He does not lack and therefore is not in need of anything good; God *is* essentially perfectly good. His love is, as a *simplex operatio*, flowing towards us, because He wants to. So

> "those *passiones* which, also formally, signify an imperfection, cannot befit God unless as a metaphor, on account of the similarity of the effect, as was said above. But those which do not signify an imperfection, are being said in the proper sense of the word of God, like love and joy, without *passio* though."[54]

Love and joy as such do not imply an imperfection, for they may well be with regard to an owned good. But desire, anger and sadness necessarily imply an imperfection: lacking a good or having what is evil. Whence Thomas says that "God loves" can be a proper statement, but that "God is angry" or "God is sad" is always a metaphor, because they imply *passio*, which does not properly befit God.

The third argument is in respect of what the love is related to: a good wanted and a person for whom one wants that good. Thomas observes that the beloved can be the loving person him/herself or someone else.[55] And this is in conformity with Mt 22,39 ("Love your neighbour as yourself"). In the case of God the good wanted is God

---

[54] ST Ia q.20 a.1 ad 2: [*I*]*lla quae imperfectionem important, etiam formaliter, Deo convenire non possunt nisi* metaphorice, *propter similitudinem effectus, sicut supra* [q.3 a.2 ad 2, q.19 a.11] *dictum est. Quae autem imperfectionem non important, de Deo* proprie *dicuntur, ut amor et gaudium: tamen* sine passione, *ut dictum est* [ad 1].

[55] ST Ia q.20 a.1 ad 3: [*A*]*ctus amoris semper tendit in duo, scilicet in* bonum *quod quis vult alicui; et in* eum *cui vult bonum. Hoc enim est proprie amare aliquem, velle ei bonum. Unde in eo quod aliquis amat se, vult bonum sibi*; cf. IIaIIae q.26 a.4, q.44 aa.7, 8.

Himself, since He is essentially perfectly good.[56] Thomas adopts Pseudo-Dionysius' definition of love as a unifying and welding force. That God loves us then means that He wills us to be unified with the divine good, with Himself that is. We find this expressed in Jn 14,23 ("Anyone who loves Me will keep My word, and My Father will love him and we shall come *to him* and make a home *in him*") and 15,9f ("I have loved you just as the Father has loved Me. Remain in My love. If you keep My commandments, you will remain in My love, just as I have kept My Father's commandments and remain in His love"). But since God is non-composed, the union cannot be in Him (*absque compositione in Deo*), but only in us. This rather enigmatic formulation is elucidated, when we read the two ways of union Thomas distinguishes in the commentary on the *Sententiae*. In the one way the lover is taking part in what is of the beloved. In the other way the lover communicates what is his/hers to the beloved.[57] Because of God's non-composedness we are to deny that a union takes place in the first way. The corollary is that we are to say that the union takes place in the second way - a fine example of negative theology, reaching a conclusion by denial.

This exposition of Thomas may lead to the assumption that God and God's love are distant, as Jüngel says, and not at all as intense as in a passionate relation of love between two human beings. Thomas indeed underlines the distance between God and us:

> "No distance is as big as the distance of the Creator from a creature."
> "We say that creatures are remote from God, because of the unlikeness of nature or grace, just like He is exalted above everything because of the excellence of His

---

[56] ST Ia q.6 a.3co: [S]*olus Deus est bonus per suam essentiam*, cf. Mt 19,17, Lk 18,19.

[57] SN III d.32 a.1 ad 3: *Uno modo secundum quod amans* [i.c. *Deus*] *transfertur in participandum ea quae sunt amati* [i.c. *creaturae*]; *alio modo ut communicet amato ea quae sunt sua*. The neoplatonic aspect of extacy in the union of love has been modified into union of love as a bond.

nature."[58]

He even says the distance is infinite; there is an immeasurable distance between the Creator and His creatures. But, Jüngel fails to see this in Thomas' theology, that at the same time God is immeasurably closer to His creatures than any fellow creature ever can be:

> "Although God is infinitely remote from a creature, He still works in all and is in all."
>
> "Not only when they [creatures] began to be, but also as long as they are, they are being preserved in being. [....] Thus, as long as a thing has being, it must be that God is present to it, in the way that it has being. In a thing being is more intimate than anything and is more fundamental than anything. [....] Therefore it must be that God is in all things, even intimately."[59]

Thus, because of His transcendence, God can be and is *infinitely* closer to us than anything else.[60]

In human relations love "with passion" is indeed more intense than without it. This does, however, not mean that God's love, being without *passio*, is less intense, for love is His essence; *all* our love is derived, received from Him.[61] And even from the viewpoint of the

---

[58] SN III d.32 a.1 ag.2: *Sed* nulla *est tanta distantia quanta Creatoris a creatura.* ST Ia q.8 a.1 ad 3: *Dicuntur tamen res distare a Deo per dissimilitudinem naturae vel gratiae: sicut et ipse est super omnia per excellentiam suae naturae.*

[59] SN III d.32 a.1 ad 2: *Deus autem quamvis in* infinitum *distet a* creatura, tamen *operatur in* omnibus *et in* omnibus est. ST Ia q.8 a.1co: *[N]on solum quando primo esse incipiunt, sed quandiu in esse conservantur.* [....] *Quandiu igitur res habet esse, tandiu oportet quod Deus adsit ei, secundum modum quo esse habet. Esse autem est illud quod est* magis intimum *cuiuslibet, et quod* profundius omnibus inest. [....] *Unde oportet quod Deus sit in omnibus rebus, et intime.*

[60] We also find this expressed in Scripture texts like W 7,24f, Is 26,12, Jn 14,23 and Ph 2,13.

[61] ST Ia q.6 a.3sc: *[A]lia omnia [creata] a Deo sunt bona* per participationem. *Non igitur per essentiam.*

union of God with us His love would be much more intense than any fellow human being's, for "the more a lover is one with the beloved, the more intense the love is."[62]

Jüngel's exposition on "God is love" is quite different from Thomas'. In his view the theology of Thomas remains after all a kind of being silent, since we do not know what love without *passio* is. The negativity of Thomas' theology would make God a distant God. Jüngel makes Thomas the harbinger of Immanuel Kant's understanding of God as the fully Unknown (der Unbekannte).[63] Jüngel's position is that God's self-revelation in the Crucified as being a saving God is discordant with not being able to say what God is.[64] Jüngel argues in favour of a Scripture oriented vocabulary in theology for the formulation of the mystery of God as a *revealed* mystery: in *positive* terms. He refers adumbrately to 1 Tm 3,16 ("He was made visible by the flesh" etc.). Jüngel describes in this mode love as the attitude (*habitus*) of self-concern, desire, and an even greater selflessness, as the occurring unity of life and death in favour of life, as the commitment to a "you", whom I want to 'have', in order to 'have' myself. This 'having' or being oneself only happens in a mutual giving away of oneself. This love is not static. It is strong as well as weak and powerless ("Schwäche und Ohnmacht") in respect of what is not love. Jesus Christ is this love of God made man, the beloved Son, come from the Father. The Spirit includes others in the love between Lover and Beloved: God's love is an overflowing love and

---

[62] SCG I c.91 n.4: Quanto *ergo id unde* amans est unum cum amato est maius, tanto est amor intensior*: Magis enim amamus quos nobis unit generationis origo, aut conversationis usus, aut aliquid huiusmodi, quam eos quos solum nobis unit humanae naturae societas. Et rursus, quanto id ex quo est unio magis intimum amanti, tanto amor fit firmior.* Unde interdum amor qui est ex aliqua passione, fit intensior amore *qui est ex naturali origine vel ex aliquo habitu,* sed facilius transit. *Id autem unde omnia Deo uniuntur, scilicet eius bonitas, quam omnia imitantur, est* maximum et intimum Deo*: cum ipse sit sua bonitas. Est* igitur *in Deo amor non solum verus, sed etiam* perfectissimus et firmissimus.

[63] Jüngel, *o.c.*, 362, 376 (265f, 276), also 381, 386 (279f, 283).

[64] Jüngel, *o.c.*, 351, 314 (257f, 231).

is extended to the lost, the sinners and the suffering.[65]

Jüngel's position may seem more appealing, for what he says is imaginable, recognizable and seems to be more Scriptural. However, Thomas also claims to be Scriptural in his theology and yet he comes to different conclusions. At first sight it seems that one of the great differences between Thomas and Jüngel as regards the love of God, is that Jüngel speaks of desire as inherent in love (note 4) and hence in God's love. Yet Thomas denies that desire is characteristic of love and underlines that we cannot say that there is desire in God's love, because of His simplicity and perfection. According to Thomas, speaking on the deep structure level, God does not need anything, whereas in Jüngel's theology God *does* and He even seems to be dependent on the love of His creatures for being God. But at the root of this there is an even more fundamental difference: from Jüngel's reaction to Thomas' approach it is clear that Jüngel has a different understanding of the negativity of Thomas' theology. Thomas would have been surprised to hear that his theology makes God look far away. For what Thomas does is nothing more than reflecting on what Scripture says. He thinks through how we are to understand it. The pivotal point is, that Thomas does in no way intend to replace or improve the first order language, that is the warm poetic, flowery language of Scripture. Therefore Jüngel's approach as an alternative to his would have made Thomas knit his brows. For from Thomas' point of view Jüngel's exposition of "God is love" is more like a paraphrase of what we read in Scripture; Jüngel uses flowery language (or metaphors, as Thomas would say) for explaining the flowery language (metaphors) of Scripture. Yet exactly these flowery words, these images need further clarification. For when Jüngel explains the love of God in terms of desire, selflessness and the beloved as essential for being who God is, immediately questions arise like what these words signify: that YHWH is dependent on His creatures for being - a loving - God? What is meant by God being selfless and giving Himself away? And how could God be (al)mighty and weak and powerless all the same?

How Thomas evaluates the flowery language of faith in Scripture will be considered in paragraph 2.3. For now it should be perspicuous that the deep structure level of Thomas' theology is not to be mistaken for our language of faith. Otherwise it might occur to someone that according

---

[65] Jüngel, *o.c.*, 340f, 430-453 (250f, 314-330).

to Thomas God's unchanging love were indeed static.

From this paragraph it is clear already that *passio* is used by Thomas in a broader sense than "suffering" alone. In order to understand better why Thomas harps upon God being without *passio*, without denying what Scripture says - that God is angry and sad etc. at times as well as passionately loving, as in Ex 3 and Ezk 16 - his understanding of *passio* will be explored, in paragraph 2.2. As was said above, Thomas designates this way of speaking of God as metaphorical. Why and what this means will be considered in paragraph 2.3.

But first something else must be clarified: we do not only faithfully speak of God as love, but of the Holy Spirit as love as well. And Jüngel, amongst others, speaks of Christ as the incarnated love of God, as was said above. How are these propositions related to one another?

2.1.3 The Holy Spirit Is Love

Whilst in 1 Jn 4 it is said that *God* is love, in the gospel according to John Christ links living a life of love with the gift of *the Holy Spirit*: Jn 14,15 - 15,17.[66] And it is not typical for our day and age that the Spirit is called or even identified with the love of God[67], for it is on the record that also for instance Doctor of the Church Gregory the Great called the Holy Spirit love.[68] And also Thomas, for instance in his

---

[66] Explained in this way in ST IIaIIae q.23 aa.2co, 3 ad 3; q.24 aa.2co, 7co.

[67] As in e.g. Coakley (1988), 124-135, Bons-Storm (1986), Kyung (1991), 37-47, Moltmann (1991), 98f (64f), Moltmann-Wendell (1995). Whence a movement in theology which speaks of God as Mother and femininity in God, a mode of speech already present in Scripture, has become stronger. Congar (1997), I,163f, in the light of this, observes a deep bond in Roman Catholic theology between the Virgin Mary and the Holy Spirit - which finds its origin in their respective roles in the mystery of salvation -, which leads to the custom of attributing to the her what should properly be attributed to the Spirit (e.g. comforter, advocate, defender of the believers).

[68] ST Ia q.37 a.1sc: *Gregorius dicit, in Homilia Pentecostes: "Ipse Spiritus Sanctus est Amor."* (*In Evang.* L.2 hom.30 par.1, ML 76,1220). Cf. Congar (1997), I,85-92, III,79-127 on Augustine, Anselm, Achard and Richard of St. Victor, Bonaventure and Thomas

commentaries to Ps 19,7 ("Rising on the one horizon he [the sun] runs his circuit to the other and nothing can escape his heat")[69] and Rm 5,5 ("The love of God has been poured into our hearts by the Holy Spirit which has been given to us"), speaks of the Holy Spirit as love, as the love of Christ and as the love of the Father and of the Son (note 53). But is love a proper name (*proprium*) of the Holy Spirit? And if so, how does this relate to "God is love"? For, as Augustine says, if "God" is the triune God, should we then not in the same way say that also the Son and the Father are love, since they are all three God? Therefore it seems that

> "no name that is predicated of a single Person *and* commonly of all three, is a proper name of a Person. Hence this name, love, is not a proper name of the Holy Spirit."[70]

In order to untie this knot, Thomas distinguishes between two ways of using the word love for God. The one is with regard to the divine essence (*essentialiter*). In this way the word love signifies the relation between the Lover and the beloved person or object, which can be in God - the love between the Father and the Son[71] - or outside God.

Aquinas.

[69] RPS ps.18 n.4, citing Sg 8,6

[70] ST Ia q.37 a.1 ag.1: *Sed nullum nomen quod de singulis personis praedicatur et de omnibus in communi singulariter, est nomen* proprium *alicuius personae. Ergo hoc nomen amor non est proprium Spiritus Sancti.* Thomas refers to the same discussion as Augustine in XV *De Trin.* (c.17, ML 42,1081): *Non itaque dixit Scriptura, Spiritus Sanctus caritas est,* [....] [*s*]*ed dixit, Deus caritas est.* The same question arises with regard to the name "Holy Spirit" for the third Person of the Trinity: "God" is holy (cf. Js 6,3) as well as spirit (cf. Jn 4,24, cited in SN I d.10 q.1 a.4 ag.1), ST Ia q.36 a.1 ad 1: [*N*]*omine spiritus significatur immaterialitas divinae substantiae* [....] [*S*]*anctus significatur puritas divinae bonitatis.* Ibidem co, citing Augustine's XV *De Trin.* c.19, ML 42,1086: [*E*]*t Pater est Spiritus et Filius est Spiritus; et Pater est sanctus et Filius est sanctus.*

[71] ST Ia q.37 a.2co: [*S*]*ecundum quod* [*diligere in divinis*] *essentialiter sumitur, sic Pater et Filio non diligunt se Spiritu Sancto, sed* essentia sua. Therefore, essentially speaking, the love of the Father for the Son cannot be the principlem of the Son's origin, REI c.5 l.3 n.3 (on Jn 5,20): *Nam secundum quod accipitur essentialiter, sic importat actum voluntatis: Si ergo esset principium originis Filii, sequitur quod Pater genuisset*

Thus *essentialiter* the love of God is parallel to God's understanding (*intelligere*). In this essential sense God's love has been discussed in subparagraph 2.1.1. And this is how Augustine speaks of the Father, the Son and the Holy Spirit as being love, as well as Jüngel, when he speaks of Christ as the love of God made man.[72] So in the essential way the word love is not exclusively used for the Holy Spirit, but equally for the Father, the Son and the Holy Spirit.[73]

The other way in which we use the word love for God is *personaliter*. We use "love" in the personal sense of the word, it signifies a going out, a *processio*, in God.[74] For the second Person we use the term "Word (*Verbum*)", to indicate what is going out *in divinis*, and the term "to speak (*dicere*)", which indicates the relation between the Word spoken and its origin. With regard to *what* is brought forth (the Word), Thomas speaks of using the term *personaliter*, with regard to *the relation* of the origin to what is brought forth (to speak) he speaks of using the term *notionaliter*.

> "For as far as we use the words *amor* and *dilectio* to
> express the relation of what comes forth by way of love to
> its origin and vice versa, by 'love' is understood the
> forthcoming love, and by 'to love' the breathing of the
> forthcoming love. In this sense 'Love' is the name of the

Filium voluntate, non natura: quod est erroneum.

[72] Jüngel, *o.c.*, 447 (326f).

[73] ST Ia q.37 a.1co: [*I*]*nquantum in amore vel dilectione non importatur nisi habitudo amantis ad rem amatam, amor et diligere* essentialiter *dicuntur, sicut intelligentia et intelligere.*

[74] ST Ia q.27 a.1co: *Quicumque enim intelligit, procedit aliquid* intra ipsum, *quod est conceptio rei intellectae, ex vi intellectiva proveniens, et ex eius notitia procedens.* [....] [*E*]*rgo accipienda est processio secundum emanationem intelligibilem, utpote verbi intelligibilis a dicente, quod manet in ipso.* Et sic fides catholica processionem in divinis. Ibidem a.4co: *Processio autem quae attenditur secundum rationem voluntatis, non consideratur secundum rationem similitudinis, sed magis secundum rationem impellentis et moventis in aliquid,* cf. OTT c.46: *Amatio autem fit secundum quandam motionem amantis ab amato. Amatum enim trahit ad seipsum amantem.* This *trahit* may remind the reader of Jn 6,44, 12,32 and also of Sg 1,4 (Vulg- Sg 1,3) and Jr 31,3.

Person and to love (*amare, diligere*) the notional term, as
'to speak' and 'to beget'."[75]

Now using "love" in the essential sense of the word, for the
triune God, as well as in the personal sense of the word, as a proper
name of the Holy Spirit, may be somewhat confusing. This confusion is
absent in respect of the second Person of the Trinity, Thomas observes.
For "God's Word" is a *proprium* of the Second Person. The name is used
in the personal sense only, for the Son, as in Jn 1, and is not used
essentialiter, for the whole Trinity.

That "love" is used in the essential sense (for the Trinity) as well
as in the personal sense (for the Holy Spirit) is due to the difference in
our understanding and speaking of the forthcomings (*processiones*) of the
Son and of the Spirit. In Jn 8,42 Christ says "I have my origin in God"
or "I have come forth from God". This is understood as concerning the
eternal forthcoming of the Son, within God.[76] Since we know of sons
coming forth from fathers, we use, in an analogous way, the terms of the
human forthcomings and relations to refer to the forthcoming and the
relation of the eternal Son in respect of the Father[77]: the term *processio*
for the eternal forthcoming from the origin, the term *generatio* to specify
the kind of forthcoming (namely of a son, as in Ps 2,7: *Filius meus es tu.
Ego hodie* genui *te*; cited by Thomas in this context), the terms *paternitas*

---

[75] ST Ia q.37 a.1co: *Inquantum vero his vocabulis utimur ad exprimendam
habitudinem eius rei quae procedit per modum amoris ad suum principium, et e converso;
ita quod per amorem intelligatur amor procedens, et per diligere intelligatur spirare
amorem procedentem: sic Amor est* nomen personae, *et diligere vel amare est* verbum
notionale, *sicut dicere vel generare.*

[76] ST Ia q.27 a.1sc: *Ego ex Deo processi* (Jn 8,42). The term *processio* is used for the
eternal forthcomings of the Son and the Spirit. What is brought forth in God is not distinct
from God (ad 2: *perfecte unum cum eo quo procedit, absque omni diversitate*) nor does it
imply a *mutatio de non esse ad esse*. These two features distinguish *processio* from
creatio. The term *missio* is used for the sending of them into creation; Christ continues in
Jn 8,42: *et veni, neque enim a meipso veni, sed illo me misit*; cf. q.43 a.1sc citing Jn
8,16, a.2sc citing Ga 4,4.

[77] Note that *in divinis* "Father" signifies the One from whom comes forth (ST Ia q.33
a.2co, ad 1), from eternity (q.10) and not, as in the context of human beings, the one
being before the Son nor the one higher in rank than the Son (qq.33 aa.1, 3), nor a man
(IIIa q.35 a.2co).

and *filiatio* to indicate the relations resulting from the forthcoming.

The term *processio* is equally used for the eternal forthcoming of the Spirit (cf. Jn 15,26) from His origin.[78] Yet, since the word *generatio* is used for the forthcoming of a child, we use the term breathing (*spiratio*) for characterizing the forthcoming of the Spirit. But as for the relational term with regard to the Spirit, the problem is that *in humanis* we do not have words to indicate the relation between a person and that person's spirit or breath leaving that person. Because of this poverty of our language (*vocabulorum inopiam*), Thomas says, putting words to this relation is a matter of contrivance.

> "Therefore we use certain periphrases to signify the procession of the third Person: also the relations that follow from this procession are called forthcoming and spiration, although these are rather words that refer to an origin than to a relation, in the strict sense of the word."[79]

Thus, only in the personal sense "Love" is a proper name (*proprium*) of the Holy Spirit.[80] Yet, again, this does not mean that the

---

[78] ST Ia q.36 a.4co: *Pater et Filius in omnibus unum sunt, in quibus non distinguit inter eos relationis oppositio. Unde* [....] *sequitur quod Pater et Filius sunt* unum principium *Spiritus Sancti*; citing in a.2 ad 1: Jn 15,26, 16,14 and Mt 11,27.

[79] St Ia q.37 a.1co: *Unde et* quibusdam circumlocutionibus *utimur ad significandam* [*tertiam*] *personam procedentem: et relationes etiam quae accipiuntur secundum hanc processionem, et processionis et spirationis nominibus nominantur, ut supra* [q.28 a.4] *dictum est; quae tamen sunt* magis *nomina originis* quam *relationis, secundum proprietatem vocabuli.*

[80] Whereas, for instance, Wisdom is not; "Wisdom" used as a name of the Holy Spirit is not a *proprium*, but what is called an appropriation. The reason why it cannot be a *proprium*, is that "wisdom" does not signify a going out in God (as knowing and loving, see below), but a being in God. Therefore it cannot be proper to one of the two forthcoming and so to say forthbringing *processiones* (cf. SN I d.10 q.1 a.1 ad 5). Hence "Wisdom" is *always* an essential name of God. Still Wisdom (and other essential names of God) is being ascribed, appropriated, to one or more of the divine Persons, by the Doctors of the Church (ST Ia q.39 a.8), in the liturgy and in Scripture itself: Wisdom is appropriated to the Son by Thomas in ST Ia q.43 a.5sc, citing W 9,10; in the liturgy e.g. where Is 11,2 is being read during Advent; in Scripture directly in 1 Co 1,24. Also the

Spirit is love, whereas the Father and the Son are not or to a lesser extent; Father, Son and Holy Spirit are, in the essential sense of the word, equally love, since *God* is love.

2.2 Not A *Passio*nate God?

The subject of this paragraph is Thomas' understanding of (*com*)*passio* and of the way we do and do not ascribe it to God and to Christ in our religious language. For Thomas does not consider the meaning of *passio* in order to find a way in which we *could* speak of God, but rather in order to interpret our actual God-talk, in Scripture and tradition, correctly, according to our faith. Next it will be clarified why *passio* includes not only corporeality, but also imperfection and what this means for ascribing *passio* to God (2.2.2) and to Christ (2.2.3).

2.2.1 *Passio* as Being Acted upon

Thomas considers what *passio* is, only in the context of a certain subject; he does not dedicate a separate *quaestio* or *articulus* to what he understands by *passio*. It may be thence that he explains what *passio* is thrice in the *Summa Theologiae*, but slightly differently every time.

In the *Summa Theologiae* a first analysis of *passio* is found in the context of the question whether knowing, as one of the mights of the human soul, is a passive might (*potentia passiva*). Here he distinguishes three ways in which *passio* is used:

> "In one way, the most proper way, when something is removed from the subject that befits it according to its nature or according to its proper inclination, like when water loses its coolness through heating and when a

---

Hagia Sophia church in Constantinople comes to mind; it was dedicated to *Christ* Pantokrator. An example of appropriating wisdom to the Spirit is Jm 3,17f (cited in IIaIIae q.45 aa.5, 6). Thomas also relates Is 11,2 to the Holy Spirit (in IaIIae q.68 a.4sc, IIaIIae q.45 a.1sc).

human being falls ill or is saddened."[81]

The example of the natural coolness of the water may be a bit strange to us, but the point Thomas makes is clear: *Passio* in the most proper sense of the word implies a loss of something that belongs to the thing (*res*). Falling ill is equivalent to losing health and eventually losing your life, whereas God created us body and soul, that we might live[82]. Being sad is most properly called a *passio*, because sadness is contrary to the natural inclination of human beings towards happiness.[83] Therefore *passio* in this most proper sense is something evil, something to be counteracted or fought against. Now on the basis of Scripture it seems also that God Himself befits *passio* in this most proper sense, for it speaks of vexing (Is 63,10, *affligere*) and grieving (Ep 4,30, *contristare*) God's Holy Spirit.[84] Also, in the former chapter, it was shown that when Christ suffers, we say that God suffers too, according to the rule of the communication of idioms. This seems to open the door to what is called patripassianism.[85]

> "In the second way, the less proper way, when something, either befitting or not befitting, is taken away from the subject. And in this way *pati* is not only used for someone falling ill, but for him/her getting better as well,

---

[81] ST Ia q.79 a.2co: [P]*ati tripliciter dicitur. Uno modo, proprissime, scilicet quando aliquid removetur ab eo quod convenit sibi secundum naturam, aut secundum propriam inclinationem; sicut cum aqua frigidatem amittit per calefactionem, et cum homo aegrotat aut tristatur.*

[82] W 1,13f, cited in ST Ia q.65 a.2 ag.1, IaIIae q.85 a.6 sc.1. Death, the separation of body and soul (IaIIae q.72 a.5co), makes the body lifeless and makes the human being cease to exist.

[83] ST IaIIae q.1 aa.2, 7.

[84] In SCG IV c.16 n.8 Thomas brings up that on the basis of these verses some may conclude that the Holy Spirit is a creature, for *in Deum tristitia cadere non potest*; why sadness, grief etc. is said to be proper to bodily creatures is explained in the course of this paragraph.

[85] A term drawn from Tertullian's works against the modalist views of Praxeas, who held that when Christ was crucified the Father also was crucified.

not only for someone feeling sad, but for him/her
rejoicing as well, and for whatever way someone is
changed or moved."[86]

At first it may seem that, whereas falling ill is called *pati* in the most
proper sense of the word, being cured is called *pati* in this less proper
sense, because the regaining of health is in accordance with what a human
being is created for: life. But apparently this is not the distinction made
by Thomas, since falling ill can be reckoned among the *passiones* in this
less proper sense of the word as well. For the difference between the
most proper and the less proper sense is in the way it is looked upon.
Passio used in the less proper sense of the word is not a negative, but a
neutral, historical qualification. *Passio* in this less proper sense is only
used to indicate that change and moves happen, for better or worse or
without improvement or deterioration. Still in this sense *passio* is accompanied by a loss: "something is taken away from the subject," be it the
illness or the health, the place where someone was etc., or one's plans
being changed, for this is a loss or letting go of one's former plans.
Therefore, in view of what we read in Scripture, it seems that *passio* in
this less proper sense of the word also befits God, for, because of the
behaviour of people God regrets and changes His mind. Gn 6,6, 1 S
15,10 and Jon 3,10 are classical examples.

The third way of using the word *pati/passio*, is the way in which
it is commonly (*communiter*) used:

"Because of this only, that something that has an aptitude
for something, receives that for which it had an aptitude,
without anything being taken away."[87]

---

[86] ST Ia q.79 a.2co: *Secundo modo*, minus proprie *dicitur aliquis pati ex eo quod
aliquid ab ipso abiicitur, sive sit ei conveniens, sive non conveniens. Et secundum hoc
dicitur pati non solum qui aegrotat, sed etiam qui sanatur; non solum qui tristatur, sed
etiam qui laetatur; vel* quocumque modo aliquis alteretur et moveatur.

[87] ST Ia q.79 a.2co: *Tertio modo, dicitur aliquid pati* communiter, *ex hoc solo quod id
quod est in potentia ad aliquid*, recipit *illud ad quod erat in potentia*, absque *hoc quod*
aliquid abiicitur. *Secundum quem modum*, omne quod exit de potentia in actum, *potest dici
pati, etiam cum perficitur. Et sic intelligere nostrum est pati.* QDV q.26 a.1co:
Communiter *quidem dicitur passio* receptio *alicuius* quocumque modo; *et hoc sequendo
significationem vocabuli. Nam dicitur a patin graece* [παθειν], *quod est recipere.*

Our getting to know is *pati* in this common sense of the word: our intellect is apt for knowledge (*in potentia*) and starts to know (*in actu*) as soon as the object is received by the intellect.[88] This is a metaphysical distinction. In this sense of the word *pati/passio* signifies growth, by receiving, towards perfection of the nature of the subject. In this sense of *pati* there is no loss, for it would not make sense to say that when one realizes one's aptitude or capacity for something one loses the aptitude or capacity through the realisation of it.

Note that the propriety of the use of the word *pati/passio* is expressed in terms of gradation[89]; none of the three is called improper by Thomas.[90]

In the *Prima Secundae* Thomas makes a different distinction. Here he distinguishes in *quaestio* 22 between two: the common use of the word *pati*, which is more properly (*magis proprie*) called "being perfected (*perfecti*)" and the proper use. And in respect of this proper way he distinguishes between one way and the most proper way. The less proper way of *quaestio* 79 is now a subdivision and is not called "less" any more, but "proper", without any further determination. Even more, here the gradation more/less is used to distinguish the common way from the

---

[88] In SN Thomas takes a different stand. For in the ST he seems to try to hold on to what Aristotle says in *De anima*: *Intelligere est pati quoddam* (cited in Ia q.79 a.2sc, q.97 a.2co: III *De anima* c.4 n.9, Bk 429b24); *Sentire et intelligere est quoddam pati* (cited in IaIIae q.22 a.1co: I *De anima* c.5 n.8, Bk 410a25). But in SN III d.15 q.2 a.1a ad 1, 2 Thomas says: *Ad primum ergo dicendum quod* non omne moveri est pati, *nisi communiter et large loquendo, sicut etiam moveri quoddam corrumpi est secundum Augustinum et secundum Philosophum in VIII Phys.. Ad secundum dicendum quod illuminatione non abiicitur aliqua qualitas, sed* tantum recipitur; et ideo non est passio. Thomas does not cite *De anima* in SN III d.15.

[89] As in ST IaIIae q.22 a.1co: *[Q]ando huiusmodi transmutatio fit in deterius*, magis proprie *habet rationem passionis, quam quando ad melius. Unde tristitia* magis proprie *est passio quam laetitia.*

[90] Contrary to what is said to be Thomas' distinction regarding *pati/passio* in the Matriti edition of the *Summa Theologiae*, vol. V, 230*: *1. Passio dicitur dupliciter, s. improprie, id est omnis receptio; et proprie, i. cum abiectione alicuius.* However, Thomas does call this third kind of *passio* "*improprie*" in CMP V l.14 n.958. The *passiones* in the proper senses of the word he discusses in l.20 nn.1065-1069.

two proper ways of using *pati*.[91]

Also in *quaestio* 97 of the *Prima Pars* Thomas makes a distinction between two: the proper way and the common way. Among the proper way is reckoned what until now is called the most proper way. The common way is described in this *quaestio* as *pati* in the sense of bringing about whatever change, even if the change is the perfection of the nature. The distinction of with or without a loss is not mentioned here, so that here the less proper use of the word *pati* is reckoned among the common way of using the word - whereas elsewhere in the *Summa Theologiae* this way is called proper (q.22) and less proper (q.79).[92] In the following I will use the terminology of *quaestio* 79 because of its distinctness.

This exposition shows that in the *Summa Theologiae* Thomas' thoughts on *pati/passio* have not been streamlined. Rather Thomas has made practical distinctions in respect of the subject to be considered: what he calls the less proper way in *quaestio* 79 can also be called proper or common, depending on the context. But what all these views of *passio* have in common is that *pati* is the consequence of an action (*actio*): the *patiens* is being acted upon, undergoes something.[93] This undergoing may be specified by "suffering", when an evil action is directed towards someone or something, so that his/her/its nature and integrity is violated. An action towards someone or something can also be experienced or described in a neutral sense, without a value judgement (good or bad). When in a particular context *pati* is used or understood in this sense, it

---

[91] ST IaIIae q.22 a.1co: [*P*]*ati dicitur tripliciter:* Uno modo communiter, *secundum quod omne recipere est pati, etiam si nihil abiiciatur a re: sicut si dicatur aerem pati, quando illuminatur. Hoc autem* magis proprie *est perfecti quam pati.* Alio modo *dicitur pati* proprie, *quando aliquid recipitur cum alterius abiectione. Sed hoc contingit* dupliciter. [*Uno modo*] [*q*]*uando enim abiicitur id quod non est conveniens rei: sicut cum corpus animalis sanatur, dicitur pati, quia recipit sanitatem aegritudine abiecta. Alio modo quando e converso contingit: sicut aegrotare dicitur pati, quia recipitur infirmitas, sanitate abiecta. Et hic est* proprissimus *modus passionis.*

[92] ST Ia q.97 a.2co: [*P*]*assio dupliciter dicitur: Uno modo* proprie*: et sic pati dicitur quod a sua naturali dispositione removetur.* [....] *Alio modo, dicitur passio* communiter*, secundum* quamcumque mutationem, *et etiam si pertineat ad perfectionem naturae.*

[93] ST Ia q.44 a.2 ad 2: [*P*]*assio est effectus actionis* (cf. q.97 a.2co); SCG II c.16 n.7: *Actus enim qui est agentis ut a quo, est patientis ut in quo*; ST IaIIae q.22 a.2co: [*I*]*n nomine passionis importatur quod patiens trahatur ad id quod est agentis.*

may well be translated by the neutral word "undergoing". It is obvious that when *pati* is used in the common sense, it cannot be translated as "suffering". In the case of knowledge "receiving" seems to cover the content: getting to know something by receiving knowledge (which presupposes an action of giving by someone or something else). Hence in all three cases "undergoing", with a further qualification if needed, seems to be what Thomas understands by *pati/passio*.

There is yet another characteristic of *passio*, that is shown by Thomas' exposition: change.

2.2.2 *Passio*: Corporeality and Imperfection

From what has been said it is clear that *passio* as the effect of an action is always accompanied by change. When the change involves a loss, either of something proper to the subject or not, it cannot be but a change in the body, i.e. a change concerning the *materia*. Properly speaking this kind of *passio* cannot include a change in the *forma*, because otherwise nothing *of* the subject would be changed, but the subject would cease to be what it is.[94] And it must be a change in a body, since

> "motion is not found but in bodies, and contrary of forms and qualities are found in beings subject to generation and corruption alone."[95]

---

[94] ST Ia q.3 a.7co: *Hoc autem etsi possit dici de habente formam, quod scilicet habeat aliquid quod non est ipsum* [....], *tamen in ipsa forma non est alienum.* Cf. q.5 a.5co: *[U]numquodque sit id quod est, per suam formam.* One could allege that this is exactly what is said in Ps 22,7: What the suffering David-figure (Ps 22,1) undergoes is such, that he loses his humanity. Yet this is what Thomas would call metaphorical use of the language (see 2.2.3), referring to the confusion and the disgrace of the person suffering; in RPS ps.21 Thomas refers to Jb 25,6.

[95] QDV q.26 a.1co: *Motus autem* non *invenitur* nisi *in corporibus, et contrarietas formarum vel qualitatum in* solis *generabilibus et corruptibilibus.* Cf. ST IaIIae q.22 a.1co: *Passio autem cum abiectione* non *est* nisi *secundum transmutationem corporalem.* Ibidem ad 1: *[I]gitur dicendum quod pati, secundum quod est cum abiectione et transmutatione, proprium est materiae: unde* non *invenitur* nisi *in compositis ex materia et forma.*

So properly speaking *passio* only befits beings that are composed of *materia* and *forma*. That an action of violence or tenderness towards a body causes a physical change is obvious. Yet, although the soul does not have *materia*[96] - it is the *forma* of a material body - it still undergoes, as was already shown with regard to Christ's *passio* (par. 1.3.3): the soul undergoes insofar as it is united with a body that undergoes. So the soul only undergoes indirectly (*per accidens*). Thomas again speaks here on a meta-physical level, concerning the deep structure of human beings.

In earlier works, but not anymore in the *Summa Theologiae*, Thomas calls these *passiones* corporeal (*corporales*). The term may be avoided in the *Summa Theologiae*, because it could be somewhat misleading. For *passiones* (*corporales*) affect the soul as well because of the union of body and soul, as was shown in the former chapter. Yet in the *Prima Secundae* Thomas speaks, as distinguished from these, of *passiones animales*. The term *passio animalis* is not confusing, since the word *passio* itself (in the proper senses of the word) implies corporeality, as was said. The term *passio animalis* then signifies that through the senses the soul apprehends something, which thereupon causes a change in the body. And this, in turn, affects the soul. Hence a *passio animalis* originates from the soul.[97] The basic *passiones* of the soul that Thomas distinguishes are love, hate, desire, aversion, enjoyment and sadness (*passiones concupiscibiles*, which have the good as their object) and hope, despair, fear, courage and anger (*passiones irascibiles*, which have the evil as their object). From our own experience we know how these may bring about a bodily change, like effecting a warm feeling, making a person restless, producing a headache or causing a psychosomatic complaint.[98]

Since in the proper sense of the word *passio* presupposes a corporeal change, the non-corporeal (*incorporea*) soul can only undergo something through the body with which it is united. So, apart from a

---

[96] ST Ia q.75 a.5co.

[97] QDV q.26 a.2co: *Alio modo ita quod* incipiat *ab anima, inquantum est corporis motor, et terminetur in corpus; et haec dicitur passio animalis; sicut patet in ira et timore, et aliis huiusmodi.*

[98] ST IaIIae qq.26-39 and qq.40-48. Their effects: q.28 aa.3, 5, 6, q.33 aa.1-4, q.37 aa.3, 4, q.44 aa.1, 3, 4, q.48 aa.1, 2, 4.

body the soul cannot undergo. But in *De veritate* Thomas observes that in our language we have in fact broadened the meaning of *passio*, so that we also speak of *passio* of the soul apart from the body:

> "In our ordinary language the use of the word *passio* is broadened, so that we speak of undergoing when whatever is hampered that befits it, like when we say that something seriously suffers, because it is prevented from moving downwards (by gravity); and when we say that a human being suffers when he/she is prevented from doing his/her will."[99]

And the will is one of the mights of the soul. Thomas calls this use of the word *passio* figurative (*transumptive*), for in this way a word implying something corporeal is used for something non-corporeal by reason of a resemblance - a clear exemple of a metaphor.[100]

Still in the common sense of the word *passio* a bodily change is not presupposed. For, as was said above, in this sense *passio* only means the movement from what the aptitude of something is for to the realisation of it, in other words the movement from being *in potentia* to being *in actu*. Therefore the term *passio* in this sense can be used for anything *in potentia*, corporeal or not, including the soul, for instance when someone

---

[99] QDV q.26 a.1co: [A]*mpliatur nomen passionis* secundum usum loquentium, *ut* qualitercumque aliquid *impediatur ab eo quod sibi competebat, pati dicatur; sicut si dicamus grave pati ex hoc quod prohibetur ne deorsum moveatur; et hominem pati si prohibeatur suam facere voluntatem.*

[100] ST IaIIae q.33 a.1 ad 1: [N]*ihil prohibet in his quae dicuntur metaphorice, idem diversis attribui secundum diversas* similitudines; IIIa q.8 a.1 ad 2: [I]*n metaphoricis locutionibus* non *oportet attendi similitudinem quantum ad omnia: sic enim non esset similitudo sed rei veritas*; In the *Summa Theologiae* this figurative or metaphorical use of the word *passio* is remarkably enough not mentioned where *passio* is considered. It is referred to, though, in the *Tertia Pars*, in the context of the almightiness of the soul of Christ, in q.13 a.4 (see 4.2.2).

begins to understand something.[101]

From this the inference is clear that according to Thomas *passio* does not befit God in *any* way. For in the proper senses of the word, *passio* presupposes corporeality. But God being or having a body, *materia*, seems to be incompatible with what we understand by "God". First of all Jesus tells us that "God is spirit" (Jn 4,24). And Thomas also accounts for it: in respect of the order of the deep structure of "God" it is obvious that we cannot hold that God is or has a body. For it belongs to "body" that it is material (*materia*). We know by experience, Thomas argues, that no body, no *materia*, moves by itself; it only moves if it *is* moved. If we then believe that God is the Creator, the First Mover, who creates of His own free will,[102] without being forced or prompted, unmoved in this sense (ST Ia q.9), we cannot hold that God is or has a body.[103]

Unless, one might say, this divine body lives and moves through a divine soul.

> "A living body does not live for as far as it is a body, for
> then every body would be alive. Therefore it must be that
> it would live by reason of something else, like our body
> lives by reason of the soul."[104]

Yet two other incompatibilities are clear. The first mentioned by Thomas is that God is the highest in reverence (*nobilissimum*). If God were a

---

[101] ST IaIIae q.22 a.1 ad 1: *Sed pati prout importat receptionem solum, non est necessarium quod sit materiale, sed* potest esse cuiuscumque existentis in potentia. *Anima autem, etsi non sit composita ex materia et forma, habet tamen aliquid potentialitatis, secundum quam convenit sibi recipere et pati, secundum quod intelligere pati est.*

[102] Cf. Is 45,10-12, 48,12-14, Rv 4,11.

[103] ST Ia q.3 a.1co: [N]*ullum corpus movet non motum: ut patet inducendo per singula. Ostensum est autem supra* [q.2 a.3, the *quinque viae*] *quod Deus est* primum *movens immobile. Unde manifestum est Deus non est corpus.*

[104] ST Ia q.3 a.1co: *Corpus autem vivum non vivit inquantum corpus, quia sic omne corpus viveret: oportet igitur quod vivat* per aliquid aliud [*quam corpus*], *sicut corpus nostrum vivit per animam.*

body, something which cannot live by itself would be more revered than something that is alive by itself, which does not make sense. Secondly, God being a living body would imply that there would be composedness, of *materia*, the divine body, and *forma*, the divine soul as its life giving principle, in God.[105] This cannot be, as was said in 2.1.1: God is totally simple, otherwise He would not be God, but a creature.

The alternative, that God would not be but would *have* a body, so that we could say "God suffers" in the proper sense of the word, cannot be held either. For in that case God's essence (*essentia*) would not be identical with His being (*esse*): God's body would be accidental and not essential to Him, which would imply time in the eternal God as well as being caused.[106] God could then also be classified, under for instance "the ones having a body", as if He were a creature.[107]

For a correct understanding of what Thomas is saying here it is crucial to see that he is not describing how God is. He is, as a negative theologian, rather showing what cannot be said of God, of whom we believe that He is the Creator. Therefore, starting from Scripture and using distinctions made in philosophy, he analyses what we say concerning God and in what way and how this is to be understood. In the case under consideration, the *passio* of God, it was shown how Thomas brings to our attention the fact that *passio* in the proper meanings of the word presupposes a body.

Thomas recognizes that Scripture not only says that God is spirit, but likewise that God is or has a body. In order to solve the problem of how to understand this, he looks at the deep structure of corporeality: corporeality implies being caused, composedness etc., implications incompatible with God's divinity and incompatible with being the Creator. On the basis of this Thomas concludes that, properly speaking, corporeality of God is to be denied. In the light of this the Scriptural texts that speak

---

[105] ST Ia q.3 a.2.

[106] ST Ia q.3 a.6co: [*O*]*mne quod est per se*, prius *est eo quod est per accidens*. [....] *Sed* nec *accidentia* per se *in eo esse possunt, sicut risibile est per se accidens hominis. Quia huiusmodi accidentia causantur ex principiis subiecti:* in Deo autem nihil potest esse causatum, cum sit causa prima. *Unde reliquitur quod in Deo nullum sit accidens.*

[107] ST Ia q.3 a.5.

of God as being or having a body are to be interpreted: corporeality is attributed to God in a metaphorical sense, because of a resemblance or an effect. In paragraph 2.3 further attention will be paid to metaphorical language as regards God's *passio*.

What may happen if one does not understand Thomas as a negative theologian in this way, can be seen in Marcel Sarot's dissertation, in which he inquires about God's body and His passions.[108] In chapter 4 he brings to the attention of his readers "a widely neglected problem": that passions presuppose corporeality. In the first two paragraphs he discusses Thomas' view on *passio* and corporeality, at least, insofar as he needs it for making his point, that passions imply corporeality. This seems to be the reason why he, commenting on Thomas, totally leaves aside the common or metaphysical sense of *passio*. But it is of the utmost importance, not only for a correct understanding of Thomas' view of *passio*, but for the subject of Sarot's own study as well: all bodies presuppose *passiones*, but not all *passiones* presuppose a body; *passio* in the third sense of the word does not. Besides, according to Thomas all *passiones* imply imperfection. Thus quite a battleground extends between Thomas and Sarot, as a representative of "perfect being theology" (see further below). Furthermore, it catches the eye that Sarot passes over in silence what Thomas understands by "God" and "body". If someone wants to know about Thomas' ideas on God and His (non-) corporeality, the obvious thing to do seems starting off with Thomas' own question of whether God is a body.[109] By doing so, the deep structure of "God" and "body" would be laid bare: a body implies composedness, being created and also imperfection. Thus being or having a body is incompatible with being God. Sarot disregards this with blithe neglect. After his eclectic discussion of Thomas' view of *passio* Sarot examines contemporary psychological concepts of emotion. On the basis of his analysis and in view of what he reads in Scripture Sarot finds it more convincing that God does experience emotions and, therefore, has a body. By arguing according to this line, it seems that Sarot rather uses Thomas

---

[108] *God, Passibility and Corporeality*, Kampen 1992, 104-119.

[109] ST Ia q.3 tit: *De Dei simplicitate*; a.1: *Utrum Deus sit corpus*; cf. SCG I c.20, II c.3, OTT c.16.

to get his, what he calls, passibilist[110] ideas across than entering into a serious discussion with Thomas.

But more fundamental is the problem of the starting point of Sarot's interpretation of Thomas' exposition. For, because Sarot does not recognize Thomas as a negative theologian, he apprehends Thomas' denial of God's passibility and corporeality as a first order statement (like "God is good" and "God is love" etc.). In brief: Sarot erroneously understands that Thomas is saying that the 'passionless' God is a cold fish.

Thomas speaks of God as a negative theologian, because he conceives God as a *mystery*, revealed, as a mystery, and hence still a mystery.[111] We do not know what God is, but we do know what He is not, as was said. Hence the categories we use in our speech regarding creation, do not fit. Therefore Thomas keeps on denying of the Creator what is proper to creatures. Reading Sarot's thesis shows that he employs a different approach. It seems that to him God is not a mystery. It rather seems that he is trying to solve the *problem* of God. A clear example is how Sarot writes about Thomas' position that God does not change. Instead of inquiring what immutability and eternity signify (in respectively ST Ia q.9 a.1 and q.10 a.1), Sarot remarks in an oblique way:

> "Although this objection [of Thomas, that God cannot change,] has a respectable tradition, *it is not necessary to pay too much attention to it*. The objection presupposes the Aristotelian scheme of actuality and potentiality [....]. Once this presupposition is abandoned, it becomes counterintuitive".

Not a very strong argument in favour of the neglect of a "respectable" tradition in one's own faith. Next Sarot continues to argue that

---

[110] Sarot, *o.c.*, 2. Sarot divides theologies and theologians into two categories: passibilist and impassibilist. Sarot describes Passibilists as the ones affirming God's passibility, meaning that they hold that God can suffer and does suffer and that He has emotions. Impassibilists would deny this. In this study I hope to make clear that such a division cannot be made. Thomas for instance, labelled by Sarot as a representative of the impassibilist view, does not deny God's true suffering - on the contrary rather; Thomas emphasizes it (see paragraph 1.4 and 2.3.4). And still Thomas says something quite different from what Sarot says, as will be shown.

[111] As expressed in Is 45,15, 19, 1 Co 13,12, 2 Co 5,7, 1 Pe 1,8.

"*God can* change in a relational way, not ascending or
descending, but neutral as to His perfection. *Just as I*
have changed, but not become less or more perfect by
marrying my wife, *God can* change without growing less
or more perfect by loving each new-born baby, respond-
ing to the free actions of human beings etc."[112]

Apparently, Sarot thinks that we (can) speak of God univocally, that is,
speak of God as we speak of creatures, just like when we describe an
object, despite Scripture's testimony that He is different (e.g. Is 40,25
and Ac 17,28f). Sarot's text quoted here shows clearly that the author
thinks he really knows, and therefore can describe, what God is. Sarot
adheres to what is called "perfect being theology", according to which
God is perfect, though not as Thomas understands it, but in the sense of
"the most perfect being", the most perfect of all beings.[113] This is,
indeed, not incompatible with having a body. Whereas the very reason
why Thomas denies that God is (or has) a body and mutable and hence
that there is *passio* in God is not that he knows what God is, but precisely
that he knows what God is *not*: a creature.

Passio in the common sense does not necessarily presuppose a
body, as was said. It befits bodily creatures and as well as angels,

---

[112] Sarot, *o.c.*, 56f, italics added, MR.
By the way, Thomas, having a different perception of God's perfection than Sarot, would
disagree with him that marriage does not change a person for the better or for the worse.
For the better, when that person is called by God to live a married life, as in Mt 19,5.
For the worse, when that person is not called to it, as in Mt 19,12; cf. SN IV d.2 q.1
a.1b, SCG III c.123 nn.5-7, IV c.78, ST Ia q.92 a.1sc, co (citing Gn 2,18 resp. 24),
IaIIae q.108 a.4 ad 1 (citing Mt 19,12, 21, 1 Co 7,35), IIaIIae q.40 a.2 ad 4, q.186 a.1
ad 4, a.4 ad 1.

[113] Sarot, *o.c.* 16-22. An ardent opponent to this type of theology is Marion, e.g. in
(1977), 261: God becomes "un étant parmi d'autres. 'Dieu' devient l'idole rayonnante où
l'Être nous ménage [....] sa divinité. Ce 'Dieu' demeure une idole, la plus haute et plus
difficile à produire, la plus glorieuse et la plus salvifique pour le *Dasein* humain; son
advenue sans doute affolerait de bonheur de *Dasein*; mais il s'agirait toujours d'une
idole."

creatures without a body.[114] Still, as the other two kinds of *passio*, it cannot be ascribed to God either, Thomas says, since it indicates growth towards perfection: from *potentia* to *actus*. Accordingly *passio* in this sense implies imperfection in the subject. Applied to God it would mean that through a process of change God and His love, His might etc. would become better, stronger etc.. However this would imply that God could become more divine and on a deep structural level composedness, time etc. and thus being created, as was said. Therefore we cannot but conclude also that this type of *passio* does not befit God.

That there is no such transition from *potentia* to *actus* in God is expressed by calling God *actus purus*. This term occurs often in Thomas' works. For a correct understanding of what he means by it is necessary to see as well that *actus purus* is not a description of what God is, but rather a metaphysical (deep structure) term, referring to the inexpressible: God's full and eternal God-ness, God's absolute perfection, incomprehensibly non-created and transcendent. The poverty and deficiency of our language for God-talk is formulated beautifully by Gregory the Great, quoted in the *Summa Theologiae*:

> "'Stammering, as we can, we let the exalted things of God resound: for what is not made or become, cannot be called perfect in the proper sense of the word,' as Gregory says. But since with regard to the things that come to be, something is called perfect because it is transferred from *potentia* into *actus*, this word "perfect" is conceived as signifying anything in which being *in actu* is not absent - whether it is perfect in the sense of perfected or not."[115]

The passive form "is transferred" (*educitur*) indicates a being moved:

---

[114] ST Ia q.50 a.2.

[115] ST Ia q.4 a.1 ad 1: [S]*icut dicit Gregorius* [*Moral.* 5,36, ML 75,715; 29,1, ML 76,477], "*balbutiendo ut possumus, excelsa Dei resonamus: quod enim factum non est, perfectum proprie dici non potest.*" *Sed quia in his quae fiunt, tunc dicitur esse aliquid perfectum, cum de potentia* educitur *in actum; transumitur hoc nomen perfectum, ad significandum omne illud cui non deest esse in actu, sive hoc habeat per modum factionis, sive non.* See also notes 16 and 20.

nothing moves or grows - from the state of being *in potentia*, or capable of/apt for something, to the state of being *in actu*, or having realized the capacity/aptitude - unless it is acted upon, in which case it undergoes something.

Thus the conclusion is that because of what is understood by *"passio"* and because of what is understood by "God" according to the Catholic faith, we have to say that no kind of *passio* is in God. The formulation of this conclusion is slightly different from the conclusion at the end of the first chapter; there, in the context of the communication of idioms, it was said that the divine *nature* cannot undergo anything. That the formulation of the conclusion in chapter 1 is more precise will be shown in paragraph 2.3. and chapter 3.

Still it remains that this conclusion seems to be opposed to what we read in Scripture. In paragraph 2.3 this issue will be discussed extensively.

Another question is raised by the words used in this subparagraph: the terminology of *potentia* and *actus* prompts us to consider this third meaning of *passio* in further detail in respect of (the non-corporeal) God and His almightiness. For parallel to Thomas' reason that there is no *com-passio* in God, since *compassio* is a *passio* (as in 1.1.2 and 1.3.2; see also paragraph 2.3), these words raise the question how there can be *omni-potentia* in God, if there is no *potentia* in Him. In other words, how does Thomas use the word *potentia* in respect of God? This will be done in paragraph 3.1.

2.2.3 Christ: Passible and Therefore Imperfect?

That *passio* implies imperfection entails the conclusion that it does not befit God. But if there truly was *passio* in Christ, does this mean that Christ was imperfect? In fact we actually never speak of Christ's imperfection. Moreover, in Ep 4,13 we read that Christ was perfect.

Yet, if Christ was truly human, nothing human was foreign to Him:

> "None of the things that God has planted in our nature
> was absent in the human nature that was assumed by the

Word of God."[116]

It is an echo of Ph 2,7: He became "as human beings are." "Truly human" implies that Christ, as any other human being, was composed of *materia*, a human body, and *forma*, a human soul.[117] As was said in chapter 1, Christ underwent the *passiones* inflicted upon him in body and soul and He lost the accidents belonging to being human, like integrity of the body, and eventually even His life. And although this happened only insofar as He allowed it to happen, His body was injured. Therefore, since the truly human Christ truly underwent *passiones* in the most proper and in the less proper sense of the word, we must hold that He was indeed imperfect, imperfect*ed* to be more precise. For, since His body was formed by the operation of the Holy Spirit, the body of Christ was perfectly human, as was said in paragraph 1.3.2. The consequence of this perfection was that He was to the highest extend sensitive to what He received through the senses. So, because being perfectly human, Christ was to the highest extend liable to *passiones*, and hence to imperfection.

Since Christ was truly human, He was liable to the *passiones* of the soul as well. But Thomas underlines that in three respects Christ did not have these as we have them: in respect of their origin, their object and their effects:

> "In us such *passiones* often precede the judgement of reason. But in Christ all movements of the sensitive appetite originated from the disposition of reason. [....] In us each time such movements do not remain in the sensitive appetite, but they pull the reason. And this was not the case in Christ. [....] His reason was in no way hampered."[118]

---

[116] ST IIIa q.9 a.4co: [S]*icut ex supra dictis patet* [q.4 a.2 ad 2, q.5], nihil *eorum quae Deus in nostra natura plantavit,* defuit *humanae naturae assumptae a Verbo Dei.*

[117] ST IIIa q.5 aa.1, 2 resp. a.3.

[118] ST IIIa q.15 a.4co: [H]*uiusmodi passiones frequenter in nobis praeveniunt iudicum rationis: sed in Christo omnes motus sensitivi appetitus oriebantur secundum dispositionem rationis.* [....] [*I*]*n nobis quandoque huiusmodi motus non sistunt in appetitu sensitivo, sed trahunt rationem. Quod in Christo non fuit.* [....] [*R*]*atio* [*eius*] *ex his nullo modo*

This is a consequence of what was said before, that the higher part of Christ's soul was not affected by the bodily *passiones*. The cleansing of the temple (Mt 21,12f par., Jn 2,13-17) may come to mind as an exception to this; was it not there that Christ let Himself go? In his commentary on Jn 2,15f Thomas gives a dual answer to this. First he cites Origen, saying that this cleansing is an example of the divine might, of Jesus that is, smothering the fury of people. Thomas refers to Ps 33,10 ("YHWH thwarts the plans of nations, frustrates the councels of peoples") as supporting this explanation. Next he elucidates why this action is an act of religion: it is connected with the honor of God, because the sinners are punished (citing Pr 5,22, Is 5,18) and the priests were there more for their own good than to honor God (citing Ezk 44,8); further He announced the end of the time of the sacrifices in the temple (citing Mt 21,43) and He condemned those selling *spiritualia* (citing Ac 8,20).[119] So although at first it may seem that Christ went beyond what is virtuous, He did not, Thomas says. He never did, because of the hypostatic union with the divine Word[120], unlike other human beings who may be carried away by their feelings and think about it only later on, maybe regretting what they did.[121] The inference of this is, that we are to hold that Christ was *morally* perfect.

This conclusion exemplifies again that Thomas does not regard

---

impediebatur.

[119] REI c.2 l.2 n.5.

[120] ST IIIa q.7 a.1co: *[N]ecesse est ponere in Christo* gratiam habitualem. [....] *Primo quidem propter unionem animae ad Verbum Dei.* Ibidem a.2co: *[S]icut in Secunda parte* [IaIIae q.110 a.4] *habitum est, sicut gratia respicit essentiam animae, ita virtus respicit eius potentia. Unde oportet quod sicut potentiae animae derivantur ab eius essentia, ita virtutes sunt quaedam derivationes gratiae.* Quando aliquod principium est perfectius, tanto magis imprint suos effectus. Unde, *cum gratia Christi fuerit perfectissima, consequens est quod ex ipsa processerint virtutes ad perficiendum singulas potentias animae, quantum ad* omnes *animae actus.* SN III d.33 intr. n.6: *Et ideo immortalis est omnino iustitia, nec in illa beatitudine esse desinet, sed* talis ac tanta erit ut perfectior ac maior esse non possit. *Fortassis et aliae tres virtutes: prudentia sine ullo iam periculo erroris, fortitudo sine molestia tolerandorum malorum, temperantia sine repugnantia libidinum.*

[121] ST IaIIae q.6 a.7 ad 3, cf. IIIa q.15 a.4co: *[I]n nobis plerumque huiusmodi passiones feruntur ad illicita: quod in Christus non fuit.*

passio as such as something negative, as long as it is not leading to sin:

> "Each time such an appetite is without sin, it is
> praiseworthy, for instance when someone longs for
> punishment according to the order of justice. And this,
> says Augustine in his commentary on Jn 2,17, is called
> anger by zeal."[122]

What may be unsatisfying in Thomas' exposition, is that he on the one hand stresses Christ's true humanity, whilst at the same time he holds that Christ never let Himself go. However, on closer consideration it is plain that letting yourself go, so to say, is not constitutive of being human. Someone who does not kick over the traces is on that account not less human. In other words, one does not become more human by sinning; on the contrary rather.[123]

Still what Thomas says is hard to imagine. Yet in the former chapter it was shown already that Thomas is not interested in the psychological side of the story. He is trying to explain what the consequences of our faith in the Incarnation are. He can only do so by using the same method as for his God-talk: negative theology. It is clear that by doing so the mystery of Christ's humanity, and divinity, is

---

[122] ST IIIa q.15 a.9co: *Quando vero talis appetitus est sine peccato, immo est* laudabilis*: puta cum aliquis appetit vindictam secundum ordinem iustitiae. Et hoc vocatur ira per zelum, dicit enim Augustinus Super Io.* [2,17 = Ps 69,10, cited in a.9co] Therefore, SN III d.13 q.1 a.2a ad 2: [*P*]*assiones, quibus caro contra spiritum concupiscit: quod in Christo non fuit; sed quantum ad alios usus, secundum quos erunt in Patris* [= *secundum ordinem iustitiae*] *plenissime in Christo fuerunt; et etiam quantum ad quosdam usus viae, qui* eius perfectioni non derogabant, *inquantum est verus viator et comprehensor.* However, later on in SN *passio* still has a negative flavour, SN III d.15 q.2 a.1c ad 2: [*P*]*erfecta virtus* non omnino *tollit animales passiones, quia et aliquando utitur eis, sicut fortitudo ira.* [....] *Sed facit ut nulla passio surgat quae rationem impediat. In Christo autem* amplius *fuit, quia in eo fuit perfecta obedientia virium inferiorum ad superiores; ideo* nulla passio *in eo surgebat* nisi ex ordine rationis. It seems that Thomas by saying this implicitly refers to Heb 4,15, 1 P 2,22 and 1 Jn 3,5, 9.

[123] As we read for, instance, in Ezk 18,4, Jn 5,14, Rm 6,16 and 1 Jn 3,9, cf. ST Ia q.63 a.9co: [*P*]*eccatum est* contra naturalem inclinationem (of angels and human beings: q.94 a.1); IaIIae q.102 a.5 ad 4: .... *immunditiam peccati, quod est* mors *animae*; IIIa q.22 a.4 ad 1: *Christus autem, simpliciter loquendo, peccatum non habuit: habuit tamen* "similitudinem peccati, in carne", ut dicitur Rom. 8,3.

deepened rather than fathomed.

Not only *passio* in the most and less proper senses of the word befits Christ, but also *passio* in the common sense of the word. In Lk 2,52 we read that Christ increased in wisdom. Since He had a human soul, He had a human intellect too.[124] Thomas distinguishes between the objects of the intellect, in order to clarify in what way Christ is also in respect of knowledge called *viator* and *comprehensor*:[125] the human mind is directed towards two: the higher things, concerning God, and the lower things, creation. Concerning the higher things the man Christ had a full, infused[126] knowledge (*scientiam inditam*). In this sense He is called *comprehensor*. But in respect of the lower things we are to say that Christ was *viator* as well, for He also acquired knowledge (*scientiam acquisitam*) during His earthly life:

> "In this respect the knowledge of Christ was brought to fullness. Not in the sense that the first fulness of His human mind (at the incarnation) had not been enough by itself; but it was becoming that it was perfected also by comparing this knowledge with deceptions."[127]

---

[124] ST IIIa q.5 aa.3, 4. Thomas says that he has changed his opinion on this point since his *Sententiae*, ST IIIa q.9 a.4co: *quamvis aliter alibi scripserim*; here he refutes his own explanation of Heb 5,8 in SN III d.14 a.3e ad 3, by taking over the argumentation of ag.3. Aristotle's thoughts (in I and II *De coelo* and III *De anima*) support Thomas' argumentation in ST.

[125] QDV q.20 a.3 ad 1: [C]*um Christus est comprehensor et viator, habuit utrumque modum considerandi*; cf. ST IIIa q.9 aa.1, 2.

[126] ST IIIa q.9 a.4co: *Scientia autem infusa attribuitur animae humanae secundum lumen desuper infusum.* [....] *Scientia vero beata, per quam ipsa Dei essentia videtur, est propria et connaturalis soli Deo, ut in Prima Parte* [q.12 a.4] *dictum est.*

[127] ST IIIa q.9 a.4 ad 2: [S]*ecundum hunc respectum anima Christi scientia impleretur: non quin prima plenitudo menti humanae sufficeret secundum seipsam; sed oportebat eam perfici* etiam *secundum comparationem ad phantasmata.* And this is also how Thomas explains Lk 2,52 in q.12 a.2, citing Doctor of the Church Ambrose (*De Incarn. Dni., sacram.* c.7, ML 16,872) as an authority.

In OTT, at the end of c.226, Thomas adds that Lk 2,52 can also be understood in this way, that Christ's wisdom among the people increased, because they were taught

The formulation a bit later in the *Tertia Pars*, where Thomas explains Mt 8,10 ("When Jesus heard this, He was astonished"), is clearer:

"Still there could be something new and unfamiliar for Him according to His experiential knowledge. And in this way some new things could occur to Him daily."[128]

"Daily" underlines that this is not something exceptional in Christ's life on earth. But this *passio*, this perfection of His knowledge, cannot be but confined to knowledge by finding out (*per inventionem*) with regard to creation; the knowledge of creation which other people acquire by studying and the so called higher knowledge concerning God were infused in Christ. Hence, Thomas says, Christ's knowledge and wisdom were not His own, but God's, as in 1 Co 1,24.[129]

After this inquiry the conclusion must be that since only God is perfect in the absolute sense of the word, it follows that everything that is not-God is by definition in this sense imperfect. Therefore, calling the man Christ imperfect is like mentioning that snow is white. Hence we do not speak of Christ as imperfect insofar as He is human, since it is redundant; imperfection is implied in Christ being a human being: body and soul.

But, since it is not obvious that a human being is, even as a

---

by Him. They were taught in stages, not at once, for then people might not attach credence to the mystery of the Incarnation.

[128] ST IIIa q.15 a.8co: *Potuit tamen esse aliquid sibi novum et insolitum secundum scientiam experimentalem, secundum quam sibi poterant* quotidie *aliqua* nova *occurere.* Whereas in SN III d.18 a.3 ad 5 Thomas still holds that *dicendum quod Christus non habeat acceptam a sensibus scientiam, sed infusam.* This leads to the conclusion that Thomas grew in his understanding of the mystery of Christ's humanity over the years.

[129] And this is how Thomas explains Jn 7,15f, in ST IIIa q.9 a.4 ad 1, and Mt 13,54f as well, in REI c.7 l.2 nn.3 (*"Mirabilia testimonia tua"* [Ps 119,129] *Verba enim Christi verba sunt sapientiae divinae*), 4. In REM c.13 n.4 (on Mt 13,54) Thomas refers to 1 Co 1,24 and 2,6ff.

human being, perfect in soul and body[130], calling a person who is perfect(ed), as in Ep 4,13 and also 2 Co 5,21 and Heb 2,10, *does* add information. The perfection meant in these texts is Christ's moral perfection. That Christ was also perfect as regards His body, is implied in texts like Mt 1,18 and Lk 1,35, where it says that Mary, His mother, conceived by the Holy Spirit, as was explained in paragraph 1.3.2.[131] And exactly the perfect composition of Christ's body made Him most sensitive to *passio*, or, in terms of this paragraph, exposed Him to the highest extent to imperfection.

In this paragraph it was shown that the word *passio* signifies an undergoing that is accompanied by a change. From this it follows that *passio* presupposes imperfection and in the proper senses of the word also a body. Hence, Thomas concludes, *passio* does not befit God, but it does befit Christ during His earthly life, insofar as He is a human being - with the exception of the higher parts of the soul, for the reasons mentioned here and in chapter 1; Christ is a true human being, but not a pure human being.

The conclusion that God and undergoing are incompatible, raises the questions how Thomas evaluates texts in Scripture according to which God does undergo *passiones*. In paragraph 2.1 it was shown that love and joy, provided that they are without *passio*, befit God in the proper sense of the word. But how then are we to understand that Scripture says of God that He detests (Ps 11,5, Is 1,24, Am 6,8) and hates (Dt 12,31, Is 61,8, Am 5,15, Zc 8,17), is jealous (Dt 5,9, Jos 24,19, Ezk 39,25), desires (Jb 14,15, Hos 6,6), is frightened (Is 7,16, "abhors" in some translations), is furious (Ex 15,7) and vengeful (Na 1,2), to mention some *passiones*, and even that He hopes (LXX-Ps 59,8, 107,9)? In paragraph 2.1.1 we came already across Scripture texts speaking of God's anger and sadness (Ps 30,6, 106,40, Is 1,24, 57,17 resp. Gn 6,6, Ps 78,40, Ep

---

[130] Texts like Jn 8,7 ("Let the one among you who is guiltless be the first to throw a stone at her"), Rm 2,1, Ph 3,12 and Jm 3,2 may come to mind.

[131] *Ibi* note 141; REI c.1 1.9 n.4: *Christus enim* in instanti suae conceptionis *fuit* perfectus Deus, et perfectus homo, *habens rationalem animam perfectam virtutibus, et corpus omnibus lineamentis distinctum, non tamen secundum quantitatem perfectam* (cf. SN III d.3 q.5 aa.2, 3, SCG IV c.44, OTT c.218, ST IIIa q.33) - otherwise the body could not have grown.

4,30) and His (great) compassion (Ex 34,6, Ne 9,17, 31, Si 2,11, Jl 2,13, Jon 4,2, Jm 5,11). Is this God not a passionate God?

The same question arises with regard to Scripture texts that speak of God as having a body. For instance Jb 11,8f speaks of God's height, depth, length and breadth; Gn 1,26 and Heb 1,3 speak of human beings, corporeal, being created in God's image; Jb 40,4, Ps 34,16 and 118,16 speak of respectively God's arm, eye and right hand - and we came already accross Ex 3,7-10 and Ezk 16,5-7: God sees and hears and is moved with pity; Is 3,13 and 6,1 speak of God standing and sitting; since one can approach God and turn away from Him, as in Vulg-Ps 33,6 and Jr 17,13, it seems that He occupies space.[132] If God is not corporeal, as was shown above, how are we to understand such texts? These questions will be dealt with in the next paragraph.

Yet another issue must be touched upon; Thomas, citing Origen, says that the cleansing of the temple was done by the divine might *of Jesus* (*divina potestas Jesus*). In chapter 4, after the consideration of the might of God, the nature of the might of Jesus Christ will be considered.

2.3 Nevertheless a *Passio*nate God?

In the foregoing it was shown that when we consider what we read in Scripture concerning the *passio(nes)* of Christ and God, we have to take a closer look at our language, at what we say and in what way. This paragraph will explain that Thomas designates ascribing *passio(nes)* to God as metaphorical language. What he understands by metaphor in our God-talk will be explored first (2.3.1). Next we will inquire what ground metaphors are used for God (2.3.2). By doing so a further answer is formulated to Jüngel's critique that Thomas presents God as distant and uncannily alien. With the results of these subparagraphs in mind Thomas' thoughts on the *compassio* of God will be considered (2.3.3). But just when the reader might think that according to Thomas God cannot undergo *passio*, that He cannot suffer, we come to the conclusion that we are to hold that this verdict is false, in the light of the cross of Christ (2.3.4).

---

[132] ST Ia q.3 a.1 ag.1-5.

2.3.1 Passionate God-talk

Right from the first page of the *Summa Theologiae* Thomas' attention on language is clear. He describes the purpose of the work as passing on what belongs to the Christian faith in a way suitable for beginners (yes!).[133] In order to do so the content of the Christian faith is to be formulated in words, human creature-words. This means that with regard to God we speak with creature-words of what is not a creature. And this is where the shoe pinches.

Thomas distinguishes three ways of proper speaking about God. One is the negative way, that is saying what God is not by denying what does not befit Him, like composedness, being moved, time etc. The second is the positive way and the third is in terms of relation between God and creatures.[134] In *De Veritate* Thomas makes another distinction regarding our God-talk. The positive words used *in divinis* can be classified into two groups:

> "One is the proper way of speech, that is when we attribute to God what befits Him according to His nature. [....] The other way is attribution according to figurative, that is metaphorical or symbolical, speech."[135]

Examples of the former are "God is love", "God is good" and "God is mighty". This is what Thomas calls analoguous language. It will be discussed in further detail in paragraph 3.4.2.

---

[133] ST intr.: *Propositum nostrae intentionis in hoc opere est, ea quae ad Christianam religionem pertinent, eo modo* tradere, *secundum quod congruit ad eruditionem incipientium.*

[134] ST Ia q.3 intr.: *Negative: Potest autem ostendi de Deo quomodo non sit, removendo ab eo ea quae ei non conveniunt, utpote compositionem, motum et alia huiusmodi.* This is done by Thomas in qq.3-11. *Affirmative*: q.13 aa.2-6. *Quae relationem ipsius* [= *Dei*] *ad creaturam significant*: q.13 a.7.

[135] QDV q.23 a.3co: *Unus* [*modus loquendi in divinis est*] *secundum propriam locutionem: quando scilicet Deo attribuimus id quod sibi competit secundum suam naturam;* [....] *Alius modus est secundum figurativam sive tropicam vel symbolicam locutionem.*

Language concerning God is called metaphorical by Thomas, when a word designating something corporeal and thus created, is used for what is spiritual and divine, which is done often in Scripture.[136]

"Just as in Holy Scripture properties of intellectual [i.e. immaterial] things are described in sensible figures according to similitudes."[137]

For instance when God is called a consuming fire, as in Dt 4,24, or a rock, as in Ps 31,3, no one understands these propositions as proper speech. But in the light of what has been said in this chapter about *passio* and God's divinity it must be said that even God's laughing, as in Ps 2,4, and regretting, as in 1 S 15,11 (which is a change, cf. 9,17), are examples of metaphorical language, since these verses presuppose a body, composedness and imperfection, which are incompatible with the divinity of God.

Thomas speaks of metaphorical language as the least problematic way of speaking positively of God. He gives two reasons. First, metaphors signify only a partial similarity, in the case of God between God and a creature. Thomas gives the example of calling God a lion, as in Jb 10,16 and Is 38,13:

"It means nothing else than that God is in a similar way powerful in His works as a lion is in his."[138]

For if a word corresponds with a thing in all respects, it is not a meta-

---

[136] ST Ia q.1 a.9co: *divina et spiritualia* sub similitudine corporalium *tradere* [....]; *[I]n sacra Scriptura traduntur nobis spiritualia sub metaphoris corporalium.*

[137] ST Ia q.51 a.2 ad 2: *Sicut enim in Sacra Scriptura proprietates rerum intelligibilium* sub similitudinibus rerum sensibilium *describuntur.* Cf. q.10 a.1 ad 4: *Deus, cum sit incorporeus, nominibus rerum corporalium* metaphorice *in Scripturis nominatur.*

[138] ST Ia q.13 a.6co: [*Omnia nomina, quae metaphorice de Deo dicuntur,*] *nihil aliud significant quam similitudines ad tales creaturas.* [....] *Sic nomen leonis, dictum de Deo, nihil aliud significat quam quod Deus* similiter *se habet, ut fortiter operetur in suis operibus, sicut leo in suis.*

phor, but the proper name of the thing.[139] This use of metaphors *in divinis*, Thomas continues, is not different from how they are used for creatures, for instance when we say that a pasture is smiling (as in Is 35,1f), meaning that it is as beautiful as a human being when he/she smiles. And since a metaphor always signifies a resemblance in a certain respect only, a particular word used as a metaphor can mean something quite different in different contexts. The word stone, for instance, used for a person, may refer to a stone on the road being a stumbling block as well as to the hardness of the stone.[140]

Still the use of metaphors in God-talk is not *un*problematic. For comparisons between God and creatures always fall short. Thomas' view of metaphors for God is not germane to the proportionality scheme (a:b::c:d), because he regards God and creature as of different orders; one is the Creator and the other a creature. In the example of God being powerful in His works as a lion is in his, we must not forget that God's power is not related to God as the lion's power is to a lion and also that the exercise of the respective powers differs. This will be clarified in the next chapter. Still a similarity referred to by a metaphor is not totally spurious. Yet because of their vagueness, that is their polysemy, Thomas rules out metaphors in definitions.[141]

---

[139] ST Ia q.33 a.3co: *[P]er prius dicitur nomen de illo in quo salvatur tota ratio nominis perfecte, quam de illo in quo salvatur secundum aliquid, quia omnia imperfecta sumuntur a perfectis. Et inde est quod hoc nomen leo per prius dicitur de animali in quo* tota *ratio leonis salvatur, quod* proprie *dicitur leo, quam de aliquo homine in quo invenitur aliquid de ratione leonis, ut puta audacia vel fortitudo, vel aliquid huiusmodi: de hoc enim* per similitudinem *dicitur.* Ibidem IIIa q.8 a.2 ad 2: *[I]n metaphoricis locutionibus non oportet attendi* similitudinem quantum ad omnia*: sic enim non esset similitudo, sed rei veritas.*

[140] QDV q.4 a.1 ad 8: *sicut lapis imponitur ab effectu qui est laedere pedem*, as in Ps 91,12; SCG I c.30 n.2: *sicut aliquis homo dicitur lapis propter duritiam intellectus*, as in Jb 6,12 and Jr 5,3.

[141] SN I prol. a.5: *Ad destructionem autem errorum non proceditur nisi per sensum litteralem, eo quod alii sensus sunt per similitudines accepti et ex similitudinariis locutionibus non potest sumi argumentatio; unde et Dionysius dicit in Epistola ad Titum, quod* symbolica theologia non est argumentativa. Cf. e.g. ST IaIIae q.33 a.1 ad 1: *[N]ihil prohibet in his quae dicuntur metaphorice, idem diversis attribui secundum diversas similitudines.* Even stronger in C1C c.1 l.3 (on 1 Co 1,17): *Tunc autem maxime modus aliquis docendi est materiae incongruus, quando per talem modum destruitur id quod est*

The second reason why Thomas considers metaphors *in divinis* the least problematic positive language, is that

> "all names that are being said of God metaphorically, are rather said of creatures than of God, for these things said of God, do not signify anything else than similarities to these creatures."[142]

In other words, in metaphorical language the way we speak, the *modus significandi*, suits what is referred to, the *res significata*. Thus metaphors used for God do not denote perfections properly, like the words "good" and "mighty" do,[143] in the absolute sense of the word, but merely comparisons with (particular aspects of) particular creatures.[144]

And yet, on the basis of Thomas' definition of metaphor *in divinis* one should not conclude that he values the cool, analytical language of theology higher than the warm, flowery, metaphorical language of Scripture, as if theology had a better language for God-talk than Scripture. For Thomas a metaphor is not *merely* a metaphor. On the con-

---

principale in materia illa, puta si quis in rebus intellectualibus velit metaphoricis demonstrationibus uti, quae non transcendunt res imaginatas, ad quas non oportet intelligentem adduci.

[142] ST Ia q.13 a.6co: *Sic ergo omnia nomina quae metaphorice de Deo dicuntur, per prius de creaturis dicuntur quam de Deo: quia dicta de Deo,* nihil aliud *significant* quam similitudines ad tales creaturas.

[143] ST Ia q.13 a.3 ad 1: *Quaedam vero nomina significant ipsas perfectiones absolute, absque hoc quod aliquis modus participandi claudatur in eorum significatione, ut ens, bonum, vivens et huiusmodi: et talia* proprie *dicuntur de Deo.*

[144] SN I d.34 q.3 a.1co: *[E]t ideo cum de omnibus quae de Deo dicimus, intelligendum sit quod non eodem modo sibi conveniunt sicut in creaturis inveniuntur, sed* per aliquem modum imitationis et similitudinis. [....] *Haec autem sunt corporalia; et ideo convenientius fuit speciebus corporalibus divina significari, ut his assuefactus humanus animus disceret,* nihil *eorum quae de Deo praedicat sibi attribuere* nisi per quandam similitudinem, secundum quod creatura imitatur Creatorem. Ibidem ad 2: *[U]t Deus dicatur ignis ex hoc quod sicut se habet ignis ad hoc quod liquefacta effluere facit per suum calorem,* ita *Deus per suam bonitatem perfectiones in omnes creaturas diffundit, vel aliquid huiusmodi.*

trary rather; for him the, often metaphorical, language of Scripture is the normative starting-point of theological reflection. And his great appreciation of metaphorical language is reflected in the first *quaestio* of the *Summa Theologiae*. Despite the fundamental dissimilarities between God and the metaphor, the use of metaphors *in divinis* is, according to Thomas, not only befitting (*conveniens*), but even "necessary" and "useful".[145] He explains this as follows. First Thomas observes that a human being begins to know through the senses; all our knowledge starts with an apprehension through the senses. This befits our nature; it is how God has made us. Hence, if God wants us to know spiritual things, it is becoming so to say, that He does so by metaphors of corporeal things.[146] It is not only becoming, for

> "it is impossible to let the radiance of God shine for us,
> unless through a variety of sacred veils that veil it."[147]

And by means of this quote from Pseudo-Dionysius' *De caelestis hierarchiae* Thomas refers to Ex 33,18-22, Nb 4,20, 1 Tm 6,16 etc.: during our earthly life we cannot see God as He is. We need many metaphors, for this reason, in order to see more of the greatness and the glory of God. For through them we catch a glimpse of it, as when a bright light shines through a veil.

Moreover, metaphors also make the word of God accessible to the unlettered (*rudes*). Thomas cites Rm 1,14 ("I [St. Paul] have an obligation to Greeks as well as other gentiles, to the educated as well as the ignorant [....] to preach the gospel"), from which it is obvious that the good news of God is not meant for the educated alone, but for all people (*communiter omnibus*). One does not need to be an academic

---

[145] ST Ia q.1 a.9 ad 1: *[S]acra doctrina utitur metaphoris propter necessitatem et utilitatem.*

[146] ST Ia q.1 a.9co: *Deus enim omnibus providet secundum quod competit eorum naturae. Est autem naturale homini ut per sensibilia ad intelligibilia veniat: quia* omnis *nostra cognitio a sensu initium habet. Unde convenienter in sacra Scriptura traduntur nobis spiritualia sub metaphoris corporalium.*

[147] ST Ia q.1 a.9co: *[D]icit Dionysius I. cap. Cealestis hierarchie* [par.2, MG 3,121]: "*Impossibile est nobis* aliter *lucere divinum radium, nisi varietate sacrorum velaminum circumvelatum.*"

theologian in order to believe. And we see that this thought is supported by e.g. Mt 13,34f; during His earthly life Christ taught many illiterate people. Thomas adds in his commentary on Boetius' *De Trinitate*, explaining 1 Co 3,1f ("I was not able to speak to you as spiritual people, [....] being still infants in Christ") that those who do not (yet) grasp the subtleties of the Christian faith, would rather be harmed than helped by the use of exclusively analytical language.[148]

But even for scholars metaphors are not in any way redundant. Thomas calls them useful (*utilis*), as an exercise. Since he does not go further into this, it almost sounds as "at least they have something to do." But in the broader context it seems that Thomas rather means that considering metaphors sharpens a scholar's theological thinking. Metaphors are also useful because they conceal the divine things from those who do not believe and laugh at them, referring to Mt 7,6 ("Do not give dogs what is holy; do not throw your pearls in front of pigs").[149]

Thomas does not speak of the usefulness and necessity of metaphors for people who are neither unlettered nor scholars. But from these extremes it is clear that Thomas esteems metaphors in Scripture and theology highly. Metaphorical language is in no way labeled inferior by Thomas; metaphors are not 'only' metaphors, but are most useful and necessary for our faith and our speech about the mystery of God.

2.3.2 Suitable Metaphors

In paragraph 2.1 it was said that, on the basis of Gn 1,26 and Rm 1,20, we draw comparisons between God and creatures. In fact this is done throughout Scripture. Comparisons are possible because God is the origin of all creation. Creation is an effect of God, of God's action. Now an agent acts in accordance with who he/she is, or, in Scriptural

---

[148] CBT q.2 a.4co, citing Lk 8,10 (cf. Mt 13,10-16).

[149] ST Ia q.1 a.9 ad 2: *Et ipsa etiam occultatio figurarum utilis est,* ad *exercitium studiosorum,* et contra *irrisiones infidelium, de quibus dicitur Mt 7,6: "Nolite sanctum dare canibus."*

language, "you will be able to tell them by their fruits".[150] Therefore,

> "when a certain effect is more manifest to us than its cause, we come to the knowledge of the cause through the effect."[151]

And this applies in particular to God, whose essence we do not know, as was said. Hence, since, according to Scripture, creation is intrinsically good, even very good[152], the inference of this is that the metaphors used must reflect something of God's goodness. Therefore metaphors which signify something sinful or evil - Thomas gives the example of the word devil - are not used for God.[153] And the same applies to God's love, might and knowledge etc.; metaphors that deny these attributes of God are unsuitable.

Thomas holds that the common-or-garden metaphors (*vilium*) are preferable to metaphors of noble bodies (*nobilium*). The latter are not unsuitable,[154] but the use of the former has three advantages. First of all, the use of these keeps the human mind from error. For it is obvious that calling God a vinedresser, as in Jn 15,1, is not proper language in respect of the divinity of God. But since the word "king" signifies something exalted and powerful, "YHWH is king," as in Ps 93,1 97,1,

---

[150] Mt 7,16, 20, cf. Si 27,6, Jm 3,12; ST Ia q.4 a.3co: *Cum enim omne agens agat sibi simile in quantum est agens, agit autem unumquodque secundum suam formam, necesse est quod in effectu sit similitudo formae agentis.*

[151] ST Ia q.2 a.2co: *Cum enim effectus aliquis nobis est manifestior quam sua causa, per effectum procedimus ad cognitionem causae.*

[152] Gn 1,31, cited in ST Ia q.47 a.2co, q.63 a.5sc, IaIIae q.9 a.6 ag.3.

[153] SN I d.34 q.3 a.2 ad 2: *[Q]uaedam nomina creaturarum sunt quae non nominant tantum id quod creatum est, sed etiam* defectum culpae *annexum; sicut nomen diaboli nominat* naturam deformatam peccato: *Et ido talibus nominibus nos possumus transsumptive uti ad significandum divina.*

[154] SN I d.34 q.3 a.2co: *Invenitur tamen etiam in nobilioribus creaturis Deus significari in Scriptura, sicut sole et stella; non tamen ita frequenter.* Thomas omits this remark in ST; rightly so, it seems, since God is called "king" quite frequently in Scripture and "king" refers to nobility.

99,1 etc., may erroneously be interpreted as proper language with regard to God's divinity, whilst it is not. A second advantage is that common-or-garden metaphors are more in conformity with the imperfect way in which we know God; they show us more how God is not than how He is. And finally, in line with Mt 7,6, they hide the divine things from those unworthy (*indignis*) of them.[155]

So very few metaphors are as such unsuitable.[156] On the basis of things or events in our world, in the light of our faith interpreted as the effect of God's action, we use metaphors to name the Unnamable.

2.3.3 A Compassionate God?

Scripture speaks of God's compassion (paragraph 2.1.1 note 46) and many experience and have experienced His compassion. That is for theologians like Jüngel the basis for ascribing suffering to God, as an expression of His love. But other modern theologians, like Metz, detect a lot of snags in this view. In contrast, Thomas' interpretation not only seems to bear the test of Metz's critique, but also seems to be more Scriptural *and* more consoling than Jüngel's. In order to see this, first Jüngel's position is set out, followed by an evaluation of it in view of Thomas and Metz.

Thomas appeals to a general experience where he says that when someone in trouble enjoys *compassio* of a friend, it is as if this person helps you bear the burden; it becomes lighter (*ideo levius fert tristitiae onus*), like when someone gives you a hand while you carry something heavy. Moreover, Thomas continues, when someone is sad with you, it is a sign that you are loved. And this makes you rejoice, which leads to an

---

[155] ST Ia q.1 a.9 ad 3. The examples from Scripture given are not explicitly mentioned by Thomas.

[156] In Scripture we even read that the metaphor of a thief is used for Christ, in Mt 24,43f, Lk 12,39f, 1 Th 5,2 and Rv 3,3. However, the point of comparison here is neither the stealing, as in Jn 12,6, where the word "thief" used for Judas is not a metaphor, but a proper name; nor is it the violence by means of which a thief may force an entry, as in Jl 2,9. The metaphor of the thief for Christ refers to the unknown hour of His coming alone; a metaphor signifies only a similarity in a particular respect. And the same applies to for instance God as a warrior and as a woman in labour (Is 42,13f).

alleviation of the pain and a mitigation of the sadness.[157] This is true for interpersonal relations. And likewise it is experienced by many in their relationships to the saints, angels, Christ and God.[158]

In line of this Jüngel speaks of *God's* compassion as His suffering along with the Crucified and the crucified. He does so on trinitarian grounds. Since the economical trinity is not another trinity than the immanent trinity, the consequence of God being love is that God is lovingly concerned with Himself: the Father loves the Son. A further inference is that God is lovingly concerned with His creation. This concern is highlighted in giving Himself to us in the Son on the cross and in this, that the Son did this out of love of the Father and of us. By saying this Jüngel criticizes what he calls the theological tradition which understood God as a merely ("schlechthin") self-concerned being. Jüngel argues that his view is in accordance with what we read in Scripture. He refers to Rm 8,32 ("God gave Him up *for the sake of all of us*") 3,16 (supposedly *Jn* 3,16 is meant, where it reads "For this is how God loved the world: He gave His only Son, so that everyone who believes in Him may not parish, but may have eternal life") and Ga 2,20 ("... the Son of God, who loved me and gave Himself for me"). On the basis of this and on the assumption that *passio* is inherent to love, Jüngel comes to the conclusion that the cross of Christ denies God's apathy and immutability[159]:

> "That the God, who is love, must be *able* to suffer and *does* suffer *beyond all limits* in the giving up of what is most authentically his for the sake of mortal man, is an indispensable insight of the newer theology schooled by Luther's christology and Hegel's philosophy. Only the God who is identical with the Crucified One makes us

---

[157] ST IaIIae q.38 a.3co.

[158] As it is formulated in ST Ia q.113 a.7 and in the *Supplementum* (which is nota bene not written by Thomas but after his death compiled from earlier works of his, esp. SN) q.94 a.2 ag.2: *Deus quodammodo miseriis nostris compatitur, unde et misericors dicitur; et similiter angeli. Ergo beati compatientur miseriis damnatorum*, cf. SN II d.11 q.1 a.5.

[159] Jüngel, *o.c.*, 505-511 (368-373).

certain of His love and thus of himself"[160] (italics added, MR)

An infinite suffering in God is too much for Thévenot.[161] As an alternative to what he calls Thomas' "strictly passive" view he opts for the interpretation of compassion as a being present with warm attachment, like Mary at the foot of the cross of her son (Jn 19,25).

As was said, according to Thomas *passio*, and therefore also *compassio*, does not befit God, since God and *passio* are incompatible. Thus even Moltmann's patricompassianism[162] or *compassio* insofar as God allows Himself to undergo any kind of *passio* does not befit Him. But first of all one needs to see that *compassio* is not the same as what we call compassion; *compassio* is used by Thomas meaning "suffering with" and "undergoing with". Indeed, the reason why someone suffers with a suffering person, says Thomas, is usually a close attachment, a friendship, as was said above. Yet, although in our word "compassion" the meaning of attachment or concern is included, and although it is closely connected with the word *compassio* as Thomas uses it, this concern is not included in the Latin term *compassio* itself. Therefore, Thomas denying *compassio* in God, neither says nor in any way means that God would be unconcerned. It is in the same way that Thomas speaks of the friendship between God and us, yet from God's side without *passio* (paragraph 2.1.1).

God is love. *Passio* is not inherent to love. That denying *compassio* in God by no means signifies a defect in His love, is also clear from what Thomas says about the (other) citizens of heaven. Where Thomas considers the loving concern of the angels with us, he formulates the thought of those who hold that, since in adversity (*mala*) *compati* is a

---

[160] Jüngel, *o.c.*, 511 (373): Daß der Gott, der Liebe ist, leiden *können* muß und in der Dahingabe seines Eigensten um des endlichen Menschen willen *unendlich leidet*, ist eine unaufgebbare Erkenntnis der durch Luthers Christologie und Hegels Philosophie geschulten neueren Theologie. Der mit dem Gekreuzigten identische Gott allein macht uns seiner Liebe und also seiner selbst gewiß. [italics added, MR]

[161] Thévenot (1990), esp. 80-82.

[162] Moltmann (1973), 359.

part of friendships between human beings, the angels, who love us with most fervent love (*ferventissima caritate nos diligunt*), must suffer with (*compati*) us when we suffer. After all, reversely, they rejoice over a repenting sinner (cf. Lk 15,7).[163] Could then not the same be said of Christ in heaven and of God, who *is* love? But Thomas shows that this contradicts what we read in Scripture:

> "In the beyond there will neither be death nor mourning
> nor sadness nor *any* pain."[164] (italics added, MR)

As if Rv 21,4 were not emphatic enough, Thomas adds "any" to the text: there is no eternal suffering. How then, Thomas wonders, are we to interpret Is 33,7, where we read of the tears of messengers of peace, in the light of this text. His answer is that, if these messengers are identified as heavenly angels, which is one of the possible interpretations of this text, it is a metaphorical saying, expressing that the angels want in general the good of humankind.

> "For thus this kind of *passiones* are (in Scripture often)
> attributed to God and to the angels."[165]

From this it is clear that, as with regard to *passio*, denying *compassio* in God (and the angels) has nothing to do with an imperfection as regards His (and their) love, but with His (and their) *impassibilitas*, as was

---

[163] SN II d.11 q.1 a.5 ag.2, 3, ST Ia q.113 a.7; in ST *damnatio hominum* is broadened to *mala eorum quos [angeli] custodiunt*.

[164] ST Ia q.113 a.7sc: [D]*icitur Apoc.* [21,4]*: Mors ultra non erit, neque luctus, neque clamor, neque* ullus *dolor*.

[165] ST Ia q.113 a.7 ad 1: *Sic enim* [SN II d.11 q.2 a.5 ad 1 adds: *fequenter in Scripturis*] *Deo et angelis huiusmodi passiones attribuuntur*. This identification would be according to the *sensus analogicus*; according to the *sensus litteralis* the messengers are (human) delegates of king Hizkia (mentioned in Is 36,22 and 37,2ff); according to the *sensus allegoricus* the messengers are the apostles and other preachers of the gospel.

explained above.[166] That Thomas denies (com)passio in God exemplifies, what Jüngel fails to see, that he is a negative theologian.

And the same applies to Christ after the resurrection, although He does not have a celestial, untouchable body, as we read in Mt 28,9 (cf. Jn 20,17), Lk 24,39, Jn 20,27 and 21,13:

> "Now the body of Christ after the resurrection was truly composed of elements. It had such qualities, that it could be touched, as is required for the nature of a human body. And therefore it was naturally touchable. And if He had not had anything additional to the nature of the human body, it even would have been corruptible (and therefore passible and mortal). However, He had something else, that made it incorruptible: yet not the nature of a celestial body, as some say [....], but the overflowing glory from the beatic soul."[167]

This overflow was prevented by Him during His earthly life, as was said in paragraph 1.3.3. And therefore neither Christ's living body, nor His soul united to it[168], experience any passio, in the most proper sense of suffering, after the resurrection. In this way Thomas formulates the mystery of Christ's true humanity after the resurrection, in the light of our faith that in the hereafter humankind will be freed of all suffering and

---

[166] SN II d.11 q.2 a.5 ad 2: [C]ompati non potest qui passibilis non est; et ideo ex impassibilitate angelorum hoc accedit quod condolere non possunt, non ex caritatis defectu.

[167] ST IIIa q.54 a.2 ad 2: Corpus autem Christi vere post resurrectionem fuit ex elementis compositum, habens in se tangibiles qualitates, secundum quod requirit natura corporis humani: et ideo naturaliter erat palpabile. Et si nihil aliud habuisset supra corporis humani naturam, fuisset etiam corruptibile. Habuit autem aliquid aliud quod ipsum incorruptibile reddidit: non quidem naturam caelestis corporis ut quidam dicunt [....], sed gloriam redundantem ab anima beata.

[168] OTT c.237: Et quia anima Christi ante mortem passibilis erat secundum passionem corporis, consequens est ut corpore impassibili facto, etiam anima impassibilis reddetur.

death.[169]

On the basis of what is said hitherto it is clear that God's impassibility of God does not allow for a Stoic interpretation: God is not apathetic, neither according to Scripture nor according to Thomas. Therefore, calling the *impassibilitas Dei* "the axiom of apathy of classical theology", as Jüngel does[170], reflects that a person confuses not only God's impassibility with Stoic apathy, but also negative theology and theism. Thus the negative theologian Thomas denies apathy in the impassible, loving and caring, incredibly close *and* distant God, as well as *passio*.

Since compassion does not signify anything evil, it is a suitable metaphor for God. When we speak of God as compassionate, we speak metaphorically, if "compassion(ate)" implies *(com)passio*. This is not necessarily the case, for Thomas also speaks of a kind of compassion which can be without *(com)passio*: *misericordia*. And in this way 'compassion', properly speaking, befits God, as will be shown in paragraphs 3.2 and 3.3.

A great concern for Jüngel, and many other theologians who attribute suffering to God, is to underline God's being-with His creation.[171] Thomas has the same concern, as was shown. But ascribing *passio* to God for this reason would have surprised him. For a 'God'-with-*passio* cannot be as close to a creature as the God-without-*passio*: the latter is, contrary to the former, absolutely free to love, without being influenced by any force or manipulation from outside Himself or hindered, distracted, (pre)occupied or withdrawn in Himself by His own sufferings, and above all not confined to a body and therefore not confined to a place and even, therefore, as Augustine puts it, whilst

---

[169] As is expressed in 1 Co 15,26, 55f, Rv 20,14, 21,4, cf. Mt 25,34-40, Lk 16,19-31.

[170] Jüngel, *o.c.*, 510f (373): "Wir haben mit der am Gekreuzigten orientierten Unterscheidung zwischen Gott und Gott die klassische Gotteslehre nun allerdings erheblich korrigiert. Denn durch die im Kreuz Jesu Christi begründete Unterscheidung von Gott und Gott sind das Absolutheitsaxiom und mit ihm das Apatieaxiom und das Unveränderlichkeitsaxiom als für den christlichen Gottesbegriff untaugliche Axiome destruiert worden."

[171] A great concern in Jüngel, see note 26, also in Sarot, *o.c.*, 15, 29, 78-102.

higher than the highest height, able to be more intimate to someone than his/her inner self.[172]

That denying *passio* and suffering in God cannot be disposed of by calling it "just a medieval relic" or something the like, is also demonstrated by Metz.[173] He reacts to Barth, Jüngel, Bonhoeffer and Moltmann, who ascribe suffering to God. Elements of Thomas' argumentation are found in Metz's critique, but also some insights not found in Thomas' theology. Metz mentions six reasons why we are to deny suffering of or in God. First, he says ascribing suffering to God looks like a gnostic reconciliation of God with suffering behind the back of the history of human suffering. Hedinger and Surin[174] call it the justification of the "creation with evil", because God Himself is partaking in the suffering. In this respect it even seems that suffering is as such a great virtue, according to Cook, critisizing Moltmann.[175] In other words, by ascribing suffering to God, one does not identify human suffering as an evil to be fought. In this study it was shown that Thomas is very clear with regard to this: *passio* in the negative, the so called most proper sense of the word, is not inherent in being human. Secondly, Metz conjectures that we do not take the negativity of negative theology seriously when we ascribe, as a reaction to it, suffering to God. As for Jüngel this critique makes sense, as was shown. Thirdly, Metz continues, ascribing suffering

---

[172] Augustine, *Confessiones* L.3 c.6 n.11, CSEL 33,53, cf. note 60.

[173] Metz (1995), 43-58.

[174] Hedinger (1972), Surin (1986), 67, reacting to Moltmann, Sölle and Jüngel.

[175] Cook (1990), 77: "Moltmann can take this kind of step and make it seem that to suffer is in itself a great virtue. Nowadays people like to overlook the suffering that is part of every great passion. People want to be perfectly happy, so they suppress suffering. They stifle pain, and rob themselves of feeling at the same time. Life without passion is poverty-stricken. Life without the readiness for suffering is shallow. We have to overcome both our fear of passion and our fear of suffering. Otherwise hope cannot be born again (*The Power of the Powerless*, 115). If taken literally and applied to God, we are doing Him a favour in allowing that he suffers and gains the helpful insights which apparently cannot be learned any other way than the hard one. Such an account of suffering comes very near to a kind of glorying in suffering itself and makes suffering and weakness almost ends in themselves."

to God is nothing more than duplicating human suffering and human powerlessness. In other words, ascribing suffering and powerlessness to God is a projection.[176] This may happen when metaphorical language is not recognized as such. Fourthly, ascribing suffering to God is saying that suffering is eternal. Jüngel is in fact asserting this, when he speaks of God's *infinite* suffering. Fifthly, the theologians criticized by Metz do not employ a method in order to *explain* the Christian faith, they follow a Hegelian way of thinking, by which they try to *determine* what the Christian faith is. In other words, their theology is more Hegelian than Christian. Finally, Metz warns that ascribing suffering to God may lead to regarding suffering - injustice, oppression, diseases etc. - as aesthetic. Hence ascribing suffering to God is even dangerous.

One could add yet another reason why God's suffering with us while we suffer does not make Him any 'closer', as Jüngel suggests. Both Thomas and Jüngel agree that the *com-passio* of a fellow human being can ease the pain of the one who suffers. Knowing and feeling that one is not the only person undergoing a particular distress, is often experienced as a relief; it brings about a bond of solidarity. But even if God experienced the same *passio* as we, He would not experience it in the same way. For a suffering 'God' suffers as God, while we suffer as human beings. Jüngel passes over this fundamental difference in silence.

Moreover, "classical" theology speaks of God's suffering which *is* of our kind. And therefore, it seems, in the "classical" view God's closeness and solidarity is even much greater than in God-suffers-as-God theologies.

2.3.4 God's True Suffering

It would be going too far to discuss Jüngel's view of the Trinity in the light of the Cross extensively in this study. But with regard to the suffering of God his point is that, because of the faithful identification of the divine Son of God with the crucified Jesus of Nazareth, which presupposes the true identification of God with the crucified Jesus, we

---

[176] Fiddes (1988), 17, warns for such a projection, but he is trapped by it himself; he employs a psychological approach. A similar move is made by Marcel Sarot, *o.c.*, as was said above.

need to distinguish between God (the Father) and God (the Son). Now if this God is love, He does not only love His creation, but also Himself. Therefore God the Father cannot but suffer endlessly in giving away His very own (Son) out of love for us.[177] And the divine Son suffers with the man with whom He is in a true union (see below).

"Since Jesus of Nazareth suffered, God suffered." It may surprise the reader after everything that has been said in this chapter, but even as a proper proposition Thomas does not deny this, provided that four (three) words are added: "as a human being (*secundum quod homo*)." Thus he says something quite different from what Jüngel says. This is under consideration in this subparagraph.

Hitherto it has become clear that *passio* befits the human nature, but that it is incompatible with the divine nature. The divine nature is *impassibile*. So when we say for instance that God undergoes sadness or anger because of an evil event, it is a metaphorical proposition, expressing that God does not will the evil to happen.
    Now in the last paragraph of the former chapter it was shown that because of the unity in person and supposit in Christ, we also say that when Christ was crucified, "the Son of God" and so even "God" was crucified, as John of Damascus does:

> "God 'has taken upon Himself those things that are proper
> to the flesh, so that God is called passible and we say that
> the God of glory has been crucified.'"[178]

These propositions are according to the rule of the *communicatio idiomatum*, as was said (paragraph 1.4).
    At first it may seem somewhat strange that Thomas identifies these propositions according to the rule of the communication of idioms not as metaphorical, but indeed as proper sayings. He does so on the basis of the Catholic faith (*secundum veritatem Catholicae fidei*), that is

---

[177] Jüngel, *o.c.*, 495-511 (361-373).

[178] ST IIIa q.16 a.4sc: *Damascenus dicit in III libro* [*De fide orthodoxa* c.4, MG 94,1000] *quod Deus* "*suscepit ea quae sunt carnis idiomata,*" *idest proprietates,* "*dum Deus passibilis nominatur, et Deus gloriae crucifixus est*".

the Christian faith as it is formulated by the oecumenical councils, concerning the Incarnation. For according to the oecumenical concils "the Word became flesh" (Jn 1,14) means that Christ was truly a human being[179] and truly God,[180] yet not, as Nestorius says, by means of inhabitation.[181] Saying that "God suffered while Christ suffered" can only be a metaphorical proposition, is Nestorianistic. For only if one denies a unity in the person and the suppositum of Christ, as Nestorius does, one cannot in the proper sense attribute suffering to Christ and God, but only metaphorically (*per quandam figurativam locutionem*). But in conformity with the oecumenical councils we are to say that incarnation means that the truly divine Son exists as a true human being:

> "But when we keep that there is only one supposit in Christ, this view is true and proper: God has become a human being, for He who was God from eternity, began to be a human being in time."[182]

As was said, in Christ there is no unity of natures, but there is a unity of person and supposit. In what way then is "God suffered, while Christ suffered" to be understood as a proper statement and in what way not? Thomas first explains the structure of our language *in humanis*: to a certain supposit, let us say "Peter", of a certain nature, in this case the human nature, a name can be ascribed, which signifies that nature concretely, for instance "human being". This is, says Thomas, a true and

---

[179] The Son of God accepted a true human body, contrary to what the Manichaeans held, and also contrary to Abelard, who denied that in Christ soul and body were united (cf. ST IIIa q.2 aa.5, 6, q.5 aa.1, 2).

[180] Christ was not, as Photinus held, God by means of participation, i.e. through grace; in this way all saints are called gods (as in Ps 82,6 and Jn 10,34). But Christ is God by nature (*naturaliter*) (cf. ST IIIa q.2 aa.10, 11).

[181] Nestorius, in trying to avoid Eutychianism (a unity of the divine and human natures in Christ), understood the incarnation of the Son as the Son putting on a coat (humanity). Yet this is a denial of the Son *becoming* man, cf. Weinandy (2000), 199ff.

[182] OCE c.21: *Sed tenendo quod in Christo sit unum tantum suppositum, haec [opinio] est vera et propria: Deus factus est homo, quia ille qui fuit Deus ab aeterno, incoepit esse homo ex tempore.*

proper way of speaking. Employed to speaking *in divinis*: "Christ" is the supposit of the human and of the divine nature. So for Him the name "human being" as well as the name "God", understood as the second Person of the Trinity, can be used.[183] When we say "God suffers" when Christ suffers, the name "God" supposits (*supponit*) for Christ, the Son of God. Thomas emphasizes vehemently that this is a true and proper way of speaking.[184]

As Schoot brings to our attention, suppositing then is understood as a *modus significandi*. For here "God" does not refer to the divine nature (*essentia*), but to the Son (*esse*). Yet "Christ", as the supposit of the human and the divine nature, is the name of the man as well as of the divine Son.[185] Since Nestorius erroneously understood the communication of idioms as an attribution of human characteristics to the divine *nature* and divine characteristics to the human *nature*, he denied its

---

[183] SN III d.11 a.4 sc.2: *Quaecumque consequuntur naturam, praedicantur de suppositis illius naturae. Sed Filius Dei est suppositum humanam naturae. Ergo consequentia humanam naturam possunt praedicari de Filio Dei.*

[184] ST IIIa q.16 a.1co, as an explanation of Ph 2,6f: *Unde, supponendo,* secundum veritatem Catholicae fidei, *quod* vera *natura divina unita est cum* vera *natura humana,* non solum *in persona,* sed etiam *in suppositio vel hypostasi, dicimus esse* veram *hanc propositionem* et propriam, *"Deus est homo":* non solum *propter* veritatem *terminorum, quia scilicet Christus est* verus *Deus et* verus *homo;* sed etiam *propter* veritatem *praedicationis. Nomen enim significans naturam communem in concreto potest supponere pro quolibet contentorum in natura communi: sicut hoc nomen "homo" potest supponere pro quolibet homo singulari. Et ita hoc nomen "Deus", ex ipso modo significationis, potest supponere pro persona Filii Dei, ut in Prima Parte* [q.39 a.4] *habitum est. De quolibet autem supposito alicuius naturae potest* vere et proprie *praedicari nomen significans illam naturam in concreto: sicut de Socrate et Platone* proprie et vere *praedicatur "homo". Quia ergo persona Filii Dei, pro qua supponit hoc nomen "Deus", est suppositum naturae humanae,* vere et proprie *hoc nomen "homo" potest praedicari de hoc nomine "Deus", secundum quod supponit pro persona Filii Dei.* And the same applies for *"Homo est Deus",* ibidem a.2, where along the same line Thomas explains Rm 9,5.

[185] ST IIIa q.16 a.5co: Nomina vero concreta supponunt hypostasim naturae. *Et ideo indifferenter praedicari possunt ea quae ad utramque naturam pertinent, de nominibus concretis: Sive illud nomen de quo intelligitur utramque naturam, sicut hoc nomen Christus, in quo intelligitur et divinitas ungens et humanitas uncta; sive solum divinam naturam sicut hoc nomen Deus, vel Filius Dei; sive solum naturam humanam, sicut hoc nomen Iesus.* Cf. Schoot (1993), 57-64.

necessity and even its possibility.[186] Likewise Jüngel, in the footsteps of Luther and Hegel, also understands the communication of idioms as an expression of the unity of *natures* in the person of Christ. For Jüngel, however, this is not a reason for rejecting it, but rather for embracing it. According to him the understanding of the communication of idioms in classical theology remains too abstract and excludes a real personal union in Christ.[187] The logical consequence of Jüngel's position is, as was said, not only that God's divine nature undergoes suffering, but even that the divine nature (love, goodness, might etc.) changes through what happens to Christ. And exactly this is the reason, why Thomas establishes:

"Properties of the human nature are *never* said of the divine nature and vice versa." (italics added, MR)[188]

And, Thomas continues, precisely suppositing as a *modus significandi* underlines the two-ness of the divine and the human nature in the one person and supposit of Christ.

As was said, according to the Catholic faith "God suffered when Christ suffered" can be true as a metaphor. It is, when by this proposition is meant that God then suffered as God (*secundum quod Deus*), in other words, that the divine nature underwent grief, sadness, anger and etc., as

---

[186] As formulated in ST IIIa q.16 a.4 ag.2: [A]*ttribuere Deo ea quae ad defectum pertinent, videtur derogare divino honori, et ad blasphemiam pertinere. Sed ea quae sunt humanae naturae, defectum quendam continent: sicut mori,* pati *et alia huiusmodi. Ergo videtur quod nullo modo ea quae sunt humanae naturae, possint dici de Deo.*

[187] Jüngel, *o.c.*, 127 (96): Er [Hegel] ist sich mit dem Luthertum einig in der Bestreitung einer *abstrakt* bleibenden, ein *wirkliches* Geschehen zwischen göttlicher und menschlicher Natur ausschließenden *Einheit der beiden Naturen* in der Person Christi. Wenn Gott Mensch geworden ist, dann müssen göttliche und menschliche Natur in der Person Jesu Christi als *mit einander kommunizierend* gedacht werden, so daß ihre personale Einheit (unio personalis) als die differenzierte Einheit eines Geschehens zu verstehen ist. [italics added, MR]

[188] SN III d.5 q.1 a.2 ad 4: [P]*roprietates humanae naturae* numquam *dicuntur de divina* [natura] *nec e converso* [....] *sed dicuntur utraeque de habente naturam, vel humanam vel divinam, quae significatur hoc nomine Deus et hoc nomine homo. Idem enim est qui utrasque naturas habet.*

a response to what happened to Christ.[189] This metaphor expresses God's love for Christ and that the people who sinned by betraying and crucifying Him, act in defiance of God's will and love.

According to the Catholic faith "the *passio* of God" is to be understood as proper way of speech in respect of the mystery of God incarnate. Then in respect of the Passion of Christ God's sufferings are understood as:

"God the Son has truly undergone as a human being."[190]

If "God" were understood as the Father or the Spirit or as the divine nature, if this proposition were in the imperfect present tense or if the reduplication "as a human being" were omitted, this proposition could not be true as a proper saying; however it could still be true as a metaphorical saying, as was said.

---

[189] E.g. in Händel's Messiah (HWV 56/23) quoting Ps 2,4f.

[190] Cf. ST IIIa q.16 aa.10, 11: *Deus Filius vere passus est secundum quod homo.*

CHAPTER 3

THE ALMIGHTINESS OF GOD

It is conspicuous to us that Thomas speaks of the *passio* of Christ as being in order. Behind the historical, visible, chaotic reality of the death sentence and execution of a just person, the Son of God even, and God who apparently does not interfere in order to prevent this, he detects the hand of God in this event. Thomas even designates it as curative, beneficial and salutary *for us*. He does so on the basis of Scripture. Thomas is in no way reluctant to say that Christ and everything was in God's hand (cf. Jb 12,10; Si 10,4); the Passion of Christ is not an attack on God's providence, but rather a part of it. The situation was never out of God's control. In Christ's Passion God is not powerless, but rather, to use a metaphor, the director on the film set, as well as - from eternity - the writer of the script. Even more, His eternally begotten Son, one in being with His Father, plays, as a human being, the leading part in the drama. Yet at the same time Thomas does not deny that evil happened, in spite of everything being in God's hand. This may seem like a contradiction or at least it raises the question of what God's might, His almightiness, is.

In the former chapters the *passio* of Christ and the *passio* of God were considered in the light of the might of God and Christ. In this chapter the might of God (*potentia Dei*) will be considered in the light of the *passio* of Christ and of God. Not only is the theme of God's almightiness present in the *quaestiones* in the *Tertia Pars* of the *Summa Theologiae* on the *passio Christi*, but it will be shown that in Thomas' exposition regarding the almightiness of God in the *Prima Pars* Thomas already refers to the Passion of Christ. From the very beginning of the discussion of God's almightiness Thomas speaks of it in view of our salvation through Christ's Passion. This will be made clear by a close reading of *quaestio* 25 of the *Prima Pars*.

As was said in the introduction of this book, almightiness is a term in our faith that requires clarification. Before Thomas speaks of God's almightiness itself, he takes two preliminary steps: are "God" and "might (*potentia*)" compatible? And is - and if so, in what way is - God's might infinite (*infinita*)? After considering God's almightiness (*omnipotentia*) in *articulus* 3, Thomas discusses in the last three *articuli* some aspects necessary for a correct understanding of what God's almightiness is (or is not).

At first sight the first two questions of *quaestio* 25 in the *Summa Theologiae* are literally the same as those of *quaestio* 1 in *De Potentia*: "Whether there is *potentia* in God" and "Whether the *potentia* of God is infinite." But on further consideration it comes out that in the *Summa Theologiae* they are more than preliminary steps in the quest for the right definitions: for in the first *articulus* Thomas thinks through the consequences of *quaestio* 3 and 11, on the simplicity of God, for our thinking of God's might; and in the second *articulus* Thomas considers the consequences of what he said in *quaestiones* 4 till 10, on God's perfection, goodness, infinity, presence in things, immutability and eternity, with regard to His might.

In this study Thomas' two preliminary steps will be considered in paragraph 3.1. Next his view of almightiness will be discussed (3.2). These first two paragraphs contain a conceptual analysis of the words might and almightiness in Thomas' theology. The third paragraph could be considered the high point of this book, for it reveals the *nexus* of Christ's Passion and God's might in Thomas' theology and scrutinizes it. After Thomas' denial of *compassio* in God, in chapter 2, it may come as a big surprise that he sees this *nexus* as via the mercy (*misericordia*) of God. The fourth and final paragraph is of a different character. It is a meta-reflection in which a closer look is taken at how Scriptural the term "almighty" is and how it functions in negative theology.

3.1 Mighty God

In this paragraph three steps will be taken. First the distinction Thomas makes between the might of creatures and the might of God will be considered: contrary to (composed) creatures (the simple) God cannot *have* might as distinct from what He *is* (3.1.1). Still Thomas holds that *we* are to make a distinction in God's might. The reason why is explored in 3.1.2. The third step in this paragraph, Thomas' second preliminary step, is the consideration of the infinity of God's might, in 3.1.3. This issue is of importance also in view of the human freedom of Christ; if the Passion of Christ was according to God's will, how free was Christ's choice then actually to do the will of His Father?

3.1.1 Might and the Might of God

God's knowing and willing are the two operations that remain in Him. The third of God's operations mentioned by Thomas, is His might (*potentia*).

> "By the might of God is understood the principle of the divine operation going out to bring about an external effect."[1]

This means that nothing that comes from God, is detached from His might. So not only deeds connected with force or violence, like evil being defeated,[2] but also creation, the Incarnation and all acts of God's love towards us come forth from His might. This raises the question what Thomas understands by might and by the might of the triune God.

Although we read in many places in Scripture that God is mighty[3], Thomas does not answer the question whether there is might in God, with a simple "yes". For Thomas distinguishes between two kinds of might, namely passive might (*potentia passiva*) and active might (*potentia activa*). He highlights that we have to say that this passive might is in no way in God, while we are to hold that active might is in God to the highest extent.[4] Something has *potentia passiva*, as we came across in paragraph 2.2, for as far as it is *in potentia*, and something has *potentia activa* for as far as it is *in actu*. *Potentia passiva* and *actus* are two sides of the same picture:

> "For it is clear that anything for as far as it is *in actu* and perfect, is an active principle of something; for as far as

---

[1] ST Ia q.14 intr.: *[P]otentia Dei, quae consideratur ut principium operationis divinae in effectum exteriorem procedentis.*

[2] As e.g. in Ex 17,8-16.

[3] Thomas cites in ST Ia q.25 a.1sc Ps 89,9, in SN I d.42 q.1 a.1 sc.1 Ps 89,9 and Lk 1,49, in SCG II c.7 n.6 Ps 71,18f and 89,9, in QDP q.1 a.1 sc.2 Ps 89,9 and Mt 3,9.

[4] ST Ia q.25 a.1co: *[D]icendum quod duplex est potentia: scilicet passiva, quae* nullo modo *est in Deo, et activa, quam* oportet *in Deo* summe *ponere.*

anything is lacking something and is imperfect, it undergoes."[5]

Something can be acted upon, undergo, insofar as it has *potentia passiva*. And *potentia activa* in return is then the principle of acting upon something having *potentia passiva*, perfecting or corrupting it. This means that in Thomas' theology *potentia activa*, or might[6], is a neutral term. For a correct understanding of what he says, it is crucial to see that in his theology might and power do not have the connotation of violence or suppression, as for instance in the definition of the sociologist Weber and the theologians Rahner/Vorgrimler and in our daily speech.[7] Because of this connotation might and power have become dirty words, so that al-might-iness is avoided or even denied of God by many a theologian.

Referring to *quaestio* 3 Thomas recalls passionately that the perfect divinity of God is incompatible with any *potentia passiva* or

---

[5] ST Ia q.25 a.1co: *Manifestum est enim quod unumquodque, secundum quod est actu et perfectum, secundum hoc est principium activum alicuius: patitur autem unumquodque, secundum quod est deficiens et imperfectum.* Cf. q.77 a.3co.

[6] Might and power are regarded as synonyms in Webster's (1986), II,1432A ([2]might). For reasons of clarity in Thomas' terminology *potentia* and *potestas* are translated as "might", whereas *virtus* is translated as "power", as was said in the Introduction of this book. For the distinction between the two, see paragraph 4.1.

[7] Max Weber, in: Wirtschaft und Gesellschaft, -Grundriß der verstehenden Soziologie, Köln, Berlin 1964, I,38, cited in Häring (1986), 364: "Macht bedeutet jede Chance, innerhalb einer socialen Beziehung *den eigenen Willen auch gegen Widerstreben durchzusetzen*, gleichwie worauf die Chance beruht." (italics added, MR); cf. Van den Eynde (2000),6. Rahner/Vorgrimler (1990), 401: "Power. The desire to enforce one's own will, to further one's own interests, to impose one's own convictions and to extend the scope of one's own freedom (*violence), often in opposition to (legitimate) counter-attempts on the part of others, is both a fundamental anthropological attribute of man (Hobbes and Nietzsche) and one of the distinctive characteristics of the structure of the State." Webster's (1986), II,1178C: "[1]power. 1a: a position of ascendancy; ability to compel obedience; control, dominion. b: military force or its equipment."

passio and that God therefore (*Unde*) is *the* active principle: *actus purus*.[8] And that, therefore, we say that there is *potentia activa* in God to the highest extent.

Thus in God there is only *potentia activa*. But what does this mean? Is this imaginable? To give an example: a motorcycle of 20 h.p. has a great *potentia passiva*; it is capable of reaching a high speed. *In potentia* it reaches a high speed. But in order to realize this capacity, the engine must be activated, be brought *in actum*, by someone. The person starting the engine has the *potentia passiva* to do so, and while he/she starts the engine he/she realizes his/her capability, bringing his/her *potentia passiva in actum*. When the motor-cyclist starts riding and accelerates, he/she brings the *potentia passiva* of the motor *in actum*: its *potentia activa* is realized, the might of the engine is *in actu*. Now Thomas would say that active might befits God neither in the sense of the motorbike, since in that case His might would be activated by something or somebody else, nor in the sense of the motor-cyclist, since in him/her there is a change from "being capable of" to "being realized". In both cases *passio* is implied, as well as - although Thomas does not mention it in this first *articulus* - imperfection and time. Yet God's active might is from-eternity-active might. And this is not imaginable, since every active might we have or experience is being brought from *potentia* (*passiva*) into *actum*, within a certain time.

After ruling out the possibility of *potentia passiva* in God, Thomas, thinking through the further consequences of *quaestio* 3 for God's might, goes on to explain that God's active might cannot be in Him as it is in us, because of His simplicity. In us, creatures, *actus* and *potentia* are distinct. But they cannot be distinct in God, since there are no distinctions in God. God's *actus* and *potentia* cannot be accidental either, since there are no accidents in God:

"Each one is divine essence, for also His existence is not

---

[8] ST Ia q.25 a.1co: *Ostensum est supra* [q.3 a.1] *quod Deus est* purus *actus, et* simpliciter et universaliter *perfectus;* neque *in eo* aliqua *imperfectio locum habet. Unde sibi* maxime *competit esse principium activum et* nullo modo *pati*; cf paragraph 2.2.2. Thomas is much more expressive here than in SCG II c.7 n.2.

something else than His essence."[9]

In other words, because of His simplicity we are to say that what God "has", is what He "is". The consequence of this is that with regard to God we cannot say, as with regard to creatures, that His activity, His knowing and willing (and therefore also His loving), or anything else in Him is better, more important or more eminent than His might. For, since all attributes are one in God, we cannot play off his attributes against one another, as Jüngel seems to do (see below).

Yet, if God's might and everything in God is the divine essence, two other differences appear regarding a creature's might: first, in creatures might is the principle of an activity in the subject - someone only thinks, if he/she *can* think - as well as the principle of an effect outside the subject. As was said above (note 1), we speak of God's might as the principle of all activities or operations outside God. But His might cannot be the principle of an activity in God, for His might as well as His activity are His essence and God's essence is not become or brought forth, but is from eternity.[10] When Thomas speaks of God's might as His essence, he calls it *potentia absoluta*, God's might as such.[11]

Secondly, we speak with regard to creatures as well as to God of might as the principle of the execution of what the will commands and the intellect directs. In creatures these three are different things (*differens secundum rem*). In God they cannot be different things, for they all

---

[9] ST Ia q.25 a.1 ad 2: [U]trumque est essentia divina: quia nec esse est aliud ab eius essentia. Cf. q.3 aa.3, 4, 6.

[10] QDP q.1 a.1 ag.1: [O]peratio Dei, qui est eius essentia, non habet principium, quia neque genita neque procedens. Still, Thomas says, we speak like this, ibidem ad 1: [R]ationis tantum, quae significatur, cum dicitur quod operatio divina est ab essentia divina, vel quod Deus operatur per essentiam suam. Cf. ST Ia q.25 a.1 ad 3: Nisi forte secundum modum intelligendi, prout divina essentia, quae in se simpliciter praehabet quodquid perfectionis est in rebus creatis, potest intelligi et sub ratione actione, et sub ratione potentiae; sicut etiam intelligitur et sub ratione suppositi habentis naturam, et sub ratione naturae.

[11] ST Ia q.25 a.5 ad 1: [P]otentiae secundum se consideratae, dicitur Deus posse secundum potentiam absolutam. Et huiusmodi est omne illud in quo potest salvari ratio entis.

denote the one essence of God; they only differ in our understanding (*secundum rationem*). This one-ness, Thomas continues, can also be expressed by saying that the might is included in the divine knowledge and the will themselves as the effective cause of operation and effect.[12] By saying this, Thomas avoids a possible misunderstanding:

> "Pseudo-Dionysius places power as a means between substance and operation. But God does not act through one or another means. We are to say that the might of God is not a means according to the nature of what it is, since it is not something distinct from His essence; only in our understanding it is. So on account of this His might may be called a means, although God does not act through a means truly different from Himself."[13]

And the same applies to our speaking of God's knowledge and will as preceding the execution of His might.[14] This is another fine exemple of how Thomas *seeks* to formulate the *mystery* of God. When Thomas speaks of God's might in this way, as bringing about an effect outside God, he calls it *potentia ordinata*.[15]

Although we speak of God's might as such and of God's ordained

---

[12] ST Ia q.25 a.1 ad 4: *Vel dicendum quod ipsa scientia vel voluntas divina, secundum quod est principium effectivum, habet rationem potentiae*, cf. SN I d.42 q.1 a.2co: *Potentia enim activa, quae sola in Deo invenitur, potest dupliciter considerari: vel quantum ad essentiam vel quantum ad actiones quae a potentia procedunt.*

[13] QDP q.1 a.1 ag.14: *Virtus a Dionysio [in lib. de Caelesti Hierarchia, c.11] ponitur media inter substantiam et operationem. Sed Deus non agit per aliquod medium.* Ibidem ad 14: *[D]icendum quod potentia Dei non est media secundum rem, quia non distinguitur ab essentia*, nisi ratione; *et ex hoc habetur quod significetur ut medium. Deus autem non agit per medium realiter differens a seipso.* Cf. ST Ia q.54 a.1co: *[I]n solo Deo sua substantia est suum esse et suum agere.* In SN I d.42 q.1 a.1 ag.2 Thomas refers to Pseudo-Dionysius as the one who says in *De divinis nominibus* that *Deus* cum sit primum agens, *non participatione alicuius, sed per suam essentiam agit.*

[14] ST Ia q.25 a.1 ad 4: *Unde consideratio scientiae et voluntatis praecedit in Deo considerationem potentiae*, sicut *causa praecedit operationem et effectum.*

[15] ST Ia q.25 a.5 ad 1: *Quod autem attribuitur potentiae divinae secundum quod* exequitur *imperium voluntatis iustae, hoc dicitur Deus posse facere de* potentia ordinata.

might, and although the effects of God's might outside Him are manifold[16], there is only one might in God. This does not mean that our words do not refer to anything, rather these different words refer to what is one and the same in God - something we cannot express in one word.[17]

3.1.2 God's Might and God's Action

Hitherto it is not clear *why* Thomas holds that we are to make the distinction as to God's might. The reader may have got the impression that Thomas rather employs a kind of philosophy concerning God's divinity than that he is engaging in theology that is speculative as well as practical.[18] For God's *potentia absoluta* cannot be experienced, since it is in God. Still we have to distinguish it from God's *potentia ordinata*. The practical value of this distinction for our faith shows where Thomas discusses the relation between what God can do and what He does.[19]

As was said, when we speak of knowing and willing, of the love, the wisdom, the justice and the might of a human being, we speak of different things. But in God, who is simple, they all must be one; all

---

[16] SN I d.42 q.1 a.2co: *[A]bsolute dicendum est potentiam divinam esse* unam*; sed tamen quod est* plurimam, *quia iudicum de unitate rei absolute est secundum essentiam eius, et non secundum id quod extra est.*

[17] QDP q.1 a.1 ag.10: *Omnis intellectus cui non respondet aliquid in re est cassus et vanus.* Ibidem ag.12: *Aut isti rationi aliquid respondet in re, aut nihil. Si nihil, ratio vana est. Si autem aliquid in re ei respondet, sequitur quod aliquid in Deo sit potentia praeter essentiam, sicut ratio potentiae est praeter rationem essentiae.* Ibidem ad 12: *[D]iversis rationibus* attribuorum respondet *aliquid* in re *divina, scilicet* unum et idem. *Quia rem simplicissimam, quae Deus est,* propter eius incomprehensibilitatem, *intellectus noster cogitur diversis formis repraesentare; et ita istae diversae formae quas intellectus concipit de Deo, sunt quidem* in Deo sicut causa veritatis, *inquantum ipsa res quae Deus est, est repraesentabilis per omnes istas formas; sunt tamen* in intellectu nostro sicut in subiecto.

[18] ST Ia q.1 a.4co.

[19] ST Ia q.25 a.5 tit.: *Utrum Deus possit facere quae non facit.* This question is closely connected with the question why there is so much suffering and misery in our world, if God is (al)mighty - a question reverberates throughout in the background of this study.

attributes denote His essence. This means that there can be nothing in His might that is not also in His will or knowledge. If one thinks this through logically, this would mean that God, who knows everything[20], therefore also wills everything and hence brings about everything that He knows and wills. Yet according to this line of reasoning God is in His operation outside Himself not acting on the basis of His free will, but out of necessity. God would not have alternatives or even a free will in respect of His creation. And inversely it would be true that God cannot do what He does not do, for instance avert the crucifixion of Christ. Then, indeed, God could be called powerless in this sense. Moreover, another consequence of this argument is, that God's will, might, wisdom, love and justice would coincide with how things evolve in this world. God would not be mightier, wiser and more just than in the order of creation and in the course of things emerging.[21] Furthermore, there would not be evil, for everything that happened would be according to the will, justice, love etc. of God. But Scripture itself testifies that God can do what He does not do. Thomas cites Mt 26,53, where Christ, being arrested in Gethsemane, says to one of His diciples who draws the sword to defend Him: "Do you think that I cannot appeal to My Father, who would promptly send more than twelve legions of angels to My defence?"

In the context of this study it catches the eye that Thomas, speaking of God's might, makes a link to the Passion of Christ.[22] And thus this question in the *Prima Pars*, whether God can do what He does

---

[20] Heb 4,13 etc.; ST IaIIae q.1 a.8 ad 2: *Potentia autem in habentibus intellectum non operatur nisi secundum voluntatem et cognitionem. Et ideo omnipotentia Dei includit* quodammodo omnium scientiam *et providentiam: Non enim posset omnia quae vellet in istis inferioribus agere nisi ea cognosceret et eorum providentiam haberet.* Cf. Ia q.14.

[21] ST Ia q.25 a.5co: *Quidam enim posuerunt Deum agere quasi* ex necessitate naturae; *ut sicut ex actione rerum naturalium non possunt alia provenire nisi quae eveniunt, utpote ex semine hominis homo, ex semine olivae oliva; ita ex operatione divina non possint aliae res, vel alius ordo rerum affluere nisi sicut nun est.* [....] *Alii vero dixerunt quod potentia divina* determinatur ad hunc cursum rerum, *propter ordinem sapientiae et iustitiae, sine quo Deus nihil operatur.*

[22] ST Ia q.25 a.5sc, citing Mt 26,53. This link is stronger in ST, where it is the only Scriptural text cited, than in earlier works. For he cites Mt 26,53 also in SCG III c.98 n.4 and QDP q.1 a.5 sc.1, but just as one of the texts cited. In SN this verse is not cited in this context (I d.43 q.2).

not do, may already prepare the way for the application of its answer to the question of the necessity of Christ's Passion in the *Tertia Pars* (1.2). Or even, as will be argued for in paragraph 3.2, this is a clue that Thomas wrote this *quaestio* 25 of the *Prima Pars*, on the might of God, in view of the Passion of Christ, and thus with our salvation in mind.

God is not being forced to do something, neither from outside, which would imply *passio*, nor from inside, which would imply *necessitas*. Hence God *must* not do something, for instance saving us, because He is mighty, good and loving. For in Scripture we read not only that He is mighty, good, loving etc., but also that God acts according to His free will.[23]

All God's actions presuppose His knowlegde and will. Of the things that God actually does towards His creatures, we are to say that they come forth from His knowing and willing[24] And, hence, they are in accordance with His essence: His knowledge, will, love, justice, mercy, might etc.. In other words: God *can* (and not: does) do something because it is in conformity with His essence (*potentia absoluta*); God *does* (and not: can) do something, because He wills it (*potentia ordinata*).[25] In

---

[23] E.g. Jb 23,13, Ps 33,9-11, 115,3, 135,6 (cited in ST Ia q.104 a.3co, IIIa q.21 a.1co), Pr 19,21, W 12,18, Is 46,10 (cited in ST IIaIIae q.83 a.9 ag.1, q.189 a.10 ad 1), Ep 1,11 (cited in ST Ia q.19 a.3sc).

[24] SN III d.1 q.2 a.3co: *[C]onsiderandum est, quando potentiae divinae aliquid adscribitur, utrum attribuatur potentiae secundum se consideratae - tunc enim dicitur posse illud de potentia absoluta - vel attribuatur sibi in ordine ad sapientiam et praescientiam et voluntatem eius - tunce enim dicitur posse illud de potentia absoluta.*

[25] ST Ia q.25 a.5 ad 1: *Secundum hoc ergo, dicendum est quod Deus potest alia facere, de potentia absoluta, quam quae praescivit et praeordinavit se facturum: non tamen potest esse quod alia faciat, quae non praesciverit et praeordinaverit se facturum. Quia ipsum facere subiacet praescientiae et praeordinationi: non autem ipsum posse, quod est naturale. Ideo enim Deus aliquid facit, quia vult: non tamen ideo potest, quia vult, sed quia talis est in sua natura.*
Hence, the rendering of Thomas' distinction by Ten Kate is incorrect, (2000), 222: "Ainsi il [= Thomas] distingue deux formes de pouvoir divin: la puissance absolue, qui peut tout faire, 'potentia absoluta', et la puissance relative, 'potentia ordinata', qui ne fait que ce qui est conforme à la nature divine, qui est remplie de bonté." What Ten Kate says concerning *potentia ordinata* applies to Thomas' definition of *potentia absoluta* as well. After all, when Thomas speaks of *potentia absoluta* here, he speaks of the *potentia*

paragraph 2.1.1 it became clear that God wills what is good, since He is love. Yet the question why God does not will or do something that is apparently or obviously good, cannot be answered by a human being, since no one can read God's mind.[26] Here we are faced with the boundaries of human knowledge. Hence,

> "those things that are of God cannot be known in themselves indeed, yet still they become manifest to us in their effects, as we read in Rm 1,20."[27]

And this must be considered as for God's might in the course of this chapter.

Still Thomas speaks of a kind of necessity as regards God's might: God can only do what befits Him and what is good and just, just as He cannot but will what is good and just. God acts necessarily in accordance with who and what He is.[28] But this can be understood in two ways. For someone could first try to make out what good is and just, and next, on the basis of this, determine what God can and cannot do. However, by doing so, one limits God's might to the current state of affairs, for we can only think of what is good and just in the context of the creation as it is now. God's might would then coincide with His

---

absoluta of *God*. So the assertion that Thomas, by making the distinction between *potentia absoluta* and *ordinata* in God, *o.c.*, 222, "risquait [....] de Lui attribuer la possibilité de pouvoir pécher" does not cut ice.

[26] Jb 15,8, 36,26, 38,1-42,6, W 9,13f, Is 40,13, 28, Jr 23,18, Rm 11,33 (cited in ST Ia q.14 a.1sc), 34 (cited in ST Ia q.23 a.8 ag.2), 1 Co 2,11 (cited in ST IaIIae q.93 a.2 ag.1), 16. Even those who *will* see God, as in Mt 5,8, cited in ST IaIIae q.8 a.7co, shall not see "everything" of His, cf. SCG III c.59 n.7: not why God does not do and never shall do certain things, although He can (Jb 11,7-9); nor the depth of God's goodness, which is the purpose of all that is made, and of His wisdom (Qo 8,17); nor the things that cohere with with God's will alone, like *praedestinatio, electio, iustificatio et alia huiusmodi quae ad sanctificationem pertinent creaturae* (1 Co 2,11).

[27] ST IaIIae q.93 a.2 ad 1: [*E*]*a quae sunt Dei, in seipsis quidem cognosci non possunt: sed tamen in effectibus suis nobis manifestantur, secundum illud Rom. 1,20.*

[28] Parallel to ST Ia q.19 a.3co in q.25 a.5 ad 2: *Deus non potest facere, nisi quod ei conveniens est et iustum.* But in the context of God's might Thomas avoids the term *necessitas*, as in IIIa q.46.

potentia ordinata. But if we accept that God acted freely when He created this world, we must hold that He could have created a different world. Therefore, Thomas proposes first to inquire what God can do (*potentia absoluta*), not determined by any circumstances outside God. And then, turning to God's action outside Himself, we can say that "God can only do what befits Him and what is just" is true if it means:

> "God can only do what would befit Him and would be good, if He does it."[29]

This implies on the one hand that the things God has created are good and that He has ordered them, according to laws of nature as we would say, in *the* way good for them - an implicit reference to Gn 1,31 ("God saw all He had made, and indeed it was very good") (*potentia ordinata*). But this implies on the other hand that the present creatures and order do not coincide with His goodness and might (*potentia absoluta*); He could have created other good things and could have placed them in a different order, which then for them would be good.[30] And the same applies to God's action in the Passion of Christ: it was shown that Thomas argues that despite the evil that also happened, the Passion of Christ, as it came to pass, reveals the goodness and the love ("for our salvation") as well as the might of God (the situation was never out of God's control, Thomas says). But the "order" of Christ's Passion does not coincide with His might; it was not all or the only thing He could do (*potentia absoluta*). God could have done something else, if He had willed it.[31]

---

[29] ST Ia q.25 a.5 ad 2: *Deus non potest facere nisi quod ei est conveniens et iustum* [....] *erit locutio vera sub hoc sensu: Deus non potest facere nisi id quod,* si faceret, *esset conveniens et iustum.*

[30] ST Ia q.25 a.5 ad 3: [L]*icet iste cursus rerum sit determinatus istis rebus quae nunc sunt, non tamen ad hunc cursum limitatur divina sapientia et potestas. Unde, licet* istis rebus quae nunc sunt, nullus alius cursus esset bonus et conveniens, *tamen, Deus posset alias res facere, et alium eis imponere ordinem.*

[31] ST IIIa q.46 a.2, cf. Ia q.19 a.3co: *Unde, cum bonitas Dei sit perfecta, et esse possit sine aliis, cum nihil ei perfectionis ex aliis accrescat; sequitur quod alia a se eum velle, non sit necessarium absolute. Et tamen necessarium est* ex suppositione: *supposito enim quod velit, non potest non velle, quia non potest voluntas eius mutari.* Implied is in this argument that God always wills what is good; "He cannot disown His own self" (2

In this way it becomes clear that Thomas makes a distinction in God's might, so that we can think of God as essentially good, just, mighty, loving etc. and at the same time realize that God's essence does not coincide with what we experience as His activity in our created world. Though we confess that God is one (*secundum rem*), we have to make a distinction (*secundum rationem*) as regards His might, because otherwise we cannot say that God could have done something (other than what He does) (*potentia absoluta*), but does not do it (*potentia ordinata*). By making this distinction Thomas places the problem in us, not in God: our intellect is inadequate.

It catches the eye that in contemporary theology this distinction in our thinking of God's might is nearly absent. "God's might" then coincides with His *potentia ordinata*. This may lead to remarkable conclusions, like that God was powerless in respect of Pilate; God did not and could not avert the crucifixion of Christ. That He, yet, protested against it.[32] Or, in more general terms, that God is not able to prevent or counteract evil, but that He does what He can in order to do so.[33] If theologians on top of this interpret the words love and might or power exclusively in the sense in which they are commonly used in our daily speech, it may happen - and it does happen - that these two, that are one in God according to our faith, are regarded as opposites. And although in Scripture God is called (al)mighty as well as love, His might usually tastes defeat, so to speak, in the light of the terrible abuse of power on a

---

Tm 2,13, cited in ST IIIa q.46 a.2 ag.3).

[32] Hedinger (1983), 57-61; he sees this in contrast with God's might at Easter and Pentecost, *o.c.*, 61-63.

[33] E.g. Burkle (1977), 121, Morin (1993), 59, Ten Kate (2000), 233f. But even Nicolas (1969), 88, 97, who does make the distinction, speaks of God's impotence, exactly because of the created order: "De ce point de vue, Dieu est impuissant. Impuissant à empêcher les stupides forces matérielles d'écraser ce roseau pensant qu'est l'homme; impuissant à contrecarrer les volontés humaines égoïstes, mechantes ou imprudentes, et à prévenir leur effects destructeurs; impuissant - c'est le mystère des mystères! - à vaincre la résistance de la volonté créée, refusant librement un amour qui ne peut être que libre."

large scale in our days and in (recent) history.[34] Or more creative solutions are found, for instance by Jüngel, who says that only in love are power and powerlessness not opposites:

> "There is, however, only one phenomenon in which power and weakness do not contradict each other, in which rather power can perfect itself as weakness. This phenomenon is the event of *love*. Love does not see power and weakness as alternatives. It is the unity of power and weakness, and such is certainly the most radical opposite to the will to power which cannot affirm weakness. Pauline 'theology of the cross' (*theologia crucis*) is, accordingly, the most stringent rejection of all deification of self-willing power."[35]

And in order to avoid a tension between God's might and God's love - a danger in Jüngel's theology because of his Weberian concept of might and his definition of love as without might ("Ohnmacht") and without violence ("gewaltlos") -, he cannot avoid a certain hierarchy or subordination in the truths of our faith: what God's might signifies must be considered proceeding from our understanding of God as love.[36]

---

[34] E.g. Berdiajew, *Essai de métaphysique eschatologique* (1946), 130f; *Von der Menschen Knechtschaft und Freiheit* (1954), 106f, cited in: Hedinger (1968), 305f. Also: Stoßwald (1994), 52-54, and Schiwy (1995). Critique from different feminist perspectives in Case-Winters (1990), 172-200.

[35] Jüngel, *o.c.*, 280 (206): "Es gibt aber nur ein einziges Phänomen, in dem sich Macht und Ohnmacht nicht widersprechen, *in dem die Macht* vielmehr *als Ohnmacht sich vollenden kann* [italics added, MR]. Dieses Phänomen ist das Ereignis der *Liebe*. Die Liebe kennt Macht und Ohnmacht nicht als Alternative. Sie ist die Einheit von Macht und Ohnmacht und als solche der wohl radikalste Gegensatz zum Willen zur Macht, der die Ohnmacht nicht bejahen darf. Die paulinische theologia crucis ist dementsprechend die schärfste Absage gegen die Vergöttlichung der sich selbst wollenden Macht."

[36] Jüngel, *o.c.*, 355 (260): "Damit wird zugleich der im traditionellen Gottesgedanken dominierende Begriff der göttlichen Herrschafft, *Allmacht* und Weltüberlegenheit der das göttlichen Wesen *strenger* aussagenden Bestimmung *Gottes als Liebe radikal untergeordnet*." This, after Jüngel has emphasized that God's love is not subordinated to His might, *o.c.*, 26 (21): "Nun soll gewiß nicht bestritten werden, daß Erbarmen und Liebe allemal Akte der Freiheit und *insofern* auch der Macht sind. Wer Freiheit vollzieht,

3.1.3 The (In)finite Might of God

In *quaestio* 3 of the *Prima Pars* Thomas construes the grammatical ground rules of negative theology. It is clear that the consequences of this *quaestio* show in the *quaestiones* 4 to 11. But it seems to me that in this *quaestio*, 25, the structure of the first eleven *quaestiones* also determines the discussion on God's might. For in the last two subparagraphs, in which the *articuli* 1 and 5 were discussed, the consequences of God's simplicity (*quaestio* 3 and 11) for our understanding of God's might were considered. In *articulus* 1 Thomas explicitly refers to *quaestio* 3. Yet although in *articulus* 2 of *quaestio* 25 Thomas only explicitly refers to *quaestio* 3, fundamental for all his theology, and to *quaestio* 7, he is in fact thinking through the consequences of the *quaestiones* 4 to 10. This shows in the three *obiectiones*, where Thomas brings up three problems. First, it seems that infinity implies the imperfection of God's might (which refers to ST Ia qq.4-6, on God's perfection and goodness). Secondly, it seems that the effect of an infinite might causes an infinite effect outside God, which is impossible, since God alone is as such (*simpliciter*) infinite (which is a clear link with ST Ia qq.7-8, on God's infinity and presence in our finite world). So since we know a cause through its effects, as was said (2.1.1), why would we call God's might infinite, if its effects are not? The third problem concerns time (as in ST Ia qq.9-10, on God's immutabilty and eternity): it seems that infinite might is so great, that its effects occur instantly, within a single moment, whilst, on the other hand, in Scripture we read that God moves creatures in time. So not only the content, but even the structure of

---

ist in Wahrheit mächtig. Umgekehrt wird man aber daraus *nicht* folgen dürfen, daß Freiheit beziehungsweise *Macht gegenüber der Liebe übergeordnete Instanz*en sind, während die Liebe Gottes gegenüber seine Allmacht und Herrschaft zu einem Epiphenomen wird." [italics added, MR, except '*insofern*']
Also Hedinger (1993), 110-126, struggles to reconcile God's almightiness with His love. His solution is the distinction between three kinds or manifestations of God's might: 1. the powerlessness (Ohnmacht) of God's love, on Good Friday, which protests against the crucifixion; 2. the might or power (Macht) of love, manifested in the resurrection on Easter morning; 3 the almightiness (Allmacht) of love, in the eschaton. However, the difficulty with this distinction is, that it suggests, to say the least, that almightiness is something different than God's might. Furthermore, by making this distinction Hedinger neutralizes the mystery of the might of God as it is revealed in the Crucified, as formulated in 1 Co 1,23-25.

his negative theology, as formulated at the beginning of the *Summa Theologiae*, is a guiding principle in Thomas' theologizing.

In order to clarify that the infinity of God's might does not imply imperfection, but rather perfection, Thomas distinguishes between infinity as Aristotle understands it, in the privative sense of the word, and as John of Damascus understands it, in the negative sense of the word. In the privative understanding the word infinity signifies quantity: an unlimited amount. It is imperfect, because it signifies not having boundaries (*fines*); there is no order to it. Imperfect is *materia* without *forma*, having much *in potentia*, but nothing *in actu*. Yet according to the Christian faith the infinity of God's might is not understood in the Aristotelian way, since God is not corporeal and His might, which is only in our thinking (*secundum rationem*) distinguished from His essence, is totally simple, as was said.

> "But the might of God is called infinite in the negative sense of the word, meaning that it is not limited to any determined effect."[37]

And in this sense infinity rather is a sign of perfection than of imperfection. Besides, if God were corporeal, He would either have been infinite in the Aristotelian sense of the word or He would have been finite. But then His might would not be infinite, for "nothing finite can have infinite might."[38]

In *De potentia* we see how this distinction is applied. If God, that is His being and essence, and therefore His might, is *realiter* distinct from creation, should He then not be limited? How could He otherwise be distinguished from creation? In order to answer this question Thomas, without explicitly referring to Aristotle and John of Damascus, sets out that there are two ways of making distinctions. The one is by distinguishing one thing from another (*per aliud*). For this it is necessary that they are of the same order (*sibi coniunctum*). Thomas gives the example of a

---

[37] CMP XII l.8 n.2550: *Non autem virtus huius* [= *divinae*] *substantiae dicitur infinita privative, secundum quod infinitum congruit quantitati, sed dicitur* negative, *prout scilicet* non limitatur *ad aliquem determinatum effectum.* Cf. ST Ia q.25 a.2 ad 1.

[38] CMP XII l.8 n.2549: *Nullum autem finitum potest habere potentiam infinitam.*

human being and an ass, both belonging to the created order. In this case both must be limited, in order to be distinguished from one another. The other way is distinguishing one thing by saying what it is not (*per se ipsum*).[39] In this way the thing to be distinguished and what it is not, are not necessarily of the same order, since it is not a distinction *between* two things, but a distinction of something *from* another thing. Thomas does not give an example, but we may think of the basic proposition "God (His goodness, love, might etc.) is not a creature." In this way "God" is not necessarily limited.[40] This second way of distinguishing is the negative way. And in this way only do we understand God as distinct and infinite.

There is yet another sense of the word, in which God is infinite and creatures are not. *Infinitas* also means "being without a *finis*", that is without an end or aim. All of creation is created towards its perfection, as its end (*finis*). And all find their ultimate end in God, who is perfect from eternity:

> "It does not befit the First Agent, who is only acting (and not undergoing anything), to act in order to achieve some aim; but He is only aimed at communicating His perfection, which is His goodness. And each and every creature is aimed at reaching its perfection, which is the resemblance to the divine perfection and goodness.[41]

At the roots of this argument lies the idea that an action is always directed

---

[39] QDP q.1 a.2 ad 7: *Alio modo* per se ipsum; *et sic Deus est distinctus ab omnibus rebus, et hoc eo ipso quia nihil addi ei est possibile;* unde non oportet quod sit finitus neque ipse neque aliquid quod in ipso significatur.

[40] QDP q.6 a.1 sc.2: [*P*]*otestas superioris non dependet a potestate inferioris, nec secundum eam limitatur. Sed Deus est* superior *quam natura. Ergo non limitatur eius potentia secundum potentiam naturae*; the Christian distinction, see 2.1.1.

[41] ST Ia q.44 a.4co: *Sed primo agenti, qui est agens tantum, non convenit agere propter acquisitionem alicuius finis; sed intendit solum communicare suam perfectionem, quae est eius bonitas. Et* unaquaeque creatura *intendit consequi* suam perfectionem, quae est similitudo perfectionis et bonitatis divinae. Cf. Pr 16,4 (cited in sc), Is 43,7 and Ep 5,1 (both cited in ST IIaIIae q.132 a.1 ag.1), Rm 11,36 (cited in SCG III c.163 n.4), 1 Co 8,6, Heb 2,10 (cited in QDV q.26 a.10 ad 7), cf. ST Ia q.1 a.7co, IaIIae qq.1-3, q.102 a.1, q.111 a.1co, IIaIIae q.81 a.1, 162 a.7.

towards an aim.[42] Although we may experience aimlessness[43] from time to time, an action is never "just happening"; the agent always has - consciously or not - a purpose, Thomas holds. By nature everything strives for its perfection as its aim:

> "All things are called perfect, in that they attain their end.
> Now, outside the end there is nothing, for the end is what
> is ultimate for each thing and what contains the thing.
> Therefore there is nothing outside the end. Thus what is
> perfect is not in need of anything outside itself, for under
> its perfection it contains everything."[44]

So achieving an aim outside Himself does not befit God, because He is not lacking anything. Furthermore, it does not befit Him, since God is the First Agent; 'before' the first action outside Himself there is nothing besides Himself to aim the action at. From this it follows that, according to Thomas, we can speak of the aim of God's might, of the end of His acting outside Himself, being nothing outside God, but God Himself.[45] An allusion to God as the aim of God's action outside Himself was already found in the analysis of "God is love," where it was said that God's love is expressed in His will to unite the beloved to Himself (2.1.2). In the following paragraphs it will be set out how this is connected with the Passion of Christ and the almightiness of God.

---

[42] ST Ia q.44 a.4co: [D]icendum quod omne *agens agit propter finem*; cf. the *quinta via* in q.2 a.3co and q.103 a.1co.

[43] As expressed for instance in Qo 1,2-2,26 and Rm 8,20a.

[44] CMP X 1.5 n.2029: [O]mnia dicuntur perfecta, eo quod deveniunt ad finem. Extra finem autem nihil est: quia finis est id quod est ultimum in omni re, et quod continet rem. Unde nihil est extra finem. Nec id quod perfectum est, indiget aliquo exteriori. Burrell (1973), 144, adds: "Aquinas tends to speak of all nature seeking its perfection - *quaelibet res quaerit perfectionem suam* - but he would be the first to recognize that seeks is used analogously, with person as the paradigm.

[45] Many theodicies get bogged down on this question: does God always achieve His aim? If one locates God's aim outside God, one could answer positively, for instance on the basis of a strong faith (e.g. Mendelssohn (1969), 68), or negatively, for instance on the basis of the experience of evil in our world (e.g. Kreiner (1997), 209f).

In respect of the infinity of the effects of God's might, Thomas first refers to *quaestio* 7, where he established that God's being (*esse*) is infinite, again, in the negative sense of the word: God's being is not "received" in and therefore not confi*ned* to a certain kind of being, like *materia* is received, and therefore limited, by a particular *forma*.[46] If, as was said, God's being is His essence and His might is nothing accidental, God's might is infinite too. But, the objection reads,

> "every might is manifested through its effect; otherwise the might would be in vain. So, if the might of God were infinite, it would be able to produce an infinite effect. This is impossible[47],

for nothing outside God is infinite. So if we cannot but say that God's might is infinite for the reasons mentioned, then either His might would be in vain (*frustra*) or the method of finding out about the cause through its effect(s) (see 2.1) must be reconsidered.

In order to find an answer, Thomas takes a closer look at the deep structure of God as agent and the effect outside God. By doing so he brings to light that

> "it is obvious that God is not a univocal agent. For nothing can correspond to Him either in type or category, as was explained above. Therefore it remains that an effect of His is always lesser than His might."[48]

In the case of a univocal action the full might of the agent is manifested

---

[46] ST Ia q.7 a.1co, referred to in q.25 a.2co.

[47] ST Ia q.25 a.2 ag.2: *Praeterea, omnis potentia manifestatur per effectum; alias frustra esset. Si igitur potentia Dei esset infinita, posset facere effectum infinitum. Quod est impossibile*.

[48] ST Ia q.25 a.2 ad 2: *Manifestum est autem quod* Deus non est agens univocum*:* Nihil *enim aliud potest cum eo convenire neque in specie neque in genere, ut supra* [q.3 a.5] *ostensum est*. Unde *relinquitur quod effectus eius* semper *est minor quam potentia eius*.
The term *univocum* is not used by Thomas in earlier works in this context. In QDP q.1 a.2 ad 2 he uses *unius generis*.

in the effect. In that case, therefore, agent and effect must be of the same cathegory, of the same kind. As an example of a univocal agent Thomas mentions a human being bringing forth a human being.[49] Thus, since we believe that the creation is not-God, we cannot but say that God with regard to creation *never* is a univocal agent.[50] So Thomas concludes that we can deduce from the effects that God is mighty, but we cannot *directly* deduce its fullness, its infinity from them.[51] If we could, we would come to the conclusion that God's might were not infinite.

In the last sentence of the answer to the second *obiectio*, commenting on the aspect of God's might being (partly) in vain, Thomas turns our whole view of might and aim upside down in respect of God:

> "In vain is what is directed towards an aim which it does not reach. Yet the might of God is not directed towards an effect as to an aim, but rather the might itself is the aim of its effect."[52]

An effect of His might, for instance creation and God's care[53] for it, is directed by God towards His might as its aim. Outside its context this may sound as if God were like a power-mad person. But not in the context of what Thomas says about the simple essence of God, in which

---

[49] It seems that by using this example he implicitly refers to the processions of the Son and the Holy Spirit, ST Ia q.27 a.1 ad 2 (cf. the Creed: *Deum de Deo, Lumen de Lumine, Deum verum de Deo vero*), a.4. Only we cannot properly call the processions a univocal action of God's might, since we speak of God's might merely in respect of the actions of God outside God, as was said.

[50] Not being a univocal agent is by the way not typical of God; it is in fact quite ordinary within creation. E.g. the power, but not the *full* power, of the sun is manifested by the growing of plants.

[51] ST Ia q.13 a.1co: [*Deus*] *cognoscitur a nobis ex creaturae, secundum habitudinem principii,* et per modum excellentiae et remotionis. See 2.1.1.

[52] ST Ia q.25 a.2 ad 2: [*F*]*rustra est quod ordinatur ad finem, quem non attingit. Potentia autem Dei non ordinatur ad effectum sicut ad finem, sed magis* ipsa est finis sui effectus.

[53] E.g. W 8,1, cited in ST Ia q.22 a.2sc, q.109 a.2co, IIaIIae q.23 a.2co, IIIa q.44 a.4sc, q.46 a.9co.

God's might is *realiter* not different from His love, goodness and all other names for it.[54] So, in this context it is clear that Thomas expresses in these two sentences nothing more and nothing less than that everything that comes from God (*exitus*) is created towards God as its aim (*reditus*; cf. 2.1.1 note 12). And thus, as a true theo-centric theologian, he points out to us in this discussion of the infinite might of God the same movement, as in the discussion of "God is love", of all creatures towards God, for our salvation (1 Tm 2,4).[55] Our might, on the other hand, *can* be in vain (*frustra*)[56], because our might is directed towards an aim outside us; if it is in order, to God.[57]

From this quotation it is also clear that God would still be infinitely mighty, if He had not created. His might (*potentia absoluta*) does not depend on whether He creates or moves something or not (*potentia ordinata*).

As for the consequences of time Thomas' answer to Aristotle's theory is similar: only In the case of an univocal agent it is true that an object moves faster as the moving might is greater and that an infinite might moves an object infinitely fast, which means that the object is

---

[54] ST Ia q.5 a.4co: [C]*um* bonum *sit quod omnia appetunt, hoc autem habet rationem* finis; q.6 a.3co: *Solus Deus est bonus per suam essentiam* [....] *cuius* solius *essentia est suum esse.* [....] *Ipse etiam ad nihil ordinatur sicut ad finem: sed* ipse *est* ultimus finis omnium rerum. And, hence, this does not mean anything different from, SN I d.43 q.1 a.1 ad 3: [P]*otentia Dei activa non est propter finem, sed est finis omnium.*

[55] Cited in ST Ia q.19 a.6 ag/ad 1, IaIIae q.91 a.5 ag.2, IIaIIae q.83 a.5 ad 2, IIIa q.70 a.2 ad 3.

[56] And this word may remind someone who, like friar Thomas, prays the Psalms daily of Ps 127,1f (Vulg-Ps 126,1).

[57] ST IaIIae q.77 a.4co: [O]*mnis actus peccati procedit ex aliquo* inordinato *appetitu alicuius temporalis boni. Quod autem aliquis appetat inordinate aliquod temporale bonum, procedit ex hoc quod* inordinate amat seipsum. [....] *Unde manifestum est quod inordinatus amor sui est causa omnis peccati.* Loving yourself is good (*debitus et naturalis*) in itself, cf. Lv 19,18, but becomes disordered when it (ibidem ad 1:) *perducit ad contemptum Dei.*

moved within a moment (*in instanti*), or out of time.[58] And God never is, as was said. Besides, this would mean that God's action towards creation necessarily implied coercion and the denial of the free human will. But, in Scripture we read that God "moves spiritual creatures through time and corporeal creatures through space and time," as Augustine says, commenting on Gn 2,8-17.[59]

Thomas then adds to his answer:

"Therefore, it does not have to be that all His power is manifested in a movement [....] and chiefly since He moves according to the disposition of His will."[60]

By mentioning God's will and thereby referring to the distinction again between God's *potentia absoluta* and *potentia ordinata*, Thomas further distances himself expressly from Aristotle; YHWH is a personal God, with a free will. Hence, that the effects of God's infinite might are not infinite is due to the order of creation, which is as it is freely willed by God Himself. Therefore the finite effects of God's might do not indicate a limitation, not even a freely willed limitation, of God's might,[61] but only

---

[58] ST Ia q.25 a.2 ad 3: [Q]uanto moventis corporis potentia est maior, tanto velocius movet: necesse est quod so fuerit infinita, moveat inproportionabiliter citius, quod est movere non in tempore.

[59] VIII *Super Genesim ad litteram* c.20, ML 34,388, cited in ST Ia q.25 a.2 ag.3. Augustine gives the exemples of God making someone remember what one had forgotten, teaching something one did not know, inspiring someone's will, respectively moving a body from the earth into heaven or the other way round or from east to west (like the sun, MR), which always implies time.

Here also the exemples given by Christ in Mt 13 may come to mind as well as what the apostle Paul says in 1 Co, that Christ is the power of God (1 Co 1,24); see chapter 4.

[60] ST Ia q.25 a.2 ad 3: Unde non oportet, quod tota virtus eius manifestetur in motu [....] et praesertim, quia movet secundum dispositionem suae voluntatis.

[61] QDP q.1 a.2 ad 13: Deus semper agit tota sua potentia; sed effectus terminatur secundum imperium voluntatis et ordinem rationis. Swinburne (1977), 132, takes another position, where he says: "An omnipotent being has the ability to choose to make himself no longer omnipotent, a power he may or may not choose to exercise." But first of all we never speak of "an" omnipotent "being"; omnipotent, or, as I prefer, almighty, is a word

the limitedness that is inherent in creation. In brief: the limitation is not in God, but in creation alone.

In the light of this it is clear that the infinity of God's might, by which God's will is executed, and thus also as regards Christ's Passion and death, by no means implies any force or coercion from the side of God or a limitation of the freedom of the man Christ to obey God's will. Since God is - infinitely - mightier than a human being, He could force him/her. But explaining Pr 21,1 ("Like flowing water is the king's heart in YHWH's hand; He directs it where He pleases"), Is 26,12 ("YHWH, [....] You have completed all our works for us") and Ph 2,13 ("It is God who brings about our willing and our doing"), Thomas elucidates that this is not what God does, when He moves someone's will. For force and coercion come from outside and go against the human will, which is naturally inclined to what is good. But when God moves the will, He *inspires* it, from inside, strengthening this natural movement.[62] The human being remains free and responsible.[63] Hence we speak with regard to the Passion of the merit of Christ.[64]

Moreover, that God is not a univocal agent means that He is not a rival of humankind; God is never party to a conflict with us. Scripture is clear that we should not think that when a human being struggles with

---

exclusively and properly used for God, as will also be argued for in paragraph 3.2. Secondly, Swinburne locates the limitation in God, which implies a change of God's being and essence, which is incompatible with the divinity of God, as was shown in chapter 2. Thirdly, according to Swinburne omnipotence is not identical with God's power. It seems that he must make a distinction between omnipotence and God's might since he neither distinguishes between *potentia ordinata* and *potentia absoluta* nor recognizes God as a non-univocal agent. The same critique applies to other works of his, e.g. (1996), chapter 6. Also Jüngel (1986), 265-275; he speaks of creation as a self-limiting act of God.

[62] Respectively in ST IaIIae q.6 a.4co, ad 1 and Ia q.105 a.4 ad 2 (*[M]overi voluntarie est* moveri ex se*, idest* a principio intrinseco*: sed illud principium intrinsecum potest esse ab alio principio extrinseco*), a.5sc and IaIIae q.9 a.6; cf. CDN c.10 l.1. This is a fundamental revision of SN II d.25 q.1 a.2, where Thomas only makes a gradual distinction between *impulsio* and *compulsio* (as resp. *insufficiens* and *sufficiens*).

[63] Cf. Dt 30,15-20, Jr 21,8 and esp. Si 15,14-17, cited in ST Ia q.22 a.4 ag.2, q.83 a.1sc, IaIIae q.10 a.4sc; in Si 15 this is explicitly connected with God's great might (*fortis in potentia*, נב ו ד ו ה (= plur.) א ם י ץ): vv 18-21.

[64] ST IIIa q.48 a.1, citing Ph 2,9 in sc.

God, he or she struggles with a peer.[65]

In this paragraph we have seen how Thomas as a negative theologian argues that, although we have to make a distinction (*secundum rationem*), we cannot but say that God's might is (*secundum rem*) one, *activa* and not something other than His essence, and therefore infinite, yes even the *finis* itself. The "infinity" of God's might implies

> "that it is not terminated by the intellect; for it is ineffable
> and unknown and it cannot be conceived, because the
> whole divine power exceeds it."[66]

It may seem that these are the reasons why we call God almighty (*omnipotens*). But in the *Summa Theologiae* Thomas' song of God's almightiness is written in another key.

3.2 "All People Together Profess that God Is Almighty."[67]

A Christian theologian from the 13th century could say this, without any doubt; it is, as we read in Scripture, revealed of old that God is almighty[68] and we profess it in the Creed. How much has changed in this respect since then. Almightiness has become such a controversial attribute of God, that it is even denied of Him by many, among them theologians. The most extreme advocate against attributing almightiness to

---

[65] Cf. 2 M 8,18, Jb 38,1-42,6, W 10,12, Is 40,12-31, Hos 12,5. This notion is absent in Ten Kate (2000), see 3.4.1.

[66] CDN c.8 1.1: *[V]irtus Dei* [....] *[q]uinto dicitur infinita, eo quod non terminatur intellectu; est enim ineffabilis et ignota, et quae cogitari non potest, divina virtus cuncta excedens.*

[67] ST Ia q.25 a.3co: *[C]ommuniter confitentur omnes Deum esse omnipotentem.*

[68] ST Ia q.13 a.1sc: *Videtur quod nullum nomen Deo conveniat. Sed contra est quod* dicitur Ex. 15,3: *"Dominus quasi vir pugnator, Omnipotens nomen eius."* IIaIIae q.174 a.6co: Dominus dicit Moysi, Ex. 6,2-3: *"Ego Dominus, qui apparui Abraham, Isaac et Iacob in Deo omnipotente, et nomen meum Adonai non indicavi eis":* quia scilicet praecedentes Patres fuerunt instructi in communi in omnipotente unius Dei.

God may be Charles Hartshorne:

> "No worse falsehood was ever perpetrated than the
> traditional concept of omnipotence. It is a piece of un-
> conscious blaspemy, condemning God to a dead world,
> probably not distinguishable from no world at all."[69]

It seems that the reason for such a statement, is what he understands by
the traditional concept of almightiness, or "omnipotence", as he calls it.
And it is particularly interesting for this study, since he foists this
'traditional' concept upon Thomas - with quite an oblique reference by the
way:

> "Without telling themselves so, the founders of the
> theological tradition were accepting and applying to deity
> the *tyrant* ideal of power. "I decide and determine every-
> thing, you (and your friends and enemies) merely do what
> I determine you (and them) to do. [....] Omnipotence is
> defined as power to absolutely determine what happens. I
> have Thomas Aquinas especially in mind here."[70]

But a similar kind of definition of what God's almightiness would
signify, is found among theologians who underline the importance of
God's almightiness, for example the Dutch theologian Abraham van de
Beek. The content as well as the casualness of the definition given by him
catches the eye:

> "If God is almighty, everything happens as he wills it to
> happen. If people have unpleasant experiences, they
> nevertheless occur in accord with the will of God. For if
> God had not willed them, they could not have

---

[69] Hartshorne (1984), 18.

[70] Hartshorne, *o.c.*, 11. Earlier on the same page instead of "absolutely" he writes
"every detail".

occurred."[71]

The origin of this perception of almightiness is not at all clear. But it seems that Van de Beek assumes that by saying this, he hits upon common ground. It seems to be his own perception too, since he does not criticize this view of almightiness.[72] But on the other hand, later on he praises Karl Barth, saying that

> "[i]t is a liberating thing not to have to speak of an omnipotent, all-encompassing Supreme Being, whose mighty hand holds within itself all contrasts and suffering of the world, and *instead* to be allowed to speak of God's concrete presence in Jesus Christ." (italics added, MR)[73]

Both of these and similar approaches may be typical of our time and make it difficult, if not impossible, to believe in "God, the *almighty* Father": first, according to these authors we obviously know what almightiness is. Second, almightiness is God's all-determining power. Third, speaking of Jesus Christ as the one living, suffering and dying with us, is regarded as an alternative way of considering the relation of (the almighty) God to creation instead of as the ultimate expression of it. At least in Van de Beek's view, for Hartshorne, retorting, totally ignores the meaning of the life and death of Christ for our God-talk.

---

[71] Van de Beek (1984), 12 (English translation: 5): "Als God almachtig is, gebeurt alles, zoals hij dat wil. Als mensen onaangename ervaringen hebben, zijn die toch volgens de wil van God. Want als God ze niet gewild had, zouden ze niet hebben kunnen gebeuren."

[72] E.g. Van de Beek, *o.c.*, 90 (90): "Overmacht wil zeggen, dat God sterker is dan de machten die God bedreigen. Almacht wil zeggen, dat alle dingen uit de hand van God voortkomen." On page 91 (91) in the small print he refers with regard to this to W. Michaelis (*Pantokrátor*, in *ThWNT* 3, page 914). But what's more, even in the reaction to his book, Heering, Van Reyendam-Beek etc. (eds.), *Nogmaals: Waarom?* (1986), none of the theologians passes critique on Van de Beek's view of almightiness.

[73] Van de Beek, *o.c.*, 225 (233): "(De betekenis van Barth voor kerk en theologie is groot geweest.) Het is bevrijdend om niet te hoeven spreken over een almachtig, alomvattend Opperwezen, wiens machtige hand alle tegenstellingen en leed van de wereld omvat, *maar* te mogen spreken over de concrete aanwezigheid Gods in Jezus Christus." (italics added, MR) Van de Beek elaborates this in n.19, 272-285 (282-294).

"'Are we to worship the Heavenly Father of Jesus (or the
Holy Merciful One of the Psalmist or Isaiah), *or* to
worship a heavenly king, that is, a cosmic despot?' These
are incompatible ideals; candid thinkers should choose and
not pretend to be faithful to both."
"[T]he suggestion heard so often that, apart from the
account of the life of Jesus, or even, apart from the Bible
as a whole, we would know nothing about God. 'Speak
for yourself,' is what I feel I must say to this."[74]

Many may not connect the name Thomas Aquinas with growth
and change in theological thought, but, as was already pointed out, in
particular in chapter 1, we find developments in his theological works
over the years, also on the *omnipotentia Dei*. After a brief overview of
this development in the first subparagraph his text about God's
almightiness in the *Summa Theologiae* will be read (3.2.2) with the issues
mentioned here in mind. They can be seen then as contemporary
questions to Thomas: is it according to him indeed so crystal-clear and
easy what almightiness is? Does it correspond with Hartshorne's
formulation of Thomas' ideas and with Van de Beek's definition? Do we
find in Thomas' text the contradiction of almightiness on the one hand
and God's presence in Jesus Christ on the other (Van de Beek) and/or
God as spoken of as a heavenly king instead of God as the holy, merciful
Father of Jesus Christ? These questions may be answered whilst it is
inquired in this paragraph whether and if so, in what way, Thomas in his
exposition on the almightiness of God makes a connection with the *Passio
Christi*.

3.2.1 Almightiness as a Word of Faith.

Looking at how Thomas in the course of time speaks of God's
almightiness in his theological works, one notices a remarkable development. Seeing this, helps the reader to understand what Thomas does
in the *Summa Theologiae*. For in the commentary on the *Sententiae* the
almightiness of God is not a distinct issue. Here it literally goes without

---

[74] Hartshorne, *o.c.*, 14 resp. 125.

saying that God is almighty because His might is infinite.[75] On the basis of what Thomas says in the *Sententiae* it is not at all clear why we use two different terms: *potentia infinita* and *omnipotentia*.

In the *Sententiae* Thomas considers *omnipotentia* in the context of God's knowing (especially predestination) and willing. In the *Summa Contra Gentiles* the consideration of *omnipotentia* is confined to the theology of creation. In this work the bottom line concerning God's *omnipotentia* is that

> "the divine power is not determined to a certain effect, but that it can simply all things: and this means that He is almighty."[76]

God's almightiness is a distinct issue here. In the explanation of the term and in the wider context of it the whole discussion on *potentia infinita* is remarkably absent; *omnipotens* is explained as *omnia potens*. Also new in the *Summa Contra Gentiles* is the explicit reference to faith and Scripture:

> "For this reason it is also that divine Scripture hands down that this must be kept in faith. For Gn 17,1 says, from the mouth of God: 'I am the almighty God; walk in the sight of Me and be perfect.' And Jb 42,2: 'I know that You can do all things.' And Lk 1,37, from the mouth of

---

[75] The question whether Gods might is infinite, is followed by the question whether the almightiness of God can be communicated to a creature (SN I d.43 q.1 aa.1, 2). Only in a subordinate clause in SN I d.43 q.1 a.2 ag.4 is it merely mentioned that God is called almighty because of the infinity of His might (*Cum ergo Deus dicatur omnipotens propter infinitatem suae potentiae, ...* - a quote from Pseudo-Dionysius *Cael. hierar.*), but this is not expounded any further, neither in the *corpus* (where the word *omnipotentia* occurs once, as a synonym of *potentia infinita*), nor in the reactions to the *obiectiones* (where *omnipotentia* occurs only once: in ad 1, as one of the examples of God's incommunicable perfections).

[76] SCG II c.22 n.6: *[D]ivina virtus non determinetur ad aliquem effectum, sed simpliciter omnia potest: quod est eum esse omnipotentem.*

an angel: 'For God no word shall be impossible.'"[77]

After the exposition and its conclusion, the authority of Scripture, God's very own word, a holy man's testimony and the testimony of an angel, confirm the truth of it.

In the following steps in the *Summa Contra Gentiles* Thomas clears up some possible misconceptions concerning almightiness. In the *Quaestiones Disputatae De Potentia* (*quaestio* 1) Thomas does this in the six preliminary steps, *before* arriving at *articulus* 7, the question why we call (*dicitur*) God almighty. Many texts from Scripture that may lie at the root of a misunderstanding or precisely run counter to a certain error, are discussed in the first six *articuli*.

But in the *Summa Theologiae* Thomas changes the whole point of view. No longer does he observe that God is called (*dicitur*) almighty, but that we all *believe* (*confitentur*) that God is almighty. In other words, Thomas identifies "almighty" as a word from the realm of faith. The *articuli* 1 and 2, on God's "might (*potentia activa*)" and "endless might (*potentia infinita*)", are tools for explaining the Catholic faith. Non-Christians also, Aristotle for instance, can come to the conclusion that there is might in God and that His might is infinite. The word "almightiness", however, presupposes faith. The consequence of this is, that almightiness cannot be discussed outside this context.

Now almightiness is not anything different from God's active and endless might. The word almightiness designates in the context of faith the one might of the triune God:

"The might of God is nothing else than almightiness."[78]

So Thomas does not establish what we believe - Is God almighty, yes or no - but he notes and records that we believe that God is almighty. Not that this puts an end to all problems concerning this attribute; it rather is the starting point of his inquiry:

---

[77] SCG II c.22 n.7: *Hinc est quod etiam* divina Scriptura fide *tenendum hoc tradit. Dicitur enim Gen. XVII,* ex ore Dei: *"Ego Deus omnipotens: ambula coram me et esto perfectus;" et Iob XLII: "Scio quia omnia potes;" et Lucae I,* ex ore angeli: *"Non erit impossibile apud Deum omne verbum."*

[78] REM c.28: *Potentia Dei nihil aliud est quam omnipotentia.*

"I answer that we must say that all people together confess that God is almighty. But interpreting almightiness seems to be difficult."[79]

A fine example of faith seeking understanding (*fides quaerens intellectum*). Hence we can say that Thomas is more theo-logical in the *Summa Theologiae* than in his earlier works.

It was said already in paragraph 3.1 that Thomas is also more systhematic in the *Summa Theologiae* than in his earlier works. The structure and his line of reasoning are more transparant here. Moreover, compared to the *Summa Contra Gentiles* it is clearer in the *Summa Theologiae* that questions about God's almightiness concern the divinity of God, and not only what is not God, creation. Furthermore, in *De Potentia* many issues discussed in *quaestio* 1 concern God's knowing and willing. In the *Summa Theologiae* (*Prima Pars*) most of these are discussed before *quaestio* 25, on the might of God, so that the preliminary steps can be fewer (only two) and more focussed on the specific problems concerning might and God.

3.2.2 What's in a Name?

Simple answers to what the word almightiness signifies, do not satisfy. For instance that it means that God can do all He wants. This is not untrue - it is characteristic (*sufficiens signum*) of almightiness - but it is not a sufficient definition (*non est sufficiens ratio*) of almightiness, since this applies to any happy person. For we feel happy when we are able to do what we want to do.[80] Also the addition that almightiness means that God does not want what is impossible - e.g. making a square circle - does not solve anything, for this is a characteristic of any wise

---

[79] The first sentence of ST Ia q.25 a.3co: *Respondeo dicendum quod communiter confitentur omnes Deum esse omnipotentem. Sed rationem omnipotentiae assignare videtur difficile.*

[80] QDP q.1 a.7 ag.3, sc.2, ad 3. And therefore Augustine's remark in *Enchiridion* c.46 that God is called almighty for no other reason than that He can do whatever He wants to do, must be understood as *a* characterization and not as *the* definition of almightiness.

person (*quilibet sapiens*).[81] But still we do not call a happy and/or a wise person almighty.

In the *Summa Theologiae* Thomas formulates four arguments according to which it seems that God cannot be called almighty, in order to clarify the meaning of the term almightiness. The focus of the first two is God, the focus of the last two is our salvation.

The first *obiectio* is that being moved and undergoing are numbered amongst "all things" (*omnia*). But since God can neither (*non potest*) be moved nor undergo anything, He cannot do "all things" (*omnia posse*). Therefore God is not *omnipotens*.[82] The same line of reasoning is followed in the second *obiectio*: not only in respect of passive things (*passiva, pati*), but also in respect of the active things (*activa, agere*) it seems that God cannot do all things. Thomas puts forward that God cannot sin or, as is said in 2 Tm 2,13, deny Himself.[83] So there are theological reasons to say that God is not almighty; in respect of what we understand by "God" we cannot - simply - say that He can do (or undergo) "all things". The third *obiectio* reads:

> "It is said of God that 'He discloses His almightiness by saving foremost and by having mercy.' Thus the ultimate thing God can do is saving and having mercy. Yet another thing is much greater than saving and having mercy, like creating another world or something the like. Hence God is not almighty."[84]

---

[81] QDP q.1 a.7 sc.3.

[82] ST Ia q.25 a.3 ag.1: *Videtur quod Deus non sit omnipotens.* Moveri *enim* et pati aliquid omnium *est. Sed hoc Deus non potest: est enim immobilis, ut supra* [q.2 a.3, q.9 a.1] *dictum est. Non igitur est omnipotens.*

[83] ST Ia q.25 a.3 ag.2: *Praeterea, peccare* aliquid *agere est. Sed Deus* non potest *peccare, neque "seipsum negare", ut dicitur II Tim.* [2,13]. *Ergo Deus non est omnipotens.*

[84] ST Ia q.25 a.3 ag.3: [D]*e Deo dicitur* [*In collecta domin.* 10 *post Pentecost*] *quod "omnipotentiam suam parcendo* maxime *et miserando manifestat." Ultimum igitur quod potest divina potentia, est parcere et misereri. Aliquid autem est multo maius quam parcere et misereri; sicut creare alium mundum, vel aliud huiusmodi. Ergo Deus non est omnipotens.*

This is a most arcane argument. For neither the connection of almightiness with saving and being merciful[85] nor the argumentation that creating another world is much greater than this as an argument against God's almightiness, is found in contemporary theology. Even more, where might is perceived as something forceful and violent, almightiness and God's saving mercy rather become opposites. But referring to an authoritative homily Thomas calls God's saving and His mercy *the ultimate* expression of His almightiness. This requires a further explanation, also in the light of what has been said of God being without *compassio*.

The fourth *obiectio* concerns a correct understanding of 1 Co 1,20: "God has shown up the wisdom of this world as folly," to which an explanatory *glossa* adds: "by showing that what it considered impossible *is* possible." Thomas rephrases this, saying that something should not be called possible or impossible because of the lower causes, but according to the might (*potentia absoluta*) of God, the first cause. But if for God everything is possible, if nothing is impossible, a problem arises:

> "When the impossible is taken away, necessity is abolished. For it is impossible that a thing that necessarily is, is not. Hence no necessity will be in things, if God is almighty. Yet this is impossible."[86]

So according to this *obiectio* the almightiness of God would deny an order of cause and effect and the laws of nature. Then almightiness would cohere with arbitrariness and chaos in creation.

Especially after reading Thomas' exposition on the *Passio Christi*, three of the four *obiectiones* in this *articulus* seem to be somehow connected with it: the first *obiectio* is about *pati* and God. In the second 2 Tm 2,13 is cited. The context of this verse is the Passion of Christ. Furthermore, the sole other places in the *Summa Theologiae* where this verse is cited, are where Thomas considers the mercy (*misericordia*) of

---

[85] An exception: Weinandy (2000), 167, referring to ST IaIIae q.30 a.4.

[86] ST Ia q.25 a.3 ag.4: *Sublato autem impossibili, tollitur necessarium: nam quod necesse est esse, impossibile est non esse. Nihil ergo erit necessarium in rebus, si Deus est omnipotens. Hoc autem est impossibile.*

God and the justice of God with regard to humankind being ordered, that is being restored to the order towards God. One of these places is *quaestio* 46 of the *Tertia Pars*, on the *passio Christi*.[87] At first sight a link between *obiectio* 3 with the *Passio Christi* may not be clear. The quotation of 1 Co 1,20, where the apostle Paul speaks of Christ crucified as the power and wisdom of God, in *obiectio* 4, is the most explicit reference to the *Passio Christi*, although the argumentation in the *obiectio* does not specifically speak of it. It could therefore be just a 'useful' quote from Scripture, as it were, taken out of its context.

The same applies to Lk 1,37, cited as the *sed contra*, which says that nothing - or "no word", as the Greek text as well as the Vulgate read - is or will be impossible to God. One could suspect that this verse is cited here, because it suits the purpose of a theologian who wants to explain the almightiness of God. But on further consideration it seems that there is more going on here. For Lk 1,37 is part of the annunciation of the birth of Christ to Mary by the archangel Gabriel, the very beginning of the mystery of Christ evolving in our world. The only two other times that it is cited in the *Summa Theologiae*, are both in connection with this mystery: first in the context of the Incarnation and later, as was shown in paragraph 1.2.2, in the context of Christ's Passion.[88] Hence the use of Lk 1,37 in the *sed contra* of this *articulus* may be another sign that Thomas is not considering the almightiness of God (merely) as a kind of speculative theology, but that he does so in view the mystery of the Incarnation and Passion of Christ, through which our salvation comes to pass.

In the *corpus* Thomas takes three steps. The first consists of two remarks, the first being that all people together profess that God is almighty, as was said above. The discussion that follows is a discussion about what we believe. In other words, Thomas does not consider the might of "an omnipotent being", but the might of the almighty God. The

---

[87] ST Ia q.21 a.3 ag.2 resp. IaIIae q.100 a.8 ad 2 and IIIa q.46 a.2 ag.3; see par. 1.2.2.

[88] ST IIIa q.3 a.3sc resp. q.46 a.2co. Note that this is not the case in Thomas' earlier works, where Lk 1,37 is cited in more general discussions on God's almightiness: SN I d.42 q.2 a.2 ag.6, SCG II c.22 n.7, QDP q.1 a.3 sc.1, a.4 ad 14, QDL V q.2 a.1 ag.1, IX q.1 a.1sc.

second remark is that it is difficult (*difficile*) to establish what almightiness, *omnipotentia* means. It is an instruction for the reader to be careful and he makes an appeal to the reader's keen intellect (*recte considere*) on this matter.

Thomas parses *omnipotentia* as *omnia posse*, that is being able to do all possible things (*posse omnia possibilia*).[89] In order to find what is understood by this, Thomas takes a second step, divided into two. He starts with the metaphysical question of what possible (*possibile*) means, which he then applies to God. Next he approaches the question what is possible for God by beginning with the divinity of God as the point of departure - using the results of the preliminary steps in the *articuli* 1 and 2.

For the first approach Thomas employs Aristotle's distinction: "possible" can be used in the relative and in the absolute sense. In the relative sense it means that something is possible for a certain might (*potentia*):

> "Just as what is subject to human might is called 'possible for a human being.'[90]

But in this sense we cannot speak of the almightiness of God, because applied to it this would either mean that God can do all that a creature can do, but God can do much more. Or almightiness would mean that God can do all things that are possible for His might, but this is circular argument (*circulatio*). In fact the text cited here (note 90) is also a circular argument. Yet in case of a human being this is not an insurmountable problem, because the might of an agent is in conformity with its nature and the nature of a creature can be known by us. "But of God we cannot know what He is," as was said. Therefore it remains that almightiness signifies that all things are *possibile* for God in the absolute sense of the word. And something is possible in the absolute sense of the word, when no absolute contradictions are implied. Hence almightiness does not designate that God could create a true human being without a

---

[89] Thomas makes an appeal to our common sense: *posse* and *potentia* are with regard to *possibilia*; *non posse* and *impotentia* are with regard to *impossibilia*.

[90] ST Ia q.25 a.3co: [*S*]*icut quod subditur humanae potentiae, dicitur esse "possibile hominis"*. Thomas refers to Aristotle's V Metaph. c.12 n.10 (Bk 1019b34).

soul or create something equal to Himself or that He could make something which truly happened in the past never to have happened.[91] In brief: what is im-*poss*ible is not subject to any *posse*.

As for the subject of almightiness Thomas first recalls earlier findings: every agent acts similar to itself (2.1.1); every active might has a possible thing as its object (as was said above); the nature of the active might is founded upon the degree of its perfection, in other words, it depends on to the extent to which it is *in actu* (2.2). Applied, in reverse order, to God's might this means:

> "Divine being, upon which the nature of the divine might is founded, is infinite being, not limited to any kind of being, but beforehand containing within itself the perfection of all being. Whence, whatever can have the nature of being is numbered among the absolutely possible things, in respect of which God is called almighty."[92]

Therefore, since there are no accidents in God, since the might of God - as well as His love, mercy, justice and any other attributes - is not anything different from His perfect being, nothing that is (*potentia ordinata*)[93] or can be (*potentia absoluta*), is excluded from His might.

---

[91] A creature without a soul is not a human being (SCG II c.25 n.13). Therefore, if Christ were truly human, He must have had a soul, as was said. A creature is *ipso facto* dependent on a higher other c.q. the Other and therefore cannot be equal to that other (ibidem n.18). As for Christ this is reflected in His obedience. See for the absolute impossibility of changing history (as in films like *Back to the Future*): ST Ia q.25 a.4.

[92] ST Ia q.25 a.3co: *Esse autem divinum super quod ratio divinae potentiae* fundatur, *est esse* infinitum, *non limitatum ad aliquod genus entis, sed* praehabens *in se totius esse perfectionem. Unde quidquid potest habere rationem entis, continuetur sub possibilibus absolutis, respectu quorum Deus dicitur omnipotens.*

[93] In the *Prima Pars* Thomas elaborates this with regard to creation, ST Ia q.8 a.1co: *Cum autem Deus sit ipsum esse per suam essentiam, oportet quod esse creatum sit proprius* effectus *eius.* [....] [N]on solum quando primo esse incipiunt, sed quandiu in esse conservatur.* Ibidem q.44 a.1co: [O]mnia alia a Deo *non sint suum esse, sed* participant esse. Necesse est igitur omnia quae diversificantur secundum diversam participationem essendi, ut sint* perfectius vel minus perfecte, *causari ab uno primo ente, quod perfectissime est.* Ibidem q.104 a.1co: *Et hoc modo omnes creaturae indigent divina conservatione. Dependet enim esse cuiuslibet creaturae a Deo, ita quod nec ad momentum*

Thence Thomas adds that it is more correct to call self-contradictory things impossible or "things that cannot be made or done" than "impossible for God". Impossibilities cannot be, are not part of everything and therefore not subject to God's might[94] or any might.

However, one could object, raising someone from the dead seems to imply a contradiction.[95] How then can we say that Christ truly died and is truly risen from the dead by the hand of God? Thomas distinguishes in the next *articulus* what is absolutely (*absolute*) contradictory from what is as such (*per se*) contradictory.[96] Bringing a dead person back to life falls under the second category. This means that it is impossible for a natural, created might. Yet these impossibilities are still subject to supernatural, uncreated might, which is the might of God.[97] For raising the dead is not absolutely impossible. What *is* impossible in the absolute sense of the word, and is therefore not subject to any might, is undoing that Christ has died on the cross after the crucifixion.[98] Hence Christ's death and resurrection as well as His humility and

---

subsistere possent, sed in nihilum redigentur, nisi operatione divinae virtutis *conservarentur in esse, sicut Gregorius dicit* [*Moral.* XVI c.37, ML 75,1143], cf. Ibidem IaIIae q.109 a.2 ad 2.

[94] ST Ia q.25 a.3co: *Ea vero quae contradictionem implicant sub divina omnipotentia* non continentur: *quia non possunt habere possibilium rationem. Unde convenientius dicitur quod "non possunt fieri" quam quod "Deus non potest ea facere".* One may think of the classical exemples "Can God make a square circle?" and "Can the God who can do all things, create a stone so big, that He cannot lift it?"

[95] ST IIIa q.53 a.3co: [*R*]*esurrectio est reparatio* a morte in vitam.

[96] ST Ia q.25 a.4 ad 1.

[97] Cf. Gn 18,14, Jb 42,2, Jr 32,17, 27, Zc 8,6, Mt 3,9, 19,26, Mk 10,27, 14,36, Lk 1,37, 18,27, Jn 11,21f.

[98] In ST Ia q.25 a.4 ad 3 Thomas gives the exemples of a woman who lost her virginity and of a sinner: God can restore the woman's virginity and He can restore the sinner to the love of God, but He cannot make that what has happened (the loss resp. of the virginity and God's love) had never happened; for this is self-contradictory and so an absolute impossibility.

humiliation and exaltation[99] are as such contradictory, but not absolutely, as long as they do not take place at the same time.[100]

The third step in the *corpus* of *articulus* 3 is to return to Lk 1,37. The "impossible for God" has been clarified and also "no word":

> "There cannot be a word for something that implies a contradiction, for no intellect can conceive it."[101]

Hence "no word" is in this context synonymous with "no thing", "nothing".

In the *corpus* no clear reference to the Passion of Christ is found. What Thomas does in the *corpus* - in step two - is to seek the meaning of the word almightiness, which is by definition the almightiness *of God*.[102] Furthermore the *corpus* shows - in step one - that this quest takes place in the context of our faith: "almightiness" is a word from the realm of our faith. Step three shows Thomas' purpose of the quest: a correct interpretation of Scripture and of our faith, especially regarding our salvation, as will be found in the answers to the *obiectiones*.

After this exposition in the *corpus* the argumentations in the first two *obiectiones* are easily refuted: since God is *actus purus* it is impossible that there should be any *potentia passiva* in Him, because *actus purus* exactly designates the absence of *potentia passiva*. God only befits *potentia activa*, as Thomas pointed out in *articulus* 1. And having

---

[99] As for instance in 2 Co 13,4, cited in ST IIIa q.53 a.4co, resp. Ep 4,9f and Ph 2,7-9, cited in ibidem q.49 a.6sc, co.

[100] Jn 3,14, read against the background of Dt 21,23 (cited in Ga 3,13), indicates a simultaneity of Christ's humiliation and exaltation. These, however, are not contradictory in the absolute sense, REI c.12 l.6 n.1 (on Jn 12,34): *Posita promissione de glorificatione Domini* [....] *"Respondit ei turba," scilicet Domino de sua morte loquenti.* Christ's humiliation and exaltation take place on a different level: The exaltation is on a deeper level, concealed in what is at first sight a humiliation - as in Is 53,4.

[101] ST Ia q.25 a.3co: *Id enim quod contradictionem implicat, verbum esse non potest: quia nullus intellectus potest illud concipere.*

[102] SN I d.43 q.1 a.2: Nothing which is not God can be almighty; see also chapter 4.

potentia passiva entails that something can undergo (*pati*) something and be moved. Hence, we should not only say, as Thomas does, "that God cannot be moved and undergo, does not contradict almightiness,"[103] but even that God cannot be moved and undergo *because* He is almighty. For undergoing and being moved are contradictory, in the absolute sense of the word, to almightiness.

In a similar way, but now formulated more strongly, positively, instead of with a double denial, Thomas points to the incompability of sinning and almightiness:

> "Sinning is failing in perfect action. Whence being able to sin is being able to fail in acting. And this contradicts almightiness. And because of this God cannot sin, because He is almighty."[104]

So sinning is in this view rather failing in action than an action. Yet in *articulus* 2 Thomas already set out that God never fails, but always achieves His goal, which God is Himself. Sinning causes a distance between the sinner and God[105] and is, therefore, the opposite of love. Thomas describes sinning as voluntarily turning away from God.[106] And so, in accordance with 2 Tm 2,13, it is impossible that God sins; it would be absolutely contradictory to the - unchangeable - love and will of God, the aim of which is the good that God is Himself.[107] Hereupon Thomas

---

[103] ST Ia q.25 a.3 ad 1: *Unde, quod non potest moveri et pati,* non repugnat *omnipotentiae.*

[104] ST Ia q.25 a.3 ad 2: *[P]eccare est deficere a perfecta actione: unde* posse peccare est posse deficere in agendo, *quod repugnat omnipotentiae. Et propter hoc, Deus peccare non potest, qui est omnipotens.*

[105] As it is expressed in Is 1,15 and 59,2.

[106] ST Ia q.94 a.1co: [V]oluntate averti a Deo, *quod est peccare.* Ibidem q.48 a.4co: *[P]eccata sunt* quasi obstacula *interposita inter nos et Deum,* secundum illud Isaias 59,2, cf. IaIIae q.71, IIaIIae q.39 a.1 ad 1.

[107] ST Ia q.20 a.1 ad 3: *[I]n eo quod aliquis amat se, vult bonum sibi.* [....] *[I]llud bonum quod vult [Deus] sibi, non est aliud quam ipse, qui est per suam essentiam bonus, ut supra* [q.6 a.3] *ostensum est.*

cites Aristotle, who holds that God can also be inclined to do evil (*prava*, as opposed to *recta*). Thomas iuxtaposes three possible *Christian* interpretations of this: 1. It is understood under the condition that He wills it - a condition under which Aristotle's opinion is true, although the condition itself never is. 2. God does something which seems evil now, but eventually turns out to be good. 3. Contrary to Christians, pagans commonly ascribe human characteristics univocally to their gods.[108] The most obvious is the third: pagans do so. The second - as the third, not found in Thomas' earlier commentary on this text in *De potentia* - may suggest a reference to Christ's Passion. For on the surface it is pure evil that God handed His Son over to be crucified. But, as was shown in paragraphs 1.1.2 and 1.2, on a deeper level it reflects the abundant goodness and the love of God for us (Rm 8,32, "God gave Him [His own Son] up for the sake of all of us", cited there).

The answer to the third *obiectio* may be as remarkable as the *obiectio* itself. Thomas endorses that "God's almightiness is shown foremost by saving and by having mercy."[109] Thomas does not mention the text from Scripture on which the homily quoted is based, but it seems that it is W 11,23: "You are merciful to all, because You are almighty." This does not really simplify the meaning of the argument, but knowing that Thomas is not just quoting "a" text, but referring to a text from Scripture, makes the argument heavier. Thomas lists three interpretations, which confirm and amplify one another. The first highlights the aspect of God, the second the aspect of our good and the third how they are related. God's almightiness is shown foremost by saving and by having mercy,

> "since through this it is shown that God has the highest
> power, that He forgives sins *freely*. For someone who is

---

[108] Aristotle, in IV *Topic.* c.5 n.7, Bk 126a34. In view of this third interpretation one could say that Thomas is more critical towards Aristotle in the ST Ia q.25 a.3 ad 2 than in QDP q.1 a.6 ad 3, where he only gives the first interpretation.

[109] ST Ia q.25 a.3 ad 3: *Dei omnipotentia ostenditur maxime in parcendo et miserando.* By placing the word *maxime* before *in parcendo* (instead of behind it), it relates equally to saving and having mercy.

bound to a higher law, is not free to remit sins.[110]
(italics added, MR)

Thus, in His saving and being merciful God shows He is the Most High, for not bound to any higher law, absolutely free - as we read e.g. in Ps 135,6 ("For I know that the Lord is great, our Lord is above all the gods. YHWH does whatever He pleases in heaven, on earth, in the waters and all the depths"[111]); being forced would imply *passio*. Being "the Most High" therefore, is, according to Thomas, inherent in being "the Almighty". Again, this does not imply that God would be 'free' to do evil, since this would imply an absolute contradiction.

In respect of our good, the second interpretation, God's almightiness is shown foremost by saving and by having mercy upon humankind, since in doing so

"He leads them to taking part in the infinite good, which is the ultimate effect of the divine power."[112]

This may remind the reader of what Thomas writes about love, as a unifying and welding force, and about the *exitus - reditus*: all that is comes from God and naturally strives to return to God, who is ultimately good, for goodness itself. Yet what Thomas does not explain here, is what the saving mercy of God has to do with reaching our final aim; is God's almightiness not enough for that?

In the third interpretation Thomas identifies all - always - free and good actions of God outside God, that is all His *mighty* deeds, as coming forth from His mercy. For He, as the first - and therefore not moved by

---

[110] ST Ia q.25 a.3 ad 3: *quia per hoc ostenditur Deum habere summam potestam, quod* libere *peccata dimittit: eius enim qui superioris legi astringitur, non est libere peccata condonare.* Cf. q.21 a.1 ad 2, explaining Ep 1,11: Deus *autem* sibi ipsi est lex.

[111] Cf. also Job 23,13, Ps 115,3, W 12,18, Is 46,10, Ep 1,11 and CDN c.8 l.1: *Psalm. XXIII,10* [Ps 24,10] *"Dominus virtutum ipse est rex gloriae"; et in multis locis dicitur "Dominus exercituum"; ex quod datur intelligi quod* si coelestes virtutes excedit, multo magis alias.

[112] ST Ia q.25 a.3 ad 3: *[Q]ia, parcendo hominibus et miserando, perducit eos ad participationem infiniti boni, qui est* ultimus *effectus divinae virtutis.*

anything outside God[113] - Mover is not endebted to anyone:

> "For nothing is due to anyone, except on account of
> something already given him gratuitously by God. In this
> way the divine almightiness is particularly made manifest,
> because to it pertains to the first foundation of all good
> things."[114]

Reading this, the first association may be creation or Mt 10,8b ("You received without charge, give without charge"). But the opposition mercy - being indebted may equally call to mind how Thomas speaks of God's free initiative as for Christ's Passion, where he opposes God's almightiness to necessity (1.2.1). By freely taking the initiative to show how much He loves us, He manifests foremost His almightiness. In any way, by saying this, Thomas denies what was said in the third *obiectio*, that creating another world would prove God's almightiness; for in our history God has *already* shown that He is almighty, namely in the Passion of Christ.

The last *obiectio* has in fact been answered in the *corpus*: almightiness signifies that God can do all possible things in the absolute sense of the word, not in the relative sense of the word. God's almightiness does not abolish the necessity of cause and effect, for this is exactly how He, in His almightiness, freely, created the world. Of the things God alone does he mentions not only creating, but also justifying. This word could be a reference to 1 Co 1,30 ("Christ Jesus, who for us was made wisdom from God, and saving justice and holiness and redemption"). And at the end of his anwer Thomas returns to the text of 1 Co 1:

> "Thus, the wisdom of the world is deemed foolish,
> because it judges to be impossible for God what is

---

[113] ST Ia q.9 a.1; this reference explains *moveri* in q.25 a.3 ag.1.

impossible to nature."[115]

Although Thomas does not explicitly mention the Passion of Christ here, by citing 1 Co 1,20 in this discussion, he seems to refer to the broader context of 1 Co 1,18-31, where we find examples of possibilities in the absolute sense of the word, and thence for God: that the One who died on a cross lives, that the One crucified in weakness manifests the might of the Almighty, that we are saved by the cross, an instrument of torture, that what seems foolish in fact reflects the wisdom of God, that what seems slight and insignificant is chosen by God.[116]

In 1 Co 1,25, however, St. Paul speaks of the *weakness* of God: "God's weakness is stronger than human strength." In the context of this sentence it is clear already that God's weakness is not like human weakness, in the sense that strength is lacking. God's weakness is of a different kind, just as God's might (1 Co 1,24) and God's foolishness (1 Co 1,23) are. Therefore Thomas explains 1 Co 1,25 as follows:

> "'God's folly is wiser than human beings' (1 Co 1,25a), as if St. Paul is saying: something divine may seem folly, but not because it would fall short of wisdom, but because it towers above human wisdom. For some people are used to consider what is beyond their comprehension folly. "A multitude of things beyond human comprehension has been shown unto you" (Si 3,25). 'And God's weakness is stronger than human beings' (1 Co 1,25b), for it is not said that there is something weak in God due to a defect of power, but on account of exceeding human power. Just as we call something invisible in sofar as it is beyond our sight. Although,"

- Thomas offers an alternative interpretation of the weakness of God -

"this could refer to the mystery of the Incarnation. For

---

[115] ST Ia q.25 a.3 ad 4: *In hoc autem reputatur stulta mundi sapientia, quod ea quae sunt impossibilia naturae, etiam Deo impossibilia iudicabat.* For Scriptural references: note 97.

[116] Cf. 1 S 16,1, 6-12 (David) and Lk 1,48 (Mary).

what is considered folly and weak in God in respect of the
assumed nature, exceeds every wisdom and power. 'Who
is like You in strength, Lord?' (Ex 15,11)."[117]

And this second, alternative interpretation we also find in Thomas'
commentary on 2 Co 13,4 ("Though it was out of weakness that He was
crucified, He is alive now with the power of God").[118] The Passion of
Christ is what is considered foolishness and weakness in God by many a
person. But exactly the Passion of Christ, Thomas says, echoing St. Paul,
is where God's wisdom and power are revealed.[119] Thomas includes in
his consideration of this mystery the critique against those who make
themselves the measure of all things, calling what they do not understand
"nonsense". Both interpretations in the text show that Thomas
acknowledges the greatness of the mysteries of God's power and the
Passion of Christ as well as the limitation of human knowledge. For St.
Paul this is the starting point of approaching them and relating to them, as

---

[117] C1C c.1 l.3 (on 1 Co 1,25): *"Quod stultum est Dei sapientius est hominibus",*
quasi dicat: Iam alquod divinum videtur esse stultum, non quia deficiat *a sapientia,* sed
quia superexcedit *sapientiam humanam. Homines enim quidam consueverunt stultum*
reputare quod eorum sensum excedit. "Plurima super sensum hominis ostensa sunt tibi.'
[Si 3,25] *"Et quod infirmum est Dei, fortius est hominibus,"* quia sc. non *dicitur aliquid*
infirmum in Deo per defectum *virtutis,* sed per excessum *humanae virtutis, sicut etiam*
dicitur invisibilis, inquantum excedit sensum humanum ("Virtutem ostendis tu qui non
crederis esse in virtute consummatus" [W 12,17]); quamvis hoc possit referri ad
incarnationis mysterium: *quia id quod reputatur stultum et infirmum in Deo ex parte*
naturae assumptae, transcendit *omnem sapientiam et virtutem. "Quis similis tui in fortibus,*
Domine?" [Ex 15,11]

[118] CIO c.19 l.2, R2C c.13 l.1, ST IIIa q.48 a.6 ad 1.

[119] Cf. Gräbe (2000), 263: "In Paul's writings weakness ('ασθενεια) is not identical
with power (δυναμις), "... sondern 'Ort' der Kraftoffenbarung (i.e. the 'place' where
God's power is manifested)" [reference to J. Jervell, *Der schwache Charismatiker,*
Tübingen 1976, 197] *Paul does not say that power reveals itself as weakness,* but *in*
weakness [reference to M.E. Thrall, *The Second Epistle to the Corinthians,* Cambridge
1994, 331]."

mysteries *of faith*.[120]

At the end of this analysis it is clear that "almightiness" signifies the one might of the triune God. Almightiness is one of the *credibilia*, that is, one of the things that is to be believed on its own account (*fides secundum se*):

> "'Faith is the substance of the things to be hoped for in eternal life' (Heb 11,1). It follows that the things that have to be believed on their own account, order us directly to eternal life. Such are the three Persons, God's almightiness, the mystery of the Incarnation of Christ and the like."[121]

How we are to understand what we believe, that God is *omnia potens*, is expounded by Thomas, employing the results of the preliminary steps, that His might must be *activa* and *infinita*, because almightiness, just as love, denotes the essence of God.

This quote from the *Secunda Secundae* (note 121) shows a link of almightiness with our salvation. It seems that the same connection is made by Thomas in *quaestio* 25 *articulus* 3 of the *Prima Pars*. For there are several indications that *quaestio* 25 is not 'just' speculative theology: Lk 1,37, in the *sed contra*, is said in view of the mystery of Christ evolving in our world; the four *obiectiones* and the replies to them contain references to aspects of the mystery of Christ's Passion, of which Scripture testifies that it was for our salvation. In chapter 1 it was shown that Thomas, in keeping with this, underlines that. No matter how speculative the terminology used by Thomas here may be, the focus of *quaestio* 25 is our salvation.

The way Thomas speaks in this *quaestio* of the mercy of God in

---

[120] As Thomas does at the very beginning of SCG IV: c.1 n.1, citing Jb 26,14: *ECCE, HAEC EX PARTE DICTA SUNT VIARUM EIUS, ET CUM VIX PARVAM STILLAM SERMONUM EIUS AUDIVERIMUS, QUIS POTERIT TONITRUUM MAGNITUDINIS EIUS INTUERI. IOB XXVI.*

[121] ST IIaIIae q.1 a.6 ad 1: *Fides principaliter est de his quae* videnda speramus in patria, *secundum illud Heb 11,1: "Fides est substantia sperandarum rerum"; ideo* per se ad fidem pertinent illa quae directe nos ordinant ad vitam aeternam: sicut *sunt tres Personae*, omnipotentia Dei, *mysterium incarnationis Christi, et alia huiusmodi.*

respect of His almightiness catches the eye. The connection he points to, is far from obvious to us. Moreover, endorsing the mercy (*misericordia*) of God is somewhat strange after such a strong denial of *compassio* in God, that came to the surface in the former chapter. Hence a closer look must be taken at what Thomas says about the mercy of God. Even more since God's saving mercy is called the pre-eminent expression of God's almightiness and Thomas' text seems to suggest that God's almightiness and saving mercy on the one hand are closely connected to the mystery of the Passion of Christ, whilst on the other hand both are closely connected with our salvation. For this reason the relation between almightiness, God's mercy and the Passion of Christ will be considered against the background of our salvation in the next paragraph, 3.3.

3.3 Your Mercy I Have Not Hidden (Ps 40,11)[122]

Throughout Scripture YHWH reveals Himself as the merciful God. Throughout the *Summa Theologiae* we find references to God's abundant mercy for us. But since nowadays in English "mercy" and "compassion" are regarded as synonyms and Thomas denies *compassio* whilst underlining *misericordia* as a property of God, we need a further explanation of how to understand God's mercy.

Furthermore, Thomas' saying that the mercy of God is the expression par excellence of God's almightiness makes us frown, just as Thomas would be dumbfounded to see how many Christians nowadays regard God's almightiness and mercy as irreconcilable. If it were only in *quaestio* 25 of the *Prima Pars* of the *Summa Theologiae* that Thomas links God's mercy up to His almightiness in this way, one could maybe look upon it as an isolated remark or as a marginal aspect of his theology. But elsewhere too in the *Summa Theologiae* and in a few other works Thomas points to this connection.[123] Therefore, in view of the apparent connection pointed at by Thomas, of God's almightiness with the Passion

---

[122] Vulg-Ps 39,11: *Non abscondi misericordiam tuam*.

[123] SN IV d.46 q.2 a.1c ad 1, XTB c.5 (referring to W 11,26), ST IaIIae q.113 a.9sc (citing Ps 145,9) and IIaIIae q.30 a.4co; elsewehere God's *omnipotentia* and *misericordia* are mentioned in one and the same breath, e.g. in ST IIaIIae q.18 a.4 ad 2 and q.83 a.15 ad 3.

of Christ a further inquiry is called for into how Thomas speaks of the mercy of God in respect of these mysteries.

Hence, this paragraph will first consider how mercy (*miseri-cordia*) befits God, whereas, as was shown in chapter 2, *compassio* does not (3.3.1). Next the focus of Thomas' speaking of God's mercy and almightiness will be examined: the salvation of humankind (3.3.2). In the final subparagraph the lines of the analysis of the *nexus mysteriorum* of the Passion of Christ and the almightiness and mercy of God come together and then will be held against the light of what we read in Scripture (3.3.3): is the *nexus* an 'invention' of Thomas or is there a Scriptural basis for it?

3.3.1 YHWH: God Who Is Concerned

At the beginning of every Eucharist and repeatedly during a service we call upon God's mercy: "Lord have mercy", "*Kyrie eleison*", "*Miserere nobis*". Whoever invokes God like this, supposes, consciously or unconsciously, that God is good and that He is lovingly concerned with us. And indeed, Scripture attests that God is merciful.[124] But what *is* mercy? Is it a synonym for compassion, goodness and love, or does it (also) mean something else?

In the *Prima Pars* of the *Summa Theologiae* Thomas considers the mercy (*misericordia*) of God in *quaestio* 21 following on the love of God. This is not surprising, since Thomas describes mercy as coming forth from love;[125] every loving person is merciful of a fellow human being.[126]

So, because God is love, He is merciful. As in the consideration of "God is love", for Thomas the problem is not *whether* God is called

---

[124] E.g. Ps 111,4 (cited in ST Ia q.21 a.3sc) and Ps 145,8 (cited in SN IV d.46 q.2 a.1a sc.1): *Miserator et misericors Dominus*. And likewise Christ speaks of God, e.g. in Lk 6,35f (cited in RSU n.1) and 15,11-32.

[125] ST IaIIae q.30 a.3 ag.3: [M]*isericordia consequitur ex caritate*, referring to Rm 12,15. And reversely, well ordered love cannot be without mercy, RSU n.1: *Dilectio enim debet esse cum miseratione. Luc. VI,36.*

[126] ST IaIIae q.51 a.2, q.55 aa.1-3, q.65 aa.2-3, IIaIIae q.30 a.3.

merciful, for that God is is part of our faith, but rather how we are to understand this. For in respect of how authorities like Augustine, John of Damascus and Aristotle write about mercy, it may seem that being merciful is incompatible with being God; mercy is described as a kind of sadness or distress about another's misery[127] or as

> "heartfelt *compassio* for another's misery, impelling to succour him, if we can."[128]

Yet *compassio* does not befit God. Therefore this definition of mercy cannot be used *in divinis*, at least not without a further qualification. Where Thomas speaks of the mercy *of God*, he avoids the word *compassio*, but speaks of it nevertheless:

> "A person is said to be merciful (*misericors*), when he is, as it were, miserable at heart (*miserum cor*); being affected with sadness at the misery of another as though it were his own. Hence it follows that he endeavors to dispel the misery of this other as if it were his own misery. And this is the effect of mercy."[129]

From this it is clear that Thomas distinguishes between two aspects of mercy. The first mentioned, is that the misery of someone else brings something about in the subject (affect). In the light of the former chapters

---

[127] ST Ia q.21 a.3 ag.1: *Misericordia enim est species* tristitiae, *ut dicit Damascenus* [*De fide orth*. L.2 c.14, MG 94,932]. *Sed tristitia non est in Deo. Ergo nec misericordia.* IaIIae q.30 a.3co: [*M*]*isericordia importat* dolorem *de miseria aliena.*

[128] ST IaIIae q.30 a.1co, citing Augustine's IX *De civ. Dei* [c.5, ML 41,261]: [*M*]*isericordia est alienae miseriae in nostro corde* compassio, *qua, utique si possumus, subvenire compellimur.* Cf. Ia q.95 a.3co: *misericordia, quae est* dolor *de miseria aliena*; IaIIae q.102 a.6 ad 8: [*P*]*assio misericordiae consurgit ex afflictionibus aliorum.*

[129] ST Ia q.21 a.3co: [*M*]*isericors dicitur aliquis quasi habens miserium cor: quia scilicet afficitur ex miseria alterius per tristitiam,* ac si esset eius propria miseria. *Et ex hoc sequitur quod operetur ad depellendam miseriam alterius,* sicut miseriam propriam*: et hic est misericordiae* effectus. We find that Thomas speaks in the same context, in SN IV d.46 q.2 a.1a, of *compassio*, since there Thomas departs from John of Damascus' definition in which this word is used.

it is clear that in this sense mercy does not befit God; being affected and saddened are *passiones*. The other aspect is that mercy incites the subject (effect). The effect of mercy is discribed as removing someone's misery. And, Thomas emphasizes, removing someone's misery befits God to the highest extent.[130] Hence, again speaking on the basis of the effects we observe, God is said to be merciful, and, again, to the highest extent (*maxime*).[131]

The ground for God's action of dispelling, is, according to Thomas' text, an ultimate concern of God with us: "as if it were his own misery." We all know that the reverse is also true: if the misery of a person does not do anything to another person, if there is no concern or connectedness, the other person will not proceed to do something about the misery. But of what kind is this connectedness or union of God with us, that He is merciful to us. Thomas, following Aristotle, distinguishes between a union of affect or love (*unio affectus*) and a union on the basis of kinship or belonging to the same group (*unio realis*).[132] Between human beings both unions are possible simultaneously and they strengthen one another. Yet since God and humankind are not of the same group or category - the former is the Creator, the latter is created - the ground for God's mercy can only be the *unio affectus*, albeit without *passio* of course.

In view of these results we are to say that according to Thomas God's mercy bears a resemblance to God's friendship. For although there are some differences (friendship is mutual, whereas mercy is a one-way communication, as will be shown; friendship is between those who are equal to a certain extent), both words signify an attitude of concern towards a beloved person. *Amicitia* signifies the provision of the beloved

---

[130] This may remind us of texts like Ps 34,5, 7, 18-20, 145,8, 19 (cited in SCG III c.95 n.7; tit.: *Quod immobilitas divinae providentiae utilitatem orationis non excludit.*), Ac 7,10 and 2 Tm 3,11.

[131] ST Ia q.21 a3co: *[M]isericordia est Deo* maxime *attribuenda: tamen secundum effectum, non secundum passionis affectum.* [....] *Tristari ergo de miseria alterius non competit Deo: sed repellere miseriam alterius, hoc* maxime *ei competit.*

[132] ST IIaIIae q.30 a.2co. Note therefore that *unio realis* cannot be translated as "real union", as in the Blackfriars edition.

with *goods*[133] and *misericordia* signifies taking away the *miseria* of the beloved. This feature of taking away the *miseria* of the beloved also distinguishes *misericordia* from *compassio*, which in Thomas' works simply means "to undergo/suffer with"[134]. Therefore *compassio* should not be translated with "compassion".

Whereas *compassio* cannot be without *passio* - *passio* belongs to the *res*, to the deep structure of *compassio* - *misericordia* can be, although in human beings it never is. And as *passio* intensifies the love of a human being,[135] even though it could never be more intense than the love of God without *passio*, since God *is* love and the source of all love, as was said, so it is for mercy: since God is merciful, He, who is without *passio*, cannot but be *maxime* merciful, even mercy itself and so the source of all mercy.[136]

Thus we speak of God's mercy from its effects, Thomas says. Scripture points to these, where it says that God provides and cares for humankind perennially[137] and that He is especially concerned for His

---

[133] Cf. paragraph 2.1.2. ST IaIIae q.25 a.7co: [*Q*]*uinque quae sunt amicitiae propria. Unusquisque enim amicus primo quidem vult suum amicum esse vivere; secundo, vult ei bona; tertio operatur bona ad ipsum; convivit ei delectabiliter; quinto concordat cum ipso, quasi in iisdem delectatus et contristatus.* Ibidem q.27 a.2 ad 3: *Philosophus ibi* [IX *De ethic.* c.4 n.1, Bk 1166a3] *ponit ad amicitiam pertinent, inquantum proveniunt ex amore quem quis habet ad seipsum, ut ibidem dicitur: ut scilicet haec omnia aliquis erga amicum agat* sicut ad seipsum. See also the similar vocabulary (*unio affectus, unio realis, unio amoris, amicus*) in ST IaIIae q.30 a.2co, on mercy.

[134] Gondreau (2002), 403, discussing the "passions" of Christ, does not mention this distinguishing aspect of *misericordia*. He translates *misericordia* with "the passion of pity" (referring to Lk 7,13, Mk 6,34 and Mt 20,34). In this way it is overlooked that according to Thomas taking away the sufferings of the other person is inherent in *misericordia* (cf. Lk 7,14f, Mk 6,34-44, Mt 20,34), so that *misericordia* is apprehended as a synonym of *compassio*.

[135] ST IaIIae q.24 a.3sc, co; see 2.1.2.

[136] ST Ia q.13 a.6, see 3.4.2.

[137] E.g. Ps 138,8, W 14,3 (cited in ST Ia q.22 a.1sc, *De providentia Dei*), Mt 6,25-34 (esp. in ST IaIIae q.55 a.6sc, co).

people in misery[138]; He sets them free.[139]

3.3.2 YHWH: God Who Liberates

A merciful person takes away the misery of the person he/she sympathizes with. But what, according to Thomas, is misery (*miseria*)? Was Christ in His sufferings miserable? And how does the sympathizing - to use this metaphor - God take the misery of His beloved away? These questions will be dealt with in this subparagraph.

First misery. In our daily use of the word it designates "a state of suffering and want that is the result of poverty or other external conditions" and "a state of great unhappiness and great distress."[140] This first meaning is not what Thomas understands by *miseria*; it rather is equivalent to *passio* in the most proper sense of the word (2.2.1). The second meaning of the word misery comes closer to what Thomas understands by *miseria*. Thomas uses the term as the opposite to happiness (*beatitudo*, *felicitas*). Happiness is a natural good; all people pursue it naturally.[141] Characteristic of happiness is perfection. Happiness is a perfect good, since perfection implies not lacking anything, as was said above (3.1.3), and lacking a good may cause unhappiness. A happy person finds pleasure (*delectatio*) in this fullness.[142] This applies foremost to God:

---

[138] E.g. Ex 3,7, Ps 98,3, 106,44, Is 57,17f, Jr 31,3 (cited in ST IIIa q.49 a.4 ad 2), 20, Lk 1,54f, 68, 78, 7,16, Ac 7,34f.

[139] E.g. Ex 3,16, 4,31, Ps 111,9 (cited in ST IIIa q.48 a.5 ag.2), Mt 1,21 (cited in ST IIIa intr., q.3 a.8 ag.3, q.37 a.2 ag.3), Lk 1,68.

[140] Webster's (1986), II, 1443C.

[141] ST IaIIae q.1 aa.2, 7.

[142] ST IaIIae q.84 a.4co: [D]e proprietate felicitatis, quam naturaliter omnes appetunt. De cuius ratione est quidem primo quaedam perfectio, nam felicitas est perfectum bonum. [....] Secundo de ratione eius est sufficientia. [....] Tertio est de conditione eius delectatio, sine qua felicitas esse non potest, ut dicitur in I et X Ethic. [c.8 n.10, Bk 1099a7 resp. c.7 n.3, Bk 1177a22].

"Happiness befits God in the supreme degree. For nothing else is understood by the term 'happiness' than the perfect good of an intellectual nature. It is proper to an intellectual nature that it knows its sufficiency in the good it possesses, that good or evil may befall and that it can master its actions."[143]

Since God is *intelligens*, since He Himself is by essence the perfect good[144] and since He does not undergo any evil (nor anything else) and since He can do all He wills, in the sense said in paragraph 3.2.2,[145] happiness *maxime* befits God. Even more:

"To have happiness naturally belongs to God alone. Therefore it belongs to God alone not to be moved towards happiness by any previous operation. Now since happiness surpasses every created nature, no *pure* creature can becomingly gain happiness without movement of operation, whereby it moves thereto."[146] (italics added, MR)

Thus our happiness is found in God. Seeking happiness equals, therefore, seeking God. Every human being naturally pursues happiness and thus God. Misery is contrary to a human being's natural inclination towards God, and therefore, Thomas says, a person naturally wants to flee from

---

[143] ST Ia q.26 a.1co: [B]eatitudo maxime Deo competit. Nihil enim aliud sub nomine beatitudinis intelligitur, nisi bonum perfectum intellectualis naturae; cuius est suam sufficientiam cognoscere in bono quod habet, et cui competit ut ei contingat aliquid vel bene vel male, et sit suarum operationum dominica.

[144] Resp. ST Ia q.14 and qq.4-6.

[145] Cf. ST IIaIIae q.30 a.1co: Miseria autem felicitati opponitur. Est autem de ratione beatitudinis sive felicitatis ut potiatur eo quod vult; nam Augustinus dicit, XIII De Trin. [c.5, ML 42,1020] "beatus qui habet omnia quae vult et nihil mali vult".

[146] ST IaIIae q.5 a.7co: Habere autem beatitudinem naturaliter est solius Dei. Unde solius Dei proprium est quod ad beatitudinem non moveatur per aliquam operationem praecedentem. Cum autem beatitudo excedat omnem naturam creatam, nulla pura creatura convenienter beatitudinem consequitur absque motu operationis, per quam tendit in ipsam.

it.[147] One may surely call this a different view of happiness. For nowadays we see many people seeking happiness where, according to Thomas, it is not to be found: in wealth and riches, in honours, fame, might or any created good.[148] This raises the question how this can come about, since we are not only naturally inclined to God, but, what's more, our will is moved by Him (Ph 2,13) as well.

Thus Thomas points out that misery is due to a defect, an imperfection, though not all imperfection leads to misery. If this were the case, every *passio* would be or cause misery. Thomas delineates that a human being's natural appetite for happiness is an intellectual striving, in other words, a human being aims at his/her *bonum naturae*, whilst and insofar as he/she knows it. The will follows upon reason[149] and the right orientation of the will is required for attaining that happiness.[150] Whence Thomas speaks of misery as a consequence of a defect of the intellectual nature, ignorance (*ignorantia*) that is. So, when someone turns away from his/her natural inclination, when someone sins, this is in this sense an involuntary act. For no one would do something of which he/she knew in advance that it would lead to unhappiness. This is not necessarily prevented by God, since the Almighty does not *force* the human will;[151] He inspires it.

The inspiration with the gift of knowledge (*donum scientiae*) of what is the true and perfect good (*verum bonum*, *perfectum bonum*) is in

---

[147] ST Ia q.94 a.1co: *Manifestum est autem quod nullus homo potest per voluntatem a beatitudine averti:* naturaliter *enim, et ex necessitate,* homo vult beatitudinem, et fugit miseriam.

[148] ST IaIIae q.2. Texts like Mt 6,19-24 (cited in ST IaIIae q.1 a.5sc, IIIa q.57 a.1co), Col 3,1f (cited in IIIa q.57 a.1co) and also the story of king Solomon's growing affluence and proportional apostasy (1 K 10-11) may come to mind.

[149] ST Ia q.19 a.1co: *[V]oluntas enim intellectum consequitur.* IaIIae q.3 a.4co: *[E]ssentia beatitudinis in actu intellectus consistit, sed ad voluntatem pertinet delectatio beatitudinem consequens.*

[150] ST IaIIae q.5 a.7co: *[R]ectitudo voluntatis, ut supra* [q.4 a.4] *dictum est, requiritur ad beatitudinem, cum nihil aliud sit quam debitus ordo voluntatis ad ultimum finem.* Ibidem q.3 a.5 ad 3: *[U]ltimus hominis finis est aliquod bonum extrinsecum, scilicet Deus.*

[151] As was brought forward in 1.3.3 and 3.1.3, cf. 2 P 2,20.

the *Secunda Secundae*[152] called comfort (*consolatio*). For by not knowing the true good, one may pursue a created good or even something evil as if it were the perfect and true good, and by doing so sin and by consequence being further removed from the true good. The insight given by inspired knowledge comforts the unhappy person, for the knowledge about what is truly good and how to find it, reunites him/her with God, makes us friends of His again[153] and thus restores a perspective in our lives; the person comforted may live again according to his/her free will, his/her natural inclination towards God. He may not take away all the pain and anxiety, but a clearer view of what the purpose of our life is, and the reunion with God as a friend, may alleviate it. Since willing a good for a beloved is an act of love, of friendship, and since it is provided to us by inspiration, this gift is appropriated to the Holy Spirit only, who is, says Thomas in the *Summa Contra Gentiles* (note 153), therefore called by Christ "the Comforter" (*Consolator*), in Jn 14,26.

Hence Thomas indicates ignorance before an act as the cause of

---

[152] ST IIaIIae q.9 a.4, on Mt 5,4: "Blessed are those who mourn; they shall be comforted". The mourning may be caused by a turning to something created as something to be pursued in such a way that the consequence is an aversion from God, as in W 14,11 (cited in co); co: *Unde in eis* [= *creaturis*] *finem constituendo, peccant et verum bonum perdunt. Et hoc damnum homini innotescit per* rectum iudicium de creaturis, *quod habetur* per donum scientiae.

[153] SCG IV c.21 n.2: *Cum igitur Spiritus Sanctus procedat per modum amoris quo Deus seipsum amat, ut ostensum est* [c.19]; *ex hoc quod huic amori* assimilamur Deum amantes, *Spiritus Sanctus a Deo nobis dari dicitur. Unde Apostolus dicit* [Rm 5,5]: *Caritas Dei diffusa est in cordibus nostris per* Spiritum Sanctum, qui datus est nobis. Ibidem c.22 n.3: *Est autem et amicitiae proprium quod aliquis in praesentia amici delectetur, et in eius verbis et factis gaudeat, et in eo consolationem contra omnes anxietates inveniat: Unde in tristiis maxime ad amicos consolationis causa confugimus. Quia igitur* Spiritus Sanctus Dei amicos constituit, *et eum* in nobis *habitare facit et nos in ipso, ut ostensum est* [c.21]; *consequens est ut per Spiritum Sanctum gaudium de Deo et* consolationem *habemus* contra omnes mundi adversitates et impugnationes. Thomas cites Ps 51,14, Rm 14,17 and Ac 9,31, that underlie these thoughts. After which he concludes: *Et ideo Dominus Spiritum Sanctum "Paraclitum", idest "Consolatorem" nominat, Ioan* [14,26]: *"Paraclitus autem Spiritus Sanctus," etc.*.

its involuntariness.[154] Saying this, Thomas does not only concur with John of Damascus and Aristotle; in Scripture also ignorance, not knowing God and His love, will, might, providence etc. is mentioned as causing someone to err[155] and to sin.[156] And this bears in particular on the sin of crucifying Christ.[157]

As for Christ Himself, did He experience misery when He suffered? Can the relation between the loving God and the suffering Christ be characterized by *misericordia*? The answer seems to be positive, for

> "The *passiones* someone undergoes are causing even more misery, if they are contrary to the entire will, as when evil befalls someone who has always striven to do well. And therefore Aristotle says that 'there is *misericordia* to the highest extent because of evil things afflicting a person who undergoes them undeservedly'."[158]

---

[154] ST IaIIae q.6 a.8co: [*I*]*gnorantia habet causare involuntarium ea ratione qua privat cognitionem, quae* praeexigitur *ad voluntarium, ut supra* [a.1] *dictum est. Non tamen quaelibet ignorantia huiusmodi cognitionem privat.* [....] Antecedenter *autem se habet ad voluntatem ignorantia, quando non est voluntaria, et tamen est causa volendi quod alias homo non vellet.*

[155] Mk 12,24 par., Jn 7,47-49.

[156] Ps 10,3f, 14,1-4 (= 53,2-5, cited in ST Ia q.2 a.1sc), 36,2-5 (cited in IIaIIae q.15 a.1co), 95,10 (= Heb 3,10), Pr 14,22 (cited in IaIIae q.6 a.8 ag.1), Jr 10,25, Ac 17,30, 1 Co 15,34, Ep 4,17-24 (verses 17f cited in SCG I c.4 n.7), 1 Th 4,5, 2 Tm 3,13-17 (cited in Ia q.1 a.1sc, IIIa q.31 a.3co), Tt 3,3f, Jm 1,15-18, 1 P 1,14. 2,19-25 (cited in IaIIae q.96 a.4sc), 1 Jn 3,5-7 (cited in SCG IV c.70 n.8 cf. n.4). And reversely, 2 Co 2,11: Someone who knows the scheming of Satan, can resist him.

[157] Lk 23,34 (cited in ST IIIa q.21 a.4 ag.2), Ac 3,17, 13,27f, 1 Co 2,8 (see par. 1.1.1; cited in Ia q.12 a.13sc, q.64 a.1 ag.4, IIIa q.36 a.1co, q.44 a.1 ag.2, q.46 a.12 ag.1; cf. q.47 aa.5, 6 and RT1 c.1 l.3, on 1 Tm 1,13), 1 P 2,7 (= Ps 118,22, cited in REM c.21 l.2, REI c.7 l.5 n.6).

[158] ST IIaIIae q.30 a.1co: [*S*]*unt adhuc magis miserabilia si sunt contra totam voluntatem: puta si aliquis semper sectatus est bona et eveniunt ei mala. Et ideo Philosophus dicit, in eodem libro* [II *Rhet.* c.8 n.2, Bk 1385b13] *quod* "misericordia maxime est super malis eius qui indignus patitur".

"Someone who has always striven to do well" and "undergoes evil undeservedly" may well remind us of Christ (The crowds about Christ, Mk 7,37: "Everything He does is good"), His trial (Mt 26,23, Mk 15,14: "What harm has He done?" words ironically put into Pilate's mouth, cf. Lk 23,4, 14f, Jn 18,38) and His death on the cross (The so called good thief crucified with Christ says, Lk 23,41: "This man has done nothing wrong"). Still the relation between the love of God and the suffering Christ cannot be called mercy (*misericordia*), since in Christ's Passion there was no misery. For two reasons we are to deny misery in Christ whilst He suffered. First of all, He underwent His Passion voluntarily, as was said in paragraph 1.1.2. Now Thomas distinguishes three ways of willing:

> "It belongs to misery that someone should undergo what he/she does not want. Now someone wants something in three ways. First by his/her natural appetite. Thus all people want to be and to live. Secondly someone wants something from deliberate choice. Thirdly someone wants something not for the sake of itself, but by reason of what it causes."[159]

This explains the deep sadness Christ felt in Gethsemane (Mt 26,38, par.) Yet the natural desire of a human being is not only to be and to live, but also happiness, as was said above, and thus God and doing His will. Secondly, we read how in the garden of Gethsemane the man Christ desired to do the will of God and also that it was a conscious will (Mt 26,39, 42, 44b, par.). In his commentary to the gospel according to Matthew Thomas refers here to Ps 116,13 (*calicem salutaris accipiam*), and citing Mk 14,36 (*omnia tibi possibilia sunt*) he denies that it would have been impossible for God to let the cup pass by.[160] In the third sense of the word Christ wanted to suffer and die, for the sake our salvation (cf. Rm 5,6, 1 Th 5,10 etc.). But on the basis of this explan-

---

[159] ST IIaIIae q.30 a.1co: [A]*d miseriam pertinet ut homo patiatur quae non vult. Tripliciter autem aliquis vult aliquid. Uno quidem* modo appetitu naturali*: sicut omnes homines volunt esse et vivere. Alio modo homo vult aliquid* per electionem ex aliqua praemeditatione. *Tertio modo homo vult aliquid non secundum se, sed* in causa sua.

[160] REM c.26 n.5

ation it seems that there was a contradiction in Christ and that part of Him wanted something else than God. In paragraph 4.2.2 a closer look will be taken at this issue.

The second reason, in close connection with this, why we are to deny misery in Christ, is that the man Christ does not befit ignorance. Although ignorance is part of human nature, by reason of the hypostatic union Christ possessed the fullness of grace and truth (Jn 1,14) so that He could enlighten those in darkness and the shadow of death (Lk 1,79); He was the perfect human being (Ep 4,13).[161] It was shown in paragraph 1.3.2 already that the higher part of Christ's soul was never deprived of the *visio beata*, so that, contrary to other human beings, His *passiones* would not lead to aversion from the good[162], which leads to unhappiness, misery.

From this it is clear that misery is the motive of mercy; misery incites to mercy. If there is no misery, there is no mercy either[163]. Hence God's love, friendship and goodness towards the man Christ cannot be called mercy, since there never was any misery in Christ; the hypostatic union was from the very beginning of His conception, through which He always had the *visio beata*. Christ is a true, but not a pure human being. By reason of the hypostatic union He had, contrary to us, happiness without movement of operation (see note 146). Pure human beings can *become* happy (*beatifica*), by participation in the divine

---

[161] The first two Scripture texts are cited in ST IIIa q.15 a.3 (ad 1 resp. sc). The last in q.39 a.3co (*Tertio...*), where Thomas connects it to Christ's moral perfection: His belief in the Trinity and fulfilling the Law (*et in his duobus perfectio vitae Christianae consistit*). In q.46 a.9 ad 4, however, Ep 4,13 is cited as referring to the perfection of Christ's body.

[162] ST Ia q.115 a.4co, cf. IaIIae q.10 a.3co, where Thomas gives the exemples of fury, fierce desire and strong emotion felt in one's body, three *passiones* also experienced by Christ: Mk 11,15-17; Lk 22,15; Mt 9,36 (cited in ST IIaIIae q.30 a.1 ad 1), 14,14 and 15,32. For, Ia q.94 a.1co: *Unde nullus videns Deum per essentiam potest* voluntate *averti a Deo, quod est peccare. Et propter hoc, omnes videntes Deum per essentiam, sic* in amore Dei stabiliuntur, *quod in aeternam peccare non possunt.*

[163] This conclusion is not explicit in Thomas' works. It is in Augustine's *Ennar. in Ps XXXII sermo II n.4* (on Ps 33,5b), with regard to the *beati* in heaven; *misericordia* belongs to the realm of the temporary, cf. ibidem *in Ps C* nn.1, 3, 12 (on Ps 101,1, 8).

happiness. This participation occurs by seeing (*visio*) God.[164] This seeing of God is interpreted by Thomas as an intellectual act: although sight (*visio*) is originally applied to the act of the sense, he says, in our everyday language it is extended to all knowledge obtained through the senses. For instance in "Let us *see* what he/she has to say".

> "Further, sight is applied to knowledge obtained through the intellect, as in those words: 'Blessed are the clean of heart, for they shall see God' (Mt 5,8)."[165]

We find this also in the Greek language where the verb *oida* (οἶδα), to know, is the perfect of *idein* (ἰδεῖν), to see.

Misery then is designated by Thomas as not seeing, that is not knowing God. We find this also expressed in Ps 42. Not seeing, not finding, not knowing God, His love, His will, His might, His goodness etc. leads to sin, aversion from God. It was said that God is to the highest extent merciful, since He takes the misery of people away. By taking a closer look at how He does this, we will understand better what Thomas understands by mercy, so that in paragraph 3.3.3 it can be examined how Thomas sees it connected with God's almightiness and with the Passion of Christ.

"There is no one who during his/her earthly life does not have a particular defect."[166] Our defects may well lead to misery, in particular our ignorance. Now defects, or imperfections, are not entities of their own. They are not "things" that could be removed, by force for instance. Rather, defects are there, where something falls short in being, in

---

[164] Cf. Job 19,25-27, Ps 27,4, Mt 5,8, 1 Co 13,12, Heb 12,14, 1 Jn 3,2.

[165] ST Ia q.67 a.1co: *Et ulterius [extensum est hoc nomen, secundum usum loquentium] etiam ad cognitionem intellectus, secundum illud Mt. 5,8: "Beati mundo corde, quoniam ipsi Deum videbunt."*

[166] ST IaIIae q.33 a.4 ad 3: *[N]ullus est in hac vita qui non habeat aliquem defectum.* Even Christ, who had a corruptible body.

perfection and so in goodness, since something is good insofar as it is.[167] Hence,

> "defects are not removed, except by the perfection of a
> particular good. And the primary source of goodness, is
> God, as was shown above."[168]

Mercy then is not only similar to friendship, but also to goodness. Yet goodness is broader than mercy; mercy is a particular kind of goodness. For contrary to mercy, goodness does not presuppose misery. It is proper to goodness to let others share in that goodness, no matter what the situation of the receiver is. Goodness does not depend on evil for its existence. Furthermore, mercy cannot but be between two intellectual beings, since we only speak of mercy if the receiver is miserable, unhappy, and the giver perceives that misery as if it were his/her own. But every creature which can communicate or receive a perfection can communicate or receive goodness.[169] Of special importance for this study is yet another difference:

> "Mercy removes the debt from a person by supplying
> him/her with a good. For we do not say that something
> which a person is indebted to someone else for, is

---

[167] ST Ia q.5 a.1co: *[B]onum et ens sunt idem secundum rem, sed differunt secundum rationem tantum. Quod sic patet.* Ratio *enim* boni *in hoc consistit, quod aliquid sit* appetibile. *[....]* *[U]numquodque est appetibile secundum quod est* perfectum*: nam omnia appetunt suam perfectionem. Intantum est est autem perfectum unumquodque, inquantum est* actu*: unde manifestum est quod intantum est aliquid bonum, inquantum est* ens*: esse enim est actualitas rei* [cf. q.3 a.4, q.4 a.1 ad 3].

[168] ST Ia q.21 a.3co: *Defectus autem non tolluntur,* nisi *per alicuius bonitatis* perfectionem*: Prima autem origo bonitatis Deus est, ut supra* [q.6 a.4] *ostensum est.* And so we read in Gn 1: everything that is, comes forth from God, and it is good, even very good in God's eyes.

[169] SN IV d.46 q.2 a.1b sc.2, co. As an example of the latter distinction: the sun communicates its light and its warmth to a plant.

mercifully given."[170]

In the case of giving something that is due, we speak of another kind of goodness: justice. As was said in the paragraphs 1.2.1 and 3.2.2, for God there was no necessity to liberate us; He was not indebted to us or to a rule or higher law. Still it may seem that God, by acting mercifully, would or could act contrary to justice. For is not mercy a mitigation (*relaxatio*) of justice? On the other hand, God cannot act contrary to Himself. Thomas cites 2 Tm 2,13 in this context[171], as in the context of Christ's Passion. Moreover, in Scripture God's mercy and justice are mentioned in one and the same breath.[172]

Thomas provides two answers. In the *Secunda Secundae* he distinguishes between mercy as a virtue and as a *passio*. Someone who is overwhelmed by feelings of sympathy for a person in misery, may indeed ignore justice. But in the case of the virtue, mercy and its accompanying feelings are regulated by reason, so that the person would not act counter to justice,[173] even becoming more zealous in his/her virtuosity. In the light of 2 Tm 2,13 and of what has been said in chapter 2 about the incompability of God with *passio*, it is clear that God's mercy is like the virtue, or rather, the virtue of mercy is like the mercy of God, the source of all mercy. But even more, as Thomas' other answer, in the *Prima Pars*, reads,

"God acts mercifully, not indeed by going against His justice, but by doing something more than justice: thus a

---

[170] SN IV d.46 q.2 a.1b co: [*M*]*isericordia removet* debitum *ab eo cui providetur; non enim dicitur misericorditer dari alicui quod ei debetur.*

[171] ST Ia q.21 a.3 ag/ad 2.

[172] E.g. in Ex 34,6f, Tb 3,2, Ps 25,10, 85,11f, 89,15 and 112,4.

[173] ST IaIIae q.30 a.3co: *Alio vero modo* [*misericordia*] *potest nominare motum appetitus intellectivi, secundum quod alicui displicet malum alterius. Hic autem motus potest esse* secundum rationem regulatus*: et potest secundum hunc motum ratione regulatum regulari motus inferioris appetitus. Unde Augustinus dicit in IX De civ. Dei* [c.5, ML 41,260] *quod* "iste motus animi," *scilicet misericordia,* "servit rationi quando ita praebetur misericordia ut iustitia conservetur: sive cum indigenti tribuitur, sive cum ignoscitur poenitenti".*

man who pays someone 200 pieces of money, though owing him only 100, does nothing against justice, but acts generously or mercifully. And likewise, if someone forgives an offence committed against him. For who forgives something, may be said to bestow a gift."[174]

And to endorse this line of reasoning, Thomas cites Ep 4,32 (*Apostolus remissionem donationem vocat: "Donate invicem, sicut et Christus vobis donavit"*) and Jm 2,13 (*misericordia superexaltat iudicum*). Thomas is not specific in *quaestio* 21 of the *Prima Pars*. But this argumentation presupposes that God's actions or at least a specific action of God meets this description.

In God's mercy also His generosity (*liberalitas*) is manifested. An action of bestowing what is good is called generous, if the giver will be none the better for it (*non propter utilitatem suam*).[175] In fact all God's good actions towards us must in this sense be called generous, since what is perfect in the absolute sense of the word cannot gain anything.

In the discussion of God's almightiness it was brought into the limelight that according to Thomas God's almightiness is manifested foremost by His saving mercy. It catches the eye how many superlatives Thomas uses while he considers the mercy of God. God is most concerned with us, dispelling our misery as if it were His very own. This expresses a maximal involvement of God; He would go to any length.

Also where Thomas speaks of the liberating mercy of God, he underlines the abundance of the Almighty's mercy: mercy is not what is due. What Thomas sets out here is parallel to the free initiative of God of which Thomas speaks in his contemplation of almightiness. Moreover, God's mercy is called *maxime* good and generous. And as for what is

---

[174] ST Ia q.21 a.3 ad 2: *Deus misericorditer agit, non quidem contra iustitiam suam faciendo, sed aliquid* supra *iustitiam operando: sicut si alicui debentur centum denarii, aliquis ducentos det de suo, tamen non contra iustitiam facit, sed liberaliter vel misericorditer operatur. Et similiter si aliquis* offensam in se commissam remittat. *Qui enim aliquid* remittit, *quoddammodo donat illud.*

[175] ST Ia q.21 a.3co, cf. SN IV q.2 a.1a co: *Sicut homo enim in repellendo miseriam alicuius considerat hominis utilitatem cuius repellit miseriam; ita et Deus per sua beneficia repellens nostram miseriam,* non ordinat hoc ad suam utilitatem, sed ad nostram.

due, justice: since God is the Most High, there is no law above the Almighty Merciful to keep or to violate.[176] What God in His mercy does for us is even much more than justice, Thomas says.

In the context of God's mercy, Thomas has not worked this out any further, neither in the *Prima* nor in the *Secunda Pars*. But, just like in the discussion of God's almightiness, there are some indications that Thomas has worked this out in the *Tertia Pars*, especially where he considers the Passion of Christ. For in this paragraph we have come across some aspects in Thomas' discussion of God's mercy that seem to refer to it. First the way in which Thomas speaks of God's concern. He describes the effect of mercy succouring a person in misery, dispelling it as if it were your own. In this sense mercy, according to Thomas, *maxime* befits God. In our words: God is a solidary liberator. In Scripture we read in many places that God comes to the aid of His people. But how much further could God have gone than His very own involvement in our misery by sharing in our humanity and by undergoing, as a human being, even humiliation and a violent death on a cross? A second lead is how Thomas speaks of our ignorance concerning God. In paragraph 1.2.3 it was shown that Thomas, discussing the fruits of Christ's Passion that come along with the liberation of sin, first mentions our knowledge of the love of God for us, in which our salvation lies.[177] Moreover, terms like liberation, forgiveness (*remissio*), debt and the abundance, or paying more than is due, also occur in *quaestio* 46 of the *Tertia Pars*, as was shown in paragraph 1.2. Finally, that 2 Tm 2,13 is cited here and besides in the context of God's mercy and justice (ST Ia q.21 a.3 ag.2 and IaIIae q.100 a.8 ad 2) only in the context of God's almightiness (Ia q.25 a.3 ag.2) and of the Passion of Christ (IIIa q.46 a.2 ag.3) can, for these reasons as regards content, be nothing more than an additional indication that these are closely related in the *Summa Theologiae*.

---

[176] In ST Ia q.21 a.1 ad 2 Thomas explains Ep 1,11, saying that God is good and therefore wants the good and acts in conformity with who He is: *Sicut et nos quod secundum legem facimus, iuste facimus. Sed nos quidem secundum legem alicuius superioris;* Deus autem sibi ipsi est lex.

[177] ST IIIa q.46 a.3co, citing Rm 5,8f: Primo *enim, per hoc* [= *Christi passionem*] *homo* cognoscit *quantum Deum hominem diligat, et per hoc provocatur ad eum diligendum:* in quo perfectio humanae salutis consistit.

3.3.3 YHWH: the Almighty, the Merciful

In this subparagraph the lines of the previous inquiry come together. First we consider in what way Thomas sees almightiness, mercy and the Passion of Christ connected: the Passion of Christ as *the* expression of God's almightiness? Next other Scriptural grounds besides W 11,23 for the connection made by Thomas will be examined.

"Mercy as the pre-eminent expression of God's almightiness" may, after this inquiry, not sound too strange anymore. In the above some similarities have come to the fore between mercy and almightiness. Both terms signify a movement from higher to lower, from stronger to weaker or even from powerful to powerless, from active to passive, from giver to receiver.[178] *All* acts of God, who is love, towards us are, therefore, characterized as merciful. However, this higher - lower scheme is exactly the reason why the word "mercy" may have a pejorative overtone. Moreover, mercy in this sense could divide humankind in haves and have-nots; it could make poor people passive and dependent and lose their human dignity, whilst they may well be regarded as inferior. Yet for a correct understanding of how Thomas presents mercy, one should note that someone who performs works of mercy merely for his/her own benefit or in order to show that he/she is superior to the other, does not act out of merciful love, but out of pure self-interest, ambition and/or pride.[179] Besides, that God is the Most High, the Almighty etc. in no way diminishes our humanity, our dignity or our freedom, as was said; God's being and acting is for our good.

In both examinations, of almightiness and of God's mercy, Thomas stresses the absolute freedom of God: no one and nothing - for instance a higher law with which God would have to comply - is higher

---

[178] *Caritas* on the other hand signifies the movement to an equal or higher good (par. 2.1.2). So when we speak of "acting out of charity" we refer to what Thomas understands by *misericordia*, not *caritas*.

[179] Thomas regards pride (as *aversio a Deo*) as the beginning of every sin (ST IaIIae q.84 a.2, sc citing Si 10,13), whereas he considers mercy the greatest (*maxima, potissima*) virtue amongst all the virtues that are directed towards the neighbour (ST IIaIIae q.30 a.4; in respect of God *caritas*, through which we are united to Him, as was said, is the greatest).

than He; no one lower, no creature can manipulate or force the Most
High in or away from His acting according to His being towards creation.
All of this would imply *passio*, which is incompatible with almightiness
and would hinder or even prevent the perfectly good and loving God from
acting to the highest extent mercifully and generously without becoming
unjust.

Furthermore, it became clear that both God's almightiness and
His mercy from the very beginning are described by Thomas as aiming at
our salvation, our happiness, the ultimate good, our union with the good
God. Whence it is surprising that the persistent prejudice is still current
that in the *Summa Theologiae* perspectives of salvation history are pushed
into the background.[180] A close reading of *quaestiones* 20, 21 and 25
unmasks this view as false.

> "It belongs to mercy to be bountiful to others and, what is
> more, to remove the defects of others. And this pertains
> foremost to someone who stands higher. Hence being
> merciful is accounted a *proprium* for God. And foremost
> therein His almightiness is said to be manifested.[181]

The consequence of this argument is that, as someone is higher and
mightier, he/she can be more merciful.[182] And, in accordance with this,
it was shown in this chapter that the name Almighty signifies that the one

---

[180] E.g. Löhrer (1967), 295ff, Rahner (1967), 325. For the view of the *Summa
Theologiae* as an approach from the history of salvation see Congar (1957), 73-122,
Seckler (1964), 33-47, Corbin (1974), 782-806, (1980), 113-138, Torrell, (1996), 150-
153.

Torrell (1996), 152, concurs with M.-V. Leroy, whilst he refines the *exitus -
reditus* interpretation of the *Summa Theologiae*, saying that the *exitus - reditus* scheme
only befits the *oikonomia*, i.e. from Ia q.44 on; Ia qq.44 - 119 concern the *exitus*, the
quaestiones in IIa and IIIa the *reditus*. The first 43 *quaestiones* in Ia concern the
theologia.

[181] ST IIaIIae q.30 a.4co: *Pertinet enim ad misericordiam quod alii effundat; et, quod
plus est, quod defectus aliorum sublevet; et hoc est* maxime superioris. *Unde et misereri
ponitur proprium Deo: et in hoc* maxime *dicitur eius omnipotentia manifestari*. This is - an
implicit - reference to *In colecta domin.* 10 *post Pentecost.*, as in Ia q.25 a.3 ag.3.

with this name is the Most High, and thence *maxime* merciful, loving, good etc. and absolutely free to express this abundantly towards us.

That being merciful is a *proprium* of God, means that God alone is merciful in the full and true sense of the word. Yet this raises questions. For this implies that when we call a human being merciful, we call him/her merciful insofar as that person is merciful like God. But, one may ask, is it in fact not rather the other way round: is it not so, that we call God merciful on the ground of our experiences with merciful people? Is not the word "merciful", or "mighty" or any human word, more proper to creatures than to God? A closer look at this question is taken in paragraph 3.4.2.

In that same paragraph also another question, in close connection with this, will be dealt with. In paragraph 2.1 it was shown how Thomas emphasizes the simplicity of God and in 3.1 how distinctions we make, and have to make, as to His being are not distinct in God.[183] But does this mean that God's mercy and almightiness are the same, as the absolute and the ordained power of God are the same? Are these - and all other - properties of God interchangeable synonyms? And if not, does Thomas then not only make a distinction *secundum rationem*, but in fact a distinction *secundum rem*?

The aspects as regards almightiness and mercy mentioned above return in Thomas' contemplation of the Passion of Christ in *quaestio* 46 of the *Tertia Pars*. What Thomas says in the *Prima Pars* in more general terms concerning God's almightiness and His merciful goodness as the utmost expression of it, is made concrete by him in this *quaestio*. For in *articulus* 1 (1.2.1) we read that in the free initiative God takes for the Passion of Christ, His absolute freedom is made manifest; no one and nothing is "higher" than the Almighty, that He would be forced in any way. Thus the Almighty was absolutely free to choose another good way to liberate humankind: *articulus* 2 (1.2.2).

It is remarkable that even in *articuli* 3 and 4 (1.2.3) the words *miseria* and *misericordia* are not used by Thomas. Yet since he is speaking of the salvation of humankind and of our happiness, he is

---

[183] Ten Kate (2000), 222: "En faisant ainsi la distinction des pouvoirs divins, entre pouvoir absolu et réalisé, il [= Thomas] risquait de mettre en péril l'unité de Dieu". This is only true for those people who misunderstood this distinction as a *distinctio secundum rem* instead of *secundum rationem*.

unmistakably referring to our misery. In fact, the whole of the *Tertia Pars* is written in this perspective, as Thomas' introduction to it shows:

> "Prologue. Since our Saviour, the Lord Jesus Christ, as the angel testified, 'while saving His people from their sins' (Mt 1,21), showed unto us in His own person the way of truth, whereby we may attain to the happiness of eternal life by rising again, ..."[184]

In the *Prima Pars quaestio* 25, in the context of almightiness, Thomas speaks of God freely forgiving our sins as the expression of having or being the highest might and in the context of God's mercy of the abundance of God's (for)giving.[185] What this abundance consists of is made explicit in the *Tertia Pars quaestio* 46, *articulus* 3: taking away our ignorance by perfecting our defects in knowledge and dignity[186] and giving us participation in the infinite good/Good, in which lies our happiness[187]. Thus we are freed from our misery and united to God by the Passion of Christ, as the ultimate - for it completes what God started in His creation (*exitus - reditus*) - expression of God's merciful love. And that this abundant generosity of God does not ignore justice, but rather is most becoming, is explicated further in respect of the cross of Christ in *articulus* 4.

The *articuli* 5 to 8 (1.3) and *articulus* 12 (1.4) of *quaestio* 46 can be regarded as elaborations on issues of almightiness, discussed in *quaestio* 25 of the *Prima Pars*. In the *articuli* 5 to 8 on the true *passiones*

---

[184] ST IIIa intr.: *Prologus. Quia* Salvator noster Dominus Iesus *Christus, teste Angelo, 'populum suum* salvum faciens a peccatis eorum' [Mt 1,21], viam veritatis nobis in seipso demonstravit, *per quam* ad beatitudinem *immortalis vitae resurgendo pervenire possimus,* ....

[185] ST Ia q.25 a.3 ad 3 and q.21 a.3 ad 2, cf. RGL c.6 1.5 (on Ga 6,16): *"Et misericordia," per quam liberentur a peccatis.*

[186] ST Ia q.21 a.3co and IIIa q.46 a.3co (*Primo; Secundo; Quarto;* resp. *Quinto*).

[187] ST Ia q.25 a.3 ad 3: [*P*]*arcendo hominibus et miserando, perducit eos ad participationem* infiniti boni, *qui est ultimus effectus divinae virtutis*; IIIa q.46 a.3co: *Tertio, quia Christus per passionem suam non solum hominem a peccato liberavit, sed etiam gratiam iustificantem et gloriam* beatitudinis *ei promeruit.*

of Christ and *articulus* 12 on the attribution of the *passiones* to the human nature and not to the divine nature of Christ we find a parallel in *articulus* 1 and in the first *obiectio* of *articulus* 3 of *quaestio* 25, on the question whether there is *potentia passiva* in God.

Finally, *articuli* 9 to 11 of *quaestio* 46 (1.2.3), are concrete examples of what Thomas says in the *Prima Pars*: that all things are in God's hand: in *quaestio* 25 *articulus* 2 he shows that God's might is infinite, not limited to act upon one particular object, and in the next *articulus* that all things (*omni-potentia*) are subject to God's might. Likewise, in *quaestio* 22 *articulus* 2 Thomas elucidates that all things are subject to divine providence (which is an exercise of God's might, since it is an action outside God).[188]

The Passion of Christ as the pre-eminent expression of God's almightiness, God's almightiness that is foremost shown in His loving mercy, God's loving mercy being revealed to the highest extent in the Passion of Christ[189] - is this an 'invention' of Thomas, or is there a Scriptural basis for these connections? Let us first examine the connection of almightiness, i.e. the might of God, with the mercy of God. The only text cited by Thomas that points to this connection is Ps 25,10: "All ways of the Lord are mercy and truth."[190] The "ways of the Lord" are interpreted by him as God's actions *ad extra*. My own first association of

---

[188] ST Ia q.22 a.2co: *Unde necesse est* omnia quae habent quocumque modo esse, ordinata esse a Deo, *secundum illud Apostoli ad Rom.13,1: Quae a Deo sunt, ordinata sunt.* Ibidem ad 4: *[N]on permittit contra eos* [= *iustos*] *evenire aliquid, quod* finaliter *impediat salutem eorum, nam "diligentibus Deum omnia cooperantur in bonum," ut dicitur Rom.8,28.*

[189] See also CDN c.10 l.1, where Thomas speaks of almightiness as of love: *Quatro, manifestat rationem omnipotentiae secundum rationem attractionis; dicitur enim magna potentiae, quae ad se aliqua* attrahere *vel convertere potest, et quantum ad hoc dicit quod convertit ad se omnia, sicut ad quamdam plantationem* omnitenentem. *In ipso enim omnia plantantur sicut in primo principio.* Here almightiness is designated as the reason of the union of the creature with God. The word *attrahere* may remind us (cf. 2.1.3 note 80) of the words of Christ in Jn 6,44 ("No one can come to Me unless drawn by *the Father* who sent Me") and 12,32 ("And when *I* am lifted up from the earth, *I* shall draw all people to Myself").

[190] ST Ia q.21 a.4sc: *[D]icitur in Psalmo 24,10: "Omnes viae Domini misericordia et veritas."*

a Scriptural text that connects God's might and mercy expressed in His deeds, is Psalm 136. This Psalm sings the praises of the woundrous deeds of YHWH: creation (verses 5 - 9), the exodus from Egypt (verses 10 - 15), leading His people through the desert (verse 16), taking possession of the Promised Land (verses 17 - 24) and His constant care for His creatures (verse 25). At the beginning and at the end (verses 1 - 4 resp. 26) the Psalm exhorts to praise God, "for", as it is repeated in *every* verse, "His mercy endures for ever." Creation and all the other works mentioned are deeds of God's might; they are totally free acts of God outside God. And in these acts God shows how utterly merciful He is: good (verse 1) and so sharing His goodness, abundantly, liberating His miserable people, who (almost) lost hope in Egypt, supplying them with food and drink when they had not got any, and continually caring for them. Thomas never cites the second part of the verses though, which says *quoniam in aeternum misericordia eius*.[191]

Another instance is Psalm 145, where God's mighty deeds are called to mind (verses 3 - 6). Of these it is said that they proclaim - which implies that they are an expression of - God's generous goodness and saving justice (verse 7). After this the conclusion follows that YHWH is good, merciful and loving to all He has made (verses 8 - 9).

Other instances in the First Testament where God's might and His mighty deeds are tied in with God's mercy are king David's hymn in 1 Ch 16 and Ps 52,10f, 59,10f and 89,2-38 (esp. verses 9, 14f, 18, 25) as well as in W 11,21-26, to which Thomas refers, as was said above, in *obiectio* 3 (ST Ia q.25 a.3) by citing a homily based upon this text (W 11,23: "You are merciful to all, because You are almighty"), and Si 18,1-14. In Ps 33,18-22, 77,9-16, 89,27, 106,1-4 and Is 54,8 the mercy

---

[191] Where we read *misericordia* in the Vulgate, it reads ד ס ח in the Hebrew Bible and ελεος in the Septuagint. ד ס ח means love, favour, goodwill, mercy, clemency and goodness and so has a broader meaning than Thomas' definition of *misericordia*. In Jr 2,2 it is even used for the love of a human being for God (Gesenius (1910), 244; Jenni/Westermann (1978), I,615). In the Vulgate it reads *caritas*. Also ם ו ח ר and ם ח ר are always translated in the Vulgate with *misericors* and *misereri*: ם ח ר (*règèm*) means "womb", whence the words refer to the motherly and fatherly love and care of God. (Gesenius (1910), 748f; Jenni/Westermann (1979), II,761-768. This comes closer to Thomas' explanation of *misericordia*. The two Hebrew words are at times used in one and the same breath (e.g. in Ps 103,4, Jr 16,5, Zc 7,9) and in strong connection with one another (e.g. in Ps 51,3, 69,17, Lm 3,22). The Vulgate then translates *misericordia* and *miseratio*.

shown in the mighty deeds of God are more specifically designated as the salvation from our distress, whereas in Ps 85,10f God's merciful might is further explicitly connected with His justice (verses 12 and 14) and His abundant generosity (verse 13). The connection of God's almightiness with the liberation of His people is found throughout Exodus and references to it, and in Jb 5,17-26 and Ps 91,1-3ff.[192]

A particular act of mercy is forgiving the defect of sin (Ps 25,7, Mi 7,18)[193] and cancelling debts (Mt 18,33). In the Second Testament the connection between having mercy and taking away a defect or lack by perfecting a good, like sight or health, is seen in many miracle stories.[194] In Mk 5,19 such a mighty, liberating action (Christ has freed a man from a legion of unclean spirits by sending them into a herd of pigs nearby) is explicitly called an act of mercy. Restoring the sense of sight may be interpreted as cure of ignorance, yet in the Second Testament only in 1 Tm 1,13f are mercy and removing ignorance expressly linked. However, in the First Testament we also find this connection in Ps 25,7, 67,2 and 119,64.[195]

That the defect or imperfection of sin is removed by the mystery of the Passion of Christ, as was said in paragraph 1.2, which is to our salvation, is found throughout the Second Testament.[196] In three instances this is expressly connected with God's might and God's mercy.

---

[192] E.g. Ex 6,2f and 15,1. Here the Vulgate reads *omnipotens* for the Hebrew ' ר שׁ resp. ה ו ה י ; in Jb 5,17 and in Ps 91,1 י ר שׁ is used. A closer look at the translation of the Hebrew words into *omnipotens* is taken in par. 3.4.1.

[193] And this is a *proprium* of the highest authority, the Most High, cf. Is 43,25, Mt 9,8 (REM c.9 1.1: [*I*]*deo Hilarius exponit: "'Qui dedit talem potestatem hominibus' ut fiant filii Dei," ut in Io. 1,12: "Dedit eis potestatem filios Dei fieri."*), Mk 2,7, Lk 7,49, Ac 5,31, Ep 4,32, Col 1,12-14.

[194] Mt 9,27-30a, 15,22-28, 17,14-18, 20,30-34, Mk 10,46-52, Lk 17,12-14, 18,35-43.

[195] Vulg-Ps 24,7 (= Ps 25,7) *iuxta LXX* speaks of *delicta iuventutis meae et* ignorantias *meas*, while *iuxta Hebr.* reads peccatorum *adulescentiae meae et scelerum meorum*. In Ps 67,2 the verb ן נ ח is used as a synonym of ד ס ח . Cf. also Hos 4,1 and 6,6, where knowing God is connected with acting mercifully.

[196] E.g. Jn 1,29, 1 Co 15,3, Ga 1,4, Ep 2,4f, 13, 1 P 2,24, 1 Jn 3,5, Rv 1,5. In the Eucharist Jn 1,29 is cited in the prayer for mercy: "Lamb of God, You take away the sins of the world, *have mercy upon us* (*Agnus Dei, qui tollis peccata mundi,* miserere nobis)."

The first two are Lk 1,46-55 and Lk 1,68-79, better known as the Magnificat and the Benedictus. These hymns highlight in respect of the mystery of the Incarnation and Passion and Resurrection of Christ[197] the manifestation of God's mercy (Lk 1,50, 52b, 53a, 54 and 1,68, 71f, 74, 77-79) in His mighty deeds (Lk 1,49, 51-52a, 54a and 1,68f, 71, 74). It is the same context in which the archangel Gabriel assures Mary that nothing is impossible for God (Lk 1,37). In the Magnificat and in the Benedictus texts from the First Testament are cited and are placed in the perspective of this mystery of salvation. The third text is 1 Co 1,18-2,5. Here St. Paul writes of the Crucified as the wisdom and the power of God, and in whom our salvation lies.

Yet despite the many and clear connections in Scripture between God's might and God's mercy, God's mercy and the Passion of Christ, the Passion of Christ and God's might, and between all three in the Magnificat, in the Benedictus and in 1 Co, despite the fact that these last two hymns have become prominent prayers in the liturgy of the Church,[198] despite the Creed of the Church, which not only connects God's almightiness with creation but equally with the mystery of Christ,[199] despite the fact that Thomas' theology in the *Summa Theologiae*, in which he demonstrates that the Passion of Christ is the expression par excellence of the almightiness of God, became so authoritative for Catholic theology, God's might is usually merely

---

[197] Cf. Schürmann (1969), 71: "Das Lied [Magnifikat] preist Gott ob seiner letzten Tat, die das Heils Israels verwirklicht (VV 50.54f) und alle Unordnung der Welt zurechtrücken wird (VV 51-53). Es spricht von *dieser letzten Tat Gottes* so, *als ob sie schon geschehen wäre*: Der prophetische Blick sieht die Vollendung der Taten Gottes schon in ihrem kleinen Anfang." *O.c.*, 86: "So ist der Psalm [Benediktus] ein *messianisches Jubellied, das auf das Kommen Jesu* (dem Johannes VV 76f zugeordnet wird; s.u.) *zurückschaut.*" Note also for instance how Lk 1,68 is referred to and elucidated in Lk 24,21ff (Kremer (1988), 33f, 240).

[198] They are prayed resepectively in the daily evening and morning prayer of the Church. The Magnificat especially has been set to music countless times throughout the centuries.

[199] The Apostolicum does this directly: God is called the almighty Father twice: once in respect of creation and once in respect of the mystery of Christ. The symbolum of Constantinople only speaks of "the Father" (who is understood as the Almighty, as it is said in the first sentence of the Creed) after recounting the the mystery of Christ.

discussed in the context of speculative theology, of "the beginning" (*creatio*, *ex nihilo*) and of how God reigns the world (*gubernatio*)[200] and not in the context of how He brings creation to its fulfilment in Christ.[201]

· The results of this study hitherto seem to confirm that Thomas' enunciation that God's almightiness is pre-eminently expressed by His saving mercy, is not a passing remark. It is not a watertight proof, but after reading what Thomas says in the contexts of mercy, there is every indication that by this enunciation he points to the mystery of our salvation through the Passion of Christ: since all actions or operations outside God are coming forth from His might, the Passion of Christ is not the only, but it is the pre-eminent expression of almightiness, the might of the Most High. This means that Thomas in *quaestio* 25 of the *Prima Pars* is not just bent on a speculative theology (*theologia*) of almightiness, but that he contemplates God's almightiness in the light of the mystery of the Passion of Christ,[202] which is the pivotal point in our history of salvation (*oikonomia*).

After examining this connection of mysteries for compability with Scripture it becomes clear that Thomas does not present something totally new or his own, original find; he rather formulates or refers to an aspect (the connection mentioned) of the mystery of the Christian faith. Yet by doing so he has not removed the mystery, as if he had solved a problem.

---

[200] Not only in our days, but in Neo-Thomism as well: E.g. Maurel (1889), 88, where only speculative aspects of ST Ia q.25 a.3 are summarized, in just eight lines, saying that God's almightiness extends to everything without contradiction and that it does not imply that God can sin. Similarly Garrigou-Lagrange (1938), 559: very brief, merely repeating a few aspects regarding *esse* and *possibilis* (from the *corpus*). He quotes from ad 3 and ad 4 too, but without any annotation. In the context of providence, (1932), 105, he refers to God's might as "une *puissance active infiniment parfaite*, c'est la *puissance créatrice*." Also: Scheeben (1933), I,598-605, esp. 599, n.349: Referring to the Creed, Scripture and Thomas he mentions creation as revealing "die spezifische That der göttlichen Macht". On this point post-Neo-Thomist theology has not really brought in innovations.

[201] In the Catechism of the Catholic Church (1993, 1995), however, in the paragraph on the name "Almighty" for God, the connections between God's mercy, almightiness and forgiving sins (n.270) and between God's almightiness and Christ's Passion (n.272) are mentioned, but unfortunately not explained any further.

[202] Esp. in ST Ia q.25 ag./ad 3, 4.

By exploring the mysteries of God's almightiness and the Passion of
Christ and pointing to the connection between the two, he rather has
deepened them: after reading Thomas' explorations we do understand
them better, *as* - connected - *mysteries*.

Referring to Scripture Thomas indicates that a good understanding
of our faith is of the utmost importance, since ignorance ends in erring
and sinning, and so leads people away from salvation. Moreover, as
Scripture also testifies, ignorance leads to despair and sadness (Ep 2,12, 1
Th 4,13), fear (Lk 1,74, Heb 2,15) and hopelessness (Rm 8,19ff). But if
so, should it then not be held as well that, conversely, a good understanding of the mysteries of our faith that God is love and almighty and
thus to the highest extent merciful and that this is shown foremost in the
Passion of Christ, is so important, because this is the source of our hope
and our trust and the way to our happiness?

In the course of this chapter some questions have come up in
respect of Christ that must be examined in further detail. That in Jn 2 (the
cleansing of the temple, in 2.2.3) and Mk 5 as well as in many other
instances, like the miracle stories, Christ is the subject of mighty and
merciful deeds, gives rise to the question whether Christ is almighty too.
And if so, how does this relate to His *passio*? For, do not almightiness
and *passio* exclude one another?

Moreover, we usually speak of God as the Almighty with
reference to God the Father. Yet in paragraph 3.2 it became clear that
almightiness is the might of the triune God. Are the Son and the Holy
Spirit then not almighty? And if they *are*, why do we usually not speak of
Them as almighty? These questions will be dealt with in chapter 4.

Until now Thomas' thoughts on almightiness have been elucidated
and examined in this chapter. In the last paragraph (3.4) attention is paid
to the language we use for our God-talk. Speaking of God entails certain
problems. In view of this study two need to be addressed here. First *the
term* almightiness. The discussion on the term almightiness cannot be
ignored. For some people are of the opinion that the word almighty/*omnipotens* is unsuitable for Christian theology, since it would be unbiblical
and originating from a non-Christian context. This will be discussed in
further detail in 3.4.1.

Finally, a closer look at *the use* of terms in our God-talk is called
for. In chapter 2 it became clear already that, when we use a word for

God, it does not fully match the meaning of that word as when it is used for a creature. Love and might, for instance, are accidents in us, whereas they denote the very essence of God; God is what He has, so to say, and has/is it in the most perfect way, unlike us. So what, then, do we say when we use such words for God? (3.4.2)

3.4 *Speaking* of Almightiness...

The last section of this chapter is of a different character. In this paragraph the term almightiness/*omnipotentia* is the focus of attention. In the first part we will not read Thomas' texts, but consider whether almighty/*omnipotens* is a suitable word for God in Christian theology. It was noticed already that the term is regarded by many, theologians and non-theologians, believers and non-believers, as problematic. This does not come as a surprise, if almightiness is apprehended as a kind of power or might as described by the sociologist Weber or the theologians Rahner and Vorgrimmler: coercion, force etc. (3.1.1). It is demonstrated that this is not what Thomas understands by almightiness. But is the term almightiness used in this sense by Christians of old? And even more fundamental, is almightiness a term that belongs to the Christian tradition at all, or is it in fact a stranger, an intruder, with which Christianity is saddled and should get rid of the sooner the better?

After the quest for an answer to this last question in 3.4.1 we inquire in 3.4.2 how Thomas interprets the Christian *use* of this term *in our speaking*: what do we say when we say that God is almighty? Is it a description of God, a metaphor or ....?

3.4.1 Almightiness, a Pagan Word?

For Thomas it was self-evident that the term *omnipotens* was used as a name of God and as a predicate for God. This turned out already in the discussion of *articulus* 3 of *quaestio* 25 of the *Prima Pars*: that God is almighty is professed "by all", in the Creed. Furthermore, in Scripture, particularly in the First Testament, God is called almighty (*omnipotens*) frequently. There was no reason whatsoever for Thomas to question the then current Latin translation of Scripture by Doctor of the Church Jerome (ca. 382 - 405 CE); the Bible Thomas had before him, was Holy

Scripture. In this translation, the *Biblia Sacra Vulgata* (Vulg), *YHWH sebaoth* and *El shaddai* in the Hebrew Bible and (*Kyrios* and *Theos*) *Pantokrator* in the Greek translation of it, the Septuagint (LXX), and in the Second Testament are usually translated by (*Dominus* and *Deus*) *omnipotens*.[203] This means that it is, to say the least, not obvious that *omnipotens* is a non-biblical word.

Yet another question is whether the term *omnipotens* as Thomas explains it in the *Summa Theologiae*, is an adequate translation of the Hebrew and Greek words mentioned. In this chapter it was shown that Thomas designates almightiness as a word from the realm of faith and that it is nothing else than the might of God. The term signifies the reign of God: that He is able to do all possible things as well as that He is absolutely free to act; there is no one and nothing above the Almighty in authority or might that might force or manipulate Him. Conversely, the term neither implies active coercion nor violence nor the abolition of the laws of nature; these are after all instituted by the Almighty Himself, according to His wisdom, love, justice etc.; almightiness and all other properties denote the very essence of the one God. Since the Almighty is God and God is love, God's might is for the good, to the salvation of His beloved, their final reunion with God that is. Are these elements also found in the Hebrew and Greek words that have been translated with *omnipotens* in Scripture?

The exegete Limbeck contends that the expression "the almighty God" is non-Biblical. His argumentation is that the Greek word

---

[203] In the Vulgate ‏שַׁדַּי‎ (‏אֵל‎) is a few times translated differently: with *Deus* (in Jb 22,3), with *Dominus* (in Jb 5,17, 6,4, 14 and Is 13,6), with *potens* (Jl 1,15), with *caelestis* (Ps-LXX 68,15) and *robustissimus* (Ps-Hebr 68,15) and with *sublimis Deus* (Ezk 1,24).

However, in Rm 9,29 (citing Is 1,9) and Jm 5,4 the Vulgate translates *Dominus sabaoth*; the Greek text reads κυριος σαβαωθ; in the Second Testament παντοκρατωρ/*omnipotens* occur outside the Revelation of John in 2 Co 6,18 only.

In LXX ‏צְבָאוֹת‎ is transcribed as σαβαωθ 65 times, 56 times of which in Isaiah. In the Vulgate this is always translated as (*Dominus*) *exercituum* (Thomas cites Is 21,10 in ST IIaIIae q.171 a.1co, Jr 32,18 in Ia q.13 a.4sc). It is the more remarkable that in the liturgy *sabaoth* has remained in the *Sanctus* (Is 6,3).

Only in the deutero-canonical book of Wisdom does the word παντοδυναμος occur, thrice. In the Vulgate this is translated with *omnem habens virtutem* (7,23) and *omnipotens* (11,17 (18), 18,15).

pantokrator is a new word originating from the Septuagint-translators, who were not able to find out the meaning of *El shaddai*. Limbeck adds, in brackets, that in our days we too cannot really fully explain the meaning of this very old name of God anymore. *Pantokrator*, he continues, does not signify, as the Latin translators convey, "Almighty (Allmächtigen)", but "the One maintaining everything (Allerhalter)". Limbeck concludes that the name "the Almighty" does not originate in the realm of the thoughts and the language of the Bible, but is derived from the world of paganism. On the basis of his interpretation of Gn 18,13f, Dt 17,8, Lk 1,36 and Mt 19,26 he presents an, according to him, Biblical view of God's might:

> "God's might does not consist in this, that He could do all things, if He only willed, *but* His might consists in His indestructible, faithfulness and orientation towards us, His creatures, *superior* to all hostile mights. By virtue of this might God can provide us with *new* life and bestow it on us time and again. God's might is His love."[204] (italics of "but" added, MR)

Unfortunately Limbeck does not explain how his denial of God being able to do what He will is related to Scripture texts that affirm that God can do what He will, like Ps 135,6 (note 111). Is God according to Limbeck not free, also not in His love for us, as in Hos 14,5, Mt 20,15 and Rm 5,15? Moreover, Limbeck contrasts God's ability to do all things with God's might as life giving. But do they necessarily exclude one another? Furthermore, it is remarkable that Limbeck first says that the meaning of *El shaddai* cannot be established and subsequently asserts that *pantokrator* and *omnipotens* are not fitting as equivalents. Limbeck also desists from determining the signification of the word *omnipotence*. Yet it was shown in the analysis of Thomas' texts that in any case the term *omnipotence* requires explanation, in our days no less than in the 13th century.

---

[204] Limbeck (1993), 77: "Gottes Macht besteht nicht darin, daß er alles tun könnte, wenn er nur wollte, *sondern* [italics added, MR] seine Macht besteht in seiner unzerstörbaren, allen feindlichen Mächten *überlegenden* Treue und Zuneigung zu uns, seine Geschöpfe. Kraft dieser Macht kann Gott uns immer wieder *neues* Leben schaffen und schenken. Gottes Macht ist seine Liebe!"

That the meaning of *El shaddai* as a name of YHWH cannot be determined exactly, is confirmed by Jenni/Westermann. The first of the eight possible interpretations discussed is "Forceful" or "Strong One" ("der Gewaltige, Starke"). And although the play upon words in Is 13,6 argues in favour of this explanation, the authors come to the conclusion that the sixth interpretation seems to have the best testimonials: "High" or "Most High".[205]

Seba means army. The meaning of *YHWH sebaoth* then extends from "Lord of Israel's armies" (e.g. Ex 12,17, 1 S 17,45 and Ps 44,10) as far as "Lord of the heavenly (e.g. 1 K 22,19 and Is 34,4) and earthly mights" (e.g. Ps 96 - 100) and "Master of all", as primarily expressed by the Greek *Kyrios Pantokrator* in the Septuagint. Without *sebaoth* the Tetragrammaton is to be translated in another way, as was said already in paragraph 2.1.1. *YHWH sebaoth* is the characteristic name of God as reigning king, throned on the cherubs.[206]

Ten Kate is another theologian who argues that *omnipotens* is a pagan term. He characterizes his dissertation as a critique leveled against the "common" or "usual meaning"[207] of almightiness - which is, according to Ten Kate, "being able to do all things". He claims, referring to Auschwitz, that this has long been superseded. He tries to demonstrate that the word *omnipotens* is older than the Greek word *pantokrator* and how the pagan import of the word *omnipotens* has been transferred to the word in the Christian context.[208] Also the Greek word *pantokrator* as used for God would be of pagan origin. *Pankrator* is etymologically derived from the world of wrestling: *pankration* ($\pi\alpha\nu\varkappa\varrho\alpha\tau\iota o\nu$), "com-

---

[205] Jenni/Westermann (1979), II,875-880. In these pages it is explained how W.F. Albright traces ‏שׁ ד י‎ back etymologically to "the One from the mountain" and how F.M. Cross also sees the name connected with the Divine Warrior. Bauke-Ruegg (1998), 331-384, esp. 347, confirms the conclusions of Jenni/Westermann.

[206] Cf. 1 S 4,4, 2 S 6,2/1 Ch 13,6, 2 K 19,15/Is 37,16, Ps 80,2 and 90,1. Jenni/Westermann, *o.c.*, II, 502-507.

[207] "Gangbare betekenis", in: Goossens, Jan (interview with Ten Kate), Almacht van God is onchristelijke erfenis uit Romeinse tijd, *Hervormd Nederland*, 29 september 2001, 18.

[208] Ten Kate (2000), 155-220.

bat", and *pankrates*, *pasikrates* (παγκϱατης, πασιϰϱατης), which is translated in this context with "getting grip of as much as you can" and "giving your all".[209]

Ten Kate considers this a more suitable image: God wrestling with the world and with the people. This aspect he also finds in the word *sebaoth*: a word which indicates combat as well as God's care for humankind.[210] But remarkably enough Ten Kate does not discuss the combination *YHWH sebaoth*. Whence the question arises how he characterizes "the combat (la lutte)" between God and the world/humankind, the "combat" of God for humankind? It cannot be like two well matched wrestlers in an arena, since the Creator and the creature are not of the same order. So what kind of a battle is God fighting?

Moreover, even if the word *pankrator* is etymologically connected with *pankration*, it is not necessary to tie it up with *pankration* as regards content. Feldmeier makes out a case for this. He sets out that *pantokrator* is not a pagan, but a typical term from early Judaism. A first indication for this is found in the Thesaurus Linguae Graecae. This authoritative book of reference mentions well over 1400 instances where this word is used. Only in less than 1% of these does it concern pagan texts, mainly prayers and hymns. In pagan philosophical or political works the word *pankrator* does not occur. More than 99% of the instances in which the word is used are religious texts of Jews in the diaspora and of Christians.

> "Early Judaism has with *pantokrator* practically exclusively reserved a word for itself - and possibly even first constructed it - in order to express in a word *God's supremacy over the world* and *His being different from the world*."[211] (italics added, MR)

---

[209] Ten Kate, *o.c.*, 5-25

[210] Ten Kate, *o.c.*, 52-55. Note that also Thomas sees God's almightiness and providence clearly connected: ST Ia q.22 aa.1, 2, esp. a.2 ad 2.

[211] Feldmeier (1997), 19: "Demgegenüber hat das Frühjudentum mit *pantokrator* ein Wort nahezu exklusiv in Beschlag genommen (und eventuell auch erst gebildet), um damit die *Weltüberlegenheit und Andersartigkeit* seines Gottes auf den Begriff zu bringen." Feldmeier adds in a note: "Sächlich parallel läuft damit die Ausbildung der Lehre von der

The hellinisation of the territory that was once conquered by Alexander the Great (356 - 323 BCE), was a catalyst for this development in theology. The hellinisation of the societies in which the Jews lived, urged them to think through the content of their own religion. That *pantokrator* occurs in a few pagan texts BCE and in some pagan incantataons from the 3rd till the 5th century CE may then rather be interpreted as influence of early Judaism on the pagan religions than the other way round.[212] Thus, just as *pankrates* was the word used by the Stoics to indicate their view of how their god reigned over the world, so *pantokrator* was commonly recognized as a name designating the God of the Bible.

Hence, the Greek word *pantokrator* is not a pagan term; it is a term from early Judaism, criticizing the then - and among certain people still - popular pagan (Greek and Roman) deterministic way of thinking, that the stars and/or a god or gods determine everything unchangeably, rigidly and arbitrarily.[213] Furthermore, the word expresses hope and faith in the God of the Bible. In situations of increasing threats, oppression and persecutions, therefore, *pantokrator* is used more often, for instance in letters[214] and in apocalyptic literature.[215] The Revelation of John is written in such a situation of distress, by the end of the 1st century CE. The word *pantokrator* occurs nine times in this book.[216] This word is later generally translated in the Latin section of

---

Schöpfung aus dem Nichts, die ebenfalls die *Überlegenheit und Unabhängigkeit* des jüdischen Gottes gegenüber der vorhandenen Wirklichkeit unterstreicht (vgl. 2. Makk 7,28; Röm 4,17). (italics added, MR)

[212] Feldmeier shows how the gods invoked in the incantations bear a remarkably great resemblance with YHWH. Feldmeier cites PMag 13,762-820 from the *Papyri Graecae Magicae, o.c.,* 20.

[213] Feldmeier, *o.c.,* 22-25, as we also see in Ovid's *Metamorphoseis* (XV, 807-812): Even Zeus/Jove, the highest god, could not but go along with what the Μοιραι (the Fates or fatal three sisters) had unalterably determined.

[214] Some exemples from papyri in Moulton, Milligan (1949), 478.

[215] Cf. also Oberlinner (1994), 299, on 1 Tm 6,15.

[216] Rv 1,8, 4,8, 11,17, 15,3, 16,7, 14, 19,6, 15, 21,22 - 7 times in combination with θεος, twice with κυριος.

the Church as *omnipotens*.[217]

Although the meaning of the Hebrew name *El shaddai* for God is not fully clear, some outlines start to show after this brief examination. First of all, *omnipotens* cannot be disposed of by saying that it is a pagan word. Ten Kate holds that the pagan word *omnipotens* is older than *pantokrator*. This is not confirmed by other scholars. But even if Ten Kate were or is correct, this does not alter the fact that *omnipotens* (as such or in combination with *Dominus* or *Deus*) is the word used by the Christians of the Latin part of the Church to translate the Hebrew words *El shaddai* and *YHWH sebaoth*, which were usually translated by the Greek speaking Jews in the diaspora and Christians with (with or without *Kyrios* or *Theos*) *pantokrator*. Thus *omnipotens* is, just like these words, used in the context of the Jewish and Christian religion, a word properly used exclusively for YHWH.[218]

---

[217] Augustine in his *In Ioannis Evangelium Tractatus CVI* n.5 elucidates that the Latin word *omnipotens* does not *etymologically* signify the same as the Greek παντοϰϱατωϱ. The latter word, he says, is philologically better (*potius*) translated with *omnitenens*, which means "maintaining everything". However, Augustine adds, Latin speaking theologians (*nostri*) explain that they signify the same (*tantumdem valere sentirent*) by the word *omnipotens*. Therefore, *ibidem*: [S]i omnipotens, utique omnitenens. In this chapter it became clear that Thomas is such a theologian (cf. CDN c.10 1.1 (expounding Pseudo-Dionysius' term *thearchia*); see note 189).

[218] As in the ancient times, nowadays the word almighty is also used by "pagans". Then the word is often used in the negative sense, for dictators and underworld characters, or in the positive sense, for sport heroes defeating their competitors impressively. In the former context almightiness signifies, in the line of the sociologist Weber, a great, dominating power, which (almost) no one can evade, so that people lose their freedom, are oppressed by (the threat of) violence. 'Almightiness' understood in this way well-nigh equals abuse of power. Since even outside the Jewish and Christian context the word almighty reminds people of God, using this word for an earthly ruler may very well lead to the apprehension that such an 'almighty' person would look like the Almighty - on the basis of which one might say: "God is not almighty," instead of "That earthly ruler is not almighty, for God alone is." It is clear that this use of the word almighty is at right angles to Thomas' explanation of it (see also ST IIIa q.13 a.1sc, discussed in par. 4.1).

In the latter context almightiness signifies human supremacy in a certain work or act, which is not a proper use of the word. In this case one may well speak of idolisation, in Marion's sense of the word, since an exclusively divine attribute is attributed - and even directly, without distance from or reference to God - to a human being. Marion

Moreover, there are some points of resemblance as regards the meaning of the Hebrew, the Greek and the Latin terms from Scripture. First of all we observe that the names *El shaddai*, *YHWH sebaoth*, *Pantokrator* as well as *Omnipotens*[219] are (translations of) the ineffable Name of God. Hence what these words signify surpasses our intellect infinitely, yet not in the first place because of *etymological* lack of clarity.[220]

In this paragraph it was said that according to Jenni/Westermann the translation "High" or "Most High" for *El shaddai* is etymologically most probable. This purport is also found in Thomas' explanation of *omnipotens*. For in the discussion of God's mercy and His free initiative to act outside Himself it showed how closely God's almightiness is connected with His absolute freedom, that is His being fully unconstrained and *not under* any obligation, since there is not such a thing. God is the most high; no one and nothing, no law or might, is above Him (cf. Heb 6,13: "When God made a promise to Abraham, He swore by His own self [Gn 22,16], since there was nothing greater to swear by"). Whether the *etymological* content of the name *El shaddai* is (also) "Mighty" or something the like,[221] is within the scope of this study not a hanging-matter, since the consequence of the meaning "Most High" is (also) that there is no one and nothing more powerful than God or (possibly) forcing Him.

Sebaoth is a word that in combination with *YHWH* refers to the might of God: there is no greater might than God's, neither in heaven, nor on earth. Withal it should be noted that Scripture testifies that this might of God is always for the protection (Ps 31,5f, 46,12) or liberation of His people from their enemies (especially Egypt and Babel) and other

---

(1977), 303: "[....] l'Être [....] devient ainsi non la lumière, mais le témoin de la lumière, c'est à dire l'icône de la distance", cf. (1991), 15-37 ((1995), 7-24).

[219] Vulg-Ex 15,3, cited in ST Ia q.13 a.1sc: Dominus *quasi vir pugnator,* Omnipotens nomen eius.

[220] Cf. ST IIaIIae q.1 a.8 ad 1: [M]*ulta per fidem tenemus de Deo quae naturali ratione inverstigare philosophi non potuerunt: puta circa providentiam eius et omnipotentiam.*

[221] Christ, being on trial before the Sanhedrin, refers to God as "Power (ἡ δυναμις, *Virtus*)", in Mt 26,64 and Mk 14,62.

sufferings inflicted upon them.[222] And this is implied as well in the word *omnipotens*, as Thomas explains.

On these grounds *omnipotens* seems to be a defensible translation of the Hebrew (and Greek) words. The words refer to the same: the might of YHWH. And insofar as we can detect the meaning of the words, there is not a fundamental difference found as for their signification. Still it is apparent that they are not without difference of accent. A first indication is already found in alternative translations of *El shaddai* and *YHWH sebaoth* in the Vulgate (note 203) and the use of for instance *excelsus* (Vulg-Ps 101,20, 137,6, Is 57,15) and *altissimus* (in the *Gloria*) besides *omnipotens*.

This insight contains a warning for us as well. Our word almightiness is a word that properly belongs to the Christian faith and in this tradition signifies the might of God. In the time of early Judaism it functioned in particular also as a critique of the belief in YHWH against pagan determinism.[223] It was and *is*, as part of our tradition, a word expressing hope and faith in YHWH[224], who is above all creation and,

---

[222] Dt 9,26, 2 S 7,23, Ps 102,21, 119,133, 147,2-6 etc.. And that God sets His people free is also in Scripture explicitly connected with His love, e.g. Ps 44,27, Is 54,8, Jr 31,2-9 (cited in ST IIIa q.49 a.4 ad 2, referring to the *passio* of Christ!) Hos 11,1-11, 14,4f.

[223] Cf. also Gräbe (2000), 16: "The Greek concept of power [$\delta\upsilon\nu\alpha\mu\iota\varsigma$] is based entirely on the idea of a natural force which, imparted in different ways, controls, moves and determines the cosmos."

[224] ST IaIIae q.64 a.4co: *Fides enim nostra regulatur secundum veritatem divinam, caritas autem secundum bonitas eius*, spes *autem secundum* magnitudinem omnipotentiae *et pietatis* eius (cf. QDV q.4 a.1co). IIaIIae q.14 a.3co, ad 1: *Ita etiam peccatum in Spiritum Sanctum dicitur irrimiscibile* secundum suam naturam, *inquantum excludit ea per quae fit remissio peccatorum. Per hoc tamen non praecluditur via remittendi et sanandi* omnipotentiae et misericordiae Dei, *per quam aliquando tales quasi miraculose spiritualiter sanantur. Ad primo ergo dicendum quod* de nemine desperandum est in hac vita, considerata omnipotentia et misericordia (cf. 2 M 7,13f (God is called the Almighty in vv.35 and 38), Ps 103,3 (cited in ag.2), 2 Co 4,7ff).

hence, also above "fate".[225] So, if almightiness is understood as what restricts and limits our freedom, if God's might is interpreted as rival to our might and is disconnected, in our minds, from His care for us - which is the case with someone like Hartshorne - we would have reverted to a pagan way of thinking, which is incompatible with the Jewish and the Christian faiths.

3.4.2 "Almightiness" in Negative Theology

We faithfully speak of God being love, almighty, merciful, good etc. We use many different names for God, although, as Thomas points out, in God there are no distinctions. God is one. This leads to the question why we actually use different names for God who is essentially one. Do these names mean the same? Are they all synonyms? And a second question is, since they are not metaphors in Thomas' sense of the word (chapter 2), what are these names: is "God is almighty" a *description* of God?

Many Different Names for the God Who Is One

"It seems that these names applied to God are synonymous names. For synonymous names are those which mean exactly the same. But these names applied to God mean exactly the same thing in God; for the goodness of God is His essence and likewise it is His wisdom. Hence these names are exactly synonymous."[226]

---

[225] ST Ia q.116 a.3: *Utrum fatum sit immobile.* Ibidem co: *[F]atum, secundum considerationem secundarum causarum, mobile est: sed secundum quod subest divinae providentiae,* immobilitatem *sortitur,* non quidem absolute necessitatis, sed conditionalem *esse veram vel necessarium, "Si Deus praescivit hoc futurum erit"* [Boetius, in *Prosa* 6, ML 63,817]; ibidem a.4 ad 2: *[F]atum refertur ad* voluntatem et potestatem Dei, sicut ad primum principium.

[226] ST Ia q.13 a.4 ag.1: *Videtur quod ista nomina dicta de Deo, sint nomina synonyma. Synonyma enim nomina dicuntur, quae* omnino idem significant. *Sed ista nomina dicta de Deo* omnino idem significant in Deo: *quia bonitas Dei est eius essentia, et similiter sapientia. Ergo ista nomina sunt omnino synonyma.*

Thomas endorses the two premisses, yet rejects the conclusion. Applied to the love and the might of God: of course His love and almightiness have the same supposition, for they both denote the one essence of God. They are the same *in God*. But these words have a different signification, for

> "the content, signified by the name, is the conception in
> the intellect of the thing signified by the name."[227]

In other words, "almighty" or "love" do not signify the essence of God directly, but only through our understanding of it (*mediante conceptione intellectus*).[228] Our understanding of love is not at all the same as of might. As was said in paragraph 2.1.1, we know God through creatures. The many different perfections in them originate from God, in whom all these are one. The many *different* conceptions of the perfections *in our mind* correspond with the one and the same, simple perfection of God (*unus re et plures secundum rationem*).

"Everything from Above Comes from Below"[229] (Analogous Language)

It seems that the consequence of this must be that we cannot speak of God and creature univocally (*univoce*), since our intellect has an imperfect understanding of God. We speak univocally of God and a creature, when we use for instance "mighty" for both in the same sense of the word. It seems that Limbeck and Ten Kate understand God's almightiness in this way, which undoubtedly contributed to their rejection of this name for God. Univocally "God is mightier", as is said in Ps 93,4, W 13,4 and, in view of Christ crucified, in 1 Co 1,25, and "God is greater", as in Ps 135,5, would be understood as if God and the powers in creation were competitive, as in Greek mythology, and God were - at

---

[227] ST Ia q.13 a.4co: *Ratio enim quam significat nomen, est conceptio intellectus de re significata per nomen.*

[228] Cf. QDV q.4 a.1 ag.2, citing Mt 15,18a.

[229] Schillebeeckx quoting the Dutch reformed theologian Kuitert, in: *de Bazuin*, 12 november 1999, 9: "Kuitert zegt altijd dat *alwat van 'boven' komt, van 'beneden' komt.*"

least one grade - mightier and greater. Or, if we call the president of the United States of America mighty and God almighty in the sense that God's might is like the president's, yet much much greater.[230]

Thomas could not have been more resolute in rejecting the possibility that we speak univocally of creatures and God:

> "Any univocal predication between God and creatures is impossible."[231]

According to Thomas we cannot say something univocally of God and a creature, since they belong to a different order or category (*genus*)[232], respectively Creator and creature. Thomas stresses that the difference between the two is not gradual, but categorical.

> "Every effect of an agent equals univocally the power of the agent. Yet because every creature is finite, it cannot equal the power of the First Agent, who is infinite. Hence it is impossible that a resemblance to God is received univocally in a creature."[233]

Furthermore, might in a creature is a quality (*qualitas*), something which it *has*, as an accident (*accidens*), distinct from what it *is*, but in God it is His very essence. Moreover, whereas in a creature might is present according to its being, that is *materialiter* and *multipliciter*, in

---

[230] This last exemple is given and rejected by Rikhof (1995), 00:59:15

[231] ST Ia q.13 a.5co: *Respondeo dicendum quod* impossibile *est* aliquod *praedicare de Deo et creaturis univoce.*

[232] ST Ia q.13 a.5 ad 2: [*S*]*imilitudo creaturae ad Deum est imperfecta: quia etiam* nec idem secundum genus *repraesentat, ut supra* [q.4 a.3] *dictum est.* Ibidem ad 3: *Deus non est mensura proportionata mensuratis. Unde* non *oportet quod Deus et creaturae* sub uno genere *contineantur*; contrary to what Aristotle says in X *Metaphys.* c.1 n.13 (Bk 1053a24-30).

[233] QDP q.7 a.7co: *Nam omnis effectus agentis univoce adaequat virtutem agentis. Nulla autem creatura, cum sit* finita, *potest adaequare virtutem primi agentis, cum sit* infinita. *Unde impossibile est quod similitudo Dei univoce in creatura recipiatur.*

God it is according to His being, that is *immaterialiter* and *simpliciter*.[234]

> "And thus, when the term 'wise' is applied to a human being, it circumscribes and comprehends in a way the thing signified; however, not when it is applied to God, for then it leaves the thing signified as incomprehended and as exceeding the signification of the term."[235]

And the same goes for mighty, love, merciful and all other names. So Thomas argues that we do not *describe* God, when we say that He is almighty. We cannot describe Him univocally, because God is infinitely far beyond our comprehension, whereas our words mirror our thoughts.[236]

Some may think we describe God in the same way as we describe a pack of sugar, when we say "God is almighty", whereas others hold that God is so completely different, that we are not able to say anything at all of God. Our words would be purely equivocal (*pure aequivoce*). In this case nothing could be said of God from creation.[237] Scripture texts

---

[234] QDP q.7 a.7co. In SN I d.35 q.1 a.4 ad 5 Thomas also brings forward the temporal aspect: God's properties are from eternity/eternal, whereas a creature's are subject to time and, therefore, to change (*corruptibilis, amitti/acquiri*).

In QDV q.2 a.11co Thomas demonstrates what the consequence is, when *esse* and *essence* are not distinguished in a creature: if in Peter *esse* (*homo*, being a certain human being) and *essentia* (*homo esse*, being human) coincided, Peter and Paul, *quibus est esse diversum*, could not be called univocally "human being"; *cum esse, quod est proprium unius rei, non possit alteri communicari*. Yet, since they share in the same nature (*essentia*), both are called univocally "human being".

[235] ST Ia q.13 a.5co: *Et sic, cum hoc nomen sapiens de homine dicitur,* quoddammodo circumscribit et comprehendit rem significatam*: non autem cum dicitur de Deo, sed relinquit rem significatam ut incomprehensam, et* excedentem nominis significationem.

[236] ST Ia q.13 a.1co: *[V]oces sunt signa intellectuum, et intellectus sunt rerum similitudines. Et sic patet quod voces referentur ad res significandas, mediante conceptione intellectus.*

[237] In QDP q.7 a.7co Thomas mentions Rabbi Moyses (Maimonides, in *Doctor Perplexorum* I c.59).

that emphasize the inequality of God and creature,[238] could be understood in this way. But, if the term might in "God is (al)mighty" would signify something totally different from the term might in "This human being is mighty", the first proposition would not mean anything. Holding that predication between God and a creature is purely equivocal, implies that it is impossibile to say anything about God from creation. In fact this is the denial of God's revelation in and through creation. This is contrary to what we believe. Thomas cites Rm 1,20 ("Ever since the creation of the world the invisible existence of God and His everlasting power have been clearly seen by the mind's understanding of created things") in order to refute this error.[239]

Thus, since "mighty" and other names cannot be simply univocally used for creatures and God, we use them equivocally. But the names cannot be *totally* equivocal, otherwise all our God-talk would be hollow. Thomas explains that within the equivocal use of our language there is a gradation: words can be used totally equivocally or partly equivocally. An example of the former is the word "might" in "The king might do this tomorrow" and in "The king has a great might." In these two sentences the word might refers to something totally different. The partly equivocal use of a word is called *analogia*. An example of the partly equivocal, analogous, use of a word, given by Thomas, is "healthy". Calling both a human being and a dog healthy, is a univocal use of the term healthy. But in calling a human being and a medicine healthy, the term healthy is used analogously: the human being *is* healthy, without illness etc., whereas the medicine *causes* health in the person taking it. And likewise urine is called healthy as a *sign* of the health of the person in question. In these cases the word healthy refers to the same, the health of this particular person that is, but in these three cases the word points to a different relation to it (being healthy, causing health, a sign of health). This example of Thomas shows that analogy is not only

---

[238] E.g. Nb 23,19, Ps 50,21, 71,19, Is 40,12-31, 46,5, Ac 17,29 and Col 1,15 (Nb 23,19 cited in SCG I c.14 n.4; Is 40,18 cited in ST Ia q.4 a.3 ag.4, q.93 a.1 ag.1, and QDV q.2 a.11 ag.1; Col 1,15 cited in ST Ia q.93 a.1 ag.2).

[239] Other texts that may come to mind are Gn 1,26, Ps 19,2, Ac 17,27-29, Ep 4,24, Col 3,10 and Jm 3,9 (Gn 1,26 cited in QDV q.2 a.11 sc.2, QDP q.7 a.7 ag.2 and 16 times in ST; Rm 1,20 cited 18 times in ST; Col 3,10 cited in ST Ia q.93 a.6sc, ad 2).

used in our God-talk, but in our everyday speech as well.

Applied to "God is mighty" and "This particular human being is mighty", the term mighty in these propositions should be understood in two ways. The one is that God's might is the cause (*causa*) of the might in the creature. God's might is the source, the origin (*principium*) of the creature's might (Ps 18,33: "This God who girds me with strength"), that is of any might of any creature. We see this also expressed in the Passion narrative in the gospel according to St. John, where Pilate urges Christ to speak, saying that he has the power to release and to crucify Him; "Jesus replied: 'You would have no power over Me at all, if it had not been given to you from above'" (Jn 19,10f).[240] And at the same time it means that the might in that creature is an indication (*signum*) of God's might. But implied is that in God might is *infinitely* more excellent - and thus not in the quantitative sense of mighty, mightier, mightiest or high, higher, highest.

> "And thus *whatever* is said of God and creatures, is said
> according to a particular relation of the creature to God as
> its principle and cause, wherein all perfections of things

---

[240] REI c.19 l.2 n.5: Thomas first endorses that Pilate did not have the power to do everything he wanted (citing 2 M 7,16): *Si enim in potestate sua totum positum erat, quare nullam causam inveniens eum non absolvit.* This in combination with the increase of his fears (*passio*) whilst he heard the crowd shouting for Christ's crucifixion (Jn 19,8) clearly shows that he certainly was not almighty, as God is. Thomas refers to Rm 13,1 (*Non est enim potestas nisi a Deo*) and Pr 8,15 (*Per Me reges regant*) in order to underline that any might/authority (*potestas*) is *data* desuper, idest a Deo, *a quo est omnis potestas*. Cf. CDN c.8 l.3: *"Laudamus Deum"*, qui excedit omnem potentiam, *"sicut omnipotentem"*, inquantum eius potentia ad omnia se extendit, [....] *"et sicut solum potentem"* ex seipso, omnes enim alii potentes non sunt ex se potentes, sed ex Deo. This may also remind us of Dt 8,17f, 32,27, 1 Ch 29,12, Ps 44,4-8, 62,12f, W 6,3, Si 10,4, Is 10,13-15, Dn 2,20f, Am 6,13, Jn 15,5, Rm 11,36 and Rv 7,2.
Cf. also QDP q.2 a.5 (*Utrum potentia generandi sub omnipotentia comprehendatur*) sc.4: [I]n quolibet genere est unum principium, ad quod omnia quae sunt illius generis, reducuntur. In genere autem potentiarum principium est omnipotentia. Ergo omnis potentia ad omnipotentiam reducitur.

pre-exist excellently."[241] (italics added, MR)

So according to Thomas this applies to our speaking of God's and a human beings' love, mercy, goodness etc. as well. And in fact hitherto in this study the reader has come across this use of language in an analogous way several times already. In chapter 2 for instance it showed how Thomas speaks of God's love without *passio*; how he speaks of God's knowledge which is without a transition from *potentia* to *actus*, as it is in us; that God is perfect, but not in the sense of perfect*ed*; how he speaks of the friendship of God without *passio*. And this chapter showed how the words "mighty" and "merciful" are used for God and human beings in an analoguous way.

But even in Thomas' discussion of the Passion of Christ we see that he interprets our language on the subject of His sufferings as analogous. For there he says that Christ as a human being truly underwent *passiones*, yet in such a way that the higher part of His soul was not affected. Hence, even in respect of Christ's humanity, there is no pure univocity of language in saying that we truly suffer and that Christ truly suffered - a consequence of Christ being truly, but not purely human.

Still "God is almighty" may seem like an improper way of naming God. For if, as was said above, we signify the essence of God only indirectly, with words that correspond to a conception in our intellect, we use words for God that befit creatures better than Him.[242] We use the term (al)mighty for God, but we know what the term mighty signifies through mighty creatures. So it seems that the term mighty as well as all other perfection words, just like metaphors (2.2), primarily befit creatures. This, Thomas says, would be true, if the word mighty in "God is (al)mighty" only meant that God were the source of the might in creatures. Then all our God-talk would be metaphorical. But, as was said above, God's might denotes His divinity, His nature as well; "God is (al)might-y" also refers to the very essence of God. So from this point of

---

[241] ST Ia q.13 a.5co: *Et sic,* quidquid *dicitur de Deo et creaturis, dicitur secundum quod est aliquis ordo creaturae ad Deum, ut ad* principium *et* causam, *in qua* praeexistunt *excellenter* omnes rerum perfectionis.

[242] ST Ia q.13 aa.3co, 6 ag.1.

view it seems that with regard to "mighty" in the proposition that God is (al)mighty, this name primarily befits God.[243]

A simple solution is not possible. It cannot be either - or. In order to overcome the impasse, Thomas makes a linguistic distinction, between the thing named (*res significata*) and the way in which it is named (*modus significandi*):

> "As regards what the name signifies, these names are primarily said applied to God rather than to creatures, because these perfections flow from God to creatures. But as regards the imposition of the names, they are primarily applied by us to creatures, which we know first."[244]

Thus, the word (al)mighty, like all other perfection words used for God, signifies the nature of God (*res significata*) itself. It is a word that properly and primarily befits God. Thomas cites Ep 3,14f ("the Father, from whom every fatherhood in heaven or on earth takes its name") in his argumentation.[245] But by stating this, Thomas does not mean that almighty, or good, merciful etc., are positive descriptions of what God is. For the way in which they are used (*modus significandi*), is ours, on the basis of what we see and according to our way of conceiving.[246] So

---

[243] ST Ia q.13 a.6 ag.3, sc (citing Ep 3,14f, which seems to imply that terms used for God and creatures are primarily used for God).

[244] ST Ia q.13 a.6co: [*Q*]*uantum ad rem significatam per nomen*, prius *dicuntur de Deo quam de creaturis: quia a Deo huiusmodi perfectiones in creaturas manant. Sed quantum ad impositionem nominis, per* prius *a nobis imponuntur creaturis, quas prius cognoscimus. Unde et modus significandi habent, qui competit creaturis.*

[245] Also 2 M 1,24f, Mt 19,17, Lk 18,19 (cf. Thomas' exegesis in SCG I c.38, ST Ia q.6 a.2 ad 2 and IIIa q.20 a.1co) and 1 Tm 6,15 may come to mind.

[246] This does not only apply to the *word* almighty, but to the *sentence* "God is almighty" as well. By means of composed sentences (subject + verb + predicate) we refer to God who is uncomposed, ST Ia q.13 a.12co: *Deus autem, in se consideratus*, est omnino unus et simplex*: sed tamen intellectus noster secundum diversas conceptiones ipsum cognoscit, eo quod non potest ipsum, ut in seipsum est, videre. Sed tamen, quamvis intelligat ipsum sub diversis conceptionibus respondet una et eadem res simpliciter. Hanc ergo* pluritatem quae est secundum rationem, repraesentat per pluritatem praedicati et subiecti*: unitatem vero repraesentat intellectus per compositionem. Ibidem ad 3: [*C*]*um*

when we speak of God as (al)mighty, we speak in an analogous way. It is a proper way of speaking of God that befits the human intellect. For although we do not know what almightiness, what God's might is, we understand it and speak of it on the basis of the mighty effects of God which we experience in creation (*Deus cognoscitur a nobis ex creaturis, secundum habitudinem principii*...), and especially in the Passion of Christ, as Thomas says, *and* as a mystery in God, in whom might and all other perfections are from eternity, in an infinitely more excellent way and in a different, i.e. non-composed, way than/from in creatures (... *et per modum excellentiae et remotionis*[247]).

This exposition shows that for a correct understanding of what we say of God (*res significata*), that "God is a rock", "God is without *passio*" and "God is almighty", we should not only pay attention to the meaning of the words and images used (*res significata*), but equally to the way in which they are used (*modus significandi*), respectively in a metaphorical way, in a proper, denying way and in a proper, analogous way. Thomas shows how we could err in our understanding of what we say of God, if His otherness is regarded as totally different, which leads to subsiding into silence, and, the other extreme, if His otherness is overlooked, which leads to conceiving God and speaking of Him as a creature, as "part of all there is". In that case "God is almighty" would not refer to a mystery, but would be a description of God as if He were a pack of sugar.[248]

---

intelligit [*quicumque intellectus*] *simplicia quae sunt supra se, intelligit ea secundum modum suum, scilicet composite:* non *tamen ita quod intelligat ea* esse *composita*. Et sic intellectus noster non est falsus, formans compositionem de Deo.

[247] ST Ia q.13 a.1co, cited in 2.1.1.

[248] Then, as Marion criticizes theism and atheism, God is no longer a question; then God has become an object, an idol, a problem to be solved, (1991), 86f ((1995), 57): "La modernité se caracterise d'abord par l'annulation de Dieu comme question [....] Quoi donc se trouve mis en jeu dans une négation ou une affirmation de Dieu? Non pas Dieu comme tel, mais la compabilité ou l'incompabilité d'une idole dite "Dieu" avec l'ensemble du système conceptuel où fait epoque l'étant dans son être. L'écart entre la compabilité et l'incompabilité importe sans doute, mais il importe infiniment moins que la constante substitution, dans l'un et l'autre cas, à un pôle absolu d'une idole. Théisme ou athéisme portent également sur une idole." *Ibidem* 197 (139): "La théologie, sauf

distingué blasphème, conforment à l'axiome que seul "Dieu parle bien de Dieu" (cf. Pascal, *Pensées* Br. §799, L. §303)."

CHAPTER 4

THE ALMIGHTINESS OF CHRIST

In this thesis it may be logical, in a sense, to consider, after the *passio* of Christ and the *passio* of God and subsequently the almightiness of God in respect of these, the almightiness of Christ. Yet speaking of Christ's almightiness probably sounds rather odd to many. Quite understandably, since we usually do not speak of Christ as "the Almighty". In the liturgy this name is only used for the Father, in the Gloria and in the Creed, or employed to address God in the prayers ("Almighty God, ..."). In theology the almightiness of Christ is virtually treated as a non-issue.[1]

However, there are some inducements for considering the almightiness of Christ. First of all, Christ is the Son of God. So if the triune God is almighty, Father, Son and Spirit are almighty. Furthermore in the Gloria Jesus Christ is called "the Most High", a name closely connected with almightiness, as was shown in the former chapter. And in the Gloria as well as in the Creed it is professed that He is sitting at the right hand of the Father.[2] Moreover, in Holy Scripture we read several times explicitly about Christ's power, for example in Mt 28,18 ("All power in heaven and on earth has been given to Me"), Jn 17,2 ("Father, [....] just as You have given Him [i.e. Your Son] power over all humanity") and Rv 5,12 ("Worthy is the Lamb that was sacrificed to receive power," etc.).[3] Also the miracle stories come to mind, for instance Mk

---

[1] Bauke-Ruegg (1998), 478f is one of the few (the only?) contemporary theologians who mentions it, referring to Bonaventure's commentary on Peter Lombard's Sententiae (I d.42 dub 6 *responsio*).

[2] Cf. Mk 16,19, Ac 7,55, Ep 1,20, Heb 1,3.13 (citing Ps 110,1). ST IIIa q.58 a.1co: *Utroque igitur modo Christo convenit sedere ad dexteram Patris. Uno quidem modo, inquantum aeternaliter manet incorruptibilis in beatitudine Patris, quae eius dextera dicitur, secundum illud Ps. 15,11* (Ps 16,11). *[....] Alio modo dicitur Christus sedere in dextera Patris, inquantum* Patri conregnat et ab eo habet iudiciariam potestam. And here Thomas refers to what was custom in his days, that the person sitting at the right hand of a king was the one assisting the king in reigning and administering justice.

[3] And also Ps.8,7 (cf. RPS ps.8 n.4) and Dn.7,14 (cf. REI c.12 l.6 n.1, ST IIIa q.59 a.1 ad 2, a.4co) have traditionally been read as aiming at Christ.

5,1-20 (as was mentioned in 3.3.3). In 1 Cor 1,23f Christ, the Crucified that is, is even called "God's power".

On the basis of this we cannot but say that from a biblical and liturgical point of view the consideration of Christ's might is plausible. Another link of Christ with almightiness is found in churches where the figure of Christos Pantokrator is depicted, after the example of the Hagia Sophia church in Constantinople, that was dedicated to *Christos Pantokrator*. This thesis will deal only with the might of Christ with regard to His Passion; Christ as the risen Lord and as the judge on the Last Day fall as such outside the scope of this study.

The first paragraph will discuss why we do not usually speak of Christ as almighty. Is it because Christ is not almighty or is there (yet) another reason? Thomas points to two matters of importance with regard to this question. The one is that we appropriate names to the three Persons of the Trinity; Thomas passes to us the grammar rule of appropriation, the importance of which is shown in Thomas' application of it to Jn 5. The other matter is that, when we speak of Christ, we must distinguish between Christ as the divine Son and Christ as a human being, as was established already in chapter 1. In the second paragraph the *quaestiones* 13 and 18 of the *Tertia Pars* are read, where Thomas considers the almightiness of the man Christ and the expression of it in doing His human will in further detail.

4.1 Like Father, Like Son?

In paragraph 3.2 it was concluded that almightiness signifies the one power of the triune God, just as the love of God is the love of the Father and of the Son and of the Holy Spirit. For, since "not any name, that is predicated in the singular of each Person and of all together, is a proper name of a Person,"[4] the almightiness of God is the might of the Father and of the Son and of the Holy Spirit.

"It says in the Creed of Athanasius: 'Almighty Father,

---

[4] ST Ia q.37 a.1 ag.1: *Sed nullum nomen quod de singulis personis praedicatur et de omnibus in communi singulariter, est nomen proprium alicuius personae.*

almighty Son, almighty Holy Spirit.'"[5]

So it is in accordance with our faith that the Father and the Son and the Holy Spirit are almighty. One may ask then why in the Creed only the almightiness of the Father is mentioned. And, in the same line of questioning, why we never speak of the Son's and of the Spirit's almightiness. For this practice may lead to a misapprehension of our faith; people might conceive almighty as a proper name (*proprium*) of the Father or might think that "almighty" befits the Father better than the Son or the Holy Spirit.

Thomas recognizes this problem.[6] He tackles it by explaining that we attribute words which denote the essence of God, like almightiness, wisdom and goodness, to one of the three Persons, in case of these examples respectively to the Father, the Son and the Holy Spirit. This is called appropriation (*appropriatio*). Appropriation clarifies the content of our faith in the triune God.[7] To expound this, Thomas first refers to the *quaestio*, where he inquired about the possibility of knowing the mystery of the Trinity of the divine Persons by demonstration. There he argues that this is not possible. The reason is that humans only know about God from the effects He brings about in creation. Yet God's creative power is the Trinity's, as of one agent, one *principium* and *causa finalis*.[8] Thus, with human natural knowlegde one cannot distinguish the divine Persons. However, one can, as pagan philosophers have done, by observing the effects in our world, come to the knowledge of God's essential attributes, as might, wisdom and goodness. In faith these are being "appropriated"

---

[5] SN I d.20 q.1 a.1sc: [*I*]*n symbolo Athanasii dicitur: "Omnipotens Pater, omnipotens Filius, omnipotens Spiritus Sanctus."* This q.1 is an exegesis of Jn 16,15, which is cited in Lombard's text.

[6] ST Ia q.39 a.7 ag.1: *Sed ea quae sunt communia tribus Personis appropriare alicui, potest vergere in errorem fidei: quia potest intelligi quod vel illi tantum Personae conveniant cui appropriantur; vel quod magis conveniant ei quam aliis.*

[7] ST Ia q.39 a.7co: [*A*]*d manifestationem fidei conveniens fuit essentialia attributa personis appropriari.* [....] *Et haec manifestatio Personarum per essentialia attributa, appropriatio nominatur.*

[8] ST Ia q.45 a.6, esp. ad 2; q.44 a.1sc (citing Rm 11,36), a.4sc (citing Pr 16,4).

respectively to the Father, the Son and the Holy Spirit,[9] in order to enliven our belief in the Trinity. Hence:

> "A resemblance in our intellect is not an adequate proof of something concerning God, because the intellect is not univocally in God and in us. Whence Augustine says in his commentary on John, that by faith we arrive at knowledge, not the other way round."[10]

So in this context we encounter again a formulation of the starting point of Thomas' theology: faith. For we are speaking of what we do not see (Heb 11,1), of the *mystery* of God (1 Co 2,6f: "We do talk of a wisdom, not, it is true, a philosophy of this age or of the rulers of this age, who will not last long now. It is of the mysterious wisdom of God that we talk, the wisdom that was hidden, which God predestined to be for our glory before the ages began").[11] Thomas brings it up here to underline that he is exploring the meaning of our faith, not describing God.

Having resumed this, Thomas takes a further step. Because of our not-knowing with respect to the divine Persons, the Trinity is in danger of remaining in the dark, being marginalized, in the sense that it would be regarded as not being of any importance in our faith. God would be regarded as discussible, *per essentialia*, as mighty, wise, good and the like, whereas with regard to the three divine Persons we would be silenced; we do not know of them through creation. Only in the *Summa Theologiae* Thomas refers to this threat, indirectly though, by expressing

---

[9] ST Ia q.32 a.1 ad 1: citing 1 Cor 2,6, of which a gloss identifies *principium huius saeculi* with *philosophorum*. Cognoverunt tamen quaedam essentialia attributa *quae appropriantur personis, sicut potentia Patri, sapientia Filio, bonitas Spiritui Sancto.*

[10] ST Ia q.32 a.1 ad 2: *Similitudo autem intellectus nostri non sufficienter probat aliquid de Deo, propter hoc quod intellectus* non univoce *invenitur in Deo et in nobis. Et* inde *est quod Augustinus, Super Io.* [6,64] [Tr. 27 par. 7, ML 35,1618], *dicit quod* per fidem venitur ad cognitionem, *et non e converso.* As Thomas' says in REI c.6 1.8 n.6: *Ex hoc enim non intelligebant, quia non credebant; Isa VII,9, secundum aliam litteram* [namely LXX]*.* Nisi credideritis, non intelligetis. Cf. ST IIaIIae q.4 a.8, q.8 aa.2, 4, 5, 8 and q.9 a.2.

[11] Both texts are cited in ST Ia q.32 a.1co. Also Is 45,15 (cited in ST IIIa q.36 a.1sc, about to whom the birth of Christ had to be made known) comes to mind.

the need to bring to light the divine Persons - he uses the word *manifesta-ri/-tatio* six times in the *corpus* of *articulus* 7 of *quaestio* 39. Still the *essentialia* are - and remain - common to all three Persons. Appropriation, therefore, is an imperfect way of manifesting the Trinity, since the appropriations are *secundum rationem tantum*. So, for the correct understanding of appropriation it is crucial indeed to avoid that appropriations are being confused with the proper names (*propria*) of God.[12]

Now the question is according to which principle words designating God's essence are appropriated to which divine Person. Thomas distinguishes two possible ways: some words are appropriated by reason of a similarity, others by a dissimilarity. He explains how in Scripture "wisdom", for instance, is in the first way appropriated to the Son, in 1 Co 1,24.[13] Not that the Father would not be wise,[14] but wisdom is appropriated to the Son, since wisdom bears a likeness to the intellect[15], from which words come forth; and "Word (*Logos, Verbum*)" is a proper name of the Son.[16] And in the same way "Creator" is

---

[12] ST Ia q.33 a.4 ag.4: *Proprium est quod uni soli convenit*. A proper name of the Father mentioned in this *articulus* is *esse ingenitum* in the sense of *principium non de principio* (co, ad 2). *Esse genitum* and *imago* are *propria* of the Son (q.35 a.2); *amor* and *donum* are, in the personal sense (*personaliter, non essentialiter*) of the word, *propria* of the Spirit (q.37 a.1, cf. 2.1.3; q.38 a.2). Unlike appropriation, ST Ia q.39 a.7 ad 1: [*E*]*ssentialia attributa* non sic *appropriantur* Personis, ut *eis esse* propria *asserantur*. For, as Thomas explains in SN I d.31 q.1 a.2co: [*Q*]*uia in personis est distinctio et ordo* realis, *sed in attributis* secundum rationem. *Unde quamvis per attributa non possimus sufficienter devenire in propria personarum, tamen inspicimus in appropriatis aliquam similitudinem personarum, et ita valet talis apropriatio ad aliquam fidei manifestationem*, quamvis imperfectam.

[13] ST Ia q.39 a.7sc; also in 1 Cor 1,30, 4,10, Col 2,3, 3,16 and Rv 5,12. Cf. SCG IV c.12.

[14] ST Ia q.39 a.7 ad 2 (referring to Augustine's VII *De Trin.* c.1 (ML 42,933)): *Filius dicitur sapientia Patris, quia est sapientia de Patre sapientia:* uterque *enim per se est* sapientia, *et* simul ambo una *sapientia*.

[15] ST IaIIae q.57 a.2: Both are *habitus intellectuales speculativi*.

[16] ST Ia q.34 a.2co: *Verbum proprie dictum in divinis personaliter accipitur, et est* proprium nomen *personae Filii. Significat enim* quandam emanationem intellectus. Ibidem q.39 a.7co: [*E*]*a quae pertinent ad intellectum, appropriantur Filio, qui procedit per*

appropriated - for properly speaking the triune God is the Creator - to the Father, to Whom being *principium non de principio* is proper.[17]

If one would expect, as I did, that Thomas interprets the appropriation of the essential name of might (*potentia*) to the Father according to the same reasoning, one would be surprised; he explains it as an appropriation by way of *dis*similarity:

> "For with us, human beings, fathers, by reason of old age, are usually weak."[18]

A rather strange reasoning, for along the same line of reasoning one could maintain the opposite: at the birth of their child fathers are, in general (*solent*), stronger than the new-born. Reading Thomas' commentary on Peter Lombard's *Sententiae* straightens out the tangle. Here he appropriates might to the Father because of similarity:

> "Might contains the notion of principle; and therefore it is appropriated to the Father, who is the principle not coming forth from a principle.[19]

Further on in the *Sententiae* he mentions the possibility of appropriation by way of dissimilarity, that is the similarity, or rather the distance of similarity, between a human being and God the Father, God the Son or

---

modum intellectus ut Verbum.

[17] *In divinis* the Son is *principium* de principio (as in the Creed: *Deum de Deo*), which means that He is born (*genitum: Filium Dei unigenitum*) of the Father (ST Ia q.27 a.2, citing Ps 2,7 in sc) and principium *de principio*, meaning that the Spirit comes forth also from Him (*filioque*) (ST Ia q.36 a.2).

[18] ST Ia q.39 a.7co: [*Q*]*uia apud nos* [i.e. *homines*] *patres solent esse propter senectutem infirmi; ne tale aliquid suspicemur in Deo.* This argument is derived from Hugo of St. Victor's *De sacramentis* (L.1 p.2 c.8, ML 176,209) (and not from Augustine, as Thomas says).

[19] SN I d.31 q.1 a.2co: *Potentia habet in ratione sua principium; et ideo appropriatur Patri, qui est principium non de principio.*

God the Holy Spirit.[20] So one and the same word, "might" for instance, can be appropriated to one of the divine Persons by way of similarity, reasoning from God to a human being, as well as by way of dissimilarity.[21]

Considering the appropriation of wisdom to Christ, Thomas cites 1 Co 1,24, where Christ, the Crucified that is, is not only called "the wisdom of God", but in one and the same breath "the power of God" as well. In the light of the above this raises some questions: if wisdom is an appropriation of Christ, is power then too? What is the similarity and/or dissimilarity in the appropriation? And if it is an appropriation, how is it related to the appropriation of almightiness to the Father? And if not, how can Christ then be called "the power of God", whilst almightiness is appropriated to the Father?

Thomas observes that the divine power is not only appropriated to the Son, but even to the Holy Spirit.[22] And according to how Thomas

---

[20] SN I d.31 q.1 a.2co: *Sicut etiam ex vestigio et imagine sumitur aliqua* [namely *imperfecta*] *via persuativa ad manifestationem personarum* (cf. ST Ia q.45 a.7: *Trinitatis vestigium in creatura*). Ibidem ad 1: *Quia haec praepositio "ad", quae venit ad compositionem vocabuli, notat* accessum, cum quadam distantia; *unde, secundum Augustinum, lib. I Retract. c.26,* homo, *qui ita imitatur Deum, quod semper invenitur distantia similitudinis, dicitur imago et* ad *imaginem. Filius autem, qui imitatur Patrem sine aliqua dissimilitudine, dicitur* imago *et non ad imaginem.*

[21] This he does in SN I d.34 q.2co with the attribution of wisdom to the Son: [*I*]*nvenitur imperitia in filiis propter iuventutis motus et propter inexperientiam, et ideo Filio Dei sapientia attribuitur*; and goodness to the Holy Spirit: [*N*]*omen spiritus* apud nos *pertinere solet ad quandam rigiditatem et inflationem, vel impetuositatem; unde dicitur Is. 2,2* [....]. *et ideo Spiritui Sancto bonitas attribuitur.*
Strangely enough Thomas in the ST does not apply this general rule where he discusses appropriation in general (Ia q.39 a.7) but only where he answers the question whether specific *essentialia* have been attributed suitably by the Doctors of the Church to the divine Persons (ibidem a.8co). Using the same exemple of *potentia* in a.7co in both cases (appropriation by way of dissimilarity *and* similarity) would have made Thomas' exposition there clear. Furthermore, in the Blackfriars edition the "*apud nos*" is not translated, which makes the text incomprehensible.

[22] ST Ia q.39 a.8co: *Virtus autem apropriatur Filio* et *Spiritui Sancto.* With regard to the Holy Spirit he does not cite Lk 1,35, 4,14, Ac 10,38 but Lk 6,19, in ag.3. Why this verse is quoted here, is not very clear at first, for the Holy Spirit is not mentioned, neither in this verse nor in the broader context. Also the only other place in the ST where

describes appropriation, power (*virtus*) can indeed be appropriated to both. For whether divine power is ascribed to one or the other depends on the character of this power: *effusing from* Christ for instance, as in Lk 6,19 and 8,46, it is to be appropriated to the Spirit, in these cases by way of similarity. God's power in a corporeal appearance, as (in) the incarnated, crucified and risen Christ[23] and as in Lk 4,40 ("…. and laying His hands on each, He cured them") and Mk 8,23 ("Then, putting spittle on his [the blind man's] eyes and laying His hands on him, ….."), cf. Jn 9,6,[24] is to be appropriated to the Son, again by way of similarity.[25]

However, since almightiness is appropriated to the Father, the appropriation of divine power to the Son and the Holy Spirit raises the question how these appropriations are interconnected. It must be noted here that the Latin word for power used in 1 Co 1,24 is *virtus*, not *potentia*. It looks like Thomas is using the words *potentia* and *virtus* as synonyms at times.[26] And although the two terms are closely connected,

---

Lk 6,19 is quoted (IIIa q.43 a.4co), is not helpful for understanding this. However, in ST IIIa q.43 a.1co Thomas cites Ga 3,5, where the Spirit *is* connected with *operari virtutes*. And in the next *articulus* (a.2co) it is made clear that "only God" (*solus Deus*) works wonders: *sola virtute divina*. Therefore it seems that, since *virtus* is a word that signifies the *essentia Dei*, it is appropriated to the Spirit in Lk 6,19, because of the way the divine *virtus* goes out from Christ: it effuses from Him, so to say, which is more befitting the Spirit (see also Lk 8,46; in both cases "*exire*"). At the same time the curing by the power of the *Holy* Spirit also resembles what the people mentioned in Lk 6,18 were cured of: torments of *unclean* spirits.

[23] Rm 1,3f and 1 Cor 1,24.

[24] All three cited in ST IIIa q.44 a.3 ad 2.

[25] Indeed the power could be appropriated to the Son by dissimilarity also, since *in humanis* fathers are usually stronger than their sons, as long as these are under-age at least. But the appropriation by similarity is more obvious in this context, since Christ, when he travelled round to proclaim the gospel and eventually was crucified, was an adult, "in the full bloom of His life", and *in humanis* grown-up sons are often (at some point) stronger than their father.

[26] E.g. in de conclusion of ST Ia q.25 a.2 ad 3, in the context of considering the infinity of God's *potentia*, without having mentioned God's *virtus* even once in the foregoing of the *articulus*: *Unde non oportet, quod tota* virtus *eius manifestetur in motu ita…* and in ibidem a.3 ad 3, discussing the *omnipotentia* of God, he says: …. *perducit eos ad participationem infiniti boni, qui est ultimus effectus divinae* virtutis. In this

they do not seem to be identical in meaning. For Thomas distinguishes the two, saying:

> "Now power (*virtus*) is appropriated to the Son and to the
> Holy Spirit, not in the sense that the might (*potentia*) itself
> of a thing is called power, but in the sense that at times
> (*interdum*) what comes forth from the might of a thing is
> called a power."[27]

Thomas gives the example of a virtuous act, as the power of an agent. With the word *interdum* Thomas apparently aims at the ordinary use of the word power. Yet as for a definition it is rather vague. In the *Prima* and *Secunda Secundae* Thomas is more precise, where he says that a power is a certain perfection of a might. The perfection, or ultimate aim, of a *potentia* is its *actus*.[28] Here, obviously, with *potentia* is meant *potentia passiva*.

In the former chapter it became clear that God's *potentia* can only be *potentia activa*; God is *actus purus*. But what then is, according to Thomas, the difference between God's power and God's (al)might(iness)? Should it not be said that, since God's *potentia* is fully in act, c.q. perfect, it therefore coincides with His *virtus*?

Thomas himself does not specifically address this. To me it seems that *omnipotentia* is appropriated to the Father, because on the one hand

---

articulus also *virtus* occurs only once. Or in ST Ia q.112 a.4co: *Virtutes et potestates dicuntur per respectum ad aliquem actum*, without any distinction or further explanation. Also in IIIa q.13 a.2sc: Of God it is said in Heb 1,3 *Portans omnia verbo virtutis suae*, whence Thomas draws the conclusion: *Ergo solius Dei est habere omnipotentiam respectu immutationis creaturarum*.

[27] ST Ia q.39 a.8co: *Virtus autem apropriatur Filio et Spiritui Sancto, non secundum quod virtus dicitur ipsa potentia rei: sed secundum quod interdum virtus dicitur id quod a potentia rei procedit.*

[28] ST IaIIae q.55 a.1co: *[V]irtus nominat quandam potentiae perfectionem. Uniuscuiusque autem perfectio praecipue consideratur in ordine ad suum finem. Finis autem potentiae actus est. Unde potentia dicitur esse perfecta, secundum quod determinatur ad suum actum.* ST IIaIIae q.129 a.2co: *Virtus est perfectio quaedam* [VII Physic. c.3 nn.4,5, Bk 246a13, 247a2] *Et intelligitur esse perfectio potentiae, ad cuius ultimum pertinet, ut patet in I De coelo* [c.11 nn.7,8, Bk 281a11, a18].

potentia, as Thomas describes it, bears the meaning of origin or source. Therefore *(omni)potentia* is as an appropriation more befitting the Father. The word *virtus* bears, on the other hand, the meaning of actually implementing, acting out. So this word is more befitting, and therefore appropriated to the Son and the Spirit, Who are being sent to fulfill the will of God.[29] This implies that God's *potentia* and God's *virtus* are identical *secundum rem* - for the words denote the one *essentia Dei*, the divinity of God - and only *(tantum)* distinct *secundum rationem*. And that, therefore, speaking of God, Thomas rightly uses *in divinis* the terms *virtus*, *potentia activa* and *omnipotentia* as synonyms.

If these appropriations are not recognized as such, but as *propria* or as descriptions, one would have to come to the conclusion, for instance, that the Father does not act towards the world directly or that the Son acts, or could act, independently from the Father.[30] This consequence of Thomas' exposition seems to be in accordance with what we read in Holy Scripture: "Whatever the Father does, the Son does too" (Jn 5,19b). And this exposition also clarifies why *in divinis* one must hold that the Son does not undergo *(patitur)*. For, as a variation on Jn 5,19b, whatever the Son undergoes, the Father undergoes too.

However, Jn 5,19 also raises questions concerning the relation between the power and might of the Father and of the Son. In paragraph 1.1.2 it has been explained that the Father did not *force* His Son to die, but that Christ died of His own free will. Yet there are texts that seem to suggest a kind of *subordination* of the Son to the Father, for example

---

[29] Jn 4,34, 6,38-40, 17,4, cf. Mt 18,14 and 1 Tm 2,4; Mk.14,36 par.; Jn 5,30, 19,28-30; Heb 10,7 (citing Ps 40,8f); and the many references in ST Ia q.43.

Now this is a clearer way of appropriating than in SN I d.34 q.2 ad 1, where Thomas appropriates *virtus* to the Father as well, namely *secundum quod in potentia radicatur*. In SN he appropriates *virtus* to the Son, following Gregory (in XXXII *Moral.* c.5 par.7), where the Father is said to operate *ad extra*: *potentia in actum exit, et ita Filio appropriatur, per quem Pater operari dicitur; unde et Filius brachium Patris dicitur, Iob 40,4* [= 40,9]: *Si habes brachium sicut Deus*. But since the power of the Holy Spirit can also be described as *potentia in actum exit*, this is not too clear. Clearer is (ibidem), though, the appropriation of *virtus* to the Holy Spirit: *inquantum* [*virtus*] *circa opus bonitatem imponit*; goodness and willing what is good are associated with the Holy Spirit (see 2.1.2, 2.1.3).

[30] In that case we would be speaking of three 'gods': ST Ia q.31 a.1 ad 4, 5; a.2.

where Christ says: "In all truth I tell you, by Himself the Son can do nothing; He can do only what He sees the Father do" (Jn 5,19a). And also further on in the same chapter Jesus says: "By myself I can do nothing; I can judge only as I am told to judge, and my judging is just, because I seek to do not my own will, but the will of Him Who sent Me" (Jn 5,30) and "I act just as the Father commanded" (Jn 14,31b).[31] And the same applies to Christ's prayer at Gethsemane (Mk 14,36 par.: "But let it be as You, not I, would have it").

In the *Summa Contra Gentiles* Thomas opens a whole arsenal of Scriptural evidence, arguing why these texts should not be interpreted as if the Son were subordinated to the Father.[32] Where Thomas addresses this particular issue in the *Summa Theologiae*, just before considering the missions of the divine persons (Ia q.43), Thomas is much more sober. And he can be, since he has already given the answer in the preceeding *quaestiones*, which he only needs to apply here. The key to the Catholic understanding of these Scripture texts is the Nicean *homoousion*. Thomas says nothing really new, when he draws the conclusion:

> "We are to hold that it is necessary to say that the Son is equal to the Father in magnitude. For God's magnitude is nothing else than the perfection of His nature. [....] And neither can it be said that the power of God the Father fell short in generating [the Son], nor that God's Son achieved perfection gradually and by change. Therefore it is necessary to say that from eternity He has been equal to the Father regarding magnitude."
>
> "The Son is equal to the Father in magnitude, in the perfection of nature that is. Therefore it remains that the Son is equal to the Father in might. And the same argument serves for the Holy Spirit regarding both of

---

[31] ST Ia q.42 a.6 ag.1, 2. Here Thomas also cites Jn 5,20a. In the sc he cites Jn 5,19b.

[32] Thomas equally refutes this Arianist interpretation and Photinus' interpretation, denying the *homoousion*: SCG IV cc.4, 6 - 9.

Them."[33]

The second "therefore" is the logical inference, since God's might constitutes His nature or essence, as was said above (3.2.1). By formulating this mystery of our faith, named coinherence (or in Greek *perichoresis*), Thomas explains to us a rule of grammar for the catholic understanding of biblical texts as mentioned above.

In the application of this rule to the texts mentioned Thomas distinguishes between *oikonomia* and *theologia*. Regarding the *oikonomia* Christ's words in Jn 5,19 are to be interpreted that one cannot speak of the Son - doing something in our created world - detached from the Father and the Holy Spirit. For, when God acts *ad extra*, it is never *either* the Father *or* the Son *or* the Holy Spirit, but always the triune God, the Father *and* the Son *and* the Holy Spirit, as was said above. Otherwise we would be speaking of three mights or powers of God or even three gods, which is not in accordance with the Christian profession of God's unity and trinity. Thomas shows by his explanation that texts like Jn 5,17-30, 8,29 ("He who sent Me is with Me and has not left Me to myself, for I always do what pleases Him"), 9,3f (".... we must carry out the work of the One who sent Me") and 14,10b ("What I say to you I do not speak of My own accord; it is the Father, living in Me, who is doing this work")[34] express the mystery of this operative unity.[35]

---

[33] ST Ia q.42 a.4co: [D]*icendum quod necesse est dicere Filium esse* aequalem Patri *in magnitudine. Magnitudo enim Dei non est aliud quam perfectio naturae ipsius.* [....] Nec *potest dici quod virtus Dei Patris fuerit defectiva in generando;* neque *quod Dei Filius successive et per transmutationem ad perfectionem advenit.* Unde *necesse est dicere quod ab aeterno fuerit Patri aequalis in magnitudine.* Ibidem a.6co: [I]*psa ratio* [....] *exigit quod Filius sit aequalis Patri in magnitudine, idest in perfectione naturae.* Unde *relinquitur quod Filius sit aequalis Patri in potestate. Et eadem ratio est de Spiritu Sancto respectu utriusque.*

[34] As explained in REI resp. c.5 l.2 nn.7ff (esp. with reference to vv. 17 (l.2 n.7), 19 (l.3 nn.1-2), 21 (l.4 n.2), 23 (l.4 n.4), 26 (l.5 n.1)) and c.8 l.3 n.9, c.9 l.1 n.4 and c.14 l.3 n.3.

[35] And with a quotation from Hilary's IX *De Trinitate* (par. 48, ML 10,319) Thomas shows that this is in accordance with the Catholic tradition, in ST Ia q.42 a.6 ad 1: *Naturae divinae haec unitas est, ut ita* per se *agat Filius, quod* non a se *agat,* cf. REI c.17 l.5 n.3, on Jn 17,22: *Sed videtur distinguere operationem suam ab operatione Patris* [....] *Sed si bene intelligatur, non ponitur hoc ad distinguendum operationem, sed*

With regard to the *theologia* one must say then that in God the Son does things personally, but never individually i.e. independently. The identity of the Son is intertwined with the Father's and the Holy Spirit's, as is also expressed in Jn 10,38 ("Believe in the work I do; then you will know for certain that the Father is in Me and I am in the Father"), 14,10a ("Do you not believe that I am in the Father and the Father is in Me?")[36] and 17,21-23 ("May they all be one, just as, Father, You are in Me and I am in You" etc.).

But still there are some Scripture texts which undeniably at the least suggest inequality between the Father and the Son. Thomas himself mentions Jn 5,20b, 5,30 and 14,31b (in ST Ia q.42 a.6 ag.2). If these texts are regarded as *theologia*, Thomas says, then they should be read as "from eternity (*ab aeterno*)": as the Father communicated to the Son divine essence, knowledge for instance, or almightiness, so He gave the Son a command (Jn 5,30, 14,31) or showed Him something (Jn 5,20) from eternity.

However, apparently Thomas does not consider this the most obvious interpretation, as he subsequently proposes yet another view of these texts, *"potius"* and therefore preferable: to read these texts according to the rule of the *communicatio idiomatum*, as referring to the humanity of Christ.[37] In his commentary on Jn 5,30 Thomas sets out why this understanding of this text is plausible, while Jn 5,19 should be

---

personas.

[36] Cited in ST Ia q.42 a.5sc. In the *corpus* Thomas explains that the Son is in the Father *et e converso* in respect of the essence (*Pater est sua essentia et communicat suam essentiam Filio*), the relation (*unum oppositorum relative est in altro secundum intellectum*) and origin (*processio verbi intelligibilis non est ad extra, sed manet in dicente*). In REI (c.10 l.6 n.5, on Jn 10,38, c.14 l.3 nn.2-4 on Jn 14,9f) only the one aspect of the unity of essence is discussed.

[37] ST Ia q.42 a.6 ad 2: *Vel* potius *referendum est ad Christum secundum humanam naturam.* In REI c.5 l.5 n.4 (on Jn 5,30) Thomas does not even mention the *ab aeterno* interpretation. He does in ST Ia q.42 a.4 ad 1, to interpret Athanasius and Hilary correctly. In REI *l.c.* he points to Jn 14,28 and 1 Cor 15,28 as refering unmistakably to the humanity of Christ. In CBT q.3 a.4 (ad 1, 3, 7f) he also interprets Ph 2,7 (2,6-8), the prayers of Christ, Mt 20,23 and Vulg-Si 24,14 (= Si 24,9) *"et omnia similia"* (unless with wisdom created wisdom is meant, then it is about the angels) in this way.

read as a saying concerning the Son as God: in Jn 5,30 the relation
between the Son and the Father is designated by the verb *audire*, to hear.
Here hearing is understood as obeying. Obeying presumes someone
giving an order and only a superior person can give an order to a person
subordinated to him/her. Since the verb *videre*, to see, used to
characterize the relation between the Son and the Father in Jn 5,19, does
not imply such a subordination[38], the *ab aeterno* interpretation lies more
upon the surface there.[39] And so it goes without saying that according to
this reasoning Jn 14,31b, where the word "command (*mandare*)" is used
to describe the relation between the Father and the Son, should be read as
concerning Christ's humanity. And likewise Jn 5,20, since the Son cannot
be shown something He does not already know for as far as He is
divine.[40]

In this way Thomas explains how these biblical texts are to be
read: doing justice to the *homoousion* of the Father and the Son and the
Holy Spirit as well as to the two natures, truly divine and truly human, of

---

[38] ST Ia q.12 a.2co: *[A]d visionem, tam sensibilem quam intellectualem, duo
requiruntur, scilicet virtus visiva et* unio *rei visae cum visu; non enim fit visio in actu, nisi
per hoc quod res visa quodammodo est in vidente.* Ibidem q.67 a.1co: *[P]ropter
dignitatem et certitudinem huius sensus, extensum est hoc nomen, secundum usum
loquentium, ad omnem* cognitionem *aliorum sensum.* And it should be noted that *in divinis*
knowledge is proper to the Son.

[39] REI c.5 1.5 n.4: *Nam audire idem est in hoc loco quod obedire. Obedire autem
pertinet ad illum cui fit imperium. Imperare autem pertinet ad superiorem.* Et ideo, *quia
Christus inquantum homo minor est Patre, dicit "Sicut audio"; idest, secundum quod
inspiratur a Deo in anima mea. De isto auditu dicit Psal. LXXXIV,9* [Ps.85,9]: *"Audiam
quid loquatur in me Dominus Deus." Supra autem* [in Jn 5,19], *quia loquebatur de se
secundum quod est Verbum Dei, dixit "Vederit".*

[40] ST Ia q.1 a.4co: *Deus eadem scientia se cognoscit, et ea quae facit.*
Besides texts that speak of the Son as equal or minor to the Father, in CBT q.3
a.4 ad 1 and SCG IV c.11 n.16 Thomas distinguishes a third cathegory: texts that only
say that the Son comes from the Father. As examples he gives Jn 5,26 and Ps 2,7. This
distinction is absent in ST, because these texts in fact do have aspects of equality as well
as inequality in them: Equality, as Thomas explains in ST Ia q.27 a.2co, since *generatio*,
the term used in Ps 2,7, is understood as *procedat secundum rationem similitudinis in
natura eiusdem speciei, sicut homo procedit ab homine et equus ab equo* (see 2.1.2);
inequality, for *in humanis* the receiver and the one brought forth are minor, in the sense
of passive and not-having, to the giver and the one bringing forth (as in SCG IV c.11
n.18).

Christ: the divine Son is not only like (*similis*) the Father, they are equal in nature (*aequalis, aequale perfecte*)[41] and thus equal in almightiness, for both are God.[42]

From the above it is clear that the distinction Thomas makes between *proprium* and appropriation is the key to understand the Creed, c.q. our faith regarding the "almightiness" and the "power" of God. But an unsatisfying feeling may remain after all. And it seems that this has to do with the consequences of his exposition for reading a text like Jn 5,19-30; one verse or even part of a verse must be interpreted as concerning Christ's humanity, another one as concerning His divinity. This may seem rather contrived and arbitrary. On the other hand, Thomas basically

---

[41] ST Ia q.42 a.1 ad 2.

[42] Yet although the almightiness of the Father is identical with the almightiness of the Son, the Father and the Son themselves are not identical, SN I d.19 q.1 a.2co: *Concedimus igitur inter Patrem et Filium esse mutuam similitudinem vel aequalitatem, quia Pater est similis Filio, et e converso: non autem mutuam adaequationem vel assimilationem, quia Filius adaequatur Patri et assimilatur et non e converso* (cf. ST Ia q.28 aa.1-3). And therefore it may seem that the almightiness of the Father is different from, i.e. greater than, the Son's. For the Father can generate a Son equal to Him, but the Son cannot (cf. ST Ia q.41 a.6 ad 1, also SN I d.20 q.1 a.1). Thomas in addressing this issue seems to be self-contradictory, where he says, ST Ia q.42 a.6 ad 3: [*M*]*anifestum est quod quidquid potest Pater, potest Filius.* Non tamen *sequitur quod* [*Filius*] *possit generare.* "*Manifestum*", because there is only one divine nature. Therefore the Father and the Son are equal in nature, ibidem a.1co: [*A*]*equale dicitur quasi per negationem minoris et maioris.* "*Tamen*", because the Father has a different relation to the divine essence than the Son. For the Father is the origin, generating (*generare*) the - equal in *essentia divina* - Son; the divine Son is the - equal in *divina essentia* with the Father - generated (*generari*): (ibidem a.3) *ordo naturae in divinis personis.* And therefore, ibidem a.1 ad 3: [*P*]*ropter hoc dicimus quod Filius coaequatur Patri, et non e converso.* In brief, the Father has almightiness as Father, as giver (*ut dans*), the Son has the same almightiness, but as Son, as receiver (*ut accipiens*), *eternally* received from the Father; it does not befit a receiver to give or the generated to generate, for then receiver and generated would be identical with the giver resp. the generator.

For the correct understanding of Thomas using words implying *passio* in his explanation (*generari, accipere*) concerning the divine Son, it must be noted that he is speaking *in divinis* here; he uses analogous language to designate this mystery. At first it may look like he is describing God, but in fact he is pointing at the *mystery* of God as we only can, excluding incorrect God-talk leading to heresy (esp. Arianism). This (ST Ia q.42 a.6 ad 3) is a very clear example of how Thomas is seeking the proper words to formulate the content of our faith: the unity and trinity of God in respect of His almightiness.

implements the grammar rules needed for a correct understanding of our belief in one God, as triune and almighty, and in the Incarnation - so denying three gods, three divine mights or powers, subordination in the Trinity as well as Christ not being truly human - in order to formulate the mystery of that faith in accordance with Holy Scripture and the Catholic tradition. And probably that is where the shoe pinches for us, because Thomas in his writings presumes this faith and knowledge of the Scriptures and the Christian tradition in his readers; at times he refers to the content of the Catholic faith, a passage from Scripture or the Doctors of the Church only with a single word. Yet before explaining the faith to us post-modern people, its content must be made known first. Moreover, Thomas reads Scripture as a theologian: his primary interest is what the texts reveal to us about God, a method we may not be accustomed to any more.

Dissecting verses from Holy Scripture may go pretty far, but what Thomas does by doing so, is passing glasses to us, in order to read the Bible and the writings of the Doctors of the Church in the Catholic way. Not that they cannot be read in any other way, but exactly because they *can* be read in another way.

4.2 An Almighty Human Being?

In paragraph 1.4 the meaning of the union of the divine and the human person and the remaining distinction between the divine and human nature in Christ in respect of His *passio* was set out: we do not only say that Christ truly suffered, insofar as He was a human being, but even that, when He suffered, *God* suffered, as a human being: the *communicatio idiomatum* as a grammatical rule to express the mystery of the Incarnation. Now because of this union one may ask whether the man Christ was almighty too.

4.2.1 All Power Is Given unto Me (Mt 28,18)

A text like Mt 28,18 seems to indicate that the man Christ is and was indeed almighty, though *after* the resurrection only.[43] Yet Thomas explains, quoting Ambrose as an authority, that the might (*potestas*) which Christ had, must have been given to Him from the very beginning of the Incarnation,[44] through the personal union with the divine Son. The might of the divine Son is almightiness, as was set out in the former paragraph. And so according to our faith we say that the man Christ was almighty.

Further, it was shown in 3.2.1 and 3.3 that almightiness is displayed to the highest extent by sparing and saving people and by being merciful, freely forgiving them their sins. And this is what is found in Christ did during His earthly life,[45] even on the cross (Lk 23,43).

However, this seems to be in contradiction with the findings in paragraph 2.2, in particular that almightiness is incongruous with *passio*: the Almighty cannot undergo anything. If the man Christ truly suffered (1.3), how then can He be called almighty?

Moreover, if, as has been set out in 3.2.1, almightiness denotes the *divine* nature, then how could the *human* being Christ, no matter how perfect He is (Eph 4,13, Heb 4,14), be almighty?[46]

Thomas' answer comes down to a correct understanding of the Incarnation, as expressed by the *communicatio idiomatum*. For we can only call the man Christ almighty in the same sense as we say that God

---

[43] ST IIIa q.13 a.2 ad 2: cf. Jerome *In Mt 28*, 1.4 (ML 26,226): [*I*]*lli potestas data est qui paulo ante crusifixus et sepultus in tumulo, qui postea ressurexit*; Thomas adds: *idest, Christo secundo quod homo*, for the eternal Son cannot be given anything additional in time.

[44] ST IIIa q.13 a.1 ag.1: Dicit enim Ambrosius, *Super Lc*. [*Glossa ordin; cf. Bedam, Homiliae* 1.1 *homil*. 1, ML 94,11]: *"Potentiam quam Dei Filius naturaliter habet, homo erat ex tempore accepturus."* [....] *Cum ergo Filius Dei ab aeterno omnipotentiam habuerit, videtur quod* anima Christi ex tempore omnipotentiam acceperit. Ibidem ad 1: [*E*]*rgo dicendum quod homo accepit ex tempore omnipotentiam quam Filius Dei habuit ab aeterno, per ipsam unionem personae.*

[45] E.g. Mk 2,5, 5,1-15, Lk 7,48, Jn 12,47 cf. Mt 1,21, Lk 2,11.

[46] ST IIIa q.13 a.1sc: [*Q*]*uod proprium est Dei*, non *potest* alicui creaturae *convenire. Sed proprium est Dei esse omnipotentem, secundum illud Exodi* (15,2f) [....]. *Ergo anima Christi, cum sit creatura, non habet omnipotentiam*; cf. IIaIIae q.178 a.1 ad 1: (*Supernaturalia*) [*q*]*uorum quidem causa est divina omnipotentia, quae* nulli creaturae *communicari potest.*

suffered when Christ did, that is on account of the Incarnation, the union of the divine Person with the human person:

> "The result of the union is, that as the man Christ is said to be God, so He is said to be almighty; not as if the almightiness of the man Christ were another almightiness than that of the Son of God, as neither is His divinity, but He is called almighty in this way, that in Christ there is one person of God and a human being."[47]

If the man Christ had been almighty on his own, there either would have been another almightiness apart from God's, which is impossible[48], or Christ would not have been truly human, for almightiness, infinite as it is, is incompatible with - finite - human nature.[49] And if Christ had not had a true human nature, He would either have been only God and His body, and therefore His *passio*, would not be real, as Docetists assert, or He would have been a "third kind", a demigod as it were. But this is not the Christian understanding of Incarnation.[50]

For this reason Thomas emphasizes with the word impossible (*impossibile*) that the man Christ was not almighty; yet because of the

---

[47] ST IIIa q.13 a.1 ad 1: ([*U*]*nio personae*) *ex qua factum est ut, sicut homo dicitur Deus, ita dicatur omnipotens:* non *quasi sit* alia omnipotentia *hominis* quam Filii Dei, *sicut nec alia deitas; sed eo quod est una persona Dei et hominis.*

[48] Cf. SN III d.14 a.4 sc.1: *Potentia habet rationem principii, ut dicitur in V Meta.. Sed non potuit communicari animae Christi quod esset principium omnium; quia* sic esset primum principium, quod est solius Dei.

[49] ST IIIa q.13 a.1co: [*M*]*anifestum est quod* potentia activa cuiuslibet rei consequitur naturam ipsius. *Et per hunc modum omnipotentia consequenter se habet ad divinam naturam. Quia enim natura divina est ipsum esse Dei incircumscriptum, ut patet per Dionysium De div. nom.* [c.5 par.4, MG 3,817], *inde est quod habet potentiam activam respectu omnium quae possunt habere rationem entis, quod est habere omnipotentiam.* SN III d.14 a.4 sc.1: *Ergo non potuit sibi* (= *homini Christo*) *communicari omnipotentia.* Ibidem ad 3: *sicut nec essentia infinita.*

[50] ST IIIa q.13 a.1co: [*S*]*icut supra* [q.2 a.1, q.10 a.1] *dictum est, in mysterio incarnationis ita facta est* unio in persona, *quod* tamen remansit distinctio naturarum, utraque *scilicet* natura retinente id quod est sibi proprium.

hypostatic union in the one supposit of Christ we cannot but call Him
almighty. Mt 28,18 then is to be understood as "All power is given unto
Me *through this union*." Since this union was in Him from the very
beginning of His earthly life, Mt 28,18 cannot refer to a new situation
after the Resurrection; it only reveals something *we* did not know yet
during Christ's earthly life.[51]

This seems to be a clear enough answer. But Thomas takes three
further steps concerning the almightiness of the man Christ. Hitherto
Thomas discussed Christ's almightiness as such (*absolute*). Next he considers His almightiness in relation (*relative*): respectively, with regard to
other creatures, His own body and His own soul. The aspect of the soul
is of special interest for this study (4.2.2).

In these three steps Thomas continues to emphasize Christ's full
humanity: Christ had a true human body and soul. The man Christ was in
forgiving people and in the miracles He wrought nothing more - and
nothing less - than an instrument of the Word of God.[52] The power to

---

[51] REM c.28: [A]*nte resurrectionem* non fuit ita manifestata omnipotentia, licet eam
habuerit; *sed tunc maxime manifestata, quando potuit totum mundum convertere.* ST IIIa
q.13 a.2 ad 1: *Dicitur autem sibi omnis potestas data* ratione unionis. A similar line of
reasoning is found in ST Ia q.13 a.7 ad 2 and IIIa q.16 a.6 ad 2, where Thomas shows
why Vulg-Ps 89,1 (*Domine, refugium factus es nobis*) should not be read as something
really new, a change in God - as if there once was a time He was not our refuge - but
rather as something new *to us*, a change in us i.e. in our knowledge; God has been our
refuge of all times (cf. Ps 90,2), but He only becomes a refuge for us, if we turn to Him
(Ps 90,3).
    In REM c.28 Thomas adds that the text can be read in another way too.
Referring to Dn 7,26 and Rv 5,12 he points to the fact that might (*potentia*, authority in
the NJB) respectively power (*virtus*) can also signify in a way the honor of a ruler
(*quemdam honorem praesidentiae*). In this sense Mt 28,18 is more like an announcement
of the enthronisation of Christ: *Constat autem quod Christus qui ab aeterno habebat
regnum mundi, ut Dei Filius,* executionem accepit *ex resurrectione; quasi dicat: "Iam sum
in possessione."* [....] *Sicut si* exaltaretur *Filius* ad exercitium potestatis *quam naturaliter
habebat.*

[52] Christ was a special instrument, though, ST III q.62 a.5co: *Principalis autem causa
efficiens gratiae est ipse Deus, ad quem comparatur humanitas Christi sicut* instrumentum
coniunctum. Miracles are beyond what must be reckoned amongst the natural powers of a
created being (cf. ST Ia qq.105 a.7, 110 a.4co). God's grace perfects these powers, in
order that e.g. one handles one's own body correctly, directs one's actions in conformity
with what is good and even may enlighten other people (ST IIIa q.13 a.2co).

work miracles may also be accorded to other people, as we read in the gospel (e.g. Lk 9,1f), in Acts (3,1-8 etc.) and in the biographies of many saints. And the same goes for Christ's power in the sacraments accorded to the ministers.[53] Yet this does not make them less human. For in this way not their own but God's saving power is manifested.[54] Through the union with the divine Son this grace was in the man Christ in the most perfect way (note 52: *instrumentum coniunctum*), so that He could even pass it on to His disciples, as in Mt 10,1 par. ("He gave His disciples the power over unclean spirits in order to drive them out and to cure all kinds of disease and all kinds of illness")[55]. Even, Mt 17,20 seems to suggest that whoever believes is almighty. For Jesus promises His disciples that if one's faith is the size of a musterd seed,

> "'nothing will be impossible for you.' What?! They were not almighty, were they?! No, they were not, since only he is truly almighty, who can do all things on the basis of *his own* power."[56]

Also in the next step Thomas underlines Christ's true humanity, citing Heb 2,17a ("It was essential that He should in this way be made completely like His brothers"). That Christ nevertheless only suffered as far as He allowed it (1.3), is said from the perspective of the union of the

---

[53] ST IIIa q.64 a.4, explaining Jn 1,16, 14,12 and 1 Cor 1,12f. These are *instrumenta separata* (ibidem q.62 a.5co)

[54] ST Ia q.117 a.3 ad 1, IIaIIae q.178 a.1 ad 1 (citing Jos 10,12, 14, Ac 5,3ff, 9,40), IIIa q.84 a.3 ad 4 (citing Ac 3,6).

[55] ST IIIa q.13 a.2co: *Si autem loquamur de anima Christi secundum quod est instrumentum Verbi sibi uniti, sic habuit* instrumentalem virtutem *ad omnes immutationes miraculas.* Ibidem ad 3: [G]*ratia virtutum, seu miraculorum, datur animae alicuius sancti, non ut propria virtute eius sed ut* per virtutem divinam *huiusmodi miracula fiant. Et haec quidem gratia excellentissime data est animae Christi: ut scilicet non solum ipse miracula faceret, sed etiam hanc gratiam in alios transfunderet. Unde dicitur Mt 10,1* [....].

[56] REM c.17 n.2: *"Et nihil impossibile erit vobis." Et quid est? Eruntne omnipotentes? Non, quia ille solum omnipotens vere est, qui* ex propria virtute *omnia potest.* Thomas compares it to a servant of the king who does something in the name of the king and not in his own name. Therefore we pray to God for strength, wisdom and all goods.

Son of God with the human being in the one person of Christ: also in the Passion the *weak* body of Christ is an instrument of God, an instrument connected to God Himself (*instrumentum coniunctum*) and therefore fully under the control of the Word of God and immeasurably, infinitely, *stronger* than the people, as in 1 Co 1,25 ("God's weakness is stronger than the people"), 27 ("God chose those who by human standards are weak to shame the strong").

> "Now, since the power of an action is not properly attributed to the instrument, but to the principal agent, in the same way almightiness is rather attributed [not "appropriated"] to the Word of God than to the soul of Christ."[57]

So although we call the man Christ almighty, Thomas brings to our attention that we only do this because of His union in person with the divine Word. It is therefore appropriate to speak of the almightiness of the man Christ, as long as it is understood according to the *communicatio idiomatum*; that through the hypostatic union Christ never stopped being truly human.

4.2.2 Here Am I, oh God; I've Come to Do Your Will (Ps 40,8)

The clear distinction Thomas has made until now, becomes more complicated when he discusses the almightiness of the soul of Christ with regard to the execution of His own human will. For, as was pointed out in paragraph 1.3.2, Christ did not suffer in the part of His soul that is directed towards God, which includes the higher part of the reason, the intellect and the will. So if the higher part of His soul did not undergo any *passio* when He suffered, it could do what it wanted without any hindrance. This is not a sufficient definition (3.2.2), but indeed indicative of almightiness.

---

[57] ST IIIa q.13 a.3co: [*A*]*nima Christi secundum quod est* instrumentum unitum Verbo Dei *in persona. Et sic subdebatur eius potestati* totaliter *omnis dispositio proprii corporis. Quia tamen virtus actionis non proprie attribuitur instrumento, sed* principali agenti, *talis omnipotentia attribuitur magis* ipsi Verbo Dei *quam animae Christi.*

"Now God is called almighty, because 'He has done all
things whatsoever He would' (Ps 115,3)."[58]

Before going deeper into this question, its purpose should be
pointed out, I think, for to us this question may seem on the one hand
redundant - has Thomas not already made his point? - whilst on the other
hand the issue at stake here seems to be pure casuistry. In other words, of
what importance is this question of whether the man Christ was almighty
as to the execution of His will? What does it matter, whether the answer
is yes or no?
    The answer to this question can be found in the text of this
quaestio, 13 of the *Tertia Pars*, itself. The careful reader may notice that
only in the fourth *articulus* the man[59] Christ is referred to as "the
Saviour":

"It is impossible that the will of the Saviour would not be
fulfilled, nor is it possible that He would want something
of which He knows it ought not come to pass."[60]

That Thomas cites these words of Augustine using the name *Salvator*
indicates that no matter how *theologia*-like this question itself - and the
questions in *articuli* 1 to 3 - may be, the focus of this *articulus* 4 and
therefore of this *quaestio* is the *oikonomia*, namely our salvation, as it is

---

[58] ST IIIa q.13 a.3 ag.1: *Sed ex hoc Deus dicitur omnipotens, quia "omnia
quaecumque voluit, fecit"* (Vulg-Ps 113,11 = Ps 115,3).

[59] ST IIIa q.48 a.1co: *Christus non solum* per suam passionem *sibi, sed etiam omnibus
suis membris* meruit salutem. Ibidem a.5co: *[A]d hoc quod aliquis redimat duo
requiruntur: scilicet actus solutionis et pretium solutum.* [....] *[U]trumque istorum* ad
Christum pertinet immediate inquantum est homo: *sed ad totam Trinitatem sicut ad
causam primam et remotam, cuius erat et ipsa vita Christi sicut primi auctoris et a qua
inspiratum fuit ipsi homini Christo ut pateretur pro nobis.* Cf. ibidem a.6co.

[60] ST IIIa q.13 a.4sc: *Augustinus dicit, in libro De quaest. Nov. et Vet. Test.* [p.1
q.77, ML 35,2271]: *Impossibile est ut* Salvatoris *voluntas non impleatur: nec potest velle
quod scit fieri non debere.*

the focus of the whole of the *Tertia Pars*.[61]

In view of this focus the perspective of the fourth *articulus* and its importance becomes clear. For if the answer to the question, whether the soul of Christ had almightiness in respect of the execution of His own, human, will, is negative, this would imply that something or someone could have stood in the way of what Christ was willing to do: to fulfill His Father's will[62]. In that case God's (eternal) plan of the salvation of humankind (Ps 33,11, Is 46,10, 1 Tm 2,4, Heb 6,17) could have been thwarted by something created (i.e. temporal). And this seems to be inconsistent with God's almightiness and with all of our faith.

But on the other hand, if the answer is positive, then it seems that Christ would not have been truly human. In this case the Incarnation never happened and Christ would not have saved us as explained in chapter 1. So on further reflection this question cannot be laid aside as if it were 'more of the same' or pure sophistry. On the contrary rather, the question posed relates to the very heart of our faith.

Having stated this, while the reader takes a closer look at the content of this fourth *articulus*, it may arrest the attention that in all three *obiectiones* a passage from each of the synoptic gospels is cited: Mk 7,24, Mt 9,30 and Lk 6,12. All three seem to indicate that Christ did not have almightiness with regard to the execution of His will. For in Mk 7,24 it says that although Christ wanted nobody to know he was in a particular house, He could not pass unrecognized. Similarly, in Mt 9,30f it is testified to that even an *urgent* warning of His - which is an expression of His will - was ignored; the two blind men cured proclaimed His deeds nevertheless. Lk 6,12 mentions Christ's night-long prayer. From other Scripture passages we know that He prayed that the Father's will would be done (the Our Father, Gethsemane). Yet there would not be any need for Christ to ask for this, if He could have fulfilled His own human will, which is doing His divine will, which is the Father's will; just as there is

---

[61] Cf. ST IIIa intr.: *Quia* Salvator *noster Dominus Iesus Christus teste Angelo,* "*populum suum salvum faciens a peccatis eorum*" (Mt 1,21) [....] *de ipso omnium* Salvatore *ac beneficiis eius humano generi praestitis nostra consideratio subsequatur.* And in the discussion of ST Ia q.25 a.3 (God is almighty) it showed that Thomas' focus in the *Prima Pars* is already Christ!

[62] The purpose of His coming, cf. Mk 14,36, Jn 4,34, 6,38, Ph 2,7f. Unfortunately in the NJB the word ὑπήκοος (obedient) in Ph 2,8 has been toned down to "accepting".

only one divine might, love etc.

In dealing with the argumentations Thomas looks like a tightrope walker: stating Christ's true humanity, against Docetism, without denying the hypostatic union of the Son of God nor the human being in Christ, against Arianism - two tendencies that are present at all times.[63] It seems that Thomas is choosing these synoptic texts especially to meet the Arianist argumentation that Christ was really only human, since these texts may be read as if Christ could not even do what He wanted to do. In general, synoptic texts seem to lend themselves better to an Arianist interpretation than the gospel according to St. John.

Thomas' answer in the *corpus* is brief and rudimentary, for it only consists of the distinction between two ways in which Christ wanted something in respect of the fulfilment of His will:

> "In the one way, as if it would be brought about by Himself. And with regard to this way it must be said that He was capable of everything He willed, for it would not befit His wisdom, if He willed to do anything of Himself that was not subject to His will."[64]

This first part of the answer suggests a postive answer to the question whether the man Christ had almightiness in executing His own will, since being able to do everything one will, is a definition of almightiness, as was said above. But Thomas' answer is a little more complicated: first of all Thomas speaks of "*quasi* brought about by Himself". In other words, we cannot speak of the man Christ apart from His hypostatic union with the Son of God. This union is such, that when the man Christ acted to fulfill His will, we must say that the Son of God acted likewise (*similiter*),

---

[63] Resp. in movements proclaiming merely "Jesus is the Lord" or merely "Jesus was an excellent man".

[64] ST IIIa q.13 a.4co: *Uno modo,* quasi *per se implemendum. Et sic, dicendum est quod* quidquid voluit potuit. *Non enim conveniret* sapientiae eius *ut aliquid vellet per se facere quod suae voluntati non subiaceret.*

in conformity with the rule of the *communicatio idiomatum*.[65]

Another aspect in this part of the *corpus* to be noticed here, is that the man Christ is said to have been willing nothing beyond His human power, if He wanted to do something "of Himself", so to say. This in contrast with other people, who at times want to accomplish what is not good for them or is beyond their power, for instance ruling the world or not dying[66], which does not really show wisdom - on the contrary rather.

The other way in which the man Christ willed something, was that it would be brought about "by means of divine power (*virtute divina*)", like the resurrection of His own body[67], setting people free by forgiving sins[68] and the miracles, things which any human being "of him-/herself" is incapable of. In this way Christ, in fulfilling His and therefore the Father's will, is the instrument of the Word of God, Thomas

---

[65] In ST IIIa q.19 a.1co Thomas answers (sc:) *Quem ad modum eadem operatio diversae est potestatis*, explaining the formulation in actum 18 of the Sixth Synod (Constantinople III): *Duas naturales operationes indivisae, inconvertibiler, inconfusae, inseparabiliter in eodem Domino Iesu Christo, vero Deo nostro, glorificamus* [in QDI a.5 sc.2 he adds:] *hoc est divinam et humanam operationem: Sic igitur* in Christo *humana natura habet propriam formam et virtutem per quam operatur, et* similiter *divina. Unde et humana natura habet* propriam *operationem* distinctam *ab operatione divina, et e converso. Et* tamen *divina natura* utitur *operatione naturae humane sicut operatione sui* instrumenti: *et* similiter *humana natura* participat *operationem divinae naturae, sicut instrumentum participat operationem principalis agentis.* For, Thomas continues, if one holds that there was only one power in Christ, it follows that He only had divine power (for it cannot be that the divine nature of Christ would be without its own *forma* and power) and that, therefore, He had not been truly human, or that there was a mixture (*confusio*) of the divine and the human nature, as the Eutychians say, SN III d.18 a.1co: *Sed ex hoc sequitur quod sua actio non fuerit neque divina neque humana, neque nobis, neque Patri conformis; et ita frustratur opus redemptionis ad quod exigitur divina actio et humana.* So, as Thomas says more explicitly in QDV q.20 a.1 ad 2, although we attribute an action to the one *suppositum* of Christ, it is more properly attributed to its nature, as the origin of the action; thus, in the case of Christ, in whom are two natures, to His divine as well as His human nature (cf. QDI a.1 ad 16)

[66] As in Mk 8,36; Ps 66,7, 103,19 resp. Ps 49,10.

[67] Therefore Thomas, in discussing Jn 10,17 (REI c.10 l.4 n.5), speaks of a *purus homo*, as distinct from Christ as *vere homo*.

[68] E.g. Mk 2,7; Ps 41,5, Is 43,25.

adds, referring to *articulus* 2. There he states that this is in order to attain the goal of the Incarnation,[69] formulated by quoting Ep 1,10: bringing everything in the heavens and on earth together under Christ, as head. Here again Thomas seems to suggest a positive answer to the initial question.

One, or I myself at least, would expect Thomas to cut the knot here, but in vain. For without a final conclusion Thomas then presents his exegesis of the synoptic texts mentioned (ad 1 - 3): the bottom line of his answer is that none of the texts indicate that Christ's will was ever not executed, in accordance with what Augustine says, as cited in the *sed contra* (note 60). Mk 7,24 can, concerning Christ's will, be understood in two ways. Thomas juxtaposes Augustine's and his own opinion. Augustine observes that this event took place in a pagan area. Since it was not the right time yet, Christ did not want His disciples to preach to non-Jews - an explanation which makes sense in the light of what follows: Mk 7,26-30.[70] However, from the fact that it did occur, Augustine concludes that He wanted the gentiles to seek and find Him. And so it came to pass. Thomas himself seems to prefer the interpretation that Mk 7,24 is not relevant in this discussion, since it is not a matter of Christ executing His human will at all, but of others either executing it or not.[71] And our salvation is not dependent on this, but on the mercy of God, as we accordingly read in Rm 9,16 ("It does not depend on what any person wants or does, but only on God having mercy").[72]

---

[69] ST IIIa q.13 a.4co: (*resuscitationem proprii corpori et alia miraculosa opera*) *Quae quidem non poterat propria virtute: sed secundum quod erat* instrumentum divinitatis, *ut dictum est*; a.2co: *anima Christi secundum quod est instrumentum Verbi sibi uniti, sic habuit instrumentalem virtutem ad omnes immutationes miraculosas faciendas ordinabiles* ad incarnationis finem: cit. Ep 1,10.

[70] Apparently after the resurrection *was* the right time: Mk 16,15, cf. ST IaIIae q.106 a.3 ad 2; Mt 28,19, cf. ST IIIa q.36 a.1 ad 2, q.42 a.1co.

[71] ST IIIa q.13 a.4 ad 1: [*H*]*aec voluntas Christi non fuit de eo quod per eum fiendum erat, sed de eo quod erat fiendum* per alios.

[72] Cited not here, but in ST IaIIae q.98 a.1 ad 3, q.111 a.2 ag.3. CRO c.9 1.3: *Omnia procedunt ex Dei misericordia*, referring to 1 Co 15,10 and Jn 15,5. This does not entail that the human will is put on the sidelines: [*E*]*x his verbis intelligendum, ut sc.* principalitas *gratiae Dei attribuatur. Semper enim actio magis attribuitur principali agenti,*

At first this same exegesis seems to befit Mt 9,30f. However, for Thomas the point of attention in Mk 7,24 is Christ's whereabouts, whereas in Mt 9,30f it is His deeds. And these must be made known to other people,[73] for their benefit (*utilitatem*). He designates this as Christ's divine will.[74] Yet concerning Christ's human will, Thomas, in the footsteps of Gregory, reads Mt 9,30f in the light of Jn 8,50: "I do not seek my own glory." By doing so, Thomas makes us appreciate the multi-layeredness of Scripture texts; they are not one-dimentional. By giving the command not to proclaim Him, Christ set an example for His disciples, that they would not seek their own glory, while working God's wonders. Thomas' view may initially seem somewhat far-fetched. But not in the context of what follows: after these words Christ cures a dumb person (Mt 9,32-34) - so that he can proclaim God's wondrous deeds too? - and sends His disciples to proclaim the kingdom of heaven in words and deeds (Mt 9,35 - 10,41). In brief: although the blind men cured seem to disobey Christ - which is outside the scope of the man Christ fulfilling His will anyway, as Thomas just said regarding Mk 7,24 - they fulfill the will of God.[75] And at the same time the will of the man Christ *is* fulfilled by Himself, namely that He sets an example for His disciples to be sent.

In reflecting on Lk 6,12 Thomas states that Christ prayed for the things that were to be done by the human will as well as for those to be done by God. By doing so, Thomas indicates that Christ's prayer may

---

quam secundario, puta si dicamus quod securis non facit arcam, sed artifex per securim: Voluntas autem hominis movetur ad bonum [....] *secundum modum naturae suae,* i.e. *per modum liberae voluntatis. Sic ergo velle* (Ph 2,13) *et currere* (1 Co 9,24) *est hominis, ut libere agentis: non autem est hominis ut principaliter moventis, sed Dei.*

[73] This is an implicit referance to texts like 1 Ch 16,9f, Ps 26,7, 96,3 and Ps 75,1, 105,2, 145,5f and also Lk 12,3.

[74] In ST IIaIIae q.174 a.6 Thomas expounds the course of the revelation of the *divina* as according to God's plan.

[75] ST IIIa q.13 a.4 ad 2: *Volebat tamen absolute, praesertim secundum* divinam voluntatem, *ut publicaretur miraculum factum, propter aliorum utilitatem.* Thomas gives a different exegesis in REM c.9 n.5: The act of proclaiming Him is in accordance with Is 63,7. But to the question whether they sinned nevertheless, Thomas does not mention their actual fulfillment of God's will; he does say that they did not sin, *quia bona fide fecerunt et ostenderent quantum sanctitatis exhibeat Dominus* - as if these are extenuating circumstances.

seem a sign of His weakness, but in fact does not say anything about the
(al)might(iness) or the weakness of His human will at all. For Christ
prayed that God would execute God's own will. By doing so, Christ set
an example.[76] He taught us to pray likewise, in the Our Father: "Thy
will be done on earth, as it is in heaven" (Mt 6,10).

> "For we pray not that we may change the divine
> disposition, but that we may impetrate what God has
> disposed to be fulfilled by the prayers of the holy ones[77],
> as Gregory says: 'By pleading' people 'deserve to receive
> what the almighty God from eternity disposed to give
> them.'"[78]

But Christ *also* prayed for the execution of His human will,

> "for the power and the operation of Christ's soul
> depended on God, 'who works in all to will and to

---

[76] In REI c.11 l.6 n.3 Thomas explains Jn 11,42 in this way too: First he denies the
necessity for Christ to pray: *Necessitatem autem orandi excludit dicens* [Jn 11,42]*: "Ego
autem sciebam quoniam semper me audis"* etc.. *Ubi* quasi obumbrate Dominus suam
divinitatem ostendit; *quasi diceret: Ad hoc ut fieret voluntas mea, non indigeo oratione,
quia ab aeterno voluntas mea impleta est; Heb 5,7.* Then he interprets Christ's prayer as
an exemplary action, referring to Jn 13,15: *Nam omnis Christi actio, nostra est instructio,*
cf. ST IIIa q.21 a.1 ad 1: *[I]dem ipse Deus existens et homo, voluit ad Patrem orationem
porrigere,* non quasi ipse esset impotens, *sed propter nostram instructionem*; ibidem q.43
a.2 ad 2, explaining Jn 14,10 (in sc): non propter necessitatem, *sed propter exemplum hoc
fecit.*

[77] Here are not meant the *sancti in patria,* but the holy people on earth, as in Jb
15,15, Ps 116,15, Ac 9,13, Rom 8,27, 1 Cor 1,2, Ep 4,12, Jd 3.

[78] ST IIaIIae q.83 a.2co: *Non enim propter hoc oramus ut divinam dispositionem
immutemus: sed ut id impetremus* quod Deus disposuit per orationes sanctorum esse
implemendum; *ut scilicet homines "postulando mereantur accipere quod eis omnipotens
Deus ante saecula disposuit donare,"* ut Gregorius dicit, in libro Dialogorum [I c.8, ML
77,188].

accomplish,' as Ph 2,13 says."[79]

And so Thomas again underlines Christ's true humanity as well as His exemplary conduct.

And this is where Thomas ends. A clear concluding answer to the question is lacking, so the reader must find - or in the meanwhile have found - and formulate it him-/herself. At first sight it seems that Thomas' answer is positive: "Yes, the soul of Christ had almightiness with regard to the execution of His will," for He always acted according to His will, even when He suffered, as Augustine says and was shown in chapter 1: in Holy Scripture we read that nobody and nothing hindered the man Christ in executing His own will, namely to obey the Father and save humankind. Hindrance is a form of *passio*.[80] *Passio* and almightiness are incompatible. So, since there was no hindrance, no *passio*, in the will of Christ, He could have been almighty in executing His will; doing all the things one wants, is a sign of almightiness (note 58). In paragraph 1.3.2 it was shown already that Christ when He suffered, did not suffer in the higher part of His soul, where the will is located. Besides, as was said above, if Christ had not had almightiness, something created could have stood in the way of God's plan of salvation. In the light of this the conclusion seems to be well-founded that the man Christ was almighty, at least with regard to the execution of His own will.

Still Thomas' answer cannot be but negative. For, if Christ was truly human, which Thomas points out elaborately here as well as in the foregoing *articuli*, one can only come to the conclusion that He did not have almightiness.[81] For almightiness denotes the divinity of God. Consequently, as was shown in the former chapter, almightiness is not a

---

[79] ST IIIa q.13 a.4 ad 3: *Quia virtus et operatio animae Christi* dependebat a Deo, *"qui operatur in omnibus velle et perficere," ut dicitur Phil.* (2,13). Cf. also note 69. And Christ's prayer is not neglected, for, SCG III c.95 n.5: (*Deus*) [v]ult *igitur* impleri desideria rationalis creaturae, quae perfectissime divinam bonitatem participat *inter ceteras creaturas*. This explanation conveys Jn 9,31 (cited in ST IIaIIae q.83 a.16 ag.1). And this applies first of all to the man Christ, (cf. REI c.9 l.3 n.8, referring to Jn 9,33).

[80] QDV q.26 a.1co: [S]*icut si dicamus* [....] *et hominem pati, si prohibeatur suam facere voluntatem*; in this context *pati* in the most proper sense of the word (2.2.1).

[81] Cf. SN I d.43 q.1 a.2, III d.14 q.1 a.4.

kind of separate or independant quality; if a human being were almighty, he or she should be from eternity and uncreated etc. as well. Yet this is logically impossible, since it belongs to the deep structure (*res*) of human beings that they are temporal and created. The non-temporal (ST Ia q.10 a.3) and uncreated is the triune God and the triune God alone.

Yet, observing in the gospel that the execution of Christ's will by Himself was never frustrated, one may ask how this could have been, if it was not by reason of almightiness. For there neither is nor has been any other human being whose will concerning him-/herself was always executed. What then was so unique about Christ that He could and did? Does Thomas do justice to the full and true humanity of Christ?

If the will of Christ was always executed, it appears that His will was always in conformity with God's, whose will is always fulfilled, according to the testimony of Scripture.[82] In chapter 2.1.1 it was expounded how God's will is inextricably bound up with His love: His will is the good of His creatures, because He loves those whom He created. God's love is greater in that it is mutual. And this mutual love we call friendship. Christ's friendship with God is characterised, as we read in the gospel, by His will to do God's good will, at all times.[83] Accordingly Thomas quotes Sallustus saying "Wanting the same is inherent in friends."[84] Therefore, if Christ always wanted what God wanted, we should say that the friendship between God and Christ was

---

[82] Ps 115,3 (cited in ST Ia q.19 a.6sc), 135,6, Jn 1,3, Rom 9,19, 1 Tm 2,4 (cited in SN I d.46 txt). Note well that despite this and although God does not give us permission to sin (Si 15,20), this does not imply that everything that happens, is what God wills (as Van de Beek suggests), as was demonstrated in paragraph 1.1.2. Cf. also Mt 23,37, cited in SN I d.47 q.1 a.3: *Utrum id quod est contra voluntatem Dei non obsequatur voluntati eius.*

[83] Jn 4,34, 5,30, 6,38-40, Heb 10,7 (citing Ps 40,8), cf. Pr 17,17.

[84] SCG III c.95 n.5: *De ratione amicitiae est quod amans velit impleri desiderium amati, inquantum vult eius bonum et perfectionem: propter quod dicitur quod* "amicorum est idem velle" [Sallustus in *Catilin.* c.20]. And ST IaIIae q.23 a.1co: [A]*micus est amico amicus.* Cf. Jn 15,34.

greater than between God and other people.[85]

In order to want unflinchingly what God wants and to act in accordance with God's loving will always, and never to be diverted from it, Christ must either have been a human being without a will of His own. This is what monoteletism holds; Christ would have had only one, divine, will.[86] But consequence of this is, that He would not have been truly (*vere*) human, which is not in conformity with our faith. Or He must have had a perfect knowledge of God's will. He could only have had this if He enjoyed the *visio beata* during His earthly life. But since the beatic vision consists of the vision of the divine essence, no human being can have it *fully* during his/her earthly life.[87] Besides, a human being's knowledge of God and His will is perfected by God's grace. Thomas cites 1 Cor 2,10 ("To us, though, God has given revelation through the Spirit") to point this out.[88] Again, Thomas cites, in the *Prima Pars*, a text which speaks of God's wisdom with regard to the crucified Christ.

Now in Jn 1,14 we read that in Christ *was* the fulness of grace, in such a way, that it could not augment:

---

[85] Since God (ST Ia q.20 a.3co:) *omnia amat uno et simplici actu voluntatis* we cannot say that God loves someone or something more intensely, but only that He loves them more in the sense that He wills and therefore provides a greater good for particular beloved. ST Ia q.21 a.4sc: [*U*]*numquodque diligit sibi simile; ut patet per illud quod habetur Eccli.* [13,19 = Si 13,15]*:* "Omne animal diligit sibi simile." Sed intantum aliud est melius, inquantum est Deo similius. And in wanting the good which God wanted, the man Christ was like God, *imago Dei*, cf. Ep 5,1, Col 1,12-15.

Also the quotation of Aristotle in ST IaIIae q.25 a.3co, *"nihil enim est ita proprium amicitiae sicut convivere"* applies foremost to Christ and God. Furthermore, the word *amicus* is related to the verb *amicio*, to surround, envelop, enclose. However Thomas does not relate this explicitly to the hypostatic union.

[86] In that case there would not have been human action in Christ, but human *passio* only (SN III d.18 a.1co). This position was condemned during the Synod of Laterans in 641 and finally during the sixth Oecumenical Council (680-681) at Constantinople (Constantinople III).

[87] As Ex 33,20 (cited in ST Ia q.12 a.11sc, cf. a.2 and IaIIae q.5 a.3) also testifies.

[88] Cited in ST Ia q.12 a.13sc, explained in co: [*P*]*er gratiam perfectior cognitio de Deo habetur a nobis, quam per rationem naturalem.* [....] *Nam et lumen naturale intellectus confortatur per infusionem lumenis gratuiti.*

"I answer that we must say that the vision of the divine essence is granted to all the blessed by way of participation in the light shed upon them from the fountain of God's Word, according to Si 1,5: 'The fountain of wisdom is the Word of God in the highest.' To this Word of God the soul of Christ is more closely connected than any other creature, since it is united to the Word in person. And therefore it receives the influence of the light more fully than any other creature[89], the light in which God is seen by the Word Himself. And that is why He sees the first truth itself in a more perfect way than all other creatures. And therefore Jn 1,14 says: 'We have seen the glory of His, as of the Only-begotten of the Father, full' not only 'of grace', but also 'of truth'."[90]

So having the fulness of grace by being united with the triune God in person, of which enjoying the *visio beata* is a consequence, does not diminish Christ's humanity. It rather is all holy ones' due, says Thomas. At the same time he explains that the man Christ is not 'just' (like) one of the holy ones; His situation is a distinct, yes even an exclusive one, yet not because of His humanity - as if Christ were super-(hu)man - but because of the kind of union of His human soul with the Word of God

---

[89] As it says in Jn 1,16, that we have received *from* the fullness of Christ (as *caput Ecclesiae*, Ep 1,10, Col 1,18, cf. ST IIIa q.8 a.1co, IaIIae q.108 a.1co, IIIa q.6 a.3 ad 3, q.7 a.1co), e.g. John the Baptist (Lk 1,15), Mary (Lk 1,28), Stephen (Ac 6,8) and the addressees in Ep 3,19 (ST IIIa q.7 a.10 ag.1, 2). Likewise Mt 17,20 (REM c.17 l.2: *"Et nihil impossibile erit vobis." Et quid est? Eruntne omnipotentes? Non, quia...*) and Mk 9,23 should be understood.

[90] ST IIIa q.10 a.4co: *[D]icendum quod divinae essentiae visio convenit omnibus creaturis secundum participationem luminis derivati ad eos a fonte Verbi Dei: secundum illud Eccli [1,5]: "Fons sapientiae Verbum Dei in excelsis." Huic autem Verbo Dei propinquius coniungitur anima Christi, quae est unita Verbo in persona, quam quaevis alia creatura. Et ideo plenius recipit influentiam luminis in quo Deus videtur ab ipso Verbo, quam quaecumque alia creatura. Et ideo prae ceteris creaturis perfectius videt ipsam primam veritatem, quae est Dei essentia. Et ideo dicitur Io. [1,14].: "Vidimus gloriam eius, quasi Unigeniti a Patre, plenum" non solum "gratiae", sed etiam "veritatis".*

and the indwelling of the Father[91] and the Holy Spirit. In brief: Christ is not different from us in respect of His human nature, but He is because of His unique union with God.

This explanation elucidates also why we call Christ not only a very wise human being, but even "the wisdom of God", in 1 Co 1,24: the one being so closely connected, united with the Word of God, fountain of all wisdom, cannot have the desire to deviate from God's wisdom, since it is fulfilling a human being's natural desire for happiness.[92] In the same way Augustine can say that Christ could not have wanted anything inappropriate, for instance something sinful or ridiculous. And since Christ in executing His own will, executed the will of God, we say that not only His power, but even His will was an instrument of God.

However, if one takes a look at the prayer and the agony of Christ in the garden of Gethsemane, the question may arise what the man Christ, inspired and in freedom as was said, actually wanted: Scripture tells us that He wanted to live and flee from the sufferings and death, but also to fulfill the will of the Father, c.q. of God. Yet the words "not as I will, but as You will it" (Mk 14,36, Lk 22,42) seem to suggest that the human will of Christ was contrary to His divine will. Or did Christ have two human wills or was there contradiction in His will? Thomas discusses these questions in *quaestio* 18 of the *Tertia Pars*, whilst he constantly refers to Lk 22,41-43 (Gethsemane) - the correct understanding of which is apparently at stake here.

The first four *articuli* are preliminary, required in order to answer the questions whether the man Christ wanted something different from God (*articulus* 5) and whether there was a contradiction in Christ's will

---

[91] In ST Ia q.36 a.1 ag.1 Thomas cites Hilary (*De Trin.* par.23,25, ML 10,253), interpreting Is 61,1 and Lk 4,18 as about the Father in Christ.

[92] As Pr 3,13-18 and 8,32-36 also testify. Cf. ST Ia q.94 a.1co: [*Q*]*uia, cum* divina essentia sit ipsa beatitudo, *hoc modo se habet intellectus videntis divinam essentiam ad Deum, sicut se habet quilibet homo ad beatitudinem. Manifestum est autem quod nullus homo potest per voluntatem a beatitudine averti:* naturaliter *enim, et ex necessitate,* homo vult beatitudinem, *et fugit miseriam. Unde nullus videns Deum per essentiam, potest voluntate averti a Deo.* Because of His union with the Word of God Christ enjoyed the beatic vision to the full during His earthly life, unlike human beings, even before the Fall (a.2co).

(*articulus* 6). The first step is to establish that we are to hold that there are two wills in Christ, one divine and one human, if we take the Incarnation seriously:

> "As was said above, the Son of God assumed the human
> nature together with all things pertaining to the perfection
> of this human nature."[93]

But in the human soul we distinguish two actions or movements which - it is rather confusing - both are called wills. The one is the will as reason, a rational movement which moves towards an aim. This aim is a freely chosen goal. This is properly called the will.[94] The second is a natural movement. Hence it is called a will by participation (*dicitur voluntas per participationem*), insofar as it is bent on obeying the will in the movement towards the aim. This movement follows the natural powers in a human being and is therefore not chosen, but of necessity. It rather concerns a means than an aim. It is the natural tendency of a human being to live and be happy. According to this 'will' - which we would rather call natural inclination or something the like - a human being naturally avoids and flees from suffering and death.

The second step, then, is to apply this to Christ, since the Son of God allowed (*permittebat*) His human body and soul to do and undergo what is proper to them:[95] as for His 'will' as nature Christ was naturally, even necessarily, inclined to escape from a deadly peril. This accounts for Christ's agony in Gethsemane and His plea for letting the cup pass - a desire that seems contrary to God's will. We all recognize this tendency in ourselves.

With regard to "as You will it" Thomas continues, saying:

---

[93] ST IIIa q.18 a.2co: [*S*]*icut supra dictum est* [q.4 a.2 ag.2, q.5 a.9, q.9 a.1], *Filius Dei humanam naturam assumpsit cum omnibus quae pertinent ad perfectionem ipsius naturae*, cf. ibidem a.1 ad 3: *Et ideo*, praeter voluntatem divinam *oportet in Christo ponere* voluntatem humanam.

[94] ST Ia qq.59 and 82: The will is an *appetitus intellectivus sive rationalis* and is *in ratione*.

[95] ST IIIa q.13 a.3 ad 1, q.14 a.1 ad 2, q.18 a.5co, cf. Ph 2,6f.

"Still at times the will could by way of reason choose these things [sensible pains, bodily hurts, death and other evils] in view of an aim, as even in one or another pure human being his/her sensuality and even his/her will as such shrink from burning, but which the will in accordance with reason chooses nevertheless for the sake of his/her health."[96]

By the formulation *in aliquo puro homine*, he makes clear that he is not pointing to something unique in Christ, but to something we come across in all human beings: for a good aim (*finis*) we may make choices, free choices, that (possibly) entail suffering and even death. In the case of Christ's Passion it was according to Christ's will "as reason", the salvation of humankind (*humanae sulus*)[97], which Thomas also mentions in this context. With the burning Thomas seems to refer to the practise of the burning clean of a wound; sin is as a wound in us, which is 'burnt clean' by the Passion of Christ. So even apart from what *is* unique in Christ, namely that because of the hypostatic union His human will was *always* in accordance with His divine will, Thomas accounts for Christ's loyalty to God's will in that distressing situation in Gethsemane.

In the sixth and last *articulus* of *quaestio* 18 Thomas expounds in the light of a text from Council Constantinople III (see note 86) as a grammer rule for understanding Lk 22,43, which could be understood as if there were a contradiction in what Christ willed. For the word agony seems to imply an attack (*impugnatio*) on the soul by a contrary tendency. However, the text from Constantinople III speaks of the free subjection of Christ's human will to His divine and almighty will.[98] This seems to

---

[96] ST IIIa q.18 a.5co: *Haec [dolores sensibiles, corporis laesionem, mala puta mortem et alia huiusmodi] tamen quandoque voluntas per modum rationis eligere potest ex ordine ad finem: sicut etiam in* aliquo puro homine *sensualitas eius, et etiam voluntas absolute considerata, refugit ustionem, quam voluntas secundum rationem elegit* propter finem sanitatis.

[97] Cf. REI c.6 l.4 n.9, on Jn 6,38, where Thomas cites 1 Tm 2,4.

[98] ST IIIa q.18 a.6sc: *[I]n determinatione Sextae Synody* [act.18] *dicitur: "Praedicamus duas naturales voluntates: non contrarias, iuxta quod impii asserunt haeretici; sed sequentem humanam eius voluntatem, et* non resistentem vel reluctantem, *sed potius subiectam divinae eius atque omnipotenti voluntati"*.

indicate the absense of such a contradiction in Christ's will.

Thomas advocates for the view that, although the natural 'will' differs from the 'rational' will and the divine will of Christ, there was no contradiction in Christ's will. He can do so, because his idea of what a contradiction is, is very strict: two contradicting items must be with regard to the same thing and in the same thing. If they are not, they only contradict one another if one obstructs or delays the other. It is clear that no contradiction is found within the divine will of Christ, which is the salvation of humankind through the Passion of Christ, as was said, nor within His 'rational' will, that is always in conformity with it, as was said (1.3), nor within the natural 'will', as was said above. Next Thomas says that the different wills did not hinder one another: Christ's will to live remained as it was notwithstanding His will to comply with God's will.[99] And as for the agony He experienced, so intensely:

> "The agony was not in Christ as regards the rational part [i.e. the higher part] of the soul, insofar as it implies a struggle of wills proceding from a diversity of lines of reasoning; like when, for instance, someone wants a particular thing whilst his reason considers it, and wants the opposite whilst his reason considers something else. For this springs from the weakness of the reason, which cannot decide which is simply the best. This was not the case in Christ, since by His reason He judged it simply better that by His *passio* the divine will concerning the salvation of the human race would be fulfilled. Still there was agony in Christ, namely as regards the sensitive part of His soul. And according to this His agony implies fear of the coming misfortune, as John of Damascus says."[100]

---

[99] ST IIIa q.18 a.6 ad 1, 2: Mt 26,41 and Ga 5,17 do not apply to Christ.

[100] ST IIIa q.18 a.6 ad 3: [A]*gonia non fuit in Christo quantum ad partem animae rationalem, secundum quod importat concertationem voluntatum ex diversitate rationum procedentem: puta cum aliquis, secundum quod ratio considerat unum, vult hoc, et secundum quod considerat aliud, vult contrarium. Hoc enim contingit propter debilitatem rationis, quae non potest diiudicare quid sit simpliciter melius. Quod in Christo non fuit: quia per suam rationem iudicabat simpliciter esse melius quod per eius passionem*

The reader came already across Thomas' emphasis on the man Christ freely choosing to do God's will and His true pain in chapter one. In Thomas' explanation of Lk 22,41-43 these lines come together. Departing from the text that Christ did experience agony and that there are two movements in Him, he employs a negative Christology, denying on the level of the deep structure what cannot be: weakness of the reason for instance, because of who He is (a perfect human being, conceived by the Holy Spirit, cf. paragraphs 1.1.2, 1.3). Furthermore it catches the eye that Thomas in this exposition is so consistent in endorsing the true humanity of Christ, that he acknowledges that the humanly natural drive in Christ can be different from God's will.

But it seems that Thomas makes it more complicated than it already is, by calling the natural drive (*motus naturalis*) in a human being "will", "the natural will".[101] For, as he himself already says, only the rational will is properly called the will, since it acts not by necessity, but by choice. If Thomas had stayed with the clear distinction he made in the *Summa Contra Gentiles*[102] or if he had used another terminology in this *quaestio*, for instance by calling this movement in a human being "natural drive" whilst declaring the then current term "natural will" unfit, it would have been clearer that besides His will there was another movement in the man Christ, yet on another level than in the reason and in the will.

So Thomas denies that the movements of the divine will and the human (rational) will of Christ on the one hand and Christ's so called

---

impleretur voluntas divina circa salutem generis humani. Fuit tamen *in Christo agonia quantum ad partem sensitivam, secundum quod importat timorem infortunii imminentis, ut dicit Damascenus, in III libro* [*De fide orth.* L.3 cc.18, 23, MG 94,1073, 1087]

[101] The confusion is even greater in REM c.26 n.5 on Mt 26,39, where Thomas says: *Constat quod Christus habuit naturalem hominis voluntatem; hoc autem est quod mortem refugiat.* For this formulation could be interpreted as if there were a contradiction in Christ's human will.

[102] SCG IV c.36 n.7: *Nam secundum rationalem partem, inest ei* [= *homini*] *voluntas; secundum sensitivam, irascibilis et concupiscibilis; et rursus naturalis appetitus consequens vires naturales. Similiter autem et secundum oculum videt, secundum aurem audit, pede ambulat, lingua loquitur et mente intelligit: Quae sunt* operationes diversae. Compared to the SN (III d.17 a.1b co), where he speaks of *dicimus* duas *voluntates, scilicet sensualitatis et rationis*, Thomas has made a nuance in the ST (IIIa q.18 a.2co), saying potest dici *quod sensualitas sit* voluntas per participationem.

natural 'will' on the other hand collide within His human will. However, what Thomas does not make explicit, they collided in the execution of these movements, the eventual result of which can be found in the gospel: Christ followed His (rational) will, which was fulfilling the will of God.

As was noticed, when the apostle Paul speaks of Christ as the power of God, he does so in his exposition of "the message of the Cross" (1 Co 1,18ff). Therefore, when he calls Christ the wisdom and the power of God, in 1 Co 1,24, he is pointing to the Crucified.

In the first chapter it became clear that Christ insofar as He was a human being, truly suffered and to the full and that by this the human race was liberated by Him. We therefore call Him the Messiah, our Saviour.[103] But Christ is not another Saviour than God.[104] For in the foregoing it was shown that Christ in His *passio* as well as in His actions, like forgiving sins and working miracles, was the instrument of God:

> "There is a twofold efficient agency: the principal and the instrumental. Now the efficient principle of the salvation of humankind is God. Since the humanity of Christ truly is the instrument of the divinity, as was said above, consequently all that Christ did and underwent are instrumental operations, in virtue of the divinity, for the salvation of humankind."[105]

So in everything the man Christ was, of His own free will, the instrument of the divine power, which is the power, the might, or the almightiness, of God: through Him (as the *instrumentum coniunctum*) and with Him (Christ cooperated with God, in obedience, voluntarily) and in Him

---

[103] As in Mt 16,16, Jn 4,25f, 42, Tt 2,13 and 1 Jn 2,22.

[104] As in 2 S 22,3, Is 45,21, 46,3f, 49,26, 1 Tm 4,10 and Tt 2,10.

[105] ST IIIa q.48 a.6co: [*D*]*icendum quod duplex est efficiens: principale, et instrumentale. Efficiens quidem principale humanae salutis Deus est. Quia vero humanitas Christi est divinitatis instrumentum, ut supra* [ST IIIa q.13 aa.2, 3, q.19 a.1 and q.43 a.2, in ch. 4.2] *dictum est, ex consequenti* omnes actiones et passiones Christi instrumentaliter *operantur,* in virtute divinitatis, ad salutem humanam.

(united with the triune God in person[106]) God wrought our salvation.[107] From this it follows Christ is called our Saviour according to the grammar rule of the *communicatio idiomatum*; the expression of faith "Jesus Christ is our Saviour" (as in Tt 2,13) then necessarily presupposes the true sufferings of Christ as well as the hypostatic union.

From this it must be concluded that judging by appearances someone might say that the man Christ in executing His own rational will - i.e. doing the will of the Father out of love, as was pointed out - was almighty, for by sight one cannot detect any difference from almightiness, since He always lived according to His own loving will, just like God does. But considering the deep structure of the man Christ, the hypostatic union and His human will, we cannot but come to the conclusion that this was because of His friendship with God, which was unsurpassable by reason of the hypostatic union, bringing in its train the full enjoyment of the beatic vision, and not because of His alleged almightiness. After all:

"He became as human beings are" (Ph 2,7).

And although Christ was not a pure human being, He was a true human being. And almightiness does not befit any - created - human being, because it is the very - uncreated - divinity of God.

4.2.3 Christ, the Loving Beloved: Two Wills, One Power

Thus considering Christ's agony in Gethsemane Thomas holds

---

[106] Cf. QDI a.1co against Nestorianism: After having explained the difference between inhabitation of the Son in us and the emptying Himself of the Son in the man Christ (as in Jn 1,14 and Ph 2,7), Thomas adds, referring to the council of Ephesus (431 CE): *Alioquin exinanitio competerit non solum Filio, sed etiam Patri et Spiritui sancto, de quo Dominus dicit Ioan. XIV* (v.17): *"Apud vos manebit, et in vobis erit"; et de se et Patre* (v.23): *"Ad eum venimus, et apud eum mansionem faciemus"*.

[107] We acknowledge this in the concluding doxology of the Eucharistic prayers ("Through Him and with Him and in Him, in the unity of the Holy Spirit, all glory and honour is Yours, Almighty Father, for ever and ever. Amen."). In praising the man Christ for what He, in union and inspired, has done for us, we praise the Almighty (appropriated to the Father) for what He, in union and inspiring, has done for us.

that there are two wills in Christ, a human, created will and a divine, uncreated will (4.2.2). But he does not speak of two mights or powers in Christ (4.2.1). At first it may seem that Thomas is of the opinion that we should faithfully hold that there are two, for, as he says in his commentary on Mt 28,18 ("All power is given unto Me"):

> "The might of God is nothing else than almightiness; and this is not given to Christ, since it does not befit Christ according to His humanity. Now something befits Him *and* as a human being *and* as God. Hence in Christ as a human being there is knowledge, a will and free judgement, and in the same way as God. Twofold, therefore, is the will in Christ, namely created and uncreated."[108]

But this does not apply to the might and power of Christ, Thomas continues. For in Mt 28,18 Christ speaks of receiving power, which may refer to the eternal gift of almightiness to the eternal Son as well as to the gift to the man Christ, in which case it refers to the consequence of the hypostatic union (cf. Jn 1,14, cited here by Thomas). But not all things that are in Christ by reason of the grace of the union need to be twofold in Christ; some *(aliis)* follow from the hypostatic union:

> "Therefore I say that might is given; not that another might were given, but that it is given because of the union with the Word; to the Son of God by nature, but to [the man] Christ by the grace of the union."[109]

It is remarkable that Thomas says *dico* here instead of his usual *dicendum est*. He makes a choice instead of drawing a compelling conclusion. To

---

[108] REM c.28: Potentia Dei *nihil aliud est quam* omnipotentia; *et* haec data non est Christo, *quia non convenit Christo secundum humanitatem. Convenit autem ei aliquid, et secundum quod homo et secundum quod Deus: Unde in Christo secundum quod homo est scientia, voluntas et liberum arbitrium, et similiter secundum quod Deus.* Duplex *ergo in Christo est voluntas,* scilicet creata et increata.

[109] REM c.28: *Unde dico quod potentia est data,* non *quia* alia potentia *sit data,* sed *data est secundum quod est unita Verbo, ut Filio Dei per naturam, sed Christo* per gratiam unionis. Cf. ST IIIa q.13 a.2 ad 1.

me it is a convincing choice. For although Thomas does not explicitly refer to a text like Jn 5,19, it resounds in this train of thought. Scripture speaks of two wills in Christ (Gethsemane), but not of two powers. Furthermore, it does not make sense to speak of two different powers or mights in Christ, since we do not ascribe a power to an instrument, a hammer for instance, or another power to a connected instrument (*instrumentum coniunctum*), a hand for instance, save to the person whom it is connected to. Moreover, an action outside a person follows upon what the will commands and the intellect directs (3.1.1); by reason of the hypostatic union His friendship with God is so strong, that the man Christ always freely chooses to do God's will. What we see Christ do and undergo for our salvation, during His life and in the Passion, is, therefore, the pre-eminent manifestation of God's might or power (appropriated to the Father), through Him, with Him and in Him, as the *instrumentum*, in the unity (*coniunctum*) of the Holy Spirit, who is love.

GENERAL CONCLUSION

This conclusion consists of five points. First we review the two hypotheses formulated at the beginning of this study, that Thomas Aquinas is a negative (5.1) and a Scriptural theologian (5.2). For the verification or falsification of these determine how the other questions are answered. In 5.3 we will formulate the answer to the main question of the book, how Thomas in the *Summa Theologiae* sees the mysteries of the Christian faith of the Passion of Christ and the almightiness of God connected (*nexus mysteriorum*) and what it means. Next the questions that were more in the background throughout the study, will be answered: "Does what we read about the *nexus mysteriorum* mentioned support calling Thomas' theology in the *Summa Theologiae* a *theologia crucis*?" (5.4). And: "Can we in faith say, and if so, what does it mean, that God suffered, when Christ suffered?" (5.5). Finally, we briefly touch upon three connections which Thomas refers to regarding the *nexus mysteriorum* mentioned and the *oikonomia*, as an opening to a further inquiry (5.6).

5.1 Negative Theology, Negative Christology

Throughout this study we met Thomas as a negative theologian, who seeks a good understanding of the mysteries of our faith, that is understanding them as mysteries, revealed and thus deepened (not solved, as problems). Thomas does not consider how we *could* speak of God, but how we are to understand what is in fact revealed of God in the history of our salvation, especially through Scripture and in the further tradition and the liturgy of the Church.

In this study "God is love" and the name "Almighty" for God were of special interest. Thomas indicates that our words "love" and "might" do not quite befit God, as when we describe objects within creation. For our word "love" used for a creature implies *passio* and "might" in a creature implies the movement from *potentia* (*passiva*) to *actus*. These aspects of love and might are proper to creatures and therefore are to be denied of God, since we by faith know that God is not a creature, but the Creator. By removing from the Creator what is proper to creatures, Thomas expresses two things: First, that we do not know what God is; we speak of the *mystery* of God. Second, that our words do not fit, because what God is, is incredibly greater than we can imagine;

His love and might are unsurpassable - not gradually, as with creatures that are compared to one another, but in a different, and for us incomprehensible way. We cannot express it properly, not because God were in the dark, but rather because He is a light too bright for us.

Still we speak of it. For that God is love and the Almighty is revealed to us through Scripture and we experience the effects of it in creation. He is love, might, mercy, justice and all perfections as well as the source of all love, might, mercy, justice and all perfections in creation. In a way Thomas turns our whole way of thinking upside down. For he says that it is not our (understanding of) love and might that determine how we are to understand God's love and might, but that true love and true might etc. are God's. Ours are received from Him. They are like His, but are not the same, since our love and might are created and therefore have an end (*finis*), not like His love and might.

This must be taken into account when we consider our religious language. Our words "love", "might" and all perfection words, are derived from what we see and understand in creation (*modus significandi*), whereas they refer to what is eternally in God, from whom all our love, might and other perfections come. In order to safeguard that we understand our religious language as concerning the *mystery* of God, Thomas makes the following distinction in our *modus significandi*: what we say, we say metaphorically or properly; when properly, denying or affirming; when affirming, univocally or equivocally; when equivocally, purely equivocally or analogously. It was shown that our affirming words for God, like love and might and all other perfection words, properly used, can neither be interpreted as univocal, as if we were speaking of one of the earthly beings, nor as purely equivocal, since then all our language would be hollow and hence all revelation would be empty. Thomas underlines the usefulness of metaphorical language concerning God. Yet in order to avoid misconceptions of our faith, we must clearly distinguish between the ways in which (*modus*) we say what (*res*) about God.

It came out that Thomas speaks likewise concerning Christ, also insofar as He is human. For he sets out that, although He became as human beings are (Ph 2,7), we cannot speak of the man Christ as of any other human being. As a true human being Christ truly suffered, and yet His situation was not exactly the same as ours, because of the hypostatic union with the divine Word throughout His life. We have seen how

Thomas does this for instance where he discusses the true and perfect humanity of Christ (conceived by the Holy Spirit), the cry from the cross "My God, my God, why have You abandoned Me?!" (Mt 27,46) and the might of Christ. Therefore not only the divinity of Christ and the hypostatic union, but even His humanity must be reckoned amongst the mysteries of our faith; we speak of what we do not fully understand, but do believe. Christ was, as we are, a true human being, but not, as we are, a pure human being. And therefore even the proper and affirmative proposition "The man Christ truly suffered" must be understood not as univocal, but as an analogous use of the language. This study confirms the thesis of Schoot[1], that Thomas offers a negative christology to us.

Thomas' theology may at times seem rather formal and it is clear that by reason of his approach some aspects that may interest us more today, remain in the background (e.g. the psychological side of the story, the historical Jesus). On the other hand, by interpreting our religious language in this way, Thomas makes his readers (more) sensitive to the insight that we may understand our faith, but that our faith concerns what we do not and cannot understand: the mystery of God, His trinity and unity, His love, His mercy, His might, His goodness etc., revealed in creation, through Christ, for our good. However, this does not lead him to pious aphasia or anti-intellectualism;[2] it rather is why Thomas' language breathes a sense of awe, that permeates his theology. Thus this 'weakness' in his theology contains a strength: Thomas' negative theology brings to our attention (anew) that theology is not a matter of solving the problem of God, but rather understanding our faith in God as a mystery, so that we might live in relation to it, so that we might live through Him, with Him and in Him.

---

[1] Schoot (1993) 103, 104f

[2] OCG c.2: [*F*]*ides nostra necessariis rationibus* probari non potest, *quia humanam mentem excedit* [....] Unde *et beatus Petrus* [1 P 3,15] *non dicit "parati semper"* ad *probationem, sed "ad satisfactionem", ut scilicet* rationabiliter ostendatur non esse falsum *quod fides Catholica confitetur*, cf. ST Ia q.3 intr.: *Sed quia de Deo* scire non possumus quid sit, sed *quid non sit, non* possumus de Deo considerare *quomodo sit, sed potius* quomodo non sit.

5.2 Scripture as Source and Criterion

The *Summa Theologiae*, which Thomas wrote as *magister in Sacra Pagina*, is, more than his earlier works, imbued with quotations from Scripture and implicit references to it. At first glance it may seem like he is just covering a theological thought with a thin layer of Scriptural authority. But a close reading of Thomas' texts from the *Summa Theologiae* has shown that Scripture does not function in it as a proof of a pre-established theological thought. Although his questions and interests may not be the same as ours, they arise from the Scripture texts and in finding an answer he is guided by what he reads in Scripture. A clear example in this study is Thomas' use of Lk 1,37 ("nothing is impossible to God"). First it seems that this verse comes out of the blue in his consideration of God's almightiness. But a close reading of Thomas' text shows a strong correlation with the mystery of Christ, which is the same context as of Lk 1,37. And the same applies to 2 Tm 2,13 and 1 Co 1,20 that are cited in the same text of Thomas on the almightiness of God (Ia q.25 a.3).

The implicit references to Scripture passages indicate that Thomas presupposes a certain familiarity with them. This insight is essential for recognizing Thomas as a Scriptural theologian. In this study the clearest example is where Thomas says that God discloses His almightiness foremost by saving people and having mercy upon them. For if the reader does not realize that the phrase from the homily cited by Thomas, refers to W 11,23 ("You are merciful to all, for You are almighty"), it may seem that the whole argument is built on quicksand. The same applies to the *nexus mysteriorum* mentioned above, which touches ground especially with the Magnificat, the Benedictus and 1 Co 1,18-2,5.

That Thomas apparently presupposes a certain knowledge of the Scriptures, applies not only to the content of his theology in the *Summa Theologiae*, but to its structure as well. For at the beginning of this work Thomas speaks without an explicit reference to Heb 2,10, 1 Co 8,6 or Rm 11,36, of theology as concerning God (*theologia*) as the source (*exitus*, in the *Prima Pars*, qq.44-119) and the aim (*reditus*, in the *Secunda Pars*, and our way to complete it, Christ, in the *Tertia Pars*:

oikonomia) of all things.[3] And in this Scripture based scheme he structures his theology.

Thomas reads Scripture as a theologian, that is he asks a believer's questions regarding the content of the faith of the Church, "in order to gain a better understanding of God and the things related to God".[4] It was demonstrated that in doing so, he uses particular concepts from neo-Platonism and Aristotle - and changes them, if required, e.g. the concept of being (2.1.1) - just as we may use and change concepts from Marxism or Heidegger to elucidate what is proper to our faith; Thomas does not hesitate to reject what conflicts with the Christian faith.[5]

In his days the common method of exegesis distinguished between four senses, four layers, of the text (*sensus litteralis*, *moralis*, *allegoricus* and *anagogicus*) and employed a christological reading (as belonging to the *sensus litteralis*) of especially the Psalms and the prophet Isaiah, as the reader came across throughout this book. The christological interpretation as a possible interpretation is not as strange as it may seem at first sight, for it reflects how these texts in fact function in the liturgy of the Church; on Good Friday, for instance, Ps 22 and Is 53 are read. Moreover, this interpretation is already found in the Second Testament[6] and in the early Church. Thomas' texts show that dogmas of the Oecumenical Councils function as interpretation rules for the texts. On the one hand this may be rather estranging, especially where this leads to a

---

[3] ST Ia q.2 intr.: [*P*]*rincipalis intentio huius sacrae doctrinae est Dei cognitionem tradere, et non solum secundum quod in se est, sed etiam secundum quod est* principium rerum et finis earum. Cf. Torrell (1996), 152 (see 3.3.3 note 180)

[4] Valkenberg (2000), 51.

[5] Thomas denies passionately what Aristotle holds, that a relation of mutual love between us and God is not possible (2.1.2), that the infinity of God's might should be understood in the privative sense of the word (3.1.3) and that we can ascribe human characteristics univocally to God (3.2.2).

[6] E.g. in the Passion and post-Resurrection narratives many references are found to Ps 22, Is 53 and other texts from the First Testament. Another famous example is how Ps 110 functions in Ac 2,29-36 and Heb 1,13, 5,5-10, 10,11-14, a Psalm that is prayed by the Church every Sunday and on every feast as the first Psalm of the Vespers.

dissection of verses. On the other hand Christians use dogmas in this way (and many probably even unconsciously) all the time, for instance when "God" is understood as the only and triune God and when "Christ" is understood as the Son of God as well as a man, born of the Virgin Mary. Just as with the texts from Scripture themselves, interpretations of them by Doctors of the Church are at times cited as authorities and at times subject to discussion: how are we to understand what is said here? In our days we are far from familiar with this method. And in particular how Thomas speaks of the role of "the Jews" in Christ's Passion and what this means, shows that what he does cannot be repeated unquestioningly.

Yet, although his theological exegesis does not satisfy anymore in view of the present exegetical insights, I would advocate for a critical revaluation of his approach. Not in order to let systematic theology outstrip current exegetical methods, but rather as an addition, as an enrichment. Not just because Thomas' method is a part of our Christian tradition, but mainly because of what it can mean for our faith today. For Thomas' theocentric and christocentric texts show a great reverence for the mystery of our faith; we speak of what we do not fully fathom. The multi-layeredness of the mystery that he lays bare makes us stand in awe, makes us aware that we do not and cannot speak of it or interpret inspired texts as expressing it univocally. Seeing that many do so, shows that strengthening this consciousness should not be regarded as dead wood. Thomas makes us more sensitive to what St. Paul writes in respect of the mystery of our salvation through Christ to the Christians of Corinth, that our "faith should depend not on human wisdom, but on the power of God" (1 Co 2,5).[7]

5.3 God's Crucial Almightiness

Being familiar with theodicies and theologies in which the profession of God's almightiness and the reality of suffering are regarded as incompatible, the answer to the central question of this study may have come as a total surprise to the reader. It certainly did to me: in Thomas'

---

[7] For, as Thomas says, commenting on 1 Co 1,19 ("As Scripture says: 'I am going to destroy the wisdom of the wise and bring to nothing the understanding of any who understand'"), C1C c.1 l.3: *[I]d quod est in se bonum, non potest alicui stultum videri, nisi propter defectum sapientiae.*

theology the connection between the mysteries of our faith of almightiness, which is God's might, God's power, and of the Passion of Christ is, that almightiness is foremost expressed and revealed in the Passion of Christ as an act of God's loving mercy towards us. Thomas speaks foremost of the almightiness of God as crucial. We have seen that there is a strong Scriptural basis for this *nexus mysteriorum* (see esp. 3.3.3).

This is quite a shocking conclusion, for it calls for a thorough revision of what we understand by might/power: God's as well as our own, which has God as its origin and aim. God's might/power, which is true might/power, from which all our might/power comes, is forgiving, life giving (as in creation), salutary. The consequence of this is, that speaking of God's powerlessness is nothing more than a denial of what we in our daily speech understand by power: in God there is no force, coercion etc.. Thomas draws our attention to the Passion of Christ, if we seek to understand what it means what we believe, that God is almighty and that He shows this foremost in Christ's Passion, by which He completes what He started in creation (*exitus*); the reunion (*reditus, finis*) with God.

Then the assumption that God's almightiness implies that evil does not happen, a view which underlies theodicies, is unmasked as not according to the Christian faith. For in the Passion narratives we clearly read that evil (betrayal, execution of an innocent person) happened, which Thomas also brings to the fore. The word almightiness, however, signifies and expresses the faith that, no matter what, everything is in God's hand, all the time.

This conclusion contains another warning: when we faithfully consider the mystery of the Passion of Christ, we should not merely look at the historical side of it, but also regard deeper levels. Otherwise the Passion of Christ may look like a gaffe of the Almighty, who is love; how could He let it happen?! Only on a deeper level we may recognize the continual and active presence of God in it, the purposiveness of the Passion, as an act of God's merciful, liberating love for us as well as an act of Christ's love (*caritas*) for the Father and merciful love for us.

5.4 Thomas' Theology as a *theologia passionis*: *theologia* and *oikonomia*

Searching for whether and, if so, how Thomas connects the

Passion of Christ with the almightiness of God, brought to light another feature of Thomas theology. Thomas' theology does not start with considering Christ crucified, and still the Crucified One is present in Thomas' theology from the beginning. Thomas presupposes his readers' knowledge of and faith in the Crucified. For it was shown that where - God's love and mercy (qq.20, 21) and His might (q.25) are discussed in the *Prima Pars* of the *Summa Theologiae*, Thomas does so in view of the suffering Christ, as the cited verses from Scripture clearly indicate. And in the *Tertia Pars*, in the context of the Passion of Christ (q.46), he works out elaborately how God's loving mercy and might are expressed concretely in our world, to the highest extent (*maxime*), and what it means for us. Because the Passion of Christ is so central in his theology and because he does not trivialize the sufferings of Christ (as a *theologia gloriae* would do), on the contrary rather, it seems that Thomas' theology in the *Summa Theologiae* can truly be called a *theologia crucis*, or better even, a *theologia passionis*.

The opening question on Christ's Passion in the *Tertia Pars* showed already that, no matter how *theologia*-like his questions may be, Thomas' ultimate concern is not knowledge for the sake of knowledge, but a better insight in the *oikonomia* of our salvation. In this study it has become clear that the same applies to the *Prima Pars*. For although (the first 43 *quaestiones* of) the *Prima Pars* is (are) commonly regarded as speculative theology concerning *theologia* (the theology of what is in God), it came out that at least as regards the love, mercy and might of God Thomas' *theologia* is thought through in view of the theology on God's acting in the history of salvation through the Passion of Christ (*oikonomia*).

Thus, the consequence of this would be that Thomas offers in the *Summa Theologiae* a *theologia* as well as an *oikonomia* that is orientated towards the Passion of Christ. However, one could add, unfortunately he has done this in such a subtle way, that this is not noticed by many (anymore).

5.5 "God suffered when Christ suffered"

The question whether we can in faith say, and if so, what it means, that God suffered (pain, grief, sadness, anger etc.), when Christ, His Beloved, suffered, is not Thomas', but clearly ours, as was said. But

Thomas can help us to find an answer. With all the outcomes of this study in mind it may be clear that this more *theologia*-like[8] question cannot have a simple answer. The proposition can be apprehended as a metaphorical way of speaking. Then the suffering of God in the proposition "God suffered, when Christ suffered" is a metaphor used to indicate the mystery of God's love, nearness, concern etc., in the Passion of Christ; in the same way it is said that God suffers when His beloved people undergo something evil. In this sense God's suffering is compared to our sufferings when a friend we dearly love suffers (*compassio*). This metaphorical way of speaking is used in the depiction of the mercy seat in which the Father, upholding the crucifix, is deeply saddened.

"God suffered, when Christ suffered" cannot, however, as a proper way of speaking refer to this mystery. For then it would imply that God underwent grief, pain, sadness etc. as God, whereas divinity is incompatible with undergoing anything (*passio*).

Still there is a sense in which the proposition "God suffered, when Christ suffered" is true as a proper way of speaking. But then it does not refer to the relation of the Father and the suffering Son, as represented in the depiction of the mercy seat, for the reason mentioned. In the proper way of speaking it can only be true according to our faith, if it refers to the mystery of God incarnate. Then "God" is understood as the Son of God. Thus, in this case "God" supposits for Christ. Hence, as a proper way of speech it is true, but a tautology: "Christ, The Son of God, suffered when Christ suffered."[9] Yet obviously this is not meant by theologians who say that God suffered when Christ suffered.

5.6 Links to the Christian Life: Faith, Hope, Prayer and the Sacraments

Whilst I was exploring Thomas' theology about the Passion of

---

[8] The form of the question is indeed as in the *theologia*, but the focus may well be the Christian life. For the answer has consequences for how people who believe or try to believe, relate to God.

[9] And it is in this sense that we say that *God* has suffered, Deus *passus est*, cf. ST IIIa q.16 a.4sc: *Deus suscepit ea quae sunt carnis idiomata, idest proprietates, dum* Deus *passibilis nominatur,* Deus *gloriae crucifixus est* (see 1.4 and 2.3.4).

Christ and the almightiness of God, his concern with the *oikonomia* became further apparent in the *Summa Theologiae* in at least three connections which he mentions. One is the link between God's almightiness (and mercy) and the theological virtues of faith and hope. Faith in the almightiness of God is the origin, the basis for a life of hope.[10] Although, Thomas says, some people are called children of despair (Ep 2,2, 5,6: *filii diffidentiae*) in respect of the circumstances of their (mortal) sins,

> "we should not despair of anyone in this life, considering God's almightiness and mercy."[11]

Faith in God's almightiness and mercy are also pointed to by Thomas as the firm ground of our prayer life - a second connection:

> "For through faith a human being comes to know of God's almightiness and mercy, which are the source whence prayer impetrates what it asks for."[12]

For, why would someone ask for mercy from a merciless person or ask for something from someone who cannot give anything or does not have anything to give?

A third connection is between the Passion of Christ and its - instrumental - power with the sacraments and the Community of faith. God's healing and reconciling power in the sacraments comes to us

---

[10] ST IIaIIae q. 18 a.4 ad 2, 3 and IaIIae q.64 a.4co.

[11] ST IIaIIae q.14 a.3 ad 1: *[D]e nemine desperandum est in hac vita, considerata omnipotentia et misericordia Dei.* Cf. IaIIae q.62 a.3 ad 2 (citing 1 Co 1,25) and RPL c.3 l.3 (on Ph 3,18), after citing 1 Co 1,18: *Et quid eveniet? Certe nobis vita per crucem Christi.*

[12] ST IIaIIae q.83 a.15 ad 3: *Quia per fidem habet homo notitiam omnipotentiae divinae et misericordiae, ex quibus oratio impetrat quod petit.*

through Passion of Christ[13], or in Thomas' own, more poetic language:

"From the side of Christ, sleeping on the cross, the sacraments flowed, namely blood and water (Jn 19,34), by which the Church was founded."[14]

These coherences mentioned by Thomas, between the mysteries of God and Christ and a Christian life, invite us to a further exploration of them, to due gratitude, praise and honor to God and for our good and happiness: a strong faith, a living hope and a wholehearted love. Therefore,

MAY THE PASSION OF JESUS CHRIST
BE ALWAYS IN OUR HEARTS[15]

---

[13] ST IaIIae q.103 a.2co, IIIa q.52 a.1 ad 2, a.8 ad 2, q.66 a.2co, q.69 a.1 ad 2 ([N]ullius *peccati remissio fieri potest nisi per virtutem passionis Christi: Unde et Apostolus dicit* [Heb 9,22] *quod "sine sanguinis effusione non fit remissio"*), q.84 a.7co; C1C intr., c.1 ll.2 (*Sic ergo, si* solius *Christio passio, si* solius *Christi nomen virtutem confert baptismo ad salvandum, verum est proprium esse Christo, ut ex eo baptismus habeat significandi virtutem*), 3.

[14] ST Ia q.92 a.3co: [D]e latere Christi dormientis in cruce fluxerunt sacramenta, idest sanguis et aqua, quibus est Ecclesia instituta.

[15] This caption (often abbreviated as "JCP") is found in many letters of St. Paul of the Cross, starting with Letter 288, dd. the 2nd August 1741, just after the papal approval of the Rule of the Congregation of the Passion he founded.

ABBREVIATIONS

Abbreviations of Biblical Books

(following the New Jerusalem Bible)

1 Ch	1 Chronicles	Jd	Jude
1 Co	1 Corinthians	Jl	Joel
1 Jn	1 John	Jm	James
1 K	1 Kings	Jn	gospel according to John
1 P	1 Peter	Jr	Jeremiah
1 S	1 Samuel	Jon	Jonah
1 Th	1 Thessalonians	Jos	Joshua
1 Tm	1 Timothy	Lk	gospel according to Luke
2 Ch	2 Chronicles	Lm	Lamentations
2 Co	2 Corinthians	Lv	Leviticus
2 K	2 Kings	Mi	Michah
2 M	2 Maccabees	Mk	gospel according to Mark
2 P	2 Peter	Ml	Malachi
2 S	2 Samuel	Mt	gospel according to Matthew
2 Tm	2 Timothy		
Ac	Acts of the Apostles	Na	Nahum
Am	Amos	Nb	Numbers
Col	Colossians	Ne	Nehemiah
Dn	Daniel	Ph	Philippians
Dt	Deuteronomy	Pr	Proverbs
Ep	Ephesians	Ps	Psalms
Ex	Exodus	Qo	Qoheleth (Ecclesiastes)
Ezk	Ezekiel	Rm	Romans
Ezr	Ezra	Rv	Revelation to John
Ga	Galathians	Sg	Song of Songs
Gn	Genesis	Si	Ben Sira (Ecclesiasticus)
Heb	Hebrews	Tb	Tobit
Hos	Hosea	Tt	Titus
Is	Isaiah	W	Wisdom
Jb	Job	Zc	Zechariah

Other Abbreviations

Ia	*Prima Pars* of the ST
IaIIae	*Prima Secundae* of the ST
IIaIIae	*Secunda Secundae* of the ST
IIIa	*Tertia Pars* of the ST
3f	3 and 4 (3ff: 3 and following ones)
a.3	*articulus* 3
a.3c	*articulus* 3c (in SN only)
a.3co	*corpus* of *articulus* 3
aa.	*articuli*
ad 3	answer to *obiectio* 3
ag.	*obiectio*
c.3	*caput* 3
cf.	confer
co	*corpus* of the *articulus*
intr.	*introductio*
L.3	*Liber* 3
l.3	*lectio* 3 (ll.3, 4: *lectiones* 3 and 4)
LXX	Septuagint
ML	*Patrologia cursus completus, series Latine*, J.-P. Migne (ed), Paris 1844-1890
MG	idem *series Graece*
MR	M.-R. Hoogland cp
n.3	number/paragraph 3
q.3	*quaestio* 3 (qq.3, 4: *quaestiones* 3 and 4)
sc.	*sed contra*
Vulg	Vulgate

BIBLIOGRAPHY

Works of Thomas Aquinas

If no edition details are mentioned, the edition used of the *Commissio Leonina, S. Thomae Aquinatis doctoris angelici Opera Omnia iussu impensaque Leonis XIII P.M. edita*, Romae 1882-. If this was not available, the text edition in Roberto Busa S.J., *Sancti Thomae Aquinatis Opera Omnia ut sunt in Indice Thomistico*, (Indicis Thomistici Supplementum), Stuttgart, Bad Cannstatt 1980, is adopted, except for Thomas' commentary on the Sentences I - III. In the text of this book Busa's abbreviations are used. The first letter indicates what type of work it is: a C stands for *Commentarium*, an O for *Opusculum*, a Q for *Quaestiones*, an R for *Reportatio* and an X for a work probably not written by Thomas.

C1C	*Super Epistolam I ad Corinthios*, Marictti 1953
CBT	*In librum Boethii De Trinitate*, B. Decker, Leiden 1959
CDN	*In Dionysii De divinis nominibus*, Marietti 1950
CIO	*In Job*
CIS	*In Isaiam*
CMP	*In libros metaphysicorum*, Marietti 1950
CRO	*Super Epistolam ad Romanos*, Marietti 1953
OCE	*Contra errores Graecorum*
OCG	*De rationibus fidei*
OTT	*Compendium Theologiae*, Marietti 1954
QDA	*Quaestiones disputatae De anima*, idem 1953
QDI	*Quaestio disputata De unione Verbi incarnati*, idem
QDL	*Quaestiones quodlibetales*, idem 1956
QDP	*Quaestiones disputatae De potentia*, idem 1953
QDV	*Quaestiones disputatae De veritate*, idem
R1C	*Super Epistolam I ad Corinthios XI-XVI*, idem
R2C	*Super Epistolam II ad Corinthios*, idem
REI	*Super evangelium Johannis*, idem 1952
REM	*Super evangelium Matthaei*, idem 1951
RGL	*Super Epistolam ad Galatas*, idem 1953
RPL	*Super Epistolam ad Philippenses*, idem
RPS	*In Psalmos (usque ad Ps. LI)*, ed. Parma t. XIV, 1863
RSU	*In orationem dominicam* , Marietti 1954
RT1	*Super Epistolam ad Timotheum*, idem 1953
SCG	*Summa Contra Gentiles*
SN	*Scriptum super libros Sententiarum Magistri Petri Lombardi*, I, II ed. P. Mandonnet, Paris 1929; III ed. M.F. Moos, Paris 1947; IV ed. Parma 1948
ST	*Summa Theologiae*
XTB	*De Beatitudine (ignoti auctoris)*, ed Parma t. XVII, 1864

Translations in the text are by the author. The English translation of the *Summa Theologiae* in the Blackfriars edition (London, New York, 1964-66) was consulted.

Secondary Literture

AERTS, LODE -- *Gottesherrschaft als Gleichnis?, -Ein Untersuchung zur Auslegung der Gleichnisse Jesu nach Eberhard Jüngel*, Frankfurt am Main 1990

AERTSEN, JAN A. -- Thomas van Aquino en de Thomas van Utrecht, -Kritische kanttekeningen bij de Utrechtse lezing van de Summa Theologiae, in: *Bijdragen* 55 (1994), 56-71.

AERTSEN, JAN A. -- "Eros" und "Agape", -Dionysiis Areopagita und Thomas von Aquin über die Doppelgestalt der Liebe, in: Tzotcho Boiadjiev, Georgi Kapriev, Andreas Speer (eds.), *Die Dionysius-Rezeption im Mittelalter*, Brepolis 2000, 373-391

ALBRECHT, BARBARA -- *Gott und das Leiden der Menschen*, Freising 1976

AMMICHT-QUINN, REGINA -- *Von Lissabon bis Auschwitz, -Zum Paradigmawechsel in der Theodizeefrage*, Freiburg (Schweiz) 1992

ANONYMUS -- *Corpus Christianorum, Series Latina*, Tomus CXL/A, Turnhout, Paris 1953

ANONYMUS -- *Constituties en Decreten van het Tweede Vaticaans Oecumenisch Concilie* Leusden 1986

ANONYMUS -- *Webster's Third New International Dictionary of the English Language Unabridged*, Vol. 1 - 3, Chicago, Auckland, Geneva, London etc. 1986

ANSELMI CP, MAX -- Intelligenza della Croce, in: *Bolletino Stauros* 8 (1982), 3-36

BARTHÉLEMIE, D. -- *Dieu et Son Image, -Ébauche d'une Théologie Biblique*, Paris 1973

BAUKE-RUEGG, JAN -- *Die Almacht Gottes, -Systematisch-theologische Erwägungen zwischen Metaphysik, Postmoderne und Poesie*, Berlin, New York 1998

BERKHOF, H. -- *Christelijk geloof*, Nijkerk 1985[5]

BIRNBAUM, DAVID -- *God and Evil, -A Unified Theodicy/Theology/Philosophy, -A Jewish Perspective*, Hoboken NJ 1989

BLANK, JOSEF -- Het begrip macht in de kerk, -Nieuwtestamentische begrippen, in: *Concilium* 1988-3 "Macht in de kerk", 20-27

BOESPFLUG, FRANÇOIS -- La Compassion de Dieu le Père dans l'Art Occidental (XIIIe - XVIIe Siècles), in: *Le Supplement, -Revue d'Étique et Théologie Morale* 172, "Mal et Compassion", Paris 1990, 124-159

BOFF, LEONARDO -- *Passion of Christ, Passion of the World, -The Facts, Their Interpretation and Their Meaning Yesterday and Today*, Maryknoll NY 1987

BONK, SIGMUND -- *Kleine Theodizee*, Regensburg 1996

BONS-STORM, MARIA (ed.) -- *Zij waait waarheen zij wil, -Opstellen over de Geest aangeboden aan Catharina J.M. Halkes*, Baarn 1986

BRACKEN, JERRY -- Thomas' and Anselm's Satisfaction Theory, in: *Angelicum* 62 (1985), 501-530

BRANDTSCHEN, J.B. -- *Laat God ons lijden*, Boxtel, Brugge 1986 (tranl. into German: *Warum läßt Gott uns leiden?*, Freiburg in Breisgau 1986)

BRETON CP, S. -- *Le Verbe et la Croix*, Paris 1981

BRETON CP, S. -- *Pour une Petite Histoire de la Théologie de la Croix*, Leueven 1986

BRETON CP, S. -- *La Passion du Christ et Sa Vertu*, Rome 1991

BRO, BERNARD -- *Le Pouvoir du Mal*, Paris 1976
BROWN, RAYMOND E. -- *The Death of the Messiah, -From Gethsemane to the Grave*, New York 1994
BÜMMER, VINCENT -- *Wat doen wij als wij bidden*, Kampen 1985
BRÜMMER, VINCENT -- *Over een persoonlijke God gesproken, -Studies in de wijsgerige theologie*, Kampen 1988
BULHOF, ILSE N., L. TEN KATE (eds.)-- *Ons ontbreken heilige namen, -Negatieve theologie en de hedendaagse cultuurfilosofie*, Kampen 1992
BURKLE, HOWARD R. -- *God, Suffering and Belief*, Nashville 1977
BURRELL, DAVID -- *Analogy and Philosophical Language* New Haven, London, 1973
BURRELL, DAVID -- *God and Action*, London, Henley 1979
BURRELL, DAVID -- *Knowing the Unknowable God, -Ibn-Sina, Maimonides, Aquinas*, Notre Dame 1986
BURRELL, DAVID -- Argument in Theology, -Analogy and Narrative, in: Carl Rashke (ed.), *New Dimensions in Philosophical Theology*, JAAR Thematic Studies 49/1 (1987), 37-52

CARETTO, C. -- *Perché Signore?, -Il Dolore: Segreto Nascosto nei Secoli*, Brescia 1985
CAROLL, JOHN T., JOEL B. GREEN etc. -- *The Death of Jesus in Early Christianity*, Peabody MA 1995
CARTER, CHARLES -- *The Easter Story in Art*, London 1936
CASE-WINTERS, ANNA -- *God's Power, -Traditional Understandings and Contemporary Challenges*, Louisville Kentucky 1990
CATAUI DE MENASCE, GIOVANNI -- Può essere compassionevole e soffrire per e con chi soffre?, in: Vittorio Possenti, *Jacques Maritain oggi, -Atti del convegno internazionale di studio promosso dall' università cattolica del centenario della nascita, Milano 20-23 ottobre 1982*, Milan 1983, 381-391
CHENU, M.-D. -- *Introduction à l'Étude de Saint Thomas d'Aquin*, Montréal, Paris 1950[3]
COAKLEY, S -- Femininity and the Holy Spirit? in: M. Furlong, *Mirror to the Church, -Reflections on Sexism*, Bristol 1988, 124-135
CONGAR, Y. -- Le Sens de l'Économie Salutaire dans la Théologie de S. Thomas d'Aquin (Somme Théologique), in: *Festgabe J. Lortz*, Vol. II, Baden-Baden 1957, 73-122
CONGAR, Y -- *I Believe in the Holy Spirit* (I-III), New York 1997
CONSTANTINI, C. -- *Il Crocifisso nell' Arte*, Firenze 1911
COOK, DAVID E. -- Weak Church, Weak God, in: Nigel M. de S. Cameron, *The Power and Weakness of God: Impassibility and Orthodoxy -Papers Presented at the Third Edinburgh Conference in Christian Dogmatics 1989*, Edinburgh 1990
CORBIN, MICHEL -- *Le Chemin de la Théologie chez Thomas d'Aquin*, Paris 1974
CORBIN, MICHEL -- *L'Inouï de Dieu, -Six Études Christologiques*, Paris 1980
CROTTY, N. -- The Redemptive Role of Christ's Resurrection, in: *The Thomist* 25 (1962), 54-106

DANE, JOSEPH A. -- Potestas/potentia: Note on Boethius' De Consolatione Philosophiae, in: *Vivarium* 17 (1979), 81-89
DAVIES, BRIAN -- *The Thought of Thomas Aquinas*, Oxford 1992

DE GRIJS, F.J.A. -- Christologie und Thomasinterpretation, in: *Bijdragen* 45 (1984), 350-373

DE GRIJS, F.J.A. -- Spreken over God en Thomasinterpretatie, in: *Jaarboek* 1984 *Werkgroep Thomas van Aquino*, Utrecht 1985, 7-38

DE GRIJS, F.J.A. -- Thomas Aquinas on *Ira* as a Divine Metaphor, in: Henk J.M. Schoot (ed.), *Tibi soli peccavi, -Thomas Aquinas on Guilt and Forgiveness*, Leueven 1996, 19-46

DEHART, PAUL JEFFREY -- *Divine Simplicity, -Theistic Reconstruction in Eberhart Jüngel's Trinitarian Glaubenslehre*, Chicago IL 1997

DE LUBAC, HENRI -- *Exegese Médiévale, -Les Quatre Sens de l'Écriture*, Paris 1959

DE MAESENEER -- *Een kwetsbare God, -Zin en onzin van het lijden*, Leuven 1976

DEPOORTERE, KRISTIAAN -- *A Different God, -A Christian View of Suffering*, Leuven 1995

DE S. CAMERON, NIGEL M. (eds.) -- *The Power and Weakness of God: Impassibility and Orthodoxy, -Papers Presented at the Third Edinburgh Conference in Christian Dogmatics 1989*, Edinburgh 1990

DE SOLMS, É. -- *Christs et Croix Romains*, Paris 1995[2]

DILLISTONE, M. -- *Jesus Christ and His Cross, -Studies on the Saving Works of Christ*, London 1953

DI MAIO, ANDREA -- La Logica della Croce in Bonaventura e Tomaso: Il Sillogismo e il Duplice Medio, in: Tito Paolo Zecca cp, *La Croce di Christo Unica Speranza, -Atti del III Congresso Internationale "La Sapienza della Croce Oggi"*, Roma 1995, 373-398

DIRKS, WALTHER -- *Christi Passion, -Farbige Bilder aus dem sechsten bis zwölften Jahrhundert erläutert W.D.* Hamburg 1963[2]

DUNBAR, DONALD R. -- On Omnipotence, *New Scholasticism* 42 (1968), 280-288

DUQUOC, CHRISTIAN -- Demonisme en het onverwachte van God, in: *Concilium* 1983-9 "Job en het zwijgen van God", 88-95

ECKERMANN, WILLIGIS -- "Einer aus der Dreifaltigkeit wurde gekreuzigt", -Von der gott-menschlichen zur Trinitarischen Sicht des Kreuzes Christi, in: Willigis Eckermann, Friedrich Janssen etc. (eds.), *Das Kreuz - Stein des Anstoßes*, Kevelaer 1998[2], 72-86

EDER, PETER -- *Ärgernis und Sinn des Kreuztodes Jesu*, Hamburg 1993

EISENBERG, JOSY, ELIE WIESEL -- *Job ou Dieu dans la Tempête*, Paris 1986

ELLUIN, JEAN -- *Quel Enfer?*, Paris 1994

ERICKSON, MILLARD J. -- *God the Father Almighty, -A Contemporary Exploration of the Divine Attributes*, Grand Rapids 1998

ESLICK, LEONARD -- The Meanings of Power, *New Scholasticism* 42 (1968), 289-292

EVANS, G.R. -- *Anselm*, Wilton CT 1989

FABER, R. -- *Der Selbsteinsatz Gottes: Grundlegung einer Theologie des Leidens und der Veränderlichkeit Gottes*, Würzberg 1995

FARLEY, WENDY -- *Tragic Vision and Divine Compassion, -A Contemporary Theodicy*, Louisville Kent. 1990

FATTINGER, JOSEF -- *In diesem Zeichen wirst du siegen*, Frankfurt am Main 1941

FELDMEIER, REINHARD -- Nicht Übermacht noch Impotenz, -Zum biblischen Ursprung des Allmachtsbekenntnisses, in: W.H. Ritter, R. Feldmeier etc., *Der Allmächtige, -Annäherungen an ein umstrittenes Gottesprädikat*, Göttingen 1997, 13-42

FERRÉ, N.F.S. -- *Reason in Religion*, London, Edinburgh 1963

FIDDES, PAUL S. -- *The Creative Suffering of God*, Oxford 1988

FRITZSCHE, HANS-GEORG -- *Und erlöse uns von dem Übel, -Philosophie und Theologie zur Rechtfertigung Gottes*, Stuttgart 1987

GALOT, JEAN -- *Vers une Nouvelle Christologie*, Gembloux 1971

GALOT, JEAN -- *Dieu, Souffre-t-Il?*, Paris 1976

GARRIGOU-LAGRANGE OP, RÉGINALD -- L'Amour de Dieu et le Mystère de la Croix, in: *L'Amour de Dieu et la Croix de Jésus, -Étude de Théologie Mystique sur le Problème de l'Amour et les Purifications Passives d'après les Principes de Saint Thomas d'Aquin et la Doctrine de Saint Jean de la Crois*, tome Ier, Paris 1929, 206-262

GARRIGOU-LAGRANGE OP, RÉGINALD -- *La Providence et la Confiance de Dieu, -Fidélité et Abandon*, Paris 1932

GARRIGOU-LAGRANGE OP, RÉGINALD -- *De Deo Uno, -Commentarium in Primam Partem S. Thomae*, Paris 1938

GARRIGUES, JEAN-MICHEL -- *Dieu Sans Idée du mal, -La Liberté de l'Homme au Coeur de Dieu*, Paris 1990

GELLMANN, JEROME -- Omnipotence and Impeccability, in: *New Scholasticism* 51 (1977), 21-37

GESENIUS, WILHELM -- *Hebräisches und aramäisches Handwörterbuch über das Alte Testament*, Leipzig 1910[15]

GILLON, L.-B. -- Tristesse et Miséricorde du Père, in: *Angelicum* 55 (1978), 3-11

GLANVILL, REGINALD -- *Jesus and His Passion*, London 1941

GNILKA, JOACHIM -- *Das Matthäusevangelium 2. Teil*, Freiburg in Breisgau 1988

GONNET, DOMINIQUE -- *Dieu Aussi Connaît la Souffrance*, Paris 1990

GONZÁLEZ FAUS, JOSÉ IGNACIO -- Wij verkondigen een gekruisigde messias, in: *Concilium* 1992-4, 68-78

GONZALES MEDINA, S. -- *La necessidad de la passión, -Un aspecto de la Theologia de la Redención en S. Thomás*, Freiburg (year not indicated)

GOOSSENS, JAN -- Almacht van God is onchristelijke erfenis uit Romeinse tijd (an interview with A.A.S. ten Kate), in: *Hervormd Nederland* 29, 29th September 2001, 18-19

GORIS, HARM J.M.J. -- *Free Creatures of an Eternal God, -Thomas Aquinas on God's Infallible Foreknowledge and Irresistible Will*, Leuven, Utrecht 1996

GÄBE, PETRUS J. -- *The Power of God in Paul's Letters*, Tübingen 2000

GONDREAU, PAUL -- *The Passions of Christ's Soul in the Theology of St. Thomas Aquinas*, Münster 2002

GREEN, PETER -- *The Problem of Evil*, London 1920

GRIFFIN, DAVID RAY -- *God, Power and Evil, -A Process Theodicy*, Philadelphia 1976

HANKEY, WAYNE -- Aquinas and the Passion of God, in: Allistair Kee, Eugene T.

Long, *Being and Truth, -Essays in Honour of John Macquarrie*, London 1986, 318-333

HÄRING, H. -- Het kwaad als vraag naar Gods macht en machteloosheid, in: *TvT* 26 (1986), 351-372

HARTSHORNE, CHARLES E. -- *A Natural Theology for Our Time*, La Salle IL 1967

HARTSHORNE, CHARLES E. -- *Omnipotence and Other Theological Mistakes*, Albany NY 1984

HAUCAULT, A. -- La Satisfaction du Christ Jésus à la Lumière de l'Encyclique Humanae Generis, in: *SMR* 3 (1960), 173-200

HAUCAULT, A. -- Le Péché est un Veritable Offence de Dieu, in: *SMR* 4 (1961), 133-184

HEDINGER, U. -- *Hoffnung zwischen Kreuz und Reich, Studien und Meditationen über die christliche Hoffnung*, Zürich 1968

HEDINGER, ULRICH -- *Wider der Versöhnung Gottes mit dem Elend, -Eine Kritik des christlichen Theismus und A-Theismus*, Zürich 1972

HEDINGER, ULRICH -- *Die Hinrichtung Jesu von Nazareth, -Kritik der Kreuztheologie, Versuche von Ulrich Hedinger*, Stuttgart 1983

HEDINGER, ULRICH -- *Kritik der Kreuztheologie, -Wider den Mythos, Jesu Ermordung bedeute das Heil der Welt*, Tübingen 1993

HEERING, J.P., L.W. VAN REYENDAM-BEEK ETC. -- *Nogmaals: Waarom, -Artikelen over en reacties op het boek van dr. A. van de Beek: Waarom? over lijden, schuld en God*, Nijkerk 1986

HENDERSON, GEORGE -- *Early Medieval*, Baltimore 1972

HESSERT, PAUL -- *Christ and the End of Meaning*, Rockport MA 1993

HICK, JOHN -- *Evil and the God of Love*, London 1970[2]

HINZ, PAULUS -- *Deus Homo, -Das Christusbild von seinen Ursprüngen bis zur Gegenwart*, Band I "Das erste Jahrtausend", Berlin 1973

HOCHSTAFFEL, JOSEPH -- *Negatieve Theologie, -Ein Versuch zur Vermittlung des patristischen Begriffs*, München 1976

HOOGLAND CP, MARK-ROBIN -- The Passionate God of Christ, -Some Remarks, in: H.J.M. Schoot (ed.), *Jaarboek 1999 Thomas Instituut te Utrecht*, Utrecht 2000, 152-158

HUBERFELT, MONIQUE -- Où est Dieu Qui Fait Justice, in: *Christus* 92 "Le Mal", Paris 1976

HÜRKEY, EDGAR -- *Das Bild der Gekreuzigten im Mittelalter, -Untersuchungen zu Gruppierung, Entwicklung und Verbreitung anhand der Gewandmotieve*, Worms 1983

IMMINK, FREDERIK GERRIT -- *Divine Simplicity*, Kampen 1987

IRSIGLER, HERBERT, GODEHARD RUPPERT (eds.), *Ein Gott der Leiden schafft*, Frankfurt am Main 1995

JANSSEN, FRIEDRICH -- Credo quia absurdum, -Der Glaube an den Gekreuzigten in Kreuzverhör der Vernunft, in: Willigis Eckermann, Friedrich Janssen etc. (eds.), *Das Kreuz - Stein des Anstoßes*, Kevelaer 1998[2], 87-102

JANßEN, HANS-GERD -- *Dem Leiden Widerstehen, -Aufsätze zur Grundlegung einer praktischen Theodizee*, Münster 1996

JENNI, ERNST, CLAUS WESTERMANN -- *Theologisches Handwörterbuch zum Alten Testament* München, Zürich 1978-1979

JOHN PAUL II -- Apostolic Letter *Salvifici doloris*, Amersfoort 1984

JOHNSON, ELISABETH -- *She Who Is, -The Mystery of God in Feminist Theological Discourse*, New York 1993

JORDAN, MARK D. -- The Modes of Thomistic Discourse: Questions for Corbin "Le Chemin de la Théologie chez Thomas d'Aquin", *The Thomist* 45 (1981), 80-98

JORDAN, MARK D. -- Aquinas' Construction of a Moral Account of the Passions, in: *Freiburger Zeitschrift für Philosophie und Theologie* 33 (1986), 71-97

JÜNGEL, E. -- *Tod*, Berlin 1971

JÜNGEL, E. -- Karfreitag - Das dunkle Wort vom "Tode Gottes", in: E. Jüngel, *Von Zeit zu Zeit, -Betrachtungen zu den Festzeiten im Kirchenjahr*, München 1976

JÜNGEL, E. -- *Entsprechungen, -Gott, Wahrheit, Mensch, Theologische Erörterungen*, München 1980

JÜNGEL, E. -- *Gott als Geheimnis der Welt, -Zur Begründung der Theologie des Gekreuzigten im Streit zwischen Theismus und Atheismus*, Tübingen 1977[2] (transl. into English: *God as the Mystery of Our World*, Edinburgh 1983)

JÜNGEL, E. -- Gottes ursprüngliches Anfangen als schöpferische Selbstbegrenzung, -Ein Beitrag zum Gespräch mit Hans Jonas über den Gottesbegriff nach Auschwitz, in: H. Deuser (ed.), *Gottes Zukunft - Zukunft der Welt*, München 1986, 265-275

KAMP, JEAN -- *Souffrance de Dieu, Vie du Monde*, Tournai 1971

KASPER, WALTHER -- *Jesus der Christus*, Mainz 1974

KASPER, WALTHER -- *Der Gott Jesu Christi*, Mainz 1982

KEATY, ANTHONY WILLIAM -- *The Holy Spirit as Love, -A Study in the Pneumatology of Thomas Aquinas*, Notre Dame IN, AnnArbor MI 1997

KITAMORI, KAZOH -- *Theology of the Pain of God*, Richmond 1965 (transl. from Japanese, 1946)

KITTEL, GERHARD, GERHARD FRIEDRICH -- *Theologisches Wörterbuch zum Neuen Testament*, Stuttgart 1949-1979

KREINER, ARMIN -- *Gott im Leid, -Zur Stichhaltigkeit der Theodizee-Argumenten*, Freiburg in Breisgau 1997

KREMER, J. -- *Lukasevangelium*, Würzburg 1988

KRELING OP, G.P. -- Het motief van de menswording, in: F.J.A. de Grijs etc. (eds.), *Het goddelijk geheim, -Theologisch werk van G.P. Kreling o.p.*, Kampen 1979, 248-257

KRESS, CHRISTINE -- *Gottes Almacht angesichts von Leiden, -Zur Interpretation der Gotteslehre in der systematisch-theologieschen Entwürfen von Paul Althaus, Paul Tillich und Karl Barth*, Neukirchen 1999

KÜNG, H. -- *Gott und das Leid*, Einsiedeln 1974[5]

KÜNG, H. -- *Das Judentum, -Die religiöse Situation der Zeit*, München/Zürich 1991

KÜNG, H. -- *Credo, -Das Apostolische Glaubensbekenntnis, Zeitegenossen erklärt*, München 1992

KÜNG, H. -- *Menschwerdung Gottes, -Eine Einfürung in Hegels theologisches Denken als Prolegomena zu einer künftigen Christologie*, Freiburg 1970

KUNTZ, PAUL G. -- Omnipotence, -Tradition and Revolt in Philosophical Theology, in: *New Scholasticism* 42 (1968), 270-279

KYUN, CHUNG HYUN -- Come Holy Spirit - Renew the Whole Creation, in: M. Kinnamon (ed.), *Signs of the Spirit, -Official Report, Seventh Assembley Canberra, Australia, 7 - 20 Febuary 1991*, Geneve 1991, 37-47

LABUSCHAGNE, C.J. -- *Zin en onzin over God, -Een kritische beschouwing van gangbare godsvoorstellingen*, Zoetermeer 1994

LACROIX, MICHEL -- *Le Mal, -Un Exposé pour Comprendre, un Essay pour Réfléchir*, Flammarion 1998

LARCHET, J.-C. -- *Dieu Ne Veut Pas la Souffrance des Hommes*, Paris 1999

LEGET, CARLO -- Aquinas on Evil. An Evaluation of and Some Reflections in Connection with Two Recent Studies, in: H.J.M. Schoot (ed.), *Jaarboek 1993 Thomas Instituut te Utrecht*, Utrecht 1994, 161-187

LEGET, CARLO -- *Living with God, -Thomas Aquinas on the Relation between Life on Earth and 'Life' after Death*, Leuven, Utrecht 1997

LEGET, CARLO -- 'Leven' in het Johannescommentaar van Thomas, in: H.J.M. Schoot (ed.), *Jaarboek 2001 Thomas Instituut Utrecht*, Utrecht 2002, 11-27

LENSINK, HENK -- 'God Almachtig' dient wegvertaald te worden, in: *Interpretatie* (juli 2000), 6-7.

LEVENSON, JON D. -- *Creation and the Persistence of Evil, -The Jewish Drama of Divine Omnipotence*, Princeton NJ 1988

LÉVI, ISRAEL -- *The Hebrew Text of the Book of Ecclesiasticus, Edited with Brief Notes and Selected Glossary*, Leiden 1904

LIMBECK, MEINDERT -- *Matthäusevangelium*, Stuttgart 1991

LINDBECK, GEORGE -- Response to Bruce Marshall, in: *The Thomist* 53 (1989), 403-406

LIPPI CP, ADOLFO -- *Teologia della Gloria e Teologia della Croce*, Torino 1982

LOUIS, RENÉ -- La Croix sur les Chemins du XIIième Siècle, in: Anonyme, *Le Signe de la Croix*, Plon 1957

LÖHRER, MAGNUS -- Dogmatische Bemerkungen zur Frage der Eigenschaften und Verhaltensweisen Gottes, in *Mysterium Salutis* II, Einsiedeln, Zürich, Köln 1967, 291-314

LONERGAN, BERNARD J.F. -- The De-hellenization of Dogma, in: *Theological Studies* 28 (1967), 336-351

MACKIE, J.L. -- Evil and Omnipotence, in: Nelson Pike (ed.), *God and Evil, -Readings on the Theological Problem of Evil*, Englewood Cliffs NJ 1964, 46-60

MACKIE, JOHN -- *The Miracle of Theism*, Oxford 1982

MACQUARRIE, JOHN -- *God-talk, -An Examination of the Language and Logic of Theology*, London 1967

MACQUARRIE, JOHN -- *In Search of Deity, -An Essay in Dialectical Theism*, London 1984

MARION, JEAN-LUC -- *L'Idole et la Distance, -Cinq Études*, Paris 1977

MARION, JEAN-LUC -- *Dieu sans l'Être: Hors Texte*, Paris 1991 (1982[1]) (transl. into English: *God without Being*, Chicago, London 1995)

MARITAIN, JACQUES -- *Saint Thomas and the Problem of Evil*, Milwaukee 1942

MARSHALL, BRUCE D. -- Aquinas as a Postliberal Theologian, in: *The Thomist* 53 (1989), 353-402

MAUREL, G., -- *Compendiosa Summa Theologica Sancti Thomae Aquinatis, Tomus Primus*, Paris 1889

MCFAGUE, SALLIE -- *Metaphorical Theology, -Models of God in Religious Language*, London 1983

MCINERNY, RALPH -- Metaphor and Analogy, in: James F. Ross (ed.), *Inquiries into Medieval Philosophy, -A Collection in Honour of Francis P. Clarke*, Westport 1971, 75-96

MCINERNY, RALPH -- Aquinas on Divine Omnipotence, in: Christian Wenin (ed.), *L'Homme et Son Univers au Moyen Âge, -Actes de Septième Congrès International de Philosophie médiévale (30 août - septembre 1982)*, Louvain-la-neuve 1986, 440-444

MCCORD ADAMS, MARILYN -- *Horrendous Evils and the Goodness of God*, Ithaca, London 1999

MCWILLIAMS, WARREN -- *The Passion of God, -Divine Suffering in Contemporary Protestant Theology*, Macon GA 1985

MENDELSSOHN, MOSES -- *Jerusalem and Other Writings*, New York 1969

MENKEN, MAARTEN -- De evangelist Johannes en de kerkleraar Thomas, -Een reactie op Carlo Leget, in: H.J.M. Schoot (ed.), *Jaarboek 2001 Thomas Instituut Utrecht*, Utrecht 2002, 29-36

MERTENS, HERMAN-EMIEL -- *Not the Cross, but the Crucified, -An Essay in Soteriology*, Leuven 1992 (transl. from Dutch: Niet het Kruis, maar de Gekruisigde, -Schets van een christelijke bevrijdingsleer, Leuven/Amerfoort 1990)

METZ, JOHANN-BAPTIST -- *Landschaft aus Schreien, -Zur Dialektik der Theodizeefrage*, Mainz 1995

METZ, JOHANN-BAPTIST -- Die Rede von Gott angesichts der Leidensgeschichte der Welt, in: Hubert Irsigler, Godehard Ruppert (eds.), *Ein Gott der Leiden schafft?*, Frankfurt am Main ²1995, 43-58

MEYER, MICHEL -- *La Philosophie et les Passions, -Esquisse d'une Histoire de la Nature Humaine*, Paris 1991

MICHIELSEN, MARJAN -- *De almachtige God en het lijden, -Een herinterpretatie door H. Berkhof en G. Greshake*, Leuven 1979

MOFFATT, JAMES -- *Love in the New Testament*, London 1929

MOLNAR, PAUL D. -- Moltmann's Post-Modern Messianic Christology, -A Review Discussion, in: *The Thomist* 56 (1992), 669-693

MOLTMANN, JÜRGEN -- *Der gekreuzigte Gott, -Das Kreuz Christi als Grund und Kritik christlicher Theologie*, München 1972

MOLTMANN, JÜRGEN -- Gesichtspunkte der Kreuztheologie heute, in: *Evangelische Theologie* 1973, 346-366

MOLTMANN, JÜRGEN -- *Trinität und Reich Gottes, -Zur Gotteslehre*, München 1980

MOLTMANN, JÜRGEN -- *In der Geschichte des dreieinigen Gottes, -Beitrage zur trinitarischen Theologie*, München 1991 (transl. into English: History and the Triune God, -Contributions to Trinitarian Theology, London 1991)

MOLTMANN-WENDEL, E. (ed.) -- *Die Weiblichkeit des Heiligen Geistes, -Studien zur feministischen Theologie*, Gütersloh 1995

MOONAN, LAURENCE -- *Divine Power, -The Medieval Power Distinction up to its Adoption by Albert, Bonaventure and Aquinas*, Oxford 1994

MORIN, DOMINIQUE -- *Le Mal et La Souffrance*, Paris 1993

MOULTON, JAMES HOPE, GEORGE MILIGAN -- *The Vocabulary of the Greek Testament, -Illustrated from the Papyri and Other Non-Literary Sources*, London 1949

MUGNIER, ABBÉ FRANCIS -- *La Passion de Jésus-Christ d'après Saint Thomas d'Aquin, Somme Théologique: IIIa, q. 46 - 49*, Paris 1932

NEUHAUS, G. -- *Theodizee, -Abbruch oder Anstoß des Glaubens*, Freiburg, Basel, Wien, 1993

NEUSCH, MARCEL -- *Le Mal*, Paris 1990

NICHOLS OP, AIDON -- St. Thomas Aquinas on the Passion of Christ, -A Reading of Summa Theologiae IIIa q.46, in: *Scottish Journal of theology* 43 (1990), 447-459

NICOLAS OP, JEAN-HERVÉ -- *L'Amour de Dieu et la Peine des Hommes*, Paris 1969

NICOLAS OP, JEAN.-HERVÉ. -- Miséricorde et Sévérité de Dieu, in: *Revue Thomist* 88 (1988), 181-214, 533-555

NIELSEN, J.T. -- *Het evangelie naar Mattheüs III*, Nijkerk 1990[4]

NÜCHTERN, MICHAEL (ed.) -- *Warum läßt Gott das zu? -Kritik der Allmacht Gottes in Religion und Philosophie*, Frankfurt am Main 1995

OBERLINNER, LORENZ -- *Die Pastoralbriefe, Erster Timoteusbrief*, Freiburg, Basel, Wien, 1994

O'LEARY CP, JOSEPH MARY -- *The Development of the Doctrine of St. Thomas Aquinas on the Passion ans Death of Our Lord*, Chicago 1952

O'MEARA OP, THOMAS F. -- *Thomas Aquinas Theologian*, Notre Dame, London 1997

OOMEN, PALMYRE M.F. -- Lijden als vraag naar God: Een bijdrage vanuit Whitehead's filosofie, in: *TvT* 34 (1994), 246-268

PEACOCKE, ARTHUR R. -- *Intimations of Reality, -Critical Realism in Science and Religion*, Notre Dame IN 1984

PESCH, O.H. -- *Thomas von Aquin, -Grenze und Größe mittelalterlicher Theologie. Eine Einführung*, Mainz 1988

PESCH, O.H. -- *Martin Luther, Thomas von Aquin und die reformatorische Kritik an der Scholastik*, Göttingen 1994

PETERSEN, B. -- *Theologie nach Auschwitz*, Berlin 1996

PHILIPPE, M.-D. -- Y a-t-il des Limits à la Toute-Puissance de Dieu? (Ia q.25 a.4, 5 et 6), in: *BCTC* 88,89 (1980), 7-24; 90 (1981), 1-22

PHILIPPE DE LA TRINITÉ -- La teologia della redenzione secondo San Tommaso d'Aquino, in: Bonaventura Rinaldi cp (ed.), *La Sapienza della Croce Oggi*, Torino 1976, I,247-253

PHILIPS, D.Z. -- On Not Understanding God, in: Mario M. Olivetti (ed.), *Teologia Oggi*, Rome 1984, 597-612

PLACHER, WILLIAM -- *Narratives of a Vulnerable God, -Theology and Scripture*,

Louisville 1994

PLANTINGA, THEODORE -- *Learning to Live with Evil*, Grand Rapids 1982

POLLEFEYT, D. -- *Niet lijdzaam toezien!, -Godsdienstige verwerking van lijden in de huidige (jongeren)cultuur*, Leuven, Amersfoort 1995

POORTHUIS, MARCEL (ed.) -- *Mijn God, Mijn God, waarom hebt Gij Mij verlaten, - Een interdisciplinaire bundel over Psalm 22*, Baarn 1997

POTT, HELEEN -- *De liefde van Alcibiades, -Over de rationaliteit van emoties*, Amsterdam 1992

RADELET, ABBÉ CAMILLE -- *Études Philosophiques de Théodicée selon St-Thomas, IIIe Volume: Opérations divines*, Bruxelles (1924?)

RAHNER, K. -- Gotteslehre, Christologie, in: *Schrifte zur Theologie IV*, Einsiedeln 1964⁴, 103-133, 137-205

RAHNER, KARL -- Der dreifaltige Gott als tranzendenter Urgrund der Heilsgeschichte, in: *Mysterium Salutis* II, Einsiedeln, Zürich, Köln, 1967, 317-401

RAHNER, K. -- Über der Verborgenheit Gottes, in: *Schriften zur Theologie* XII, Zürich, Einsiedeln, Köln 1975, 285-305

RAHNER, K. -- Fragen zur Unbegreiflichkeit Gottes bei Thomas von Aquin, in: *Schriften zur Theologie* XII, Zürich, Einsiedeln, Köln 1975, 306-319

RAHNER, KARL, HERBERT VORGRIMLER -- *Dictionary of Theology*, New York 1990 (transl. from German: *Kleines Theologisches Wörterbuch*, Freiburg 1976)

REDMOND, HOWARD -- *The Omnipotence of God*, Philadelphia 1964

REY, BERNARD -- *Nous Prêchons un Messie Crucifié*, Paris 1989

RICHARDSON, ALAN, JOHN BOWDEN -- *A New Dictionary of Theology*, London 1991

RICHTER, HORST E. -- *Der Gotteskomplex, -Die Geburt und die Krise des Glaubens an die Allmacht des Menschen*, Reinbek (Hamburg) 1979⁴

RIKHOF, H.W.M. -- Voorzichtig spreken over God, -Een lezing van enkele quaestiones uit de Summa Theologiae, in: *De Praktische Thomas, -Thomas van Aquino: De consequenties van zijn theologie voor hedendaags gedrag*, Hilversum 1987, 57-73

RIKHOF, H.W.M. -- *Over God spreken, -Een tekst van Thomas van Aquino uit de Summa Theologiae*, Delft 1988

RIKHOF, H.W.M. -- Das Geheimnis Gottes, -Jüngels Thomas-Rezeption näher betrachtet, in: *Zeitschrift für dialektische Theologie* 6 (1990), 61-78

RIKHOF, H.W.M. -- De almacht van God, in: KRO/RKK, *Katechismus van de Katholieke Kerk* video cassette 1A "De geloofsbelijdenis" n.7 (00:58:03 - 01:07:52), Hilversum 1995

RIKHOF, H.W.M. -- Trinity in Thomas, -Reading the Summa Theologiae against the Background of Modern Problems, in: H.J.M. Schoot (ed.), *Jaarboek 1999 Thomas Instituut te Utrecht*, Utrecht 2000, 83-100

RITTER, W.H., F. Feldmeier, W. Schoberth, G. Altner, *Der Allmächtige, -Annäherungen an ein Umstrittenes Gottesprädikat*, Göttingen 1997

ROBINSON, H. WHEELER -- *Suffering Human and Divine*, London 1940

ROCCA, GREGORY -- The distinction between *res significata* and *modus significandi* in Aquinas' theological epsitemology, in: *The Thomist* 55 (1991), 173-197

RODENBERG, OTTO -- Vom Schmerz Gottes, -Ein Beitrag zur biblischen Anthropologie Gottes, in: E. Lubahn, O. Rodenberg (eds.), *Das Wort vom Kreuz*, Gießen, Basel 1988

ROSS, ELLEN M. -- *The Grief of God, -Images of the Suffering Jesus in Late Medieval England*, Oxford 1997

ROSSNER SJ, WILLIAM -- Toward an Analysis of "God Is Love", in: *The Thomist* 38 (1973), 633-667

SAGNE, JEAN-CLAUDE -- Jezus' uitroep op het kruis, in: *Concilium* 1983-9 "Job en het zwijgen van God", 59-67

SALVATI CP, GIUSEPPE MARCO -- La Croce del Risorto, -Via alla ontologia del mistero, in: Fernando Taccone cp (ed.), *La Teologia della Croce nella Nuova Evangelizzazione*, Roma 1992

SAROT, MARCEL -- *God, Passibility and Corporeality*, Kampen 1992

SCHEEBEN, MATTHIAS JOSEPH -- *Handbuch der katholischen Dogmatik I*, Freiburg in Breisgau 1933

SCHILLEBEECKX, E. -- Ergernis van onze lijdensgeschiedenis en mysterie van heil, in: *Schrift* 36 (1974), 226-231

SCHILLEBEECKX, E. -- *Jezus, het verhaal van een levende*, Baarn 1982[9]

SCHILLEBEECKX, E. -- Overwegingen rond Gods weerloze overmacht, in *TvT* 27 (1987), 370-381

SCHILLEBEECKX, E. -- *Om het behoud van het evangelie*, Baarn 1988

SCHIWY, GÜNTHER -- *Abschied vom allmächtigen Gott*, München 1995

SCHNACKENBURG, RUDOLF -- *Das Johannesevangelium 2. Teil*, Freiburg, Basel, Wien 1971

SCHNEIDER, THEODOR -- Gottesbild und Kreuzopfer, in: Wolfgang Beinert (ed.), *Gott - ratlos vor dem Bösen*, Freiburg in Breisgau 1999

SCHOBERTH, W -- Gottes Allmacht und das Leiden, in: W.H. Ritter, R. Feldmeier etc., *Der Allmächtige, -Annäherungen an ein umschrittenes Gottesprädikat*, Göttingen 1997

SCHOONENBERG, PIET -- *De Geest, het Woord en de Zoon, -Theologische overden-kingen over Geest-christologie, Logos-christologie en drieëenheidsleer*, Averbode, Kampen 1991

SCHOOT, HENK -- *Christ, the Name of God, -Thomas Aquinas on Naming Christ*, Leuven, Utrecht 1993

SCHOOT, H.J.M. -- Friars in Negative Christology, -Thomas Aquinas and Luis de León, in: T. Merrigan, J. Haers (ed.), *The Myriad Christ, -Plurality and the Quest for Unity in Contemporary Christology*, Leuven, Paris, Sterling VA 2000, 329-348

SCHÜRMANN, HEINZ -- *Das Lukasevangelium 1. Teil*, Freiburg in Breisgau 1969

SCHWARZ, HANS -- *Evil, -A Historical and Theological Perspective*, Minneapolis 1995

SCHWARZWÄLLER, KLAUS -- *Kreuz und Auferstehung, -Ein theologisches Traktat*, Gütersloh 2000

SECKLER, MAX -- *Das Heil in der Geschichte, -Geschichtstheologisches Denken bei Thomas von Aquin*, München 1964

SENIOR CP, DONALD -- *The Passion of Jesus in the Gospel of Matthew*, Wilmington DE 1985

SENTIS, L. -- *Saint Thomas d'Aquin et le Mal, -Foi Chrétienne et Theodicée*, Paris 1992
SEPIERE, MARIE-CHRISTINE -- *L'Image d'un Dieu Souffrant, -Aux Origines du Crucifix*, Paris 1994
SERTILLANGES OP, A.-D. -- *Le Problème du Mal, -L'Histoire*, Paris 1948
SERTILLANGES OP, A.-D. -- *Le Problème du Mal, -La Solution*, Paris 1951
SIA, MARIAN F., SANTIAGO SIA -- *From Suffering to God, -Exploring Our Images of God in the Light of Suffering*, New York 1994
SILVESTER, HUGH -- *Arguing with God, -A Christian Examination of the Problem of Evil*, London 1971
SIMONIS, WALTHER -- *Woher kommt das Böse? ... wenn Gott gut ist*, Graz, Wien, Köln 1999
SIWEK SJ, PAUL -- *The Philosophy of Evil*, New York 1951
SLOYAN, GERARD S. -- *The Crucifixion of Jesus, -History, Myth, Faith*, Minneapolis MN 1995
SOBRINO, JON -- *Christology at the Crossroads, -A Latin American Approach*, New York 1978[2] (transl. from Spanish, 1976)
SOKOLOWSKI, ROBERT -- *The God of Faith and Reason, -Foudations of Christian Theology*, Notre Dame, London 1982
SONTAG, FRIEDERICK -- *Wie frei ist Gott?, -Nachdenkliches zu menschlichen Erfahrungen*, Frankfurt am Main 1986 (transl. from English: *What Can God Do*, Nashville TN 1979)
SOUTHERN, R.W. -- *Saint Anselm, -A Portrait in a Landscape*, Cambridge 1990
SPARN, WALTHER -- *Leiden - Erfahrung und Denken, -Materialen zum Theodizeeproblem*, München 1980
STACKHOUSE JR., JOHN G. -- *Can God Be Trusted? -Faith and the Challenge of Evil*, New York 1998
STOßWALD, V. -- Gottes Allmacht, -Ungedeckte Ausreden, in *DPfrBl* 94 (1994), 52-54
SURIN, KENNETH -- The Impassibility of God and the Problem of Evil, in: *Scottish Journal of Theology* 35 (1982), 97-115
SURIN, KENNETH -- *Theology and the Problem of Evil*, New York 1986
SUURMOND, P.B. -- *God is machtig, maar hoe?, -Relaas van een godservaring*, Baarn 1990
SWINBURNE, RICHARD -- Omnipotence, in: *American Philosophical Quarterly* (10), 1973, 231-237
SWINBURNE, RICHARD -- *The Coherence of Theism*, Oxford 1977
SWINBURNE, Richard -- *Is There a God?*, Oxford 1996
SWINBURNE, RICHARD -- *Providence and the Problem of Evil*, Oxford 1998

TEN KATE, A.A.S. -- *Avec Dévouement total, La Lutte de Dieu contre Toute Puissance: Origine et Evolution de la Toute-Puissance*, Bergen op Zoom 2000
TEN KATE, A.A.S. -- Alles wordt mogelijk, -Kanttekeningen bij de almacht van God, in: *Interpretatie* (december 2002), 11-13
TERNANT, P -- *Le Christ est Mort 'pour tous', -Du Serviteur Israël au Serviteur Jésus*, Paris 1993
TESFAI, Y. (ed.) -- *The Scandal of a Crucified World, -Perspectives on the Cross and Suffering*, Maryknoll NY 1994

TE VELDE, ROELF AREND (ed.) -- *Over liefde en liefde, -Beschouwingen over liefde (amor, amicitia, caritas) volgens Thomas van Aquino*, Nijmegen 1998

THALER, ANTON -- *Gott leidet mit, -Gott und das Leid*, Frankfurt am Main 1994

THÉVENOT, XAVIER -- La Compassion, -Une Réponse au Mal, in: *Le Supplément, - Revue d'Étique et Théologie Morale* 172 "*Mal et Compassion*" (1990), 79-96

THOMASSON, BILL -- *God on Trial, -The Book of Job and Human Suffering*, Collegeville Minnesota 1997

TORRELL OP, JEAN-PIERRE -- *Saint Thomas Aquinas, -The Person and His Work*, Vol. 1, Washington D.C. 1996

TÜCK, JAN-HEINER -- *Christologie und Theodizee bei Johann Baptist Metz, -Ambivalenz der Neuzeit im Licht der Gottesfrage*, Paderborn, München, Wien, Zürich 1999

TURNER, DENYS -- *The Darkness of God, -Negativity in Christian Mysticism*, Cambridge 1998

VALKENBERG, W.G.B.M. -- "By the Power of the Passion of Christ": The Place of Christ in Aquinas' Theology of Peanance, in: Henk J.M. Schoot (ed.), *Tibi soli peccavi, -Thomas Aquinas on Guilt and Forgiveness*, Leuven, Utrecht 1996, 151-174

VALKENBERG, WILHELMUS G.B.M. -- *Words of the Living God, -Place and Function of Holy Scripture in the Theology of Thomas Aquinas*, Leuven, Utrecht 2000

VALKENBERG, PIM -- Johannes, Thomas en de andere leerlingen, -Aantekeningen bij Thomas' interpretatie van Johannes 8 en 20, in: H.J.M. Schoot (ed.), *Jaarboek 2001 Thomas Instituut te Utrecht*, Utrecht 2002, 37-52

VAN BAVEL, T.J. -- Schoonenberg's paradoxaal spreken over God, in: *TvT* 31 (1991), 246-264

VAN BAVEL, T.J. -- Spreken of zwijgen over God bij Augustinus, in: *TvT* 37 (1997), 132-149

VAN DE BEEK, A. -- *Waarom?, -Over lijden, schuld en God*, Nijkerk 1984 (transl into English: Why?, -On Suffering, Guilt and God, Grand Rapids Michigan 1990)

VAN DE BEEK, A. -- *Jezus Kurios, -De Christologie als hart van de theologie*, Kampen 1998

VAN DEN BRINK, G. -- *Almighty God, -A Study of the Doctrine of Divine Omnipotence*, Kampen 1993

VAN DEN BRINK, G., M. SAROT (eds.) -- *Understanding the Attributes of God*, Frankfurt am Main 1999 (transl. from Dutch: Hoe is Uw Naam, -Opstellen over de eigenschappen van God, Kampen 1995)

VAN DEN EYNDE, SABINE -- Maar zij vreesden de Levende, -Omgaan met macht en onmacht in bijbelverhalen, in: *Interpretatie* (juli 2000), 8-10

VAN DER VEN, JOHANNES ANTHONIUS -- *Entwurf einer empirischen Theologie*, Kampen 1990

VAN DER VEN, P. -- Almachtig alleen nog als bijwoord, *Trouw* 3rd August 1996, 10

VAN DRIEL, L. -- *Over het lijden en God, -tussen Kushner en Calvijn*, Kampen 1988

VANN, GERALD -- *The Pain of Christ and the Sorrow of God*, Oxford 1947

VARILLON, FRANÇOIS -- *L'Humanité de Dieu*, Paris 1974

VARILLON, FRANÇOIS -- *La Souffrance de Dieu*, Paris 1975

VÄTERLEIN, CHRISTIAN (ed.) -- *Die Zeit der Staufer II*, Stuttgart 1977

VERCRUYSSE SJ, JOS E. -- Der gekreuzigte Gott, in: *Gregorianum* 55 (1974), 371-378

VERNEAUX, ROGER -- *Problèmes et Mystères du Mal*, Paris 1956

VERNETTE, JEAN -- *Si Dieu Était Bon, -On ne verrait pas tout cela. Face au Problème du Mal: Souffrance, Maladie, Mort, Cataclysmes; la Réponse de l'Église*, Paris 1991

VOSMAN, FRANS -- Het leven getekend, het leven betekend, -Goede gronden voor de kerkelijke uitspraak "Het leven is altijd een goed", in: Martien Pijnenburg, Frans Vosman (eds.), *Tegendraadse levensvisies*, Assen 1996, 63-85

WADELL CP, PAUL J. -- *Friendship and the Moral Life*, Notre Dame IN 1989

WALKER, DAVID A. -- Trinity and Creation in the Theology of St. Thomas, in: *The Thomist* 57 (1993), 443-455

WALTHER, R. (ed.) -- *God heeft wel honderd namen*, Baarn 1986

WEATHERHEAD, LESLIE D. -- *A Plain Man Looks at the Cross, -An Attempt to Explain in Simple Language for the Modern Man, the Significance of the Death of Jesus*, London 1945

WEINANDY OFM CAP, THOMAS G. -- *Does God Change? -The World's Becoming in the Incarnation*, Still River MA 1984

WEINANDY OFM CAP, THOMAS G. -- *Does God Suffer?*, Edinburgh 2000

WEISHEIPL, JAMES A. -- *Friar Thomas d'Aquino, -His Life, Thought and Work*, New York 1983

WESTBERG, DANIEL -- Emotion and God, -A Reply to Marcel Sarot, in: *The Thomist* 60 (1996), 109-121

WESTLAND, J. -- *God, onze troost in noden, -Een gesprek met hedendaagse theologen over de vragen rond God en lijden*, Kampen 1986

WHALE, J.S. -- *The Christian Answer to the Problem of Evil*, London 1950[4]

WIERSINGA, HERMAN -- Een bloeddorstige God?, in: *Schrift* 36 (1974), 218-221

WIERSINGA, HERMAN -- *Verzoening met het lijden?*, Baarn 1975

WILES, MAURICE F. -- *God's Action in the World*, London 1986

WISSINK, J.B.M. -- Enkele theologische reflecties over de negatieve theologie, toegelicht aan de hand van Thomas van Aquino, in: Ilse N. Bulhof, Laurens ten Kate (eds.), *Ons ontbreken heilige namen, -Negatieve theologie in de hedendaagse cultuurfilosofie*, Kampen 1992

WISSINK, J.B.M. -- Wil God bloed zien?, -Wie doet er genoeg voor wie?, in: *Schrift* 149 (1993), 151-154

WISSINK, J.B.M. -- Aquinas: The Theologian of Negative Theology. A Reading of *ST* I, qq.14-26, in: H.J.M. Schoot (ed.), *Jaarboek 1993 Thomas Instituut te Utrecht*, Utrecht 1994, 15-83

WISSINK, J.B.M. -- "De sacramenten geven de kruisgenade die ze betekenen", -Over het verband tussen het heilswerk van Christus en de sacramenten, in: A.H.C. van Eijk, H.W.M. Rikhof, *De lengte en de breedte en de hoogte en de diepte, -Peilingen in de theologie van de sacramenten*, Zoetermeer 1996, 234-261

WISSINK, J.B.M. -- Satisfaction as Part of Penance, According to Thomas Aquinas, in: Henk J.M. Schoot (ed.), *Tibi soli peccavi, Thomas Aquinas on Guilt and Forgiveness*, Leuven 1996, 75-95

ZAHRNT, H. -- *Wie kann Gott das zulassen?, -Hiob, der Mensch im Leid*, München 1985
ZENGER, ERICH -- *Durchkreuztes Leben, -Hiob, Hoffnung für die Leidenden*, Freiburg, Basel, Wien, 1981
ZOFFOLI, ENRICO -- *Mistera della Soffrenza di Dio?, -Il Pensiero di S. Tomaso* (Studi Tomistici 34), Citta del Vaticano 1988
ZUBIZARRETA CP, JOSÉ RAMON -- *Theologia della Croce*, in: Bolletino Stauros 10 (1984), 3-21

INDICES

Names

Subjects

actus purus 121, 154, 186, 248
almightiness
    and mercy 181, 188f, 194-221
    and passio 180f, 187
    and the Passion of Christ XVI,
    1, 28-47, 181f, 191
analogous language XVIII, 84, 130,
231-9, 254, 282f
angels 120f, 139f, 158
Anunciation 37, 182
appropriation 107f, 202, 241f, 244-9,
280
attribution 103, 130, 147, 214
Auschwitz XIII, 224

beatitude, happiness 199-201, 212-4,
220
belief → faith
Benedictus, hymn 218, 284

casus diaboli 30
Chalcedon 24, 47, 78
Christ
    abandonment 18, 20-28
    beatitude 67-70, 205
    body after resurrection 141
    comprehensor 69, 126
    death 1, 4f, 9
    depiction 47f
    divinity 2, 47f, 54, 66, 71-80,
    253, 256, 264, 266, 274, 283
    example 41f, 45, 59
    free will 5, 7, 16-18, 29, 31,
    34, 39, 69f, 79, 151, 204f,
    249, 260-80
    goodness 46
    human being 7, 19, 47, 53f,
    71-80, 125, 128, 205, 236,
    253, 255-80, 282
    impassibility 79
    in control 70
    instrument of God 25860, 265,

272, 277
joy 65-68
justice 42
knowledge 69, 126-8, 205
loud voice 4f, 9
love 11, 13, 17, 42, 46, 79,
287
Messiah 277
might 6f, 9, 129, 220, 240-80,
chapter 4
miracles 9, 220, 240, 258,
264
obedience 10f, 13, 16f, 42,
47, 70, 253, 262, 277
→ *Passion of Christ*
perfect 53, 122-9, 205, 276
power of God 246, 277-80
powers, higher and lower 58f,
69f
powerless 80
prayer 27, 37, 250, 252, 262,
266f
Saviour 214, 261, 277
solidarity 27
strength 55, 70
suppositum, supposit 7, 9, 72,
146f, 264
two wills 19, 272-9
viator 66, 68f, 126
weakness 9, 27, 51, 69f, 192,
267
will → *free, two*
wisdom 126, 244
Christian distinction 88
Christian life 42-44, 289-91
christological meaning 5, 23, 285
christological perspective XV
Church, community of faith 44, 218f,
281, 285, 290
confort, *consolatio* 202
communicatio idiomatum 72, 74-76,
145-8, 252, 256, 264, 278
compassio, compassion 22, 27, 56,
60, 95, 108, 137-44, 151, 194-6, 198,
289

SUMMARIUM

Hoc studium rationis in fide christiana omnipotentiae Dei cum passione/Passione Christi huius crisis recentis fidei ratione habita et adiumentum in quaerendo emergi ex ea fecit. Magna quaestio quare invitus Dei tantae passiones in hoc mundo sint, omnium temporum est. In Occidente autem ea antehac initium se ad investigationem conferendi, hoc tempore ratio ad frangendum pactum et fidem dimittendum facta est. Nomen Dei Omnipotens in hoc praecipue difficile esse videtur. Alii aliud nomen nominis omnipotentis vicem quaerunt sive de omnipotentia non iam loquuntur, sed de Dei amore. Hoc autem cuidam credenti quaerenti vel quaerenti credendum non est dissolutio, cum hoc nomen traditionis nostrae pars sit et amplius quaestio rationis Deo cum passionem eius dilectorum remanet. Haec quaestio passionem/Passionem Christi, Dei Filii dilecti sine peccato, vidente urgens fit.

Non solum mihi, Passionistae, membrae Congregationis in cuius spiritualitate Passio Christi medius locus est, crisi fidei nostri ex parte passionis/Passionis Christi obviam procedendum luce clarius est, quia christiana fides et sacra Scriptura totum circa eam torquent. Ad accipiendum meliam intelligentiam nostri fidei de nexo mysteriorum inter Dei omnipotentiam et passionem/Passionem Christi, verba Thomae Aquinatis de illo exquisita sunt, imprimis in eius Summa Theologiae. In hoc perrectum est utique a duabus cognitionibus in priis studiis in Thomas Instituto, Thomam theologum negativum et biblicum esse.

In primo capite, de passione/Passione Christi, primo quomodo rationes Christo cum Deo et aliis qui adfinem fuerunt evento sint. Thoma hoc considerante, Christum enectum esse patet, sicut in sacra Scriptura legitur, sed hoc neque Deum eum tradere neque Christum sua propria voluntate istam passionem accipere tollit. Ergo omni ex parte Deus in agendo crudelis vel cogens non fuit, sed inspirans. Praeterea, ad consilium fidei omnia continenter in manu Dei fuisse Thomas impense animum nostrum attendit. Simul malum a persecutoribus Christo factum esse non negat. Quo aperte est omnipotentiam quodcumque malum impedire non significat vel implicat, sed omnia in manu Dei esse.

Ita Thomas animum nostrum praeter sensum historicum ad sensus depressiores quorum christologicum narrationis Passionis attendit. Consequentes incarnationis intelligendo nostro clamorem Christi in cruce (Mt XXVII, XLVI) et Dei passionem Christo patiente contemplatur. Qaestionem in medio huius studii oculis lustrante, in nexo necessitati passionis/Passionis Christi cum Dei libertate defigendum est. Cum hic de necessitate in aliud agatur, quod est in finem a Deo libere eligitum,

Thomas notionem convenientiae prefert harmoniam demonstrantem. Tametsi severitas passionis Christi nullo modo neglecta est a Thoma; fuse de Christi passione secundum corpus et animam vera et gravissima loquitur. Unionis autem hypostaticae in Christo causa ipsum in altiora parte animae passum esse negato; quoad eius anima ad "Patrem" directa, minime impeditus fuit. Eius passio ut manus ad peccatum tendat eum non adduxit, sicut aliis hominibus fieri potest. Eo passio humana, sed tamen passio alicuius alii hominis non exacte eadem fuit.

Thomas etiam Christum passum quoad Filium divinum esse ardente pernegat, nam Deus et passio inter se discrepant. Hoc mirum videtur: Si Deus pati non possit, quomodo amor sit (I Io IV, XVI)? In capite secundo, de passione Dei, ostenditur Thomam, Deum sine passionem esse dicentem, Deum quasi gelidum esse non ponere, sed Deum creaturam non esse; passio creaturae est. Notio patiendi a nobis ut accipere sive recipere intelligenda est. Thomas nullum modum patiendi Deo convenire posse demonstrat, quia quisque corpus vel imperfectionem et compositatem ponit. Quae in simplice et perfecto et bono et aeterno Deo esse non possunt. Mutatio in Deo eum non vel quasi minus vel plus Deum fuisse ante mutationem aut post eam non iam vel plus Deum esse significet.

In homine amor semper cum passione confluit. In amore autem passio non inhaeret; secundum Thomam amor est quod voluntatem ad bonum movet. Amor unionem amantis cum amato vel amati cum bono vult. Scripturam nihilo setius de patiendo Dei loqui, metaphorice intelligendum est, quia aliter Deus numero creaturarum habeatur. Per animi perturbationem et compassionem Dei eius propinquitas incogitabilis designatur. *Descriptiones* Dei, sicut obiecta describuntur, non sunt. Deus enim mysterium est et ideo plene cognitus non potest. Solum proprie de Dei passione loquitur, cum de mysterio passionis Dei incarnati in Iesu Christo loquimur.

De potentia Dei loquens Thomas iterum theologus negativus se manifestat: "Potentia" Dei dicitur, sed non exacte eadem quam potentia creaturae est. Thomas priis cognitionibus in Summa Theologiae de scientia et lingua in divinis pro contemplatione Dei potentiae utitur et Deum potentiam habere distinctam a eo quod est negandum esse concludit. Attamen ista distinctio in intellecto nostro facienda est, ut potentiam Dei et cur non omnia facit qua possit, utique contemplari possimus. Praeterea, potentia - infinita - Dei alii ordinis esto, non potentiis creatis aemula.

Concepto potentiae sicut in loquendo nostro de Deo usu per praecedentes passus explicato, Thoma de omnipotentia loquente, sonus mutatur: Omnipotentia notio fidei, non philosophiae est, et nihil aliud nisi potentiam JHWH significat. Non autem est terminus, sed eius meditandi de ea principium est: Quemadmodum omnia potens in fide intelligendum est? Difficile dictu, secundum Thomam. Iam ex obiectionibus et sed contra et potissime verbis allatis Scripturae, Thomam quaerere Passionem Christi observantem perspicuum est - perspicientia non offensa in ullo opere aliorum theologicorum vel philosophorum. Itaque hic theologiam Thomae theologiam passionis esse patet. In eius expositione summe conspectum est eum referre homiliam pondus habentem, cuius fundamentum versum Sapientiae non nominat, in qua omnipotentiam suam parcendo maxime et miserando (non "compatiendo"!) manifestare dicitur. Explicationes Thomae sunt tres, altera iuxta alteram posita. I. In libere peccata dimittendo Deum altissimum potentiae vel auctoritatis esse ostenditur; nemo et nihil eum maxime esse misericordem impedit vel cogit. II. Hoc agens Deus homines ad participationem infiniti boni perducit, quod ipse est. Hic actus finis, ultimus effectus, motus creationem incipientis est (exitus - reditus). III. Inceptum ad actionem apud Deum esse ostenditur, sicut semper erat; omnia Dei opera misericordia sunt. Sic lector ad intelligentiam ducitur quod in Prima Parte Summae Theologiae de omnipotentia et misericordia Dei dictum (quaestione XXV), explicatum esse in Tertia Parte de Passione Christi (quaestione XLVI): Passio Christi ultima manifestatio Dei omnipotentiae atque ipsius amoris, virtutis unitivae et concretivae. Nexui omnipotentiae Dei cum eius amore misericorde et Passione Christi fundamentum clarum est in Scriptura.

Nomina Hebraica *El shaddai* et *JHWH sebaoth* Deo communiter in graece *Pantokrator* et in latine Omnipotens et in neerlandice *Almachtige* sive *Alvermogende* redduntur. Haec nomina sunt, quae antiquitus spem et fidem in JHWH exprimunt et determinatum modum putandi Graecum improbant. Thomas autem nos verbo potentiae Deo uti analogice dicit, nam Deo praeter intellectum nostrum, eum univoce describere non possumus. Unde "potens" dictum de Deo et de aliquo homine, Deum principium potentiae illius hominis et etiam potentiam Dei illam ipsius infinite excedere significat. Mysterium Dei permanet. Hoc modo *verbum* potens potius Deo aliquo homine convenit. Simul autem *usus* ipsius verbi potius nobis convenit, quia de Deo loquimur sicut intelligimus. Idem ad "amorem", "misericordiam" et omnia nomina proprie dicta de Deo pertinet.

Si Deus est omnipotens, et Pater et Filius et Spiritus omnipotentes sunt. Nos tamen communiter praeter Deum solum Patrem omnipotentem nominare, appropriatio dicitur: De omnipotentia Patris loquimur exempli gratia quia nomen potentiae sensum principii in se habet et hic patri melius convenit filio sive spirito. Filio et Spiritui Sancto autem nomen virtutis Dei datur (puta I Cor I, XXV); virtus enim ex potentia procedit. At contra, homini Christo nomen omnipotens tantum convenire potest propter unionem hypostaticam cum Verbo Dei, sicut Filium divinum passum esse (communicatio idiomatum) dicimus. Tametsi homo Christus propriam voluntatem habuit, praeter voluntatem divinam - Thomas nobis Gethsemane commemorat - de ipsius propria potentia vel virtute non loquitur; a se facere nihil potuit (Io V, XIX).

Cum de Deo tum de Christo loquentem in hoc studio Thomam theologum negativum cognovimus. In Summa Theologiae sacra Scriptura et fons et criterium et principium struens (exitus - reditus) ostenditur. Thomae modus Scripturam legendi theologice mirum nobis videtur, at simul nos facilius tangi a tabulatis atque magnitudine mysterii fidei nostri facit. Conclusio inaudita Passionem Christi summe manifestationem Dei omnipotentiae esse, ad penitus emendandum considerationes nostras de potentia, et Dei et nostri omnino a Deo, et de ratione eis cum passione in mundo et in vita christiana nos permovet.

Marke Robin a Terraedita Sinea, C.P.

(*Summarium in Latinum sermonem conversum a huius studii scriptore*)

PRINTED ON PERMANENT PAPER • IMPRIME SUR PAPIER PERMANENT • GEDRUKT OP DUURZAAM PAPIER - ISO 9706

N.V. PEETERS S.A., WAROTSTRAAT 50, B-3020 HERENT